W9-BZE-734

The Cybergypsies

The Cybergypsies

A True Tale of Lust, War, and Betrayal on the Electronic Frontier

Indra Sinha

VIKING

VIKING
Published by the Penguin Group
Penguin Putnam Inc., 375 Hudson Street, New York, New York 10014, U.S.A.

Penguin Books Ltd, 27 Wrights Lane, London W8 5TZ, England

Penguin Books Australia Ltd, Ringwood, Victoria, Australia

Penguin Books Canada Ltd, 10 Alcorn Avenue, Toronto, Ontario, Canada M4V 3B2

Penguin Books (N.Z.) Ltd, 182-190 Wairau Road, Auckland 10, New Zealand

Penguin Books Ltd, Registered Offices: Harmondsworth, Middlesex, England

First American edition
Published in 1999 by Viking Penguin, a member of Penguin Putnam Inc.

1 3 5 7 9 10 8 6 4 2

Grateful acknowledgment is made for permission to use the following copyrighted works:
"Animula" from *West of Elm* by Roger Garfitt, Carcanet Press, 1974.
By permission of the author.
"Beware, that night is back" (retitled "Leaves and Birds") by Raf Atul Hussaini, translated by Satinath Sarangi. By permission of Raf Atul Hussaini and Satinath Sarangi.
"Cry" by Rzgar Goran. By permission of the Kurdish Cultural Centre.

LIBRARY OF CONGRESS CATALOGING–IN–PUBLICATION DATA
Sinha, Indra.
The cybergypsies: a true tale of lust, war, and betrayal on the electronic frontier / Indra Sinha
p. cm.
ISBN 0-670-88630-0
1. Internet (computer network)–Social aspects. 2. Subculture. 3. Interpersonal communication. 4. Online chat groups. 5. Online etiquette. 6. Sinha, Indra. I. Title.
HM851.S56 1999
306.4'6–dc21 99-33077

This book is printed on acid-free paper.
∞

Printed in the United States of America
Set in Palatino

For Viktoria

Satanbug

It's 3 a.m. and I'm online to Jesus Slutfucker. JS informs me that he's typing one-handed, knuckling open a beer with the other. Needs a drink, he tells me. He just got home to find his girlfriend throwing her clothes into a case. She said she was sick of being shackled to a sleazeball, his lifestyle was doing unspeakable things to her head, she was leaving. To emphasise the point, on the way out she stuck a knife in his arse. JS is a nurse, so he knows he's barely scratched, but in any case, it's not the knife that hurt.

i 'm b etter off w i tho u t t he bitch ...

He's trying to tough it out, but the bugger's clearly had a shock. I can tell he's upset by the way he's typing, characters detonating on my screen in bursts of venom. What the hell, JS says, wounded or not, he'll celebrate her departure with a few more beers and then settle down to a serious night's buttkicking on the net. Well, in Oklahoma City where he's hunched over his keyboard it's just after nine, so he has the night ahead of him. For me night's nearly over. Something – the moon? my imagination? dawn? – is silvering the sky over the Sussex woods to the east. I've been on the computer for six straight hours and am yearning for bed. My eyes are burning from trying to focus the blue flicker of the screen, but JS is getting into his stride and there's something I want to find out. I type:

>Geno, friends here in Britain are shitting themselves about a virus called Satanbug. It's clever and nasty - apparently has come from the US. Do you know anything about this one?

A pause while the satellite relay to the States kicks in. This is the question I've waited up to ask. Jesus Slutfucker, aka Geno Paris, self-styled 'technopath', is proprietor of one of the biggest virus collections on the net: all the common viruses you'll find on any bug-exchange bulletin board, plus hundreds of exotic specimens, various unidentified species culled from the wild and not a few he has written himself. He has links to every major partisan group in the virus underground. If anyone knows about Satanbug, it will be Geno. The wait is longer than usual. He's thinking. Then the screen comes to life and characters flash across.

>*you know it's a funny thing, bear, you're the second brit in two days who's asked me about satanbug...*

>*Who was the other?*

>*lady logged in here from the uk, asked if i had it... strange girl... her name is slasha something or another... i did not believe she was a she, or really calling from the uk, so i voiced her...*

>*You spoke to her?*

Slasha must have been exceptional if Geno made a transatlantic voice call from his own phone. Roaming the pre-internet net is expensive, which is why so many of its denizens are there courtesy of someone else's phone bill. The first task for a hacker, long before he starts breaking into other people's computers, is to find a way to do it at someone else's expense. It's almost a law of net life. To survive for long as a serious net nomad, you need to be a hacker. Or rich. As a non-hacker who has travelled the nightsky roads for years, my finances are in serious trouble. This call to Geno in Oklahoma City is, for example, costing me a fortune. Our bills, since I began my nocturnal electronic wanderings, have become so terrifying – the largest so far was £2,000 in a single quarter – that I've had to start hiding them from Eve.

>well she was for real... but weird... one of the first things she told me was that she didn't really like american men because they did not know how to cane a girl the way a british gentleman did... i swear that was almost her exact words...

I'm so astonished that I forget to reply.

> hey bear, you still alive...?

Typed communication is always tedious. There's nothing worse during one of these sessions than sitting twiddling your thumbs waiting for the ether to respond. Eventually I muster some words.

>Geno... the Brits do have quite a reputation for this sort of thing. The French call it 'le vice anglais'. But this Slasha... what did she want with Satanbug?

I feel that he's leaning back in his chair, laughing.

>i knew the brits rep for this type of behavior but i did not think that their women actually enjoyed it... :) strange lady... she asked for access here and in return she gave me some viruses... a couple i don't think i had...

This too is odd. The only viruses he hasn't got are the kind you don't catch from computers.

> she uploaded a photo of herself - a home made gif... she's about 36, i think she said, and the gif would seem to support that, and blondish, looks dyed... see if I can find it. hold on...

Halfway across the world, Geno can't hear me sigh. It's 3.12 a.m. I leave for work at seven, but of course there is now no question of logging off. Curiosity has locked its wrestler's biceps round my neck. Actually it is more than curiosity. What I'm experiencing is a sort of jangling paranoia. Is it possible that my line is tapped? Sometimes it seems as if all the connections on the net are alive to one another and that information flows through regardless of how you try to dam it up. It finds its own way, leaks along the wires and out onto the airwaves. Information, as would-be hackers never tire of telling us, wants to be free. But certain kinds of intelligence are hard to come by. It has taken me a year to work my way into the virus nets, to get to know the people who write cancerous code and send it out into the world to mutate other people's data. My idea had been to shop these folk, but it's not that simple. There are no laws against writing viruses, only against using them. My motives are easy to misunderstand, so I've told no-one, not even my 'friend' Nasty Ned the Net Nark, of my virus adventure. Geno is my secret. Or so I'd thought until tonight.

Unaware of my sudden consternation (panic is vulgar), Mister Slutfucker vanishes from the screen to delve in the hidden part of his bulletin board, the grandly named *Oklahoma Institute of Virus Research*. It isn't a 'real' place. It has no existence in space-time. It is a computer-generated mirage, a cloud castle, a Fata Morgana, yet real people meet here and start things which ricochet into the real world. Geno's board is a piece of software that lets my computer, via a modem, call his. Once past the electronic portcullis, identity and password verified, I'm genuinely inside his system, or the bits of it which he allows me to see.

Being inside someone else's computer is like wandering round their house. Geno's storerooms, where he has gone looking for the picture of mysterious Slasha, are stacked high with things not intended for public inspection: computer viruses, alphabet bombs, trojan horses, virus-generating and mischief-making machines. (Surely 'mechanic' comes from the same root as 'méchant'?) I tap a key, and Geno's viruses present themselves on my screen, rather like a wine list in a good restaurant – names, vintages, descriptions – lacking only prices. Viruses are the ultimate freeware.

BACKFIND.ARJ	4757	09-26-93	Trojan, overwrites hard drives. Written by some SAD fuck to take down a mutt called Geoff
BACKTIME.ZIP	605	09-12-93	Prague inf., makes time run backwards
BADBOY2.ZIP	1068	09-12-93	Stealth virus, variant "Make me better"
BADBRAIN.ZIP	2822	10-02-93	Brainless virus by Hellraiser
BWOLF.ZIP	2520	10-02-93	Beowulf. Kind of a lame little virus I wrote when I was drunk

Next door, bits of bomb-making equipment lie scattered, as if abandoned by some hastily departed cyber-terrorist.

G2-070B.ZIP	47705	09-13-93	Dark Avengers Virus Writing Program
GWKTROJ.ZIP	4370	09-13-93	Kinda lame trojan maker
INSIBV2.ZIP	34984	09-13-93	Fairly good ansi bomb maker
IVP-V17.ZIP	40610	09-13-93	Instant Virus Production, latest version
MPC091B.ZIP	46178	09-13-93	Virus creator
MTE091.ARJ	11100	09-26-93	MTE Polymorphic engine
TPE11.ZIP	8709	09-02-93	TPE another Mutation Engine
VCL.ZIP	166650	09-13-93	Virus Creation Lab
ZIP-TROJ.ZIP	2203	09-13-93	Ansi bomb, formats disk when unzipped

I imagine the viruses as bombs made by bearded anarchists, innocent-seeming brown paper parcels done up with string and plastered with smudgy foreign stamps, the trojans as rocking horses stuffed with high explosive.

MEGATROJ ZIP	11650	07-13-91	A lethal and destructive trojan, use at your own pleasure
TROJ-1 ZIP	7598	02-19-91	Trojan horse from The Hill People HQ
TROJANS ZIP	38447	07-13-91	Trojan horses from The Immortal Grounds, Sysop: Toxic Waste
ARIHAK93.ZIP	63368	11-13-93*	ARiSToTLE's instant 500-virus creator
BOGUS.ZIP	124469	09-13-93	Bogus Msg writter *(sic)*

Bogus Message Writer is one of Geno's own méchantisms, a device which enables him to pepper the net with thousands of scatological messages, each of which appears to come from someone he dislikes. ARiSToTLE's viruses-while-u-wait creator (ARiSToTLE is a flamboyant virus collector from Virginia), I picture as a collection of multicoloured tubes and pipes, like a Würlitzer jukebox. I once tried it. It chuntered for hours before spawning a swarm of viruses that looked like a drawerful of silverfishes, thus:

αϒιΣƒ101.zip	668	14/08/93	10:31
αϒιΣƒ102.zip	662	14/08/93	10:32
αϒιΣƒ103.zip	661	14/08/93	10:32
αϒιΣƒ104.zip	664	14/08/93	10:32
αϒιΣƒ105.zip	669	14/08/93	10:32

You ask innocently: Bear, what is a computer virus? It is a tiny program, a scrap of code that burrows into other programs, then makes copies of itself to infect further hosts, like a biological virus. It needn't be destructive. If you're simply interested in replication, your virus will probably be harmless. It's easy, however, to include instructions that erase or mangle data, or cause the characters on your victim's screen to cascade tinkling into a heap at the bottom. Rumour has it that Satanbug is a nasty virus. But however mean a virus may be, a trojan horse is nastier, because its intention is always hostile. Viruses play a mischievous game of catch me if you can. Trojans lie. They masquerade as harmless programs, but when you run them, they may wipe your hard disk, delete files or, as Geno puts it, 'tunnel down and fuck the FAT' (the file allocation table which tells your computer where to find its files). Particularly cruel was *Story Book,* which told its victims, 'Watch your child smile as Homely (the G-rated) Clown happily tells his story.'

'Joy,' says Geno, 'is creative and stylish destruction.'

Oddly, in all the time – several months – I've been calling Geno's board, I have never asked him what he looks like. In my mind he shapeshifts. Sometimes he's large, blond, moustachioed. At other times short, wiry, dark. He has long hair tied back in a ponytail, or a Yul Brynner No.1 cut. In reality, I know nothing about him save what he sends to my screen. I feel we're mates, yet I've never even heard his voice. It's a strange kind of friendship, which blossoms like a bat-pollinated durian flower, always in the dead of night.

Light thickens,
And the crow makes wing to the rooky wood,
Good things of day begin to droop and drowse
And night's black agents to their preys do rouse.

These lines come to me, and I think of what I've become.

3.21 a.m. in the weald of Sussex. In the field outside my window, a small animal, probably a rabbit, screams as its life is ended by a fox. There are far more lethal creatures abroad, but no-one dreams that they exist.

The night, my love, is full of invisible pathways, crisscrossing the globe, bounced off the stratosphere by orbiting comsats. Along them wander an odd gypsy folk, ceaselessly exploring, always on the lookout for new systems, new people, new information. They congregate, these travellers, at the oases and caravanserais of cyberspace: this bulletin board, that multi-user game. Fifty million people connected to the net, yet all over the world you meet these same few. You come across their spoor on systems in South Africa and Argentina. You bump into them at online parties in San Francisco or Stockholm. You hear rumours that they've hacked a High Street bank, or were last seen heading Amazonwards to track down illegal mahogany cutters with satellite-linked bulletin boards. Faster than the jet set is this net set. They can flit from London to San Francisco to Finland in seconds, and have friends, on whom they regularly call, in places like Sarajevo, Bombay and Vladivostok. Some are hackers, virus writers – you may never know who they really are. Some may be known to you as scientists, housewives, musicians, policemen, yet in other guises you have probably fought them on multi-user games or flirted with them in that haven of deep roleplayers, the Vortex. These people are the cybergypsies, the explorers of cyberspace. Theirs were the first camps in cyberspace. They mapped it and made its links. They named the constellations of its night sky. They share your secret life, and guilt.

3.25 a.m. Here in Britain respectable computer folk have long since climbed the wooden hill. Earnest techies, calling each others' boards to keep up with the latest anorak talk, are sleeping now. The universities have quietened down for the night and their network, the JANET, is just a whisper. In the City of London, fifty miles north of us, big commercial networks are running their inhuman data transfers, banks and corporations trading digits with, here and there, like a fly on a precipice, the odd hacker patiently trying to find a way to crawl in.

At this hour, the only hotspots are the really dedicated multi-user games and certain offbeat bulletin boards. On Shades, the serial killers will be lurking, hoping to ambush unwary necromancers and enchanters come to gather easy points in the dead of night. The roleplayers at the mysterious Vortex will still be playing out their bizarre fantasies. The software pirates are busy, but their boards are always busy all night. On the porno boards, lusts will be subsiding as patrons are forced by tomorrow's approaching workday to drag themselves away from their keyboards to solitary beds.

Then there are the people like me, the addicts, who drift round the globe with the tide of darkness. 9.25 p.m. now in Oklahoma City. East Coast America is just coming online. The partying on The WELL, in San Francisco, won't be in full swing for maybe six hours yet. Nothing significant ever happens on the net before midnight. The catch is that midnight is sweeping round the world at speeds up to and including 1,000 mph. Some modem jockeys like to ride the cusp of darkness round the globe. If you're addicted enough, have unlimited funds and access to chemicals, you can make night last forever, because it's always night somewhere on the net.

3.27 a.m. Geno's back.

>found it, yeah, it comes back... she had a kind of cultured british accent (if I am any judge, because all I have to go on is the movie my fair lady and my brief setting down in scotland when i was in the air force) but another thing she likes to talk about is how that riding crops are really too nasty to use on human beings, unless that they really deserve it... :)

>This is very peculiar Geno. Really extremely strange.

>yeah, but i must admit this slasha, or sasha is entertaining...

>You've no idea how fucking weird this is.

>come on, thought you limeys would be used to this kind of thing... hey, tell you what, i'll squirt you her picture along with the virus... okay stand by to receive satanbug and slasha...

It's too late at night to explain that it's not the sado-masochism that's weird. There are lots of S&M-ers on the net. They meet in places like the Vortex, which has a facility, Madame Pompadora's, devoted to the art of pain. No, what is weird is that hours earlier, I'd first heard of the Satanbug virus from a British bulletin-board operator called Josh, whose girlfriend is Carmine. And Carmine is a slender blonde whose bedtime reading is Skin Two catalogues, who attends clingfilm and candlewax parties with the keener Vortex players and, if this isn't clear enough, is known to have a fondness for the lash. Last time I saw Carmine, she was sheathed in a black rubber dress that clung like a condom, sucking vodka through a leather mask that sprouted nails like porcupine quills.

Can it just be coincidence that, one day after Slasha's chat with Jesus Slutfucker, Josh calls me to ask about Satanbug? Slasha gave Geno a copy of Satanbug. Could it have been marked? All it would take is a tiny change to the code – like a radioactive trace put into the bloodstream – so that its route back into the UK could be traced? But why suspect me? Josh doesn't know I know Geno. Surely he doesn't imagine I'm the channel by which American viruses are entering Britain? Tired worries scrape the inside of my skull like metal buttons clattering round in a laundromat. Pointless. Geno is about to send me Slasha's picture. I'll soon know if it was Carmine. I sit and watch the Satanbug virus drip into my system.

Searching ZIP: SAT-BUG.ZIP - CV BBS - NuKE WHQ - 514.425.4540

Length	Method	Size	Ratio	Date	Time	CRC-32	Attr	Name
7104	Implode	5131	28%	30-01-93	16:55	e6591831	—w-	TEST1.COM
4215	Implode	2847	33%	21-02-93	21:53	d0853e51	—w-	SAT-BUG.COM
2186	Implode	1147	48%	21-02-93	22:01	11060a6b	—w-	SAT-BUG.DOC
13505		9125	33%					3

The bug arrives zipped, compressed, ergo safe. Amazing how many 'experts' don't realise that viruses can't infect you unless you actually run them. The tiny *.com* files in the zip envelope are the monsters: *sat-bug.com* is the virus itself, *test1.com* is an infected file. Geno's typing back to me:

>there are two satanbug viruses, i think... i am really not sure who wrote the first one, i think it was viper or priest but various people have claimed responsibility, strange you should mention it, i got the second version from the brit girl who likes to have her ass beat and then again today from brother jack. both seem to be the same and undetectable... okay here comes slasha.

'Bear, what are you doing?'

My heart leaps like Basho's frog. My wife is standing in the doorway in her nightie, shading her eyes against the light.

'Eve!' I say lamely, 'I thought you were asleep.'

'I can't sleep. What are you doing?'

'Just finishing some writing. I'll be up in a minute.'

'It's three-thirty, you've got work in the morning.'

'Don't worry about it.'

She's frowning. I can't tell if she's upset.

'You're not writing. What are you really doing?'

Searching ZIP: SLASHA.ZIP - Oklahoma Institute of Virus Research

Length	Method	Size	Ratio	Date	Time	CRC-32	Attr	Name
49592	Stored	49592	0%	11-20-93	22:45	e4e07671	—w-	SLASHA.GIF
49592		49592	0%			1		

Luckily she doesn't come any nearer. The picture of Slasha has just arrived, Geno is back online, busy hammering his keyboard, the letters come skittering across the screen:

>...maybe all brit women like to be beat i dunno :) american women seem not to like it so much, one redneck up here just got his dick cut off (real big in the news) for beating and raping his wife...

Eve is shivering. I get up, go over and put my arms around her. She doesn't respond. From the corner of my eye I watch Mr. Slutfucker's outpourings scattergun across my screen.

'I'll be up in a second,' I tell her. 'Promise.'

Eve says quietly, 'You do this every night.' She removes herself from my arms and is gone.

I wait till I'm sure she's back in bed, then examine the gif. A blowsy, puffy faced woman stares out of the screen at me. Nothing like Josh's ex-girlfriend. Coincidence, after all.

Castle Perilous

From the rest of the world it's invisible. Driving by in the lane, we don't know it's there. All we see are trees – oak, ash, hawthorn, hazel, hornbeam, cherry – raising leafy battlements and towers. But there's a gate. Ducking, we enter a cave of leaves, at the far end of which is a smudge of light. Roots writhe at our feet. Eve peers into the green chaos, pulls back a branch to reveal the perfect rose-shape of a camellia.

'We'd be crazy to take this on,' she says. 'We'll never cope.'

We're within feet of the house before we see it, its walls hung with clay-tiles in the style of the Sussex Weald, bricks greened by the gloom of the trees. Paint is flaking from its window frames, squares of cardboard stand in for missing panes of glass. The front door is sentried by brambles that drop soft, spiky spears to bar our way. Everywhere, things drip on us and the light is green. I fall in love with it immediately.

We find the owner Grolius – an old man with a shock of white hair that explodes in all directions from under a sailor's cap, beard to match – sitting on a log by the back door.

'That's right, front door doesn't open,' he says, when we explain our abrupt appearance. 'Off its hinges. Frame's all rotten, wants replacing. I've had to nail it shut.'

He seems dejected to learn why we've come. The house is on the market, he tells us, because his wife wants to move.

'She's fed up, wants to see the back of it. Told me I had to bloody well get the place smartened up. Well, it does need a lick of paint here and there. Bit of weeding maybe. Though I don't like killing things.'

Such is apparent. He walks us round a garden in revolution, an uprising of flowering, seeding weeds. Everywhere, things are tied up, tied back or tied together – nothing is pruned. No blade has ever been taken to these plants, no stem severed, no sap shed, no root from its mother's womb untimely ripp'd.

'It's lovely,' Eve says, and I can tell she's not keen.

'Bless you. There's not many would agree,' says Grolius, tying one more knot into a cats-cradle of twine that is trying unsuccessfully to confine a climbing rose.

'Had a couple here two days ago, walked round with their noses in the air. Caught 'em giving dirty looks to the daisies in the grass. Can't rightly call it a lawn I daresay. To me grass without daisies is like a night without stars. They went off saying "Sorry, don't think it's really quite us".'

'Don't worry Mr Grolius, we're not put off,' I tell him, not looking at Eve. 'It's charming, your garden.'

'It's a real bit of old Sussex,' says Grolius proudly. 'Land's never had nothing done to it. Not the garden, not the paddocks. No chemicals, no fertilizers. The plants here's been growing in these parts since time out of mind. Got some rare ones. That one, there. Rare one, that is.'

Eve whispers to me, 'It's a grape hyacinth.'

She can name them all, lungwort, toadflax, lilac, syringa, peony, thrusting from the wreck of what had once been a horticulturalist's garden. A garden fork stands rusting in a bed of roses, bindweed twining up its shaft: Eve mutters that it would make a perfect cover for a book called 'The Idle Gardener'.

The orchard is as overgrown as the rest of the place: about twenty apple and pear trees with brambles rearing in their branches and, lost in blackberry jungle, six rotting hen houses.

'I'm leaving the hens,' says Grolius. 'There's only five left. Don't want no extra for them. But I want you to know they was family pets.'

Eve gives a little laugh.

'Don't worry,' she tells him, 'we wouldn't eat them.'

'One other thing,' he says, waving at an elder tree which is growing through the broken frames of a once elegant greenhouse, offering its bitter plates of white flowers to us as we pass, 'you'll think me odd for saying so, but the elder, if you want her out, even if you want to break a branch of her, you must ask her pardon first.'

'Be honest with you,' says the old man, leading the way back to the house, 'she has got it all worked out, my wife, when people come to view the place. Tricks learned off the estate agent. Get the coffee brewing. Real beans, got to grind 'em first, instant won't do. Stick Mozart on the gramophone. Flowers all over the house. But I never did any of that because I didn't want anyone to buy it.'

Eve glances at me in dismay. Grolius, wading chest-deep in cow parsley, stops to push at a leaning laburnum.

'I did my best to put 'em off,' he tells us. 'It's why I don't mend things. Break my heart to leave this place, Mrs . . . ?'

'. . . Bear,' says Eve, horrified yet relieved by these disclosures. 'Don't you worry, Mr Grolius, we won't buy it. Will we, Bear?'

'No,' I say. 'Oh no, certainly not.'

But this makes Grolius even more mournful. 'Oh dear. Oh dear, I thought you liked it. Don't you like it, Mrs Bear?'

'Well, yes, it's lovely,' says trapped Eve.

'Then you will have it' says Grolius. 'No, I insist. It's no good me trying to hold onto it. See, the thing is, Mr and Mrs Bear, to be frank, I can't hold on. Me and my wife, we're separating. She's found a place she wants and she needs the money quick.'

His eyes moisten. He tells how he and his wife no longer speak. They live in the house like two strangers, cook for themselves, do their own washing, avert their eyes and no longer bother to mumble greetings when they pass. They communicate by note. I catch Eve's glance and guess what she's thinking, which is what I'm thinking, that this will not ever happen to us.

As we leave, all we can see of Grolius in the undergrowth is the sailor's cap, hair going off like fireworks, and a waving arm. Later, we realise we hadn't really noticed the house, except that it was dark and smelt of damp and apples – the typical smell of an unheated English country cottage.

'We can't live there,' Eve says firmly. 'It's falling to bits. The walls are damp, there's a horrible black mould up near the ceilings. There's no proper heating. The children will get ill. The garden's a wilderness. There's too much to be done, and you're away in London all the time. We'd never cope.'

The day before we move in Grolius telephones full of apologies that another apple tree has blown down. And we needn't worry about the hens because, well, the old fox, he's scoffed the lot.

Our packing cases, thirty tea-chests of books, leave no room in the house. We take the two small children and huge dog and go outside to explore.

Grolius's log is still outside the back door, a limp wet object flattened upon it.

'Look, Bear,' Eve says, 'he's left you his cap.'

Without the exotic presence of Grolius, the place reverts to what it really is, a damp house in a soggy wilderness. I'm also aware that Eve only agreed to move because I promised her I'd work hard to restore the house and help her coax a garden from the wild. She doesn't say so, but I know she's regretting the comfortable little house we left behind, friends miles away. For a whole month after our move it rains continuously, but we nonetheless set to, pruning and digging. Under the ashes of a bonfire, I find an old midden and fork out things that must have been thrown away when the house was young, a belt buckle formed of rust, a china doll's hand and angular bottles of dark blue glass embossed with the name of a long ago paregoric.

Beyond the orchard a green lane runs to a meadow where the grasses are up to Eve's shoulders. We tread paths through and trample a dell in the centre. We lie hidden, in a circle walled with grass, and make love with only the passing clouds as witnesses. Afterwards, with her head cradled on my shoulder, Eve sleepily murmurs, 'Bear, what did Grolius mean about the elder?'

The day after we move in our four-year-old daughter jumps around the floor of the drawing room.

'Ooh look, like a bouncy castle.'

Something our surveyor has missed: in one corner the floorboards spring a good four inches. Lifting them reveals the joists to be black and spongy. An odour like mushrooms. Wet rot. The whole lot will have to come out.

I earmark the small room next door as a study and move my boxes in. Books, stationery, computer, and a small box containing the modem.

Geno's board, with its zoo of artificial life and arsenal of cyber-weaponry, makes me think of Jamrach's, an emporium which flourished in the London of a century ago. It stood in notorious Ratcliffe Highway, 'a skirmish of crimps and foreign sailors with long knives', Jack the Ripper's part of town: a place of twopenny whores, lascar curry houses and opium dens; Doctor Watson visited it in *The Sign of Four* ('So help me gracious, I have a wiper in this bag, and I'll drop it on your 'ead if you don't 'ook it!'). Jamrach's offered for sale a menagerie of lions, tigers and bears, panthers and elephants, alligators, monkeys, parrots and (w=v)ipers, accompanied by 'the largest and most varied collection of arms, curiosities and savage and civilised art brought together for trade purposes in the world'. Stacked in corners were fantastic gods and goddesses, strange arms and armour, wonderful carvings in ivory, priceless gems of old Japanese pottery, a life-size golden Buddha, shrunken heads, a clay mask with violently protruding tongue, gorgeous seashells, pasha's tails, crania bearing signs and tokens of violent death, among them the skull of an undoubted cannibal.

Just such a jumble are the bulletin boards of the cybergypsies, a glorious chaos of objects, trophies, curios and booty brought back by travellers from remote regions of the metaverse. Shrunken heads, cannibalism, strange gods, sacred masks, wild animals – yes, you'll find all these in cyberspace, as well as other things you wouldn't necessarily expect: Neanderthal remains, curare, cobra and rattler venoms, blueprints for atomic bombs, immortality potions, iron neck-collars, slave helmets, leather underwear, and latter day Burkes and Hares purveying real human skulls, whole skeletons, arms, legs, etc. ('Everything clean & in good condition, with no holes'.)

Listen, Eve. There's a cave in the hillside, hollowed out by the lick of a watery tongue on limestone. It runs back twenty feet, then narrows to a crack from which, according to tradition, lost underground passages depart for the world of faery. Nothing otherwordly about the place now. The dirt floor is littered with the usual tourist wrack, crumpled cola cans, cigarettes dissolving into splats of horse-manure, pre-owned condoms and an embrasure of sooty stones where visitors – boyscouts, new age travellers, gypsies, tramps, take your pick – have lit many fires. In one corner a child has dropped a pink plastic bracelet. On the walls – no Pêche Merle this – generations of graffitists have left messages of the utmost puerility.

Whoever wrote this, he was a sexist
Joey is a wanker
Effie loves her own finger

Some older scratches further back in the cave: a date, 1781, and initials which look like S.T.C.

All of this Laura Hunter, Lorelei to her friends, regards with weary disgust. Emerges, stands blinking in the sunlight looking across to where the land slopes to a flatscape of fen and dyke. There is her goal, an ivy-strangled castle which totters rather than rises from a moat over which mists hover like strips of ether-soaked gauze. It's everything she detests.

Lorelei levers her heels with fastidious revulsion from the Oxfordshire loam. Living in London, she has not seen fields for years and is surprised that there are so many left. She's here to scout locations for a fashion shoot. The art director wanted a castle, so Lorelei, mainly to get out of the office, has volunteered to do the recce. She's a junior copywriter in a London ad agency famous for the startling campaigns it created – surreal posters for Benson & Hedges cigarettes, funny TV commercials for Hamlet cigars and Heineken lager. The agency is in its third golden age, living on its own myths in a world where glasses of Cinzano will forever drench Joan Collins's décolletage and gruff Yorkshire folk always use Hovis for their butties. Lorelei's contribution to the Hovis ads is one line, spoken by a flour-dusted baker to a boy who has rowed three miles to buy a loaf: 'Ee lad, yer not 'alf as green as yer cabbage looking'.

In the real world there is fear of recession and the agency's backers, locked in sullen conclave, are talking of 'downsizing', but advertising folk are used to living high on the hog and are in the habit of mistaking eccentricity for talent, so they turn a blind eye when Laura borrows her boss the head of copy's hired Porsche and abandons it, driver's door flung wide, at Heathrow airport because, as she later points out, she has no idea where the car park is, no time to find out and no intention of missing her flight to New York, after all she's only going for the weekend. That, anyway, is how she tells it. New York is a typical Lorelei bolthole. She has friends in Greenwich Village who'd known Mapplethorpe and Warhol. *'Linger on, your pale blue eyes,'* sings Lou Reed in her ear and suggests they go roust out Moe Tucker in Georgia. She dances with Mick Jagger (no, someone cooler, David Bowie) during a cyberslut night at Jackie 60 (thi is a slip-up, not everything she says can be taken at face value, but who among us is entirely what we seem?), until her skin glistens like armour, shouting to him on the crowded dance floor that she is going to discover the secret of immortality.

A cynic might say that Lorelei lives out a set of clichés. Hers is exactly the sort of life you'd imagine for a girl as smart, intelligent and attractive as she appears. She's bright, a double first from Cambridge in Eng. Lit., and naturally she's attractive – twenty-three, slim, a natural blonde – men's jaws plummet past their balls at her very description. Lorelei likes medieval French poetry, the music of Thierry Robin, clothes, parties, dancing, fast cars and sex, provided the sex isn't heavy and the lover not too serious and vice versa. If a thinking man had to design an ideal girl, it might well be Laura H.

This then is the amazing bint who stands surveying the falling-down castle, comparing it to other castles she knows. She thinks of Carcassonne in the Languedoc, razed in the anti-Cathar crusade of Simon de Montfort in 1209, restored as nineteenth-century fantasy by Violet le Duc; Sleeping Beauty's Castle in Orlando, created as a first generation fantasy by Walt Disney; Castle Drogo, a beetling granite crag on the edge of Dartmoor, William Randolph Hearst's castle, a sort of portmanteau castle-of-castles assembled from bits of real buildings, glued together by pastiche, including details from the Doge's palace in Venice. Castles have always been fantastic. Never were they designed purely to be functional, but always, even in the middle ages, to express dreams of power or unction. This is true, Lorelei reflects (Eve, if you're wondering how I know what she's thinking, just take my word for it), for every castle she can think of, imaginary or real, from Fata Morgana's cloudy keep to the crenellations described by Tristram Shandy's Quixote-inspired Uncle Toby with flourishes of his walking stick; Macbeth's castle – 'heaven's breath smells wooingly here'; Monty Python's castle of the Holy Grail, from whose ramparts enemies were pelted with tandoori'd chicken-legs; the grim battlements of Bunratty Castle in County Clare, provided with 'murder holes' for pouring boiling oil onto enemies; and Carcassonne itself, from whose eyries defenders could shit from a great height upon besiegers. (Laura-Lorelei's imagination is caught by Carcassonne's doom: brought about by a faith which taught that the world was made by an evil creator, that human spirits are fragments of deity imprisoned in flesh, and must escape the universe of mass, energy, space and time.)

Far below her, in the area enclosed by the castle walls, Lorelei sees something strange, a little girl skipping along in an old-fashioned Alice-in-Wonderland party dress. Chasing a hoop? Surely not. Perhaps it's a Mad Hatter's tea party. The child vanishes from view, but her presence is reassuring. Lorelei takes off her shoes and runs down the hill, puts them on again when she reaches the path at the bottom and steps out onto the rotten drawbridge wondering if her heels will spike through the powdery timber.

Someone else is there, a young man with a rucksack. He is throwing morsels of bread into the water for outsize carp that appear from the depths, opening O mouths to suck the crumbs down green whirlpools.

Hello, the young man smiles. Seems pleasant, and Lorelei is glad to have company. He asks if she plans to enter the ruined courtyard and if he might accompany her. She agrees and is still wondering what they will talk about when he runs round in front and sweeps from under his jacket a rusty blade the length of a sword. Lorelei does not have time to scream before he hacks off her head.

She is reborn three seconds later minus half her points, her innocence shattered. She has learned the first lesson of cyberspace: that although everything around her, including herself, is fantasy, the terror is real.

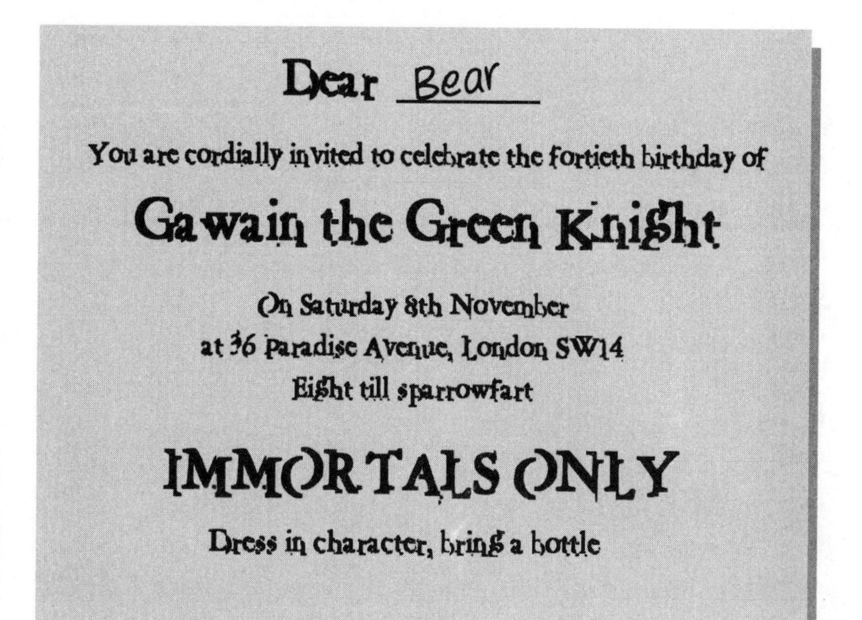
Dear Bear

You are cordially invited to celebrate the fortieth birthday of

Gawain the Green Knight

On Saturday 8th November
at 36 Paradise Avenue, London SW14
Eight till sparrowfart

IMMORTALS ONLY

Dress in character, bring a bottle

The assassination of a prince of the virtual realms at this party would spark off the First Wyrd War.

Great Tew

Lorelei died and was born again in a place called Shades, a remote region of cyberspace, little visited by tourists. Shades is a multi-user game, a place where unusual folk come to escape 'reality' (Eve, note the ass's ears I affix to that vulgar word) and to enact agonies and ironies upon one another. A place, I say, but the cave, landscape, castle and underlying labyrinth of Shades are no more than words on a screen, descriptions to be navigated solely by the compass of the imagination. They are, nonetheless, completely real to the characters who inhabit them. Such lands are discovered only by chance. Each player finds his or her own way there. For me, the path to the murder scene beneath the castle walls led directly from a spot in the 'real' world. I can even supply the grid reference: 51°58′N, 1°35′W, Ordnance Survey SP 296309. It was at this place, at 4.10 on a cold afternoon fifteen years ago, that a wormhole from cyberspace opened up and sucked me in.

I'd spent the morning driving round the lanes of north Oxfordshire near the village of Great Tew, looking for signs to a circus. Third time past the same old man wheeling his bicycle up the same lane, I stop to ask for directions and then realise I have forgotten the name of the farm.

'Where Chipperfield's Circus has its winter quarters,' I tell him, 'a farm where they have lions and bears and things.'

The old fellow looks me up and down.

'Don't get lions in England,' he says.

'This isn't a normal farm,' I say, speaking more slowly. 'It's where the circus spends the winter. They have all sorts there, tigers, lions, elephants . . .'

The ancient man shakes his head. 'Won't find elephants round here, s'all sheep and dairy.'

'It's a fucking circus.'

The old man's lips wrinkle back from his gums revealing half a dozen discoloured teeth, and a thick tongue slides forward through the largest available gap.

'Hehehehe,' he cackles, 'sorry. Well, wouldn't you?'

Like Lorelei, I am on an advertising shoot. Our mission is to take portraits of a bear and a bull. We will blend them together to make a picture sequence showing the bull transforming by degrees into the bear. The pictures will illustrate an ad for a thing called a modem, which lets your computer telephone another computer for the latest share prices. Use this modem thing, our idea is, and don't get caught out when a bull market turns bearish. The fact that you can check share prices from a computer on your desk or at home seems to me incredible. That you can even have a computer at home is amazing. I have never met anyone who has used one, either at home or at work: I'm going to be the first person I know to try one out. Before heading for Oxfordshire I had visited the Bristol office of the Apricot computer company. On the back seat of my car is a large box containing a computer called an Eff-One, Apricot's answer to Apple's newfangled Macintosh. The modem and the magical disk are sitting on the passenger seat in a plastic bag as I follow the old git's directions ('Back the way you come, bear left not as in bear haha, go on 'bout a mile and a half and look out for elephant do.').

Actually it *is* bear shit we have to watch for. Stinks like dog dung, only more so. Bear droppings are dark and fibrous, with that bitter-sour reek so insulting to the nostrils when you step in it. Sooty the black bear is young and unused to lights. She defecates a lot, dropping merds a foot wide. The small art director complains of the reek and Stak, our dapper Greek photographer, who never loses an opportunity to talk about wine, chips in that he would far rather be inhaling the bouquet of a good claret (albeit his favourite 'claret' – nothing is ever what it seems – is a cabernet sauvignon-syrah-mourvèdre-grenache blend from the Beka'a Valley).

'We'll give her a break,' the trainer, Jim, tells us, 'She's young and cuddly as a pup, but bears are unpredictable. You can't tell what she's feeling from the look on her face. She could just *go*.'

We go instead. Stroll round the farmyard. Steaming animals, hay smells, the ever present dung-reek, smoke from a wood fire. Along the fence stands a row of travelling animal wagons, cages on wheels. Some are huge – what beasts must they be for? We enter a field and a dozen grazing animals look up. Not cows, camels.

'Keep calm,' says Stak. 'They are *to*-ta-lly harmless.'

He bends, uproots some grass and walks towards them. A she-dromedary, misliking his hubris, or perhaps mistaking his intentions, works up a big gob of green slime and lets fly. Stak leaves fast, camel closing behind (exit pursued by a camel) teeth lunging for the seat of his pants, art director and I helpless with laughter.

After the shoot, Stak offers to take a picture of us in front of the lion's cage. We pose proudly.

'Can't get you both in,' Stak says. 'Step back a bit.'

The art director's shoulder touches the cage, the lion gives a furious roar and charges the bars. Stak doubling up in a fit of giggles. 'Bugger, missed it' he says. 'You both leapt right out of frame.'

I get in my car to go home and drive away in the wrong direction. Twenty to four.

The Rollright Stones

Picture a lane glittering under a watery sun, lined with elders that reach out to scrape woody nails along the car. I am lost. Stop to take bearings, consult a map. It feels as if all day I've been roaming this countryside. The sun is low, the trees casting long shadows across the road. There's a chill in the air. In the manner of the best fairy tales I emerge from a reverie to find myself staring at a circle of weathered stones. In the failing light they look incredibly ancient, like rotten stumps of teeth that the wind has stuck its tongue unto.

I get out of the car and am walking towards the circle when an elderly woman materialises from the shadows.

'So sorry,' she says, 'I was having a cup of tea. It's twenty pence to see the stones.'

She takes my small coin and, licking her forefinger and thumb, carefully tears a leaf from a book of tickets. Then, since I am her only visitor that afternoon, she comes over to join me by the stone circle and tells me their story.

'A very long time ago,' she says, 'an earl and his followers were approaching this spot, just like you a minute ago, when up jumped this ugly old witch, barring the way. She declared:

> *"Seven long strides shalt thou take,*
> *And if Long Compton thou canst see,*
> *King of England thou shalt be."*

'Well, the earl was thrilled. He was already where we are, almost on top of the hill. Long Compton's just the other side. He shouted:

> *"Stick, stock, stone,*
> *As King of England I shall be known."'*

The old lady pauses and peers up at me. She is wearing a straw hat about seven sizes too large for her.

'Take you, you're a big chap. You'd think you could get to the top in a few strides. Be honest, you would, wouldn't you?'

I nod.

'Ah! Got you!' she cries in triumph. 'Got you, she would have, that old witch. Lump of stone you'd be. That'd be you standing there, all oolitic. You see, just as the earl took the last stride, into view popped a small mound – and what do they call it when the moon blots out the sun? – an eclipse. Yes, well this mound just rose up out of the hillside and eclipsed Long Compton. The crone laughed and shrieked:

"As Long Compton thou canst not see,
King of England thou shalt not be.
Rise up stock and stand still stone,
For King of England thou shalt be none.
Thou and thy men hoar stones shall be,
And I myself an eldern tree."

'When he heard these words, the earl felt his muscles start to stiffen and realised that his body was turning to stone.'

'Look.' She points across the lane to a stooping shape eight feet high. 'That's his lordship. His knights were cowards. They're down the hill in the other direction. Must've hung back, waiting to see what would happen, but that didn't save them from the witch.'

She beckons me to the centre of the stone circle.

'The common soldiers had more courage but less sense. They surrounded the witch to taunt her, or maybe to poke her with their pikes, and here they all are to this day – a bunch of poor old oolitic limestones.'

'What happened to the witch?' I ask.

'Oh her?' says the old woman with a strange smile. 'She's still here.'

'She turned herself into an elder tree. Why do you think the elders round here are so overgrown? It's because the locals don't dare to cut them back. And you know what else? Under the stones is a cave of the fairy folk and from time to time someone stumbles across the opening and vanishes, never to be seen again.'

'It's a good story,' I say, 'but I've heard it before.'

Homer used bits of it in *The Odyssey*, Tolkien in *The Lord of the Rings*, Pratchett in *Wyrd Sisters* and Shakespeare in *Macbeth*. The Rollright witch surely inspired the three hags who flagged down Macbeth, causing Banquo to give that great start of alarm (well, it had to be visible from the gods): 'What are these, so withered and so wild in their attire, that look not like the inhabitants of th'earth, but yet are on't?' The heath encounter, foul hag, promise of kingship, equivocating double-talk that betrays, faery cavern, connivance of nature (earth mounds, or woods, that move) in the hero's downfall – all are found in *Macbeth*. Shakespeare must have known the story of the Rollright witch, for Stratford-on-Avon lies a handful of miles to the north.

'Knew about her? I should think so', says the old woman with a good deal of scorn in her voice. 'Of course Bill Shakespeare knew all about that witch. She was far better known than he was.'

Five centuries before Lorelei's death and resurrection, a child was born in a cave by a river. Ursula Sontheil entered the world after a labour during which not just her mother's waters but the caul of the sky broke; her mother's cries of pain were translated into lightning flashes; her farts and the drumming of her heels on the earth floor became claps and rumbles of thunder. This was the stormy summer of 1488 and the baby girl would be better known as Old Mother Shipton, the most famous beldam of her day. She was eldest of a trio of seers. Nostradamus was born fifteen years later near Avignon and, in London twenty-four years after that, the wizard John Dee, who lived to be a contemporary of Shakespeare. The prophecies of Nostradamus and Dee are obscure, but Mother Shipton's was a lucid style of sybilry. She unambiguously foresaw the Great Fire of London, the French Revolution, the motor car and the internet. (You see, Eve, this is not entirely irrelevant. A denizen of the usenet newsgroup *sci.maths* has shown that Nostradamus forecast the Pentium Bug, lambasting Intel and Bill Gates by name. John Dee's contribution is harder to pin down, but his invocations, babbled in an unknown angelic tongue, inspired Aleister Crowley, and other gnostics, including the spiritual heirs of the Cathars, with what results we see today throughout the world wide web. Shipton, Nostradamus, Dee – proto-cybernauts all.)

Much taken with the old lady's tale, I begin scanning the ground for a little fragment of stone – one nobody could possibly mind me taking – for good luck. In the gathering gloom, when the witch's back is turned, I prise a small chip from the muddy field. Had it originally flaked off one of the Rollrights? No way to tell. I put it in the glove compartment and, mind buzzing, drive home to Sussex and Eve. Eve and I need luck. Lots of it. We are about to move to a house we've been arguing over for months, a place so run down that it has been on the market for a year, so overgrown that from the road it's invisible, hidden behind salutes of green leaf-smoke fired at the sky by woody, irresponsible cannons.

In a Sussex hedgerow

The mind plays tricks, sees shapes in hedges, things that aren't there. Or maybe they are there, for Sussex, on evenings when the woodsmoke closes in, is a shape-shifting magical countryside. Its trees and hedges are transforming themselves under my tired eyes to stilt-legged magicians and witches. I should heed the warning signs and stop to rest, but don't. At some point the road slides away from underneath me and whirls round and round; the car's headlights, revolving like a lighthouse beam, pick out a hedge of ash trees that come spinning from the night, slide past the bonnet and smash into the rear. When the car finally becomes quiet, I find myself in darkness, lying flat on the floor. My seat has absorbed an impact which might have killed me had the car hit head first. I sit up to find a wrist-thick spear of ash raking through a shattered window. Crawl out of the passenger door, unhurt save for a scratch. Before leaving the wreck, I remember to retrieve the little piece of Rollright stone.

The car is a write-off but the computer, which had been in the back seat, works when I plug it in. There is no sign of the modem or disk, they must have been lost in the crash.

I'd probably never have touched a modem again, if four days later, Eve hadn't come into the room holding a magazine.

'You'll never believe this,' she says.

There is an article about the Rollright Stones. It says that anyone who tries to remove a piece of the Stones draws down a curse upon themselves – a curse which will only lift if the stone is returned. A man from Banbury took a chip from one of the stones – and returned to his cart to find its wheels locked solid. A young soldier took a piece of a Rollright stone to India – and was soon dead of typhus. A farmer from Little Rollright once removed a capstone to bridge a stream . . . As Eve reads I can almost hear the old woman's voice:

'The moment they got the ropes round that stone, strange groans and cries of pain started coming up out of the earth. It took a team of twenty horses to drag the stone down to the bottom of the hill. It didn't want to go, and it crushed a man. In the end they got it lying across the stream and went sorrowfully home. But by morning the stone had flipped over and was lying on the bank. They went at it again and another man died and next morning the stone was flipped over again. Well, no matter how stupid you are, you learn in the end. The farmer realised that he must take the stone back. And do you know, just one horse pulled it all the way back up that field as easy as you like into its proper place.'

At the weekend we hire a car, get the children in and drive back to the stone circle. I take the fragment of stone from my pocket and, with a sincere apology to Old Mother Shipton, tread it into the turf.

'There you are,' says a voice. 'I knew you'd be back. You left this behind.'

She hands me the bag with the disk and the modem.

130.43.43.43

130.43.43.43 was the IP number of an internet 'gopher', an archive of texts, called *wiretap.spies*. Into this machine, half a decade ago, a person or persons unknown placed verses looted from a translation of *Kama Sutra*; and not any common-or-perfumed-garden *Kama Sutra*, but one that Eve and I had worked on together in an effort to break out of the poverty trap and because we wanted to travel.

In the seventies Eve was an editorial assistant in a publishing firm and I was a junior copywriter in a London advertising agency. Somehow we persuaded her company to commission me to make a new translation of the text, and Eve to find pictures. This gave us the chance to spend six months running round India, pestering museum keepers and gallery owners, meeting some odd people: the elderly Englishman with a reputation as an international art smuggler; a sinister tantric poet. On a steam train from Lucknow to Bombay, Eve read me her favourite lines of John Donne's:

Let sea-discoverers to new worlds have gone,
Let maps to other, worlds on worlds have shown,
Let us possess one world, each hath one, and is one.

We spent two months in Bombay puzzling over Vatsyayana's text with a tiny Sanskrit professor who limped and had a passion for English horse-racing. One day we took a boat to Elephanta Island where we were adopted by a guide with the startling pale eyes you sometimes see in Maharashtra. Mindful of efficient work practices, he led us round the caves at breakneck speed.

'Can you tell us something about this one?' Eve asked, stopping briefly before a huge figure carved in the rock.

'Madam, it is a god.'

Eve moved to the next figure. 'And this?'

'Madam, this is also a god.'

'Yes, but what are their names?'

'How is it mattering, madam. Ultimately all gods are one.'

I took her to see Ravi Shankar play. As the music heated up, afficionados in the audience uttered appreciative cries of 'wah wah' and clicked their tongues in delight – precisely the same sound an English mother makes to scold a misbehaving child.

Eve turned and glared at the enraptured gentlemen behind us. 'If they don't like it,' she whispered, 'why did they come?'

We went to meet the folks at a hashish den hidden in a maze of back lanes in the city's bazaars, a place where some years earlier I had spent a lot of time. On the way back in a taxi, we were stopped by a girl selling jasmine garlands and bought her entire stock. It cost about £1 and Eve was hidden by the flowers, wreathed like a maharani on her wedding day. (Have I remembered to say we were just married? The trip to India doubled as our honeymoon.) We were in love and liked, as much as wandering the real world, roaming the territories of each other's minds.

My face in thine eye, thine in mine appears,
And true plain hearts do in the faces rest;
Where can we find two better hemispheres,
Without sharp north, without declining west?
Whatever dies, was not mix'd equally;
If our two loves be one, or, thou and I
Love so alike, that none do slacken, none can die.

Our *Kama Sutra* was published by Hamlyn and, sadly, is still in print. Predictably the pirates on *wiretap.spies* stole only the section on the sexual positions. What they missed, apart from the point, was one of the most extraordinary uses of language in the book and unquestionably the sweetest experience.

The language of birds

The ecstatic utterance of birds as recorded by Vatsyayana in *Kama Sutra*:

> अम्बर्थाः शब्दाः वारणार्थ मोक्षणार्थाश्चलमार्थ स्ते ते चार्थ योगात पारावत परभ्रित हारीत शुक मधुकर दात्यूह हंस कारण्डव लावक विरुतानि सीत्क्रित भूयिष्टानि विकल्पशः
>
> The best translation is Meg Ryan's in *When Harry met Sally*.

The electronic post arrives bringing a letter (yes, a genuine ee-by-gum-mail) from Jarly, who is a Yorkshireman and writes:

>Bear darling, if tha fancies mekkin a few changes to yer bank balance, here are't codes for NatWest:

Telephone number: 061 833 0091
Baud rate: 1200/1200 7N1
TTY Xmodem
4 x " followed by <RETURN>
<RETURN>
D1 <RETURN>
4 x " followed by NNATDEM287UCC <RETURN>
3 x "
A21280011164 <RETURN>
5 x " followed by 9900 <RETURN>
2 x " ACCESS <RETURN>
2 x " followed by OPER01 <RETURN>
2 x " followed by TESTOP <RETURN>

>If it's nation's pockets tha want to pick drop in on't Bank of England on 01 583 3000

CALL 79
ID BOE001

Please, don't even think about it. Hacking banks is not a sound idea unless you're an expert, besides which the dialling codes and modem speeds show this stuff to be years out of date. What the Bank of England data – password deleted, reason fear of treason, for which you can still be executed in the Tower of London – does reveal is that the B of E belonged to System 79 of an antediluvian network called Telecom Gold, the same system to which Apricot's magic bull-to-bear software connected me late in 1984. There were in those days three British Telecom nets much used by the UK cybergypsies: Gold, Prestel, and Micronet. Someone hacked Prince Philip's Prestel mailbox about the time I joined Gold.

Jarly is my first friend on the net. He says he's twenty-two. I am a dozen years older, but if it makes no difference to him it makes none to me.

'So Bear, how long have you been using?'

'Using what?'

'Onlining. It's like mainlining, only more addictive.'

'I'm not addicted,' I say.

'You will be,' says Jarly.

Jarly claims to be a part-time postman and a roadie for a heavy metal band. Neither can be true since, as he frequently tells me, he's a Gloriaria Estefanfan – hard to believe but I have seen her picture on his wall. He lives in a bare north London attic that smells of pickle and leaks. (No, no, Eve, not smells like leeks, the room leaks, but that story is for later.) A permanent state of war exists between Jarly and his landlord, who lives in the flat below. Jarly is usually months behind with the rent and large folk with bent noses are forever knocking on the landlord's door wanting cash.

'Your problem,' I tell him, 'is you spend too much time on Shades killing people.'

'Be reasonable, Bear, I can't give that up. It's my life.'

'Couldn't you cut down?'

'Doesn't fuckin' work. Ask any sixty-a-day bloke. Ask a junkie.'

'You're on too much Jarly. Every time I log in, there you are. Or if you're not already there, you sogonr appieanr.'

So*g*on*r* app*i*ea*n*r? Oh, soGonR appIeaNr.

This happens when he starts typing back to me while I am still in the middle of typing to him.

I have to admit he's right.

'Aye,' says he, 'tha's not so green as tha's cabbage lookin.'

Jarly spends a minimum of eight hours a day on Shades, which is, depending on your outlook, a game, a world, or a way of life. Shades is offered by all three BT services and Jarly has an account with each. I know that his last telephone bill was well into four figures, with time charges for Gold and Prestel/Micronet probably adding the same again. How he pays them I don't know, given that he hasn't time to work. Actually I do know. Jarly's habit, when one account begins to stagger under the burden of debt, is to abandon it and open a new one in a variant of his name, Jarly, Charlie, Sharlene, Sherry, Jerry: a sort of slash and burn existence, entirely appropriate to a cybernomad.

He also makes a small living selling immortality. (Eve, this will not make sense if I try to explain it now.)

There's a note from Jarly at the end of the hacking stuff. 'Someone's gotta be daft enough to try it and, Bear lad, your need is greater than mine.'

Rain rain go away

I connect for the first time on a drab December day, water running down the newly glazed window panes of my study. Outside is the joyful dripping wilderness. Inside the walls are neatly papered, books sorted on shelves that still smell of sawdust and pine resin. Eve and I did this together. We tackled the study first because I have so much work to get through. I've promised that as soon as I have time, I'll build her a kitchen to replace the woodlouse-ridden units we pulled out and burned on the first day. I turn on the machine, click Apricot's magic software into its slot. Out in the rain I can see Eve, fair hair tucked under a sou'wester, booted feet wide apart in what had once been a flowerbed, stubbornly forking at the Sussex clay. The machine emits a high pitched whistle, followed by the kookaburra cackle of a modem exchanging electronic greetings. Then there's text rolling up the screen, welcoming me to something called Telecom Gold.

One of the first things I discover is that Apricot's vision of instant intelligence is seriously flawed. The databases of share prices and company information are hard to negotiate, slow, and cost several quid a minute – ridiculously expensive. Apart from chucking money away on these, there isn't very much else to do on Telecom Gold. I go to something called the Noticeboard. It proves to be an electronic pinboard where users leave notes for one another. The messages are listed in date order: the most recent first, then back through yesterday, last week, last month. They are not very interesting. People spend a lot of time posting variations of 'Hi. I'm here. Are you there?' Their names intrigue me. Molesworth and Pooh hobnob with Neuromancer; Bond007 with the inexpressible horror of Great Cthulhu (given to posting *h'nglui mglw'nafh Cthulhu R'lyeh wgah'nagl fhtagn* which, as any fule kno, means 'In his house in

R'lyeh, dead Cthulhu lies dreaming'); Country Girl, Bouncy, Zimmerman, Branwell (Brontë), Chesh the Cheshire Cat, Shadow – each talking to the rest several times a day from offices all over Britain, a couple in Ireland, many in Europe. Despite the banality of their chitchat, it is soon apparent that these geographically scattered folk share a curious intimacy. They are a community. Gradually, over the next few weeks I learn some of the stories behind the names. Branwell is deaf. Country Girl is blind. Bouncy is in love. It's like being part of a soap opera. I'm soon logging in at all hours, in eager to catch the latest gossip. Dracula wasn't on last night, but has checked in at 8.30 this morning full of bonhomie. What can this mean, except that his date with Little Miss Muffet has ended with breakfast?

Sudeep is in his pyjamas scouring his teeth. He sighs. Early shift tomorrow, but there's something on the radio he's loth to miss. The midnight concert is a performance of the rare *raga* Rageshri by *sarod* maestro Ustad Bahadur Khan. Sudeep is a music connoisseur, but a police inspector's salary does not run to fancy equipment. He sets up his battery-powered cassette recorder and positions the microphone as near as he can get it to the radio. As the station's eerie flute motif signals midnight, he presses the 'record' button, holding his breath, better to hear the first notes of the *sarod* steal out into the quiet night air.

The way a classical *raga* works is that the instrumentalist, the *sitar* or *sarod* virtuoso, begins a slow exploration of the scale. This is like a meditation. It can last an hour, but for radio performances is generally much shortened. When the performer feels that he has wrung what emotion he can from the notes, he nods for the *tabla*, the hand drum, to join in. Rhythm now provides the focus, as both performers improvise within a strict cycle of beats, the soloist demonstrating his mastery of the various set pieces and ornaments demanded by tradition. After this the music can move to a faster gait, calling for a more instinctive performance; the instrumentalist will make shining runs, the beat quickens again, doubles, the *tabla* player's fingers blurring over his drums, the sarodist's fingers flying on the strings; the sound becomes a continuous singing tone, in the midst of which are little rushes and runs, like rivers of bright flame inside a fire; the *raga* reaches its climax when the two instruments blur and become one, and then it stops. But on Sudeep's tape, the sound does not stop.

Early in the recording, the music begins to be accompanied by unusual sounds. The *sarod's* deep-throated tones – twenty-five strings ringing on a neck of polished steel – are interrupted by the thud of a door, muffled distant shouts. The *tabla,* coming in, cuts through the interference, but not for long. Within a minute, the tape is recording cries and yells. Doors banging. Footsteps pounding in the lane outside. Rageshri is a sombre *raga,* it should be heard in silence. But now, inside the house, there is a cough, then a startled cry. A woman calls out in alarm. A child screams. A man's deeper voice, very close, tries to restore calm, disintegrates into retching. In a moment of respite, the *sarod* sobs under Bahadur Khan's clever fingers. The child screams again and the woman shrieks something unintelligible. More coughing. An older child urgently speaking. The music is eclipsed by coughing very close to the microphone. Outside sounds too are louder. The woman begins to weep. The children are wailing, the music is completely drowned. The woman cries, 'Oh mother, I'm dying.' A dry scraping sound. Someone runs across the room. Vomiting. The door of Sudeep's house opens and noise rushes in, a thunder of feet and hundreds of voices all at once. Hubbub inside too. Frantic feet, a crackle as the radio is knocked, and then the goose-hiss of white noise. Still the tape winds on slow spools. If it were videotape, it would see what comes creeping in, pressing foggy fingers on the window, beating through the open door in waves. It would see the light grow pearly and fade to white. But the machine in Sudeep's abandoned house, its metal circuitry unaffected, records only the dismal groans and shrieks, gradually diminishing, and, in the end, silence . . .

Bear, imagine that when you're two your mother dies – you're too young to realise – but your father remarries three months later cos he says you need a mother. So you see, it is for your benefit – the ungrateful, wicked, daughter – that he ignores the criticism of his family. 'Bugger their lace-curtained souls.' His family had asked him to wait. They wanted a decent period of mourning. No chance. When my brother was born, five months after the marriage, they had to say he was premature . . . Are you listening . . . ?

Until I was eight I thought Angela was my mum. There was no reason not to – that's the best way I can put it now. We were just a normal family. Dad, Mum, me and Tim. Until my aunt came to visit. My father's sister, who'd been in Canada for years. She looked at me and said, 'You look just like your mother.'

I laughed and said, 'I'm nothing like Mum.'

I was dark you see, while Angela was sort of mouse, but got blonder every year.

'Oh, I meant your real mother,' said my aunt.

I started laughing at the joke. My aunt looked at Dad. He was furious, I could see that. But he was controlling himself. He was a big man, with big hands, sort of gruff, like you'd imagine an engine driver. His fists were clenched tight.

I got scared. I said, 'Mum?'

Angela looked wretched. Then I knew it was true. I felt sick. Horrified. Then Angela started crying. I wanted to shake her and say, 'Mum, why won't you say it's not true?'

The aunt sat there, taking it all in. She said, 'I'm sorry. I thought you'd have told Clare by now.'

I'll never forget that evening. Everyone trying to act natural . . . Dad turning on the telly for the football . . . My aunt made an excuse and went upstairs. Dad took me aside and said, 'Your mum's upset. Forget what your aunt said. She's out to cause trouble. One day I'll explain. You're a good little girl, Clare. Don't let this bother you. Put it out of your mind. Forget it.'

I caught my aunt next day. She was packing to leave. I said to her, 'Tell me about my real mother.'

She stopped in the middle of folding a jumper and asked, 'Haven't they said anything?'

'Dad says we're not to talk about it. In case it upsets me.'

She sat me down and looked at me. 'Queer little thing, aren't you?' she said. 'You're just like her, you know . . .'

Bear, does it make you nervous, me walking up and down like this? Say if the smoke's bothering you . . .

Things got back to normal, but they weren't the same. Angela would hug and cuddle me, saying that she really *was* my mother, even if she wasn't my *real* mother, if you see what I mean. But after that, I began noticing things. Trivial things, but clues. If there was a scrape of baked beans left in the pan, Angela would dollop it onto her son's plate. If we were quarrelling it was always 'Oh Clare let him have it stop bothering him Clare Clare, don't make him cry.' He always got the last biscuit and the first ride when we went to the seaside. Now I knew why. They said Tim was spoilt because he was the younger one. But I knew that wasn't the real reason. It was because my brother was the real child.

I was a step-child. I didn't fit in my family. My brother had a real dad and a real mum. Angela had a real son and a real husband. Dad had a real wife and real children. They were a normal family – it was me who was out of step. When I thought back I realised that it had always been like this. I'd just never noticed. How the hell had I been so stupid? God, they must have thought I was really dumb.

I used to be awake in my bed at night – this was when I was older – Bear, are you really, truly comfortable, lying there? . . . I remember that room so well. The yellow sodium light outside the window turned the whole world grey, the street grey, curtains grey, my bedspread grey. The walls were thin and I used to hear the bed creaking next door, the cough, the groan of springs as she got up afterwards – never him, she had a light tread – the running of water in the bathroom. I thought, that's where your power comes from. That's how you took him from my mother. Your magic is in your . . . that word we don't like to say. I would lie in my cold bed, touching myself for comfort. I used to feel guilty, but not about that. About not having the guts to say what my aunt had told me.

Sometimes I'd talk to my real mother. I'd say, 'Did you know what was going on with Dad and Angela? Is that why you died?' I'd ask, 'How did you do it? How could you pull that off?' You see, Bear, she didn't do anything obvious like a bottle of pills or slitting her wrists in the bath. Not her. She died of pneumonia caught while walking her dog in a snowstorm. I can't even kid myself that she deliberately walked out into a blizzard, because it was June. Years later I looked up the report in the local newspaper. The weathermen were as amazed as everyone else at the freak weather over Leith Hill. Bear, I've no proof but I know my mother wanted to die. She'd willed that snow (which proves there's magic in the world). There is magic, Bear, if you know how to find it – how are you feeling now? – a wounded heart can conjure a thunderstorm out of a clear sky and ice from midsummer.

I wanted so much to know my mother. When I went away to university I tried everything – hypnosis, LSD, rebirthing – that might bring back a glimpse, a smell, a feeling. That's also when I discovered men. The first time someone said they loved me, can you imagine what that was like? Men will say anything to get you into bed, and how badly I wanted to hear them say it. During my first year I ended up sleeping with a lot of people. Not for sex. I'd get sex out of the way, so I could get beyond it. Sex doesn't matter, it isn't as important as love. Bear, you understand why I'm telling you these things? I don't want secrets between us. I want you to know everything about me. Everything, no matter how bad . . . Once I was in a bar and these two men began chatting me up. I went back to their hotel. They were salesmen, sharing a room. I got into bed with one while his friend lay in the other bed. When we'd finished, my one went to the bathroom and the other one climbed into bed with me. I let him. Just lay there while he did it. I was thinking about Angela and how the fairy tales are wrong. Because you see, the really wicked thing is, she probably did her best to love me.

Clare, still naked from the waist down, paces back and forth, smoking her umpteenth cigarette as she offers these explanations for her peculiar life. Lying on her sofa with my eyes closed, fighting to breathe, I wonder, does she really expect me to believe her.

Aphrodite foods and supplies

APHRODITE FOODS AND SUPPLIES, the sign glows faintly blue in the dingy north London half light, is an emporium owned by Jarly's landlord Dimitri. It juts from the ground floor of the tall Victorian building in whose bleak attic Jarly leaves his body while he is off wandering the cyberverse. From its open doors emanate, now and at most o'clocks, mournful eastern Mediterranean musics.

I am here to dine chez Jarly, an invitation he issued on Shades in a fit of bonhomie after he'd killed someone we both disliked. I don't think I was expected to turn up, because Jarly seems surprised to see me. There's no food in the flat, hence the visit to Dimitri's.

'Go ahead,' says Jarly with a wave, 'choose anything you like.'

Around the walls are arrays of tins that have the feel – a slight taint about the metal, oily discolorations of the label – of having sat in warehouses at Limassol for several years. They bear names in Greek script which decode to things like *kalamares, hathapodi, houmous, dolamadakia, imam*. Jarly walks down the aisle rapping the tins and jars with his knuckles, picking up packets, examining them briefly and putting them back.

'Checking the calories?' I ask, because it's what I do.

'Don't be a middle-class git, Bear.'

'So, Jarly. Who is your big mate?'

We pull up before a counter presided over by a stocky balding man who, judging by the scowl that crosses his face when he catches sight of Jarly, must be Dimitri himself.

'Dimitri, this is Bear.'

His landlord is gruff but polite to me – well, I am twice Jarly's age, grey-haired, dressed in the suit which I had been forced to wear to a business meeting earlier in the day.

'I hope Jarly isn't giving you trouble, Mr Dimitri.'

'Jarly give me trabble, I give him dabble.'

Seems Dimitri is pleased with this, or has said it before, because he repeats it.

'Jarly, you give me bladdy trabble, I give you bladdy dabble.'

On the wall behind the proprietor hangs a fading map of the eastern Mediterranean showing the extent of present day Greek influence, and Cyprus, an island the shape of a swordfish, across whose belly runs a red and bloody cut. Dimitri, catching my glance, asks, 'You ever been to Cyprus, Mr Bear?'

'Once, a few years ago.'

'Yes? Enjoy yourself? Great place. Music, great. Food, great. Wine, great. You like fishing, fishing's great. Not just Cyprus fish. Fish swim through the Suez Canal to visit Cyprus. Big ocean fishes. Sharks too. Think I'm joking?' After a pause, 'Hey, Mr Bear, you know why I call this place Aphrodite's? Because Aphrodite, the goddess of love, was born in Cyprus. You know this? Just near Paphos, where I am building my house. Homer says so. You know Homer, Mr Bear?'

'Only that the dawn has rosy fingers and ancient Greek wine must have been blue.'

Dimitri looks puzzled. 'You know how come Homer knew Cyprus? Because Cyprus was a Greek island.'

'Fucking figs,' says Jarly, slapping his head, and vanishes down an aisle.

'Don't get me wrong, Mr Bear,' says Dimitri, 'I don't say we Greeks are the only Cypriots. Always we have welcomed guests. King Richard the Once, he got married in Limassol. Saint Andrew came to Cyprus. When I was a boy, before the Turks invaded, my father would take us to the monastery of Saint Andrew and we would fill bottles with the holy water . . .'

It's an odd thing, and it won't do to tell Dimitri, but I already know this story and the place he's describing. Two years ago, Eve and I went to northern Cyprus, the part occupied by Turkey, to see our old friends Todd and Lori, who were teaching at the University of the Eastern Mediterranean in Famagusta – Gazi Magosa as the Turks call it. One day they took us on a long drive to their favourite beach. We went out along the Karpas peninsula to the very tip of the swordfish-beak, past hamlets where chickens scratched in the dirt, the remains of Greek communities enclaved by the invading Turks. The only traffic for miles was tractors. Todd told us that there were only about a hundred Greeks left in the Karpas. Dipkarpas, the largest village, was one street with a hardware shop and two cafés at which a few elderly men sat over their coffees. On one side of the street was the Greek café, on the other, the Turkish. Turkish Cypriots were forbidden to settle in Dipkarpas, said Todd, but the Turkish government had encouraged people from the mainland to go there, promising them a house, some land and a tractor. A lot of these people were hicks from the interior, who had never known electricity. In Dipkarpas they fitted right into the earthy lifestyle, but in cosmopolitan Magosa, where mainlanders were housed in modern apartments abandoned by fleeing Greeks, they put chickens in the washing machines and strewed straw on the marble floors to warm them. These stories were told to him, Todd said, not by Greeks, but by scoffing Turkish Cypriots.

It was a long, dusty drive through the Karpas. By late afternoon the last of the land was overwhelmed by the ocean and we came to the monastery and the holy spring. We heard its story from a very old lady dressed in black, whom we found filling candlesticks in the church. She gave us candles to light and showed us where to fill our bottles. But what I chiefly remember is neither history nor holy water, but the simple pleasure of saying *'kalimera'* to someone who rarely heard her own language on an outsider's lips.

'Pay for the fuckin' figs, Bear, and while you're about it, why don't you get some of that red wine? But fuck's sake hurry up.'

'Hahaha,' says Dimitri, 'Jarly is saving all his money to pay last month's rent. You know why he got no money Mr Bear? Because he tap tap tap on that computer all day.'

'What's the big rush, Jarly?' I say when we're back outside. 'Anyway, I thought you were entertaining me to dinner. Is this it? Figs and bladdy Mavrodaphne?'

'An' if tha believes that tha'll believe anything,' says Jarly. He lifts his sweater to reveal, beneath his wasted ribcage, a sucked-in hollow where his stomach ought to be, and slides from his waistband a large rounded object still coated in frost.

'I've hacked us a chicken.'

Bear, I don't want any secrets between us. Secrets are barriers. I went home from college wearing my disgrace like a suit of armour, but when Angela opened the door, all I saw was a grey woman whose life hadn't gone as she'd planned. I felt quite sorry for her. This lasted three days. On the third day we were talking about my course: poetry and drama. Angela recited a poem she'd always liked. It was about a cat, an awful poem, sugary and sentimental. This desire to hurt her just rose up in me. I said, 'That's not real poetry, this is poetry.' I picked up a magazine I'd brought back and began reading out a poem I liked. Angela got up, grabbed the book from my hands, ripped the page out and tore it into tiny pieces. Her face was twisted and hateful. I backed away. She followed me. She stalked round the room after me saying, 'Clare is clever. Clare is wise. Clare is always right.' With each step she threw bits of poem at me like confetti and when it was all gone she left the room. No-one else said anything. I picked up the pieces. I was crying. I sat at the kitchen table and tried to sellotape the bits together. I couldn't do it, my hands were shaking so much. Then I got my stuff and walked out of my father's house. I've never seen her since.

Exit Clare with bare behind. Watching the twin globes of her backside waltzing a retreat, I'm thinking that somehow I must drag myself off her sofa and into my car. I must get home. But in a few moments she returns and with a sad smile hands me an envelope full of torn scraps. 'One odd thing,' she says. 'Later, I arranged the pieces, like a jigsaw, but mistakenly assembled them the wrong way up. There was a beautiful poem – which I'd never noticed before – on the reverse.'

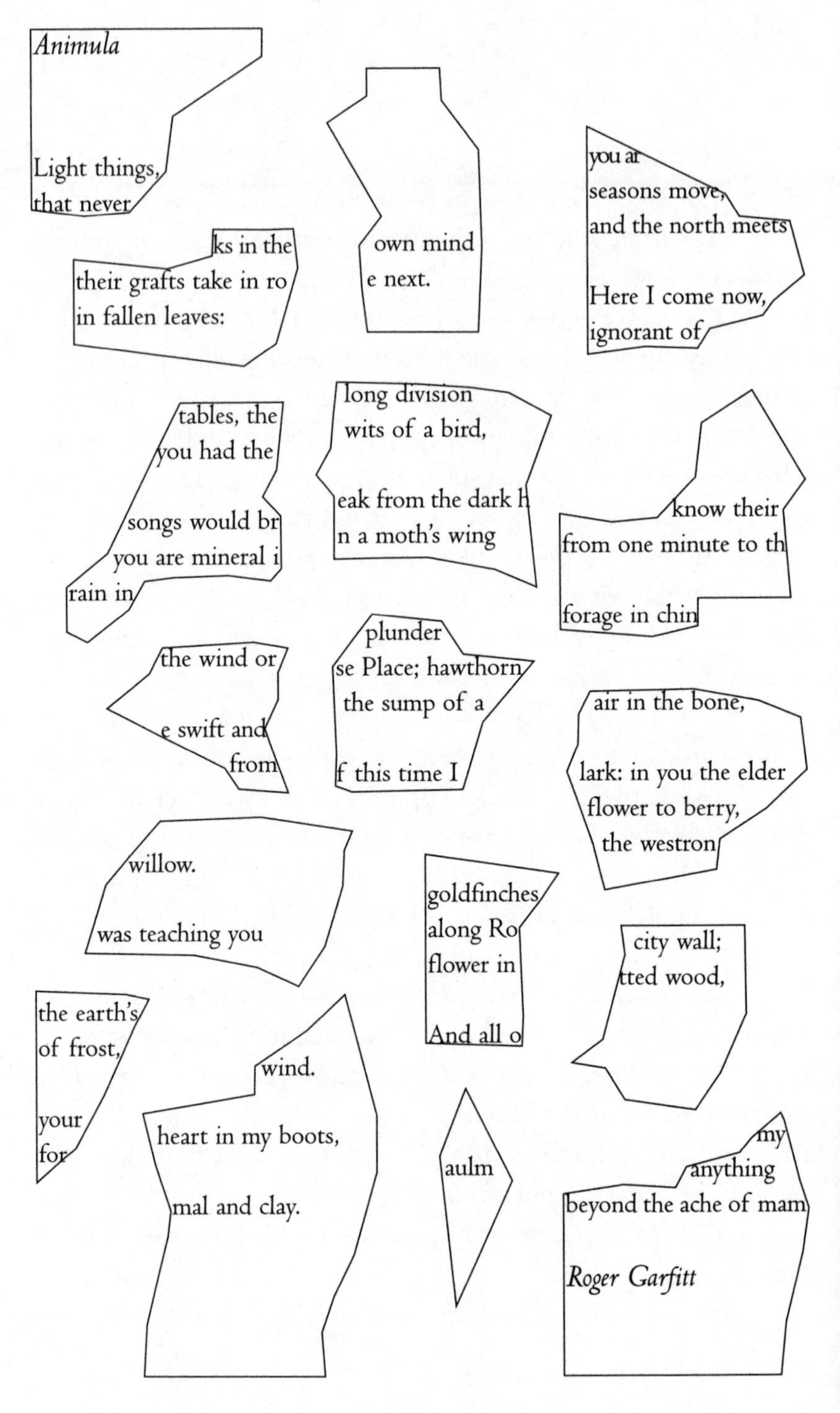
Animula
Light things,
that never
own mind
e next.
you ar
seasons move,
and the north meets
Here I come now,
ignorant of
ks in the
their grafts take in ro
in fallen leaves:
tables, the
you had the
songs would br
you are mineral i
rain in
long division
wits of a bird,
eak from the dark h
n a moth's wing
know their
from one minute to th
forage in chin
the wind or
e swift and
from
plunder
se Place; hawthorn
the sump of a
f this time I
air in the bone,
lark: in you the elder
flower to berry,
the westron
willow.
was teaching you
goldfinches
along Ro
flower in
And all o
city wall;
tted wood,
the earth's
of frost,
your
for
wind.
heart in my boots,
mal and clay.
aulm
my
anything
beyond the ache of mam
Roger Garfitt

Lilith says 'That's Calypso.'

The 'meet' at the Goat and Compass is mainly of Shades players with a sprinkling of those who belong to the secret society of the Vortex – maybe sixty people crowded into a smoky pub off the Gray's Inn Road. Lilith is in her fifties, tall, with fading fair hair pulled back into a bun and kind eyes that turn down softly at the outer edges. She wears gold-rimmed half-moons perched on the end of her nose and her expression, as she gazes over them and across the room, is a mixture of compassion and amusement, with something perhaps hard at its centre. She might easily be taken for a headmistress, a magistrate, or a judge at a village dog show, were it not for the fact that she is wearing leather trousers and smoking a monstrous stogie.

'Hoyo de Monterrey gauge 47,' she says, noticing my interest. 'Ask Zerubabel, he taught me to smoke.'

She takes a long drag, aims the glowing tip of her cigar at a woman on the far side of the room and after a long pause says in a series of smoky hiccoughs, 'That's Calypso. The only woman in history to go on holiday with her husband and three lovers.'

The woman, as if overhearing this remark, although she can't have, turns towards us. She's extremely pretty, hair falling like dark silk to her shoulders. There's a small crowd around her, some of whom I know from the early Telecom Gold days. No other women. As she glances in our direction, I catch – or perhaps I imagine it – a green flash of eyes.

'Five of them,' says Lilith, 'in three gypsy caravans. Horse-drawn painted wooden wagons. Cally and hubby up front, Cabbalist and Chorley next, Morgan on his own bringing up the rear. The amazing thing is, none of the men knows about the others.'

Somewhere along here, among these neat houses, tidy gardens and cherry-blossom-showered pavements of a zero-dogshit zone, Clare lives. For more than half an hour I have been lost in a labyrinth of identical streets named, typically for an estate built on green fields, after the trees and flowers they have replaced. Holly Avenue, Elm Drive, Bluebell Close, Cedar Road, Beech Road, Hawthorn Road, Meadowsweet Rise. It's a neighbourhood full of people who mow the lawn on Sundays, catch the 8.01 to Waterloo every weekday, on Saturdays drive to supermarkets stacked with food and know beyond doubt that they are leading *normal* lives . . . Except that this place can't possibly be normal because Clare lives here. Clare is the least conventional person I know. Do the neighbours know about her? Do their curtains twitch to whispers of her reputation? Do they have any idea that she is immortal? Which of these prodigiously timbered replicas of Ann Hathaway's cottage shows signs of being inhabited by a witch? (Oh why the hell did I forget to bring her address?) The houses appear all exactly alike until you look closely, when you see how each, in small ways, proclaims its individuality. Here a pottery plaque warns *cave canem*. There a hedge has been clipped into the shape of a lopsided bird, or tipsy dinosaur. In a window across the road, there's a model . . . Wait a minute . . .

On the windowsill stands a gaily painted model of a traditional gypsy caravan...

. . .This is it. The real life home of Calypso the Shades witch. Lugging my old Apricot out of the car, I am caught in a storm of petals, tumbling in the breathless air like powdery precursors of snow.

He met Calypso (this is my retelling of Lilith's retelling of Cabbalist's story) soon after she started playing Shades. She was a natural charmer who had a trick of hanging on his every word and gazing at him with huge green eyes (remember, Bear, this was in cyberspace). Steve – his real name – had been around roleplaying games on the net for years, and suspected that Calypso in real life would turn out to be dumpy, fifty and probably male. But he was wrong. When Clare – her real name – turned up to a meet he saw that she really was pretty, with dark hair, eyes as vast and green as any lovelorn single man could desire – and she knew how to use them too. Unfortunately she'd brought her husband along, but he was a quiet fellow who didn't seem to mind the attention his wife got from other blokes.

It is always important to draw the distinction between player and character (said Lilith, lecturing). On Shades, Steve might be Cabbalist the Wizard, complete with immortal swagger, but in that strange and fearful dimension that Shades players call real life, he was just Steve, a banker and, many thought, a bit of a something-that-rhymes-with-it. He had reached his mid twenties with no social life apart from that lived through the computer screen and his sexual experience involving other people was limited to one-handed typing. (This is Lilith's wickedness, I disclaim responsibility.) He knew how to flirt with cyber females (cool guys do this in terse unpunctd lwr cs remrks) but hadn't met many real women. So when Clare turned the green lamps of her eyes upon him, Steve was overwhelmed. She not only seemed to like him, but unlike the few girls he had tried chatting up at work, didn't appear to find his manner weird and his talk boring. She listened with interest to his tales of computer errantry, battles with wraiths and morlochs, magical skirmishes with necromancers in the dead of night and strategies for waging war against fellow players. She asked many questions and behaved as if she were in the presence of a master.

Steve, or more accurately his wizard, Cabbalist, began helping Calypso with advice, guiding her round the game, and making her gifts of fabulous jewel-crusted daggers, black pearls, strangely glowing crystals and all the other treasures that lay hidden in the land. When she confided to him that she was too bad at fighting ever to reach witch, he suggested that she tell him Calypso's ID and password. Using his own account, he would log on as her and play her character. In this way Calypso quickly gained points and powers and within three months stood on the threshold of immortality. It is tedious and laborious work, amassing points in Shades. The same routines must be repeated over and over. On an empty game, with no-one else competing for treasure, an expert can make about 7,500 points an hour, but people were almost never alone. Steve found it hard to score half of that, meanwhile fending off attacks from other players and the ghoulish automatons that roamed the game with murder in their hearts. He was not a first rank duellist – fighting in Shades is an art in itself – and points were inevitably dropped fleeing to preserve life.

Steve could only play Calypso when Clare wasn't using the character. Nothing would irritate him more, after he'd spent three or four hours adding 20K to Calypso's score, than logging in next day to discover that she'd got into a fight and lost it all again. As weeks passed, the assailants grew fewer (except for Jarly, whose killers always attacked on sight) and losses were more than offset by Calypso's popularity, which drew a constant stream of baubles and gewgaws from mortals and invisible immortals. The gifts were often accompanied by kisses, hugs and whispered endearments, against all of which Steve had to steel himself, thanking the donors in monosyllables. Playing her character broke every rule of the game. If caught he'd be hauled before the game's archwizards, have his wand snapped over his head and lose his immortal life.

Steve soon had new worries. He was playing three or four hours a day (at a cost to himself of £3 an hour) and witchhood was still far off. To please Calypso, he started spending more time on the game. He was often late for work and his boss remarked on the dark rings under his eyes. But Calypso didn't seem to appreciate either his help or the risks he was running. Steve didn't like the way she would flirt with other male players. She was capricious. There were times when he'd come onto Shades and find her already there. He'd say hello and she would ignore him. Even when he loaded her with gifts that would once have made her gasp in wonder – the unicorn's horn, princess's crown, hermit's hoard of jewels and gold – she'd mutter taciturn thanks and wrap the silence back around her like a cloak.

Steve took Calypso's score to 196,000 and suggested that she might enjoy completing the job herself. He took a day off work to be there when typographical peals of bells rang out over the game proclaiming 'Calypso has reached immortality'. But this was one of those times when she was being taciturn and to his congratulations made no reply. It also peeved Steve that when Calypso became a witch she immediately changed her password.

'The most telling thing about this story,' Lilith said, 'and my wrists ache, Bear dear, from the effort of typing it all to you, is that if, by hitting you very very hard over the head with a golf club or forcing a bottle of Ukrainian peppered *horilka* down your throat, I could make you see double, and if you were then to re-read what I've typed, inserting the name Morgan alongside that of Steve, then everything I've told you, bar some minor details, would still be true.'

Old time cybergypsies rarely talk of 'surfing the internet'. They tend to think of present-day netsurfers as tourists, flown in their millions to the gaudy electronic resorts of the world wide web by package tour operators like Compuserve and America Online. Cybergypsies detest the commercialisation of the internet and some *still* avoid it altogether. It's important to understand that when cybergypsies speak of 'the Net', they're not thinking of any one network, and certainly not just of the internet, which is a rag-bag collection of networks and stand-alone systems, some parts connected by trans-continental and sub-oceanic cables, others by the digital equivalents of string and chewing gum. Contrary to common belief, the internet is only *part* of the global computer matrix and was until recently, for cybergypsies, probably the least interesting. Cybergypsies like free-flowing, live, subtle interaction and internet chat is banal and brutish, compared with the range of expression afforded by Shades, or a Fidonet bulletin board. Under the fingers of a maestro like Branwell, the keyboard can be as eloquent as a human voice, with nicely timed pauses, silences, disingenuous Freudian slips, and droll changes of mind. In the heyday of Shades, the cybergypsy universe consisted mainly of privately run bulletin board networks. Fidonet at its peak had 50,000 boards and perhaps 5,000,000 users around the world. Other nets were tiny: three, four or six boards dedicated to a purpose. There were many solo systems. Some networks were, and remain to this day, secret, their existence unguessed at, never publicised. Cybergypsies roam the internet end to end, but it is these obscure nets which were their homes and heartlands.

The internet became accessible in Britain, via the university net JANET, in 1984 (the year of *Neuromancer,* the Apple Mac and my visit to the Rollright Stones). I came to it three years later through Greennet, a network for bringing together activists and progressive organisations. Through Greennet I discovered internet newsgroups and the exhileration of telnetting. Riding the telnet is like piloting a beam of light. Think of where you want to be, and in a flash you're there. Hackers liked it because it helped them cover their tracks. I used it to visit fun systems like the WELL in San Francisco. Demon, started by friends of Lilith's, was first to offer fellow cybergypsies full internet access at £10 a month, but for a long time there were only a couple of thousand of us. The software was hard to use and if you were outside London it was a long-distance call. Even Demon did not start until June 1992.

Surfing the Internet was an article, written by Jean Polly of the WELL, that began circulating on cybergypsy bulletin boards later that year. Polly raved excitedly about MUDs, internet newsgroups, telnetting and exchanging email across continents. He enthused about having during a single day visited Minnesota, Texas, California, Cleveland, New Zealand, Sweden, and England. His article barely mentioned the world wide web – which was then still a twinkle in the eye of its inventor, Tim Berners-Lee – but gave Tim's phone and fax numbers for anyone interested in finding out more about his crazy vision. A year after Polly's article appeared, roughly the time I was getting to know Geno, there were fewer than two hundred websites (at the instant of writing there are more than two and a half million). By 1994, hundreds of internet service providers had appeared, about sixty percent of them started by cybergypsies who were ex-Fidonet bulletin board sysops.

Fidonet had begun in 1984 when a San Franciscan netgypsy called Tom Jennings wrote a bulletin board program and called it 'Fido' in honour of the 'mongrel' computer he had built from odd scraps and other people's cast-off bits. Jennings had realised that, since local phone calls in the US are free, a network of faithful Fidos spanning the country could pass mail and files along from one to another without ever incurring a cent in phone charges. The idea soon spread beyond the US and by the early nineties Fidonet was a worldwide network with its own netmail delivery system and thousands of themed 'echoes'. Because Fido sysops were spending their own money, they evolved super-efficient ways to speed mail and echoes around the world. Fast, accurate file transfer protocols like Z-modem, 'mailers' like FrontDoor which automatically sent and received 'packets' of netmail and echomail in a few seconds: these cybergypsy-authored programs were superior to anything the major software houses possessed. What Fidonet could not do was deliver live chat at local call rates. In those days, when hardly any of us had internet accounts, if we wanted to chat to the sysop of a bulletin board across the world, it was an international phone call. For this reason, most people used to content themselves with posting to Fidonet echoes, which are strings of messages and replies on particular subjects.

Fidonet's *Virus* echo was particularly active, with dozens of new messages every day. There was war in cyberspace between the 'elite' and the 'lamers', a kind of Star Wars fought with viruses, ANSI bombs and trojan horses. Many of the messages on *Virus* were from 'lamers' terrified of the digital evil that would one day erupt on their screens, laugh in their faces and fuck up their hard disks. Advising these folk were a hard core of anti-virus software salesmen who, like quack psychiatrists, were able to make a living by simultaneously fuelling anxiety and offering a cure for it. They portrayed virus writers on the one hand as attention-seeking brats who could not program to save their lives, and on the other as desperate and dangerous experts, threatening the very security of the nation. (After Satanbug took down a US Secret Service computer for three days, men in dark suits knocked on hackers' doors up and down the country looking for traitors.) The hackers retaliated with ever more devious viruses and mockery. Some of the viruses rampaging around in the wild were 'goat files', created by the anti-virus folk to attract and catch passing viruses as a tethered kid attracts tigers. Others were harmless lab experiments which had somehow got loose, but the hackers never missed a chance to allege that the antivirus people were deliberately releasing them to create hysteria. The following satirical message was posted to *Virus* to needle the anti-virus organisations whose members were making a fortune out of the constant virus scares.

```
Message #2832 - Virus discussion
   Date: 09-07-93 12:41
   From: CARO Central
     To: All
Subject:: Viruses for profit
_____________________________________________

@MSGID: 1:13/13.0 2c8cb9ca

        +    +    +
        |    |    |    +--+  o   o
        |    |    |    |     +   +
        |    |    |    |     |   |
         \-/      +    +     +   +

NuKE INTERNaTiONaL! FOR VIRUS RESEARCHERS ONLY!
not to be used for illegal purposes

AS aDVERTISED IN pC MaGAZiNE, NuKe INTERNaTiONAL @TM
SELLS VIRII. fROM oKC THE VIRUS CAPATIAL OF THE WORLD
(SeE LATEST VERSION OF hACK REPORT)

FOR A LIMITED TiME oNLY: For only $50.oo NuKE will sell you:
-oVEr 2,000 cataloged viRiI
-iNSTRucTIOnAL ELECTRONIC MAGAZINES AND JOURNALS HOW TO
WRITE VIRII -hACK REPoRTS 40HEX AND OTHERS
-iCED vIRII WILL NOT BE PICKED UP BY ANY SCANNER
-***tROJANS***tROJANS*TROJANS***
-aLL THE LATEST GREATEST vIRRI WRITTING PROGRAMS
-aLL THE gREATEST tROJAN WRITTING PROGRAMS
-vIRUS UTILITES SUCH AS NOWHERE MAN'S FAMOUS uTLITIES
-tWICE THE VALUE OF aristotle's COLLECTION, MORE VIRII
LESS COST

-Send Check Money Order OR CASH to (specify if you want
1.4 or 1.2 disks) Please add $2.50 postage and handling:
```

```
   NuKE iNterNational, P.O.BOX 19196,
                           OKLAHOMA CITY, OK. 73144

ALL ORDERS WITH MONEY ORDER OR CASH ARE MAILED THE DAY
RECIEVED PERSONAL CHECK ORDERS ARE NOT MAILed UNTIL THE
CHECK CLEARS THE NuKE BANK

--  Vx Toss Version 666
 * Origin: Still selling Viruses after all these years!
(1:209/209)@PATH:  147/34  7  18  666  7  209/209  170/400
253/165 257/100 441/80 86
```

(Note the dig at ARiSToTLE, who had recently offered for sale his entire virus collection, complete with instant virus creator kit.)

I'd always thought viruses were written by bored students. The first one had been a programming exercise by a university lecturer called Fred Cohen. But four thousand viruses later, the virus authors were organised into networks which, like those of hackers, software pirates and other misunderstood minorities, operated from private bulletin boards whose numbers were not always easy to find. If you did get hold of one, and logged on, you were given a thorough grilling before they let you see anything interesting. There were lots of virus groups, Phalcon/Skism, Youth Against McAfee, in England the Association for Really Cruel Viruses (stupid name, it got their leader, Apache Warrior, busted), Trident in Holland, Immortal Riot in Scandinavia and, straddling the planet, with nodes as far apart as Argentina and Australia, there was NuKE which numbered among its members the famous Nowhere Man and talented TäLoN. Who were these guys? For months I had been trying to penetrate into the heart of NuKE and Geno, aka Jesus Slutfucker, was the closest I'd come.

Calypso's taciturnity on Shades was doubly puzzling to Steve because, as Clare, she readily agreed to meet him in 'real' life. He took her to lunch at a restaurant which he could not really afford, but it was worth it to see her eyes, over the rim of her wine glass. In the taxi on the way back to her office, his arm slid round her and then they were kissing, oblivious to the sniggering cabby. ('There is a magic in the kisses of an inexperienced youth,' said Lilith, 'he's full of eager goatlust, yet you can still sense his shyness.') They met several more times, each encounter culminating in furtive subvestmental fumblings, before Steve felt confident enough to propose to Clare that they go to a hotel. She smiled but did not refuse. One of the lads at the bank had told him about a place in King's Cross where rooms could be hired by the hour. One lunchtime, instead of taking her to a restaurant (they were by now slumming it in tavernas and pizzerias), he plucked up courage and led her over the dingy threshold and up the threadbare stair-carpets of the Imperial Lake Hotel. Clare raised no objection and, when it came to the point, was curiously submissive to his wishes.

She said, 'If it's important to you it makes me happy too.'

She smiled and held his eyes with her green gaze as he climbed on top of her. It was his first time. He hadn't told her, but it didn't take her long to guess. She found it funny, which wounded Steve. ('Oh you should have seen his face when he told me this. *Na yevô lítso stoílo posmotryet.')*

'Of course she was more experienced than me . . . then', Steve had said resentfully to Lilith. 'Well, she *is* married isn't she?'

The holiday grew out of an idea Chorley the Caveman Necromancer had for an expedition to some grottoes in the north Yorkshire dales, to see if they could get a game going in real caves and tunnels. But potholing holds little appeal for people whose spelunking is done by the tap of keys in crisp-packet and coke-can littered bedrooms. Somehow the idea turned into a caravan holiday – real wooden gypsy caravans pulled by real horses rented from real Romanies – what could be more appropriate for a bunch of cybergypsies? Clare wanted to go. Unfortunately the husband had to come too, but she pestered Steve to join Chorley and promised him that they would find chances to be together. Steve was not keen on Chorley, but Clare said that he would be a useful smoke-screen. The rendezvous was in Appleby-in-Westmorland near the Yorkshire border. At the last minute, Morgan turned up uninvited and a third caravan had to be found for him.

They set out on a typical summer day of rain showers, draughts of warm sunshine and wild churnings of light over the distant Lake District fells to the west. The flaw in their plan immediately became obvious. There were three caravans: in the first Calypso and her husband, Alain. Bringing up the rear was Morgan. In the middle caravan were Steve and Chorley. Steve, yearning for Calypso, found Chorley's inscrutably cheerful manner irritating. Chorley was some years older than Steve, nearer to the age of Calypso and her hubby. In 'real' life, he was a wine broker who, unlike Steve, was not short of money. The problem was Chorley's car.

Chorley's car was an old Riley that rattled and smelt of leather and oil. It had brought Chorley, scarfed and goggled, up the motorway from London and was now accompanying the caravans because Calypso had insisted they must keep a car with them for emergencies. What Calypso, indeed all of them, had overlooked was the fact that whether it was crawling along near the caravans, or driving ahead to scout a place to stop for the night, the car needed a driver. As Calypso, full of apologies, explained that she could not drive, the car always claimed one of the men. This left three men to manage three caravans; ergo each must inevitably spend most of the day on his own.

'We're on holiday,' Clare said. 'We can't have everyone lonely and bored.' She proposed that she should ride with each of the drivers in turn and if she hadn't spent her time flitting between the wagons with sandwiches and thermoses of soup, it would have been a dismal business for all of them.

On the second afternoon Clare sent Alain off in the car on a fish and chip hunt. What could be more natural than that Steve should step up to sit beside her and take the reins of her wagon? The creaky wooden structure behind them blotted out Chorley on the second van and Morgan bringing up the rear. Alain was gone a couple of hours. By judicious use of a blanket, they were able to accomplish most of the things they were used to doing together in the clammy beds of the Imperial Lake Hotel.

That night, with the vans drawn up in a farmer's field and horses turned out to graze, they ate fish suppers round a small fire that Chorley and Alain built. Clare kept their glasses filled with a wine from Chorley's cellar and then sat staring into the fascinating flames as though they were a gypsy enchantment. Alain and Chorley talked about investments. Steve, cocooned in afterglow, was content to remember Clare's body under the blanket. Morgan said hardly a word, but sat on the edge of the firelight casting, as he so often did on Shades, a huge and brooding shadow.

Later in their caravan, Steve was horrified to hear Chorley out of the darkness begin singing loudly:

'In Scarlet Town where I was born
A girl with red red lips-o
Made many a youth cry well a day
Her name was fair Calypso

'Twas in the merry month of June
Love's fever did him grip so
Sweet Steven came from the south countree
And courted sweet Calypso'

They managed just one long afternoon together. It was Morgan's turn in the car and Steve was driving the hindmost van. Clare was with him as he lagged further and further behind the others and then took a wrong turn. They parked out of sight in a convenient copse and tethered the horse where she could graze. Lying in the narrow wooden bunk, after he had convulsed her slender body with orgasm after orgasm ('His technique was improving' I said. 'Or her acting', said Lilith), Clare told him of the tragic death of her mother in a car crash when she was eight years old and how she had been brought up by an unloving stepmother. They were lucky not to be caught. Scarcely had the nag been harnessed and persuaded to get underway again than the Riley appeared, piloted by an over-solicitous Morgan who insisted that Clare drive back with him because 'We have all been worrying, Cally, but especially your old man.'

In Whitechapel with Don McCullin, the photographer. It is hard to believe that the original White Chapel once stood here among the pleasant fields and orchards. By the early 1600s, slaughter houses, fish farms and factories of various trades were being built to the east of the City, so that the prevailing west winds blew the smells away from the prosperous 'west end'. Two more centuries and Whitechapel had grown to a grim slumscape, a vast and squalid stew housing the latest waves of immigrants, among whom were landless Irish fleeing the potato famine, and Russian and Polish Jews fleeing nights of long knives. Today's Whitechapel, its houses still black with the soots of a century ago, is a quarter Bengali. The working men's cafés have been replaced by restaurants that look all alike, with mirrors, plastic flowers and oriental arches made of plywood, studded with coloured lightbulbs. Where Jewish ritual slaughtermen once plied their *kosher* trade, Muslim *halal* butchers now prepare their meat. In both *kosher* and *halal* slaughter, the animal's throat is slit and the blood drained while the victim is still conscious. But Whitechapel's most famous butcher is thought to have strangled his victims before he cut their throats. Of all the walking stories that have inhabited this charnel house over the centuries, only five are regularly remembered and retold, one for each of Jack the Ripper's victims.

Don and I are looking for vagrants who will not mind having their photograph taken. We're doing an ad about homeless people for the Metropolitan Police. The idea came from a famous picture of Don's, which he calls his 'Neptune man'. It is of an old tramp with a strong handsome face, cracked open and blackened, not by the sun but by sleeping too close to open fires. Don won't let us use this picture, so we decide to shoot a new one. It won't be very hard.

Mrs Thatcher's government has closed dozens of mental hospitals and the patients have ended up on the streets. Everyone comments on how many beggars there are in London these days. Underneath Waterloo Bridge, the homeless have built themselves dwellings of cardboard and sacks, packing cases and sheets of corrugated iron. The place is known as 'Cardboard City'. This is where I assume we'll be going, but Don, who has recently done a picture essay on London's homeless for one of the Sunday magazines, thinks we should go to Whitechapel.

'The Waterloo people have got used to photographers,' he says.

We are walking through a little maze of alleys near what was once Flowery Dean (Flower & Dean Street) when we are accosted by a man pushing a dustcart. He says that if we are on the Ripper trail, he knows of a derelict house nearby where men living rough have discovered a diary written by Jack the Ripper crammed into a gap in the lath-and-plaster wall. (Soon after this a Ripper 'diary' was purported to have been found by workmen in Liverpool and proved a short-lived publishing sensation.) The dust-wallah offers to show us the place in return for a fee. We decline and he goes off in search of Americans.

'Did you see he had a USAF pilot's badge in his cap?' Don says. His photographer's eyes notice everything.

We enter Durward Street – it used to be called Buck's Row – where the Ripper's first victim, Polly Nichols, was found dying on the cobbles, guts hooked from her body by an upswept knife. Along the north side are boarded-up terraced houses with grimy broken windows. To the south is a wasteland of mud and rubble in which a single building remains. It is a gaunt ruin, its roof half off, its gable wall pierced by small holes. As we come near, we see that the upper floor has caved in and the interior is a mess of fallen beams and masonry. Don ducks inside and I follow him. There is a frantic scuffling, like that of a giant rat. Someone is inside. Then a figure shifts in the shadows, an old man, filthy, bearded and drooling, with melting eyes and the most beautiful face you ever saw. He cowers back as we stoop to enter the ruin.

'Don't be afraid,' says Don.

The old man stands up. A dribble of spit runs down from the corner of his mouth onto his coat.

'Dunno you,' he says in a weak voice.

'We're taking pictures.' Don shows him the camera. 'I'd like to take your picture. Is that okay?'

'Not safe here,' mumbles the old man. 'Not any more.'

'What happened?' asks Don, looking for the best angle.

'A fella got killed.'

He gestures at a mess of timber dangling from a hole in the floor above. 'Sleeping upstairs. Killed while he was sleeping.'

The old fellow looks at us with head on one side, like a crazy old bird. I wonder if he can grasp what we are asking him. But then he grins and brushes down the front of his coat.

'Just a minute. Want to look me best.'

The session begins, the tramp sitting on a pile of bricks, half-lit by a shaft of dusty light from above. Nearby there is a tin with a candle stuck in it and a pile of yellowed newspapers. In front of his boots, which look as if they have been chewed by some starving animal, is a circle of half bricks in which are some charred sticks.

We've been there ten minutes when Don says to me quietly, 'Don't turn around. Look on the floor for something you can use as a weapon, but don't pick it up till I tell you.'

Fear flickers through me. I can feel it building up in my body like static. Don, still clicking, murmurs, 'There's a stick on the ground, couple of feet to your left. Know where it is in case you have to grab it. There's a couple of heavy-looking guys heading this way.'

One part of me is calm, as if this has happened a hundred times before. A weird fantasy starts inventing itself in my mind.

>*The Scottish Tramp attacks you barehanded.*
>get stick
>*You have taken the heavy stick.*
>ret stick
>*You start to use the heavy stick.*
>*The Scottish Tramp has stolen the heavy stick from you.*
>*The Scottish Tramp thrusts at you with the heavy stick.*
>st stick tramp
>*Your attempt to steal the stick from the Tramp fails miserably.*
>*A blow from the Tramp lands solidly.*
>look
>*Burnt out warehouse.*
>*Picking your way through the burnt out timbers you eye what remains of the roof with caution, as it looks likely to cave in at any time. You get very black and dirty. There is a brick lying on the ground here.*
>g brick
>*You have taken the broken paving brick.*
>ret brick
>*You start to use the brick.*

The ad that took Don and me to Whitechapel was one of a long line the agency has produced to attract recruits for the Metropolitan Police. Over the years, we've spent an enormous amount of time talking to policemen, going on patrol with them. I spent a week wandering round Southall learning about the misdeeds of an Asian gang called, unless I had misheard, the 'Tooting Nuns'. The Nuns revved up and down the High Street in cars and motorbikes flying horsetail insignia. One had recently attacked a rival gang member and split his head open with a hammer in front of a lunch time crowd buying *filmi* songs, *idli* and *sari* borders. It all sounded most unlikely. 'Them Nuns is everywhere,' the officer who was showing me round muttered darkly. 'They recruit in school playgrounds. Use threats to make the youngsters join. Poor bloody parents don't know what to advise.' I told him I would like to talk to a parent about the problem, so he took me into a shop where a smirking hand-wringing proprietor bade us welcome, offered us tea and miniature fried *samosas*. 'This is Mr Bear from Scotland Yard,' said the copper by way of introduction. 'He'd like to ask you a few questions about gangs.' The poor man was paralysed with horror.

'Sir . . .,' he said, tears of sincerity brimming in his lower lashes, 'Sir, I would rather my own child was dead, dead I tell you, than in such a gang.'

'Got you there, didn't he?' my copper sniggered as we left.

In the same line of duty, I've gagged at the saucepan, on display in Scotland Yard's Black Museum, in which Dennis Nilsen boiled his victims' heads, leafed through scene-of-murder photographs at the Streatham CID office and listened to a Chief Superintendant in Brixton describe police work as 'a cascade of tragedies'.

'Twenty bloody years staring down the toilet bowl.'

A copper I meet in Brixton tells me that not only are London's police stations not online to one another, many of them do not even have computers. (Eve, this is no longer true.) I start talking about the net. He tells me about the hospital that was hit by a virus and lost all its records. This is a legend that everyone has heard but no-one can verify.

'Ah, but *could* it happen?' he asks.

After this conversation I decide that I will try to infiltrate NuKE and other virus-writing groups, with a view to discovering their secrets and grassing them up. I know zilch about viruses, or ASM programming (assembler code), but it doesn't matter. On the whole, members of virus groups don't do anything as radical and dangerous as actually write viruses. They just swap them. Failing real viruses, pseudo-viruses. The virus-exchange bulletin boards are full of bugs that aren't in the least bit infectious. Some won't run at all. It's very easy to fake a virus. Just take any relatively small .exe or .com file and rename it to something terrifying. Now upload it to your local VX board. Hardly any sysops will dare to test it. They will just stash it away with the rest of their collection, which is nothing more than a list of file names over which, like the dirty pictures in the adjacent directory, they gloat in private. In applying to NuKE World HQ for admittance, I don't even bother to upload fake files. There is not a single reason why they should admit me and – given that I am planning to leech their secrets and then denounce them to the Feds – every reason why they shouldn't.

NuKE InFoForm Questionnaire

Your Validation to this BBS heavily revolves on the answers of this questionnaire. None of these questions are HARD, as I am conjuring the questions for this questionnaire right now, right out of my head.
NOTE: THERE'S ONLY 13 Questions! (Very Simple) They are basically on your opinion! There's NO RIGHT or WRONG Answer! Just GOOD and COMPLETE and SPECIFIC Answers! Thank you! AND NO "FUCKING" around. Any dumb

answer, will get you DELETED! AND ALSO: NOTHING Illegal or corrupt is taken, NO CODE POSTING, No Cards#, you name it, any of this material will be turned over to the local law enforces. YOU HAVE BEEN WARNED!

Do you wish to continue [y/n]: *Yes*

Name us three BBSes you tend to call often. That will vouch for you.

[BBS Name]	[Number]	[SysOp]	[Affliation]
(3 lines)			
BlackDog	*081X8X7X8X*	*K. Dog*	*H/P/A/V*
Flying Teapot	*060X7X8X4X*	*K.S.*	*Warez*
Ok.Inst.Vir.Research	*XXXXXXXXXX*	*Geno Paris*	*NuKE*

Where did you get this Phone Number? By Whom? or where? BE EXACT!
from a friend in NuKE

What do you EXPECT to get from this system? Why are you calling here? BE VERY SPECIFIC, don't post To meet People, Msgs...etc you can call ANY BOARD for that! (3 Lines)
to hone knowledge about viruses
to exchange viruses
to perfect skills in relation to viruses

This System is a [NuKE] WHQ, Do you know anything on this organization? As this BBS is dedicated on the NuKE idea, and we don't need anyone that is disinterested. (3 Lines)
i have heard nuke rubbished by the anti-virus crowd, but i reckon that those people are arrogant and nuke has the edge...i like that. i would like to be part of it.

What is a COMPUTER VIRUS for you? Do you have a view on them?
Do you like them? Hate them? Why? (Be Specific) (3 Lines)
an interesting intellectual exercise. i think they are fascinating. i don't hate them, actually i doubt if people who are researching into these things have time or inclination to go wrecking systems

What is your view on the AntiVirus community? Do you hate them?
Do you like them? Why? (Be Specific) (2 Lines)
i don't hate them, they are complacent, or maybe they just appear that way. some, at any rate. vhey are very opinionated. some are okay. they too have their useful function.

Do you understand ASM (Assembly) Language? If yes, what? (2 Lines)
un peu

This system contains users from ALL parts of the world, And we gather here to brainstorm and talk, can you be an 'Active' supporter of the group? Are you willing to participate? or Help us in anyway? (Also what way can you help us by) (3 Lines)
i could join in, yeah, but at this cost (calling from the UK), i would have to be a millionaire, so offline mail is better for me. i can help with research, to some extent, but obviously you guys know more than i do... which is why i am here.

What computer are you using? IBM Compatible? And what OS System? (MS-DOS, PC-DOS, DR-DOS, OS/2?) (2 Lines)
a pc 386 clone, dos5
that's ms-dos 5, good old billgates

Do You know we do not tolerate any `Illegalities?' we are not NARCs But for legitimate reasons, we do not take that, this BBS is for the purpose of [NuKE] with the idea of Self-Knowledge advancements No POSTING on illegalities, NO UPLOADING of Illegalities... Do you understand this? And are willing to comply by this? (1 Line)
yes no problem

This BBS contains a Legitimate Collection of `Computer Viruses' and Related Sources and Text files on them! All Viruses are LABELLED as Viruses! So there can be no MISUNDERTANDING! So you CANNOT SAY "I didn't know what I was Downloading!" ALL Viruses here are EXPECTED to be used in a LEGITIMATE fasion (sic), for research, and understanding and/or Testing. If you are unsure or unable to meet with the following Answer `NO' bellow (sic), but if you find that you are responsible enough to understand Viruses on a Mature Level, Answer `Yes' bellow and we will grant you the Virus Section!

So did you understand the above? (Yes/No) *yes*
So do you want access to the Virus section? (Yes/No) *yes*

Thank you Very Much. For the questions. All Applicants are Validated within 24 hrs. So call back after 24hrs to abtain Full Access to this system.
~~~~~~
NOTE: you will NOW WRITE a Message to the Sysop, add ANYTHING you wish inside there, Your background is nice. IF [NuKE] wishes to contact you,
~~~~~~

what number can we reach you at?
Ex: XXX-XXX-XXXX or +XX-XX-XXX-XXXX
Phone Number: = *+44 XXXX XXX XXX*
Ask for Whom: *Bear*

You will now send a new user letter to the SysOp. This letter is required, and cannot be aborted. If you choose to not put anything in it, you will probably not be noticed, and thus not validated. In this message, it is required that you write about yourself, and why you think you deserve access to the system. Just remember, no matter what you put in this message, chances are you'll get validated.
-= PAUSE =-

To: Rock Steady #2
Title: New User Application
Enter your message now, Private EMAIL [LOCAL] #0. You may use up to 200 lines. Press /S to save, or /? for a list of commands.
[--+--1--+--2--+--3--+--4--+--5--+--6--+--7--+--]
okay, well i am fascinated by the subject of computer viruses...and have been studying up what i can on my own...as you know, it is not easy to come across viruses in the wild or to get infected files passed on, but what one or two came my way, i have done my best to open up and suss out how they work and what they were all about...frankly assembly ain't my strong point and this is a bit of a bastard, but anyhow, some progress...then i was reading the virus echoes and came across an advert which listed nuke...sounded interesting, at the same there was a discussion about vnuke's test scan of various av systems... i found the av leaders to be rather complacent and the rest of the av crowd seemed to take a closed minded position, whereas the nuke position was more exciting and imaginative, well i decided there and then that i would like to make contact and see if i could join you and really learn something...so there you go...i'll call back with high hopes... ciao, bear, bye for now

Command (?=Help): ®h¥5ʃj)m⁄Õ¢⁄äjMÖŸïÅjïÕÕÖùï˝⁄íUuÅ"⁄¥5≤⁄äjˇYes
Saving message...<<

'He'll never swallow all this bullshit,' I tell myself, but twenty-four hours later I log back, and I'm in.

>look
>*Burnt out Timber warehouse.*
>*Picking your way through the burnt out timbers you eye what remains of the roof with caution, as it looks likely to cave in at any time. You get very black and dirty. There is a brick lying on the ground here.*
>g brick
>*You have taken the broken paving brick.*
>ret brick
>*You start to use the brick.*
>*Sabbath has stolen the brick from you.*
>*Sabbath thrusts at you with the brick.*

Sabbath is the most feared killer on Shades, with a huge lust for blood. He is played by a friend of Jarly's called Graeme. I meet him one day at Gawain's, a large youth in a Motorhead tee-shirt, lank hair hanging halfway down his back. He has written a program called *Ripper* which allows him to enter macros – whole strings of commands – with one or two key presses. Thus pressing *alt+c* might generate 'get shortsword, go northeast, cut the wall with the shortsword, climb up, go out, feed the bone to the cub'. This is a sequence of commands to be executed in the middle of a sand strewn Roman arena. You leap down, unarmed, into a tunnel which leads to an arena where a large and hungry lion is pacing. Lying on the sand ahead is a bloody bone with tattered shreds of flesh still attached. Beyond this is the gate beyond which the lion waits. Once through this gate there is no way back. Inside the arena, a dinted but serviceable short sword lies on the sand and further off in a different direction, a golden helmet. The helmet is what you've come for. But first you have to avoid the lion and get the sword. If the lion attacks, you have little chance of survival. Graeme's program speeds you through the lion's den and out of trouble. But the real use of *Ripper*, the true purpose for which Graeme designed it, is murdering other players. Some multi-user games view the idea of 'player killing' with revulsion. Homicides are treated with the same horror as in ancient Greece, banished, fair game to be hunted down and killed without mercy. Not so in Shades. Fighting is the fun of the game. Killing one's friends is as natural as breathing. One murders daily with a song in one's heart.

Fighting in Shades is practised with as much dedication as any obscure eastern martial art. It's so important that we have seminars on it. In most MUDs of the Lambda and Diku sort, players belong to a race and a guild, and acquire special armour, weapons, skills and magic. In a fight, these are tallied against those of the opponent. The outcome is pretty much predetermined. Shades is not like that. Shades is like the real world, random and unpredictable. Fighting skill depends entirely on the players. Their level determines how hard they can hit, but tactics, surprise and luck can enable a small player to bring down the biggest in the game. Unlike most other games, Shades allows players to steal each other's weapons. Timing is crucial. You must steal the weapon and use it just before your own blow goes in, and try to make sure that you have got it when your opponent's blow falls. You must keep careful track of your stamina and your opponent's as they fall towards the death-point of zero. You must know always where the Strange Little Girl is, because strength and stamina are restored by touching her. The complexity and freedom of action on Shades have led to several distinct schools of fighting. Some teach multi-weapon combat, attacking with longsword and deadly ninja fighting cabbage or mild unassuming rat and brick. Others rely on the use of spells like 'fumble' which causes the opponent to drop what he is carrying, 'strip' which denudes him of weapons, and 'butterfingers' which ensures that anything he picks up will slide harmlessly out of his fingers. You can also 'force' your opponent to do things, drop his weapon, for instance, or hand it to you. If you are defending against his attack, you can force him to flee. You can even force your opponent to execute a 'where is everything?' command. If this works, it leaves him watching helplessly while a list of every single object on the game scrolls slowly up his screen. By the time it has finished, so is he. 'Force where all' is considered very vile, although its exponents point out that everyone has the same opportunity to use it. The real reason for most players' dislike of it is that it spoils the fantasy. It steps outside the game's carefully painted illusions and tampers with the under-stage machinery. The problem with all of these fine tactics is that they must be typed and if you're a bad typist, you are dead. Graeme is a terrible typist, which is why he invented:

```
*********************************
*   RIPPER III: The Final Conflict *
*                                 *
*               v1.0              *
*     written by Graeme R         *
*    designed by Graeme R         *
*            and Roger Davies     *
*********************************
```

Ripper enables players to automate their fighting. For example, instead of slowly and laboriously typing 'steal rat from Sabbath', you just press F4. *Ripper* turns Graeme and his friends into super-killers. Jarly, particularly, becomes addicted to the shedding of blood. Suddenly every player on Shades wants *Ripper.* But Graeme has written it for his own computer, which happens to be an Atari ST. It will run on nothing else. An underclass develops of people who neither have 'f-key software' nor that other most desirable fighting tool, a 'fast' modem. Determined to keep up in the arms race, I spend several hundred pounds on an Atari ST, telling Eve I need it for desktop publishing. I also buy, for three hundred quid, a 2,400 bps modem, but this I don't mention at all.

'Bear, I'm spending eight hours every day on Shades. Costing a fucking fortune, what with long distance calls and time charges on top. I've tried cutting down and it's like ciggies, it doesn't work. So I decided to stop it. Just cut off. I just sat up in my room and did programming.'

Jarly lives in a tiny bare attic which Dimitri had advertised as 'a commodious studio apartment with built-in kitchen'. The 'kitchen' is a cheap plywood cupboard which holds a few pots and some bits of crockery and cutlery. On it stands a small electric oven with a ring on top. The ring is caked with burned-on carbon deposits and the whole thing looks extremely unsafe. (We defrost the chicken by immersing it in a pan of boiling water.) The rest of the furnishings consist of a pine chair, a table carrying his computer and modem and a bed which looks as if Messalina has just entertained a legion in it. Pinned to one wall is a bullfight poster, the souvenir of a long ago trip to Spain and above his bed are some pictures torn from magazines, of Gloria Estefan. His only other possession is a hi-fi with two large speakers which sit on thick layers of newspaper ('Otherwise the fucking things vibrate and jump about').

'Park your arse, Bear, while I get this chicken stuffed,' Jarly says, handing me a dirty plastic tumbler of Mavrodaphne. 'Only watch out for the fucking . . .'

Too late. One of the legs of the bed is bent under and if you sit on the edge, the whole thing dips alarmingly. There is what looks like a pool of blood on the floor.

'Have you got a cloth – something to wipe the floor?'

'Just use one of them, it's what I do,' he says, waving at a pile of soiled tee-shirts in the corner.

Our hacked chicken, cooked with figs and Mavrodaphne, is rather disgusting but Jarly wolfs it down. He's anxious to get the meal finished, he tells me, in order to be rid of the evidence should Dimitri come knocking at the door.

'I've to be careful not to pinch too much stuff from down below,' he says. 'The bastard comes in when I'm not here. He suspects me, but he can't prove a thing.'

Unusually for a cyber addict, Jarly is thin. This is because he's starving. He tells me that for the last week there's been nothing to eat except cornflakes and a jar of mango pickle. He spoons pickle onto the dry flakes, dribbles in a little water and mixes it all up with a teaspoon. He's had this for breakfast, lunch and supper. I recall times when I've met Jarly on Shades and he has been weak with hunger, made worse by the fact that Dimitri's kitchen is right underneath his room and rich Cypriot cooking smells waft up through the wide gaps in the floorboards.

Jarly can't afford food but one of the first things he did after he moved in was to have a telephone line installed. Not a telephone, just the line. ('Don't need a phone. Don't want buggers ringing me. All my mates are on-line. Just need a gateway to the net.') On the tobacco-smogged wall, amid splots of insect gore and smeared crescents of some rich dark stuff which surely can't – or can it? – be shit, the socket gleams incongruously white. To most people it is just something they unthinkingly plug a phone into – but to Jarly it is a gateway to heaven and to hell. Into it vanishes every penny that he can earn, borrow, or claim in social security benefits. From it comes pleasure, knowledge, pain. It is a plastic vulva awaiting his modem jack, a hollow vein awaiting a needle, a synapse whose long copper nerve – axon and dendrite – receives and transmits signals that connect Jarly's brain to a vast and chaotic world of the imagination. Jarly's real life is not 'real' life but the life which is lived in the worlds to which this tiny hole in the wall leads.

Jarly has tried many times to stop, to break his modem habit. He's tried everything he can think of but, lying on his narrow bed, he knows that sooner or later he will succumb to the whispering of the little mouth in the wall. He describes to me the self-hatred and sweetness of the inevitable moment of surrender, of giving in, letting go, of busy fingers conjuring a fix, the buzz of the modem coming to life, the whistle of connection sliding like a needle into his brain, and the rush of relief as he floats into the game.

'It isn't *like* a drug. It *is* a fucking drug. The pleasure chemicals that happen when you do drugs, Bear? Well the same fuckers are triggered by the modem.'

Jarly claims to suffer withdrawal symptoms if he is away from Shades for long. His body is tired and full of aches, he can't keep still, his legs and arms hurt, his head aches and feels too heavy to hold up, his neck and shoulder muscles knot and burn, his eyeballs feel as if they've been sandpapered, he is constantly tired but his sleep is broken by threatening dreams and he wakes exhausted. To me this sounds more like the effects of eight hours on Shades than a few hours away from it, but Jarly swears he really does want to give up the game.

'There's no future in being a twenty-four year old Shades addict, Bear,' he tells me, and I am not sure whether he sees the funny side of what he's saying. Probably not, because he continues, 'Believe it or not, I do think there's a life after Shades.'

I don't believe him. For one thing, wouldn't he miss the killing? Jarly is a serial murderer, one of those who kill for pleasure. His characters are expert and violent wielders of longsword and axe, hacking their opponents apart in sprays of imagined blood. These fights are no sporting contests, where the outcome is of as little importance as 'death' in a paintball game. They are desperate affairs, because so much is at stake. It may have taken someone a hundred hours of play, much of it sneaked in office time at the risk of their job, and cost hundreds of pounds to get a character to high level. Then along comes Jarly who – because he is an expert who is constantly inventing new, nastier tactics – guts them. A few strokes of the longsword and months of play go for nothing. I have seen people scream, cry, sob, become hysterical, slide into depression, do stupid and unforgivable things, after being killed on Shades.

When we've eaten, Jarly says to me, 'Bear, I really asked you here because I wanted you to see how things are with me. I'll be honest, I need to ask you a favour.'

Uh-oh. I know he's strapped for cash. He'll ask for money.

'I can't go on this way,' says this new, responsible Jarly, 'Shades addiction is killing me. I've been trying to give it up, Bear, but it's hard, man, worse than ciggies. I've got to get some fucking brass together and I need some help. What I need . . .'

He stops and looks at me, as if embarrassed to go on.

'Yes?'

'What I really need, Bear, and you could help me here, is. . .'

Ingredients: For this you need one chicken, about ten fresh ripe figs (squashy and overripe is okay if you don't look), half a bottle, or better still a whole bottle, of Mavrodaphne (a syrupy Greek red wine a bit like curried port) and (ideally) a dollop of ground coriander seed, a pinch of cayenne pepper, about a teaspoon each of ground cumin and ground black pepper. Plus salt, two large onions chopped, bay leaves, grated lemon, chopped parsley and crushed garlic to taste.

Method: Chop, mangle, mince and mix together everything that isn't chicken. Insert into chicken.

Cooking: Place in an oven preheated to 180°C, gas mark 4, until chicken is crisp brown on outside, or until overcome by hunger, whichever is the sooner.

Gypsy Caravanserai (Morgan's story)

He's been on Shades for three days without a break, except when he falls asleep at his keyboard and anyone who is nearby sees 'Morgan the le Fay Wizard fades out . . .' But he's soon back, resuming his vigil outside the pub. He is waiting for Calypso.

On the third afternoon, I beg Morgan to log off and sleep, shave, have a bath. All of us spend too much time in Shades, but no-one, not even Jarly, has ever done a seventy-two hour jag before.

'Bear, I'm okay. I'm tired, but I'm clear in my mind.'

'About what, you silly sod?'

'Clear that she's avoiding me. She feels guilty I suppose. I want to tell her she's no need . . .'

Of course he can only be talking about Calypso.

'Hang on,' he says, 'let's go to my place.'

And I'm whirling through the Shades air, summoned by Morgan to his hideaway, the room he was given when he became a wizard.

Morgan & Calypso's Hideaway (1024)
You are in a cheerful room with the uneven whitewashed walls of an old farm cottage. A fire crackles merrily in the grate before which are two comfortable armchairs with brightly coloured throws and cushions on one of which lounges Calypso's black cat, Bustopher. Around the room are many tokens of Morgan and Calypso's love for each other. On the windowsill stands a gaily painted model of a traditional gypsy caravan.

'She told me she'd have to give up Shades, because her husband was worried about the bills.'

'Not your problem.'

'Is and isn't,' he says.

'Morgan, what have you done?'

'I was trying to help . . .'

'Not you too,' I say, thinking of all the hours Cabbalist had invested in pleasing Calypso.

'You don't understand, Bear. Everyone thinks they can judge her, but they're wrong.'

'All right then, help in what way?'

'Ease the burden a bit.'

'You gave her money?' I ask.

'No,' he says. 'Not like that. My Micronet bills.'

'Racked up by running round the game in Calypso's frillies?'

'Nah, didn't do very much of that,' he says. 'Didn't have time or I would have . . .'

'How much?'

'Oh bugger it, okay. I'm not sure, but probably not more than 2K. Thing is you see . . . well, I let her use my account.'

'What?!'

Lending your account to a Shades addict is like handing a credit card to a junkie. At £3 an hour, with a seriously addicted player spending up to eight hours a day on the game, the damage will start at £500 to £700 a month. And Calypso had been on a lot.

'Morgan, close your account. Today.'

'Please don't overreact.'

'Listen to me Morgan. Talk to Lilith. There's a list of people as long as your arm who've been playing Calypso.'

After a long silence he says, 'Yeah, I have been worrying. The last bill was over £3,500.'

'She's given your account details to other people,' I tell him, 'and god knows who they've passed them on to. There could be dozens of people playing at your expense. Shut the account.'

'I don't think she's like that, Bear. You don't know her like I do.'

'How well do you know her, Morgan?'

'Believe me,' he says, 'I know her pretty well. Take my word.'

Is this a trace of innuendo? I do hope so. Signs of humour are signs of sanity. At times like this I regret the limitations of cyber communication. I can't see Morgan's face, can't read his expression. If – at the far end of the connection that runs from my modem through suspended and buried telephone wires, zips along miles of coiled metal cables, enters bundles of plastic spaghetti looped in sooty tunnels where trains roar in the darkness, traverses the fizzing electron exchanges of the city, threads its way to the heart of the massive computer in which the sprites of Shades perform their myriad tasks, receiving, sorting, stamping, swapping and posting packets of information, leaves by another set of tunnels and pipes, follows a different route out to the suburbs, is lifted into the air to race along miles of telegraph wire swooping in shining scallops from pole to pole tracking road and railway in frozen moonlight, until it comes at last to a connector on a wall of the house where Morgan lives, drilling through the brick, ingressing to a telephone jack, a wire, modem, screen close enough to be misted by his breath – there had been the briefest tremor of a smile, I have missed it.

We've met in the flesh only twice, Morgan and I. At one meet we sat at the bar, and all the time we talked he was dipping his finger into a pool of spilt beer and tracing liquid faces: circle for face, dots for eyes, dash for nose, half moon mouth, always curved down. He's a big guy, as big as me, with a softness about his features that makes him seem weak, as though a veil of fine gauze hangs before the large dark eyes, his plump and slightly upturned nose, chubby lips and the rolling acres of his chin. But Morgan is not weak. Not at all. On the contrary, he has a stubborn strength, but never uses it on his own behalf. What looks like weakness is actually kindness, but of that cloying kind which is more often rewarded by irritation than gratitude. This at least is the thanks he gets from Calypso.

'I know her well,' he repeats. 'Remember I spent a lot of time with her here. Then we were on holiday in Yorkshire.'

'You saying you slept with her?'

'You know I can't answer that.'

'So you did. But when? She must be a superwoman.'

'She's a very unhappy woman, Bear, who is entitled to a bit of happiness. And that goes for me too.'

'She led you all a dance. Ask Lilith.'

'No, that's not true. If you mean she spent time on the holiday with all of us, well she had to. There were four men, three caravans and a car. Each of us was on our own most of the day. So she'd come and sit with each one in turn. Nothing wrong with that.'

'Why are you so miserable then?'

'Well, after we got back she hardly talked to me and now she has not been on the game for days.'

'I heard that you and she didn't get on very well.'

'We decided beforehand that we'd appear to quarrel so nobody would guess what was going on between us.'

'You've got all the answers.'

'And you're misjudging her.'

'One of us is.'

Jarly lets go

'What I really need, Bear, is a job.'

'A job? What sort of job?'

'In your advertising agency. Anyone can think up the kind of crap you see on the telly.'

Jarly tells me about the incident which to him symbolises the depth of his degradation. He's on Shades in search of a victim when he's jumped by a particularly vicious mobile. (A computer generated character which can attack and even kill players. The Crow, the Deer, the Sprite, the Mouse, the Bear, the Morloch: these are some of the Shades mobiles. Most of these cyber-beings can be killed with the major weapons, the rusty longsword, sabre or mild unassuming rat.) Happily for Jarly his battle is taking place on a path where the Strange Little Girl wanders, because 'touching' or 'grabbing' the Girl instantly restores health. Jarly replenishes the stamina the monster is draining from him. The Girl drifts onward.

Jarly is still under heavy attack, his strength again being sapped when, to his dismay, a powerful rival appears on the game. Bad news. He can do nothing until his fight is over. To make things worse a situation which has been nagging at him for some time chooses this moment to become intolerable: he can no longer ignore the fact that he's bursting for a piss. Jarly, trapped at his keyboard until the mobile is despatched, prays that the enemy (one of Barbarella's) will not sneak up and attack him before he has the chance to quit for a swift relief dash. He hangs on, fighting the exquisite agony in his bladder, rocking back and forth, clenching his thighs, working his sphincters for all they're worth, his chair-legs rat-tatting on the bare floorboards. The worst happens. As the mobile dies the enemy attacks and Jarly, screaming with frustration, has no option but to remain and fight. The disgrace of running is more than he can bear, the thought of being defeated by his arch rival is unendurable. Barbarella has 'low-stammed' Jarly, which is to say attacked him when he is below full strength. Despite this, his skill is such that her character is down to his last gasp, another blow will finish him off when . . . the Strange Little Girl drifts in and restores both to full strength.

By now Jarly's bladder is stretched beyond endurance. He must think of something, anything, to take his mind off it. As a boy he'd supported Leeds United. Was only a nipper, went with his dad to Elland Road. Soccer. What a game. How had it started, kicking a pig's bladder blown up taut – no! no! no! – think of something else. University! He'd got into multi-user computer games at Essex, home of EssexMUD. Fighting there was similar to Shades. Shades was written by an Essex MUDder. At Essex he'd lived in one of the tall residential towers. There was a craze for dropping condoms filled with water – no! no! no! – occasionally piss – for God's sake no! – onto passers by. A condom filled with water could expand to a wobbling balloon over a foot long – no! no! no! no! Jarly can't wait, has to go, must quit, cannot stay. But he's winning, his enemy's stam in single figures, one blow will do it. One last blow, and that blow is due to fall. Jarly lifts his weapon . . . and the Strange Litt. . . Teeth clenched, sobbing with frustration and then with relief as a thick rope of urine unravels down his leg, lakes across the floorboards and begins vanishing into the gaps between them, Jarly is yelling with triumph because he has struck his man down, it is his rival's blood that is running down his legs and onto the floor.

Dimitri from downstairs is banging on the ceiling and then at his door, shouting for him to turn off the tap.

I call Geno to find him lamenting that the fuckers at NuKE have gone soft. He's just checked the latest Hack Report, which records all new virus infections reported from the wild. For months, the only new outbreaks have been his own.

>we are losing it bear, from a standpoint of where there is plenty of writing going on, but no one is doing any infecting (except me) shit I think I am the only person that I ever hardly read about in the hack report anymore... not that I am banging my own horn, but shit. It is getting sad...

>hehe, so the rest have taken the line that mike is talking about, of researching, not infecting?

Mike is Michael Paris (no relation to Geno) who runs the CRiS (Computer Research Institute) board up in Chicago. He's a virus researcher with links both to hackers and anti-hackers. You can get clean, well-presented and documented virus specimens from his board if you're willing to sign on as a researcher. If I really want to learn virus programming, I should probably spend more time there, but at £1 per minute it isn't as entertaining as Geno.

>Well there is plenty of people out there writing new stuff. Have you seen Offspring yet? Damn good little spawning virus, but I and a very few others are the only ones putting them into anything. It is really getting sad. I mean somewhere along the line these people have lost the reason for viruses... they are not to play with they are to spread...

>I see that satanbug is still rampaging around...

>Yeah it fucked up a secret service computer. We need more of that kind of action. I am almost willing to say that all the virus swappers are not helping the situation either all they are doing is letting the anti-virus people get their hands on the new stuff like satanbug faster...

>Geno, do you think the anti-virus mob have got access into groups like NuKE etc?

>To some degree, yes. I know for a fact that there are several anti-virus people in NuKE that Rock Stupid has let in. Tiphoid Mary is a member of VirNET for gods sake and there are others. That fucking F__________ is a non-programing idiot who gives everything straight to MacFee...

Tiphoid, ironically, was later kicked out of VirNET for being a member of NuKE. MacFee (sic) is McAfee the anti-virus man.

>well, why did Rocky let them in then?

I don't tell Geno that thanks to my friendship with him, Rock Steady has admitted me, a secret if clueless double agent, to NuKE.

>He is a moron. The last NuKE journal pissed the hacker\phreakers off, because Nowhere Man's article was almost straight out of 2600 mag, also the fucker is a virus thief, he has stolen one of mine that I gave him.

>ah Geno, if only the public knew the tribulations of being a virus writer...

Next year in Jerusalem

The New York HQ of a large computer company is hit by the Jerusalem B virus. The virus infects only ten files, but every machine connected to the network has to be checked. It takes a team of administrators, technicians and security folk two working days and cost around $5,000. On this basis, the Oklahoma Institute of Virus Research contains enough destructive code to trash every system in the US. Stashed in a chamber marked 'J', I find hundreds of mutant strains of the Jerusalem virus.

J-1361.ZIP	1216	09-12-93	jerusalem modification 1361
J-1605.ZIP	1338	09-12-93	jerusalem modification 1605
J-1735.ZIP	1478	09-12-93	jerusalem modification 1735
J-1813.ZIP	1346	09-12-93	jerusalem modification 1813
J-4KA.ZIP	3961	09-12-93	jerusalem mod
J-A204.ZIP	1377	09-12-93	jerusalem (1808.a.204)
J-AC2900.COM	3000	02-24-92	jerusalem (anticad.2900)
J-AC2900.ZIP	2196	09-12-93	jerusalem (anticad.2900)
J-AC3004.COM	3104	01-01-80	jerusalem (anticad.3004)
J-AC3012.EXE	3604	03-19-89	jerusalem (anticad.3012)
J-AC3012.EXE	3604	03-19-89	jerusalem (anticad.3012)
J-AC4KA.COM	5911	06-01-89	jerusalem (anticad.4096)
J-AC4KCH.COM	5096	08-31-90	jerusalem (anticad.4096.chinese)
J-AC4KDA.COM	14096	02-06-91	jerusalem (anticad.4096.danube)
J-AC4KMO.COM	4138	12-20-90	jerusalem (anticad.4096.mozart)
J-ACTOBA.COM	6471	06-03-91	jerusalem (anticad.2900.tobacco)
J-ACTOBA.ZIP	4192	09-12-93	jerusalem (anticad.2900.tobacco)
J-ANARKB.COM	5909	03-18-91	jerusalem (1808.anarkia.b)
J-ANARKC.COM	6928	03-11-91	jerusalem (1808.anarkia.c)
J-ANTISC.COM	1607	02-09-92	jerusalem (antiscan)
J-BARCEL.COM	5363	04-03-91	jerusalem (barcelona)
J-CARFLD.COM	2516	08-31-90	jerusalem (carfield)
J-CLIPPR.EXE	2437	07-29-90	jerusalem (clipper)
J-CNDER.ZIP	3260	09-12-93	jerusalem (1808.cnder)

J-CTRIP6.COM	1817	01-01-80	new or modified variant of jerusalem
J-CTRIPS.COM	1817	02-19-91	jerusalem (1808.captain trips.skism)
J-CZECHB.COM	1737	03-11-90	jerusalem (czech.b)
J-DRAGON.COM	5384	06-03-91	jerusalem (1808.triple)
J-EINSTN.COM	1438	05-12-91	jerusalem (einstein)
J-EINSTN.ZIP	933	09-12-93	jerusalem (einstein)
J-F13416.COM	432	08-19-89	friday the 13th (416)
J-F13416.ZIP	491	09-12-93	friday the 13th (416)
J-F13VB.COM	604	01-01-80	friday the 13th (540.b)
J-F13_V2.COM	452	09-19-89	new or modified variant of friday the 13th
J-FEB7.COM	1818	02-10-92	jerusalem (1808.february 7th)
J-FEB7.ZIP	1356	09-12-93	jerusalem (1808.february 7th)
J-FLAGEE.COM	1818	02-10-92	jerusalem (1808.flag ee)
J-FREREA.ZIP	1477	09-12-93	jerusalem (1808.frere.a)
J-FRI15.EXE	6464	12-30-90	jerusalem (1808.friday 15th)
J-FUMCHU.ZIP	1810	09-12-93	jerusalem (fu manchu)
J-GP1.COM	2869	10-29-90	jerusalem (gp1)
J-GRLINX.ZIP	1431	09-12-93	jerusalem (groen links)
J-INJECT.EXE	12080	01-07-91	j-inject trojan
J-JAN25.EXE	6928	03-11-91	jerusalem (1808.january 25th)
J-JVT1.COM	1855	10-31-90	jerusalem (1808.jvt1)
J-KYLIE.ZIP	1812	09-12-93	jerusalem (kylie)
J-MENDOZ.ZIP	1565	09-12-93	jerusalem (1808.mendoza)
J-MIKY.ZIP	3470	09-12-93	jerusalem (miky)
J-MOCTEZ.ZIP	4320	09-12-93	jerusalem (moctezuma)
J-MULE.ZIP	1788	09-12-93	jerusalem (mule)
J-MUMY10.EXE	10513	12-20-90	jerusalem (mummy 1.0)
J-MUMY12.EXE	10743	01-03-89	jerusalem (mummy 1.2)
J-NAZI.ZIP	3955	09-12-93	multiple infections: jerusalem (1808.standard) and cascade
J-NOV30.ZIP	1628	09-12-93	jerusalem (november 30th)
J-PHENOM.COM	2048	03-15-91	jerusalem (1808.phenomen)
J-PLO.ZIP	1459	09-12-93	jerusalem (1808.p)
J-PSQR.ZIP	1317	09-12-93	jerusalem (psqr)
J-PUERTO.EXE	6928	03-11-91	jerusalem (1808.puerto)
J-SK2.COM	1817	01-01-80	jerusalem (1808.captain trips.c)
J-SK3.COM	1817	01-01-80	jerusalem (1808.captain trips.d)
J-SK4.COM	1817	01-01-80	jerusalem (1808.captain trips.e)
J-SK5.COM	1817	01-01-80	jerusalem (1808.captain trips.f)
J-SK6.COM	1817	01-01-80	jerusalem (1808.captain trips.g)

J-SK7.COM	1817	01-01-80	jerusalem (1808.captain trips.h)
J-SK8.COM	1817	01-01-80	new or modified variant of jerusalem
J-SK9.ZIP	1378	09-12-93	new or modified variant of jerusalem
J-SKISM.COM	1817	01-01-80	jerusalem (1808.skism)
J-SPAIN.ZIP	1447	09-12-93	jerusalem (1808.spanish)
J-SS110.ZIP	1128	09-12-93	jerusalem (solano.subliminal.1_10)
J-STTD.ZIP	6995	09-12-93	jerusalem (1808.standard)
J-SUB_0.ZIP	1384	09-12-93	jerusalem (1808.captain trips.subzero)
J-SUMS1.ZIP	1373	09-12-93	jerusalem (1808.apocalypse)
J-SUMS2.ZIP	1638	09-12-93	jerusalem (1808.frere.c)
J-SUMS3.ZIP	1348	09-12-93	jerusalem (1808.0ffd)
J-SUMS4.ZIP	1513	09-12-93	jerusalem (1808.frere.c)
J-SUNDY2.ZIP	1577	09-12-93	jerusalem (sunday ii)
J-SUNDYC.ZIP	1479	09-12-93	jerusalem (sunday.c)
J-SUNDYD.EXE	2644	08-31-90	jerusalem (sunday.d)
J-SUNDYE.COM	1668	12-25-89	jerusalem (sunday.e)
J-SURIV3.EXE	6928	03-11-91	jerusalem (suriv 3)
J-SWISS.EXE	2496	12-16-90	jerusalem (1808.swiss)
J-TRIPLE.ZIP	3273	09-12-93	jerusalem (1808.triple)
J-WESTWD.ZIP	1364	09-12-93	jerusalem (westwood)
J-YELLOW.COM	2387	07-11-91	jerusalem (yellow)

Geno explains to me that it is the pitiful incompetence of the virus writing crowd that accounts for the hundreds of Jerusalem offspring. The original Jerusalem virus had been written in Haifa in the eighties. It went off with a bang every Friday 13th. For years it was the commonest computer virus 'in the wild', which made it the perfect laboratory specimen for would-be virus writers to examine and disassemble. Most of the Jerusalem clones were created by a virus-writing gang called Phalcon/Skism, much feared by the anti-virus establishment, who portray them as a sinister clique of cyber-terrorists. Actually, says Geno, they are 'second-rate programmers barely old enough to masturbate'. All they did was take the Jerusalem virus apart and put it back together again in dozens of minutely varying iterations, most of which were duly given new, terrifying sounding names and launched as new creations. Geno tells me that he has tested all of them, most do not work.

'Bear, it's Chorley an . . . an I'm telling yer straight up don't get offended cos I'm fucking drunk. In fact I'm *fucking* drunk. I've got this giant bloody bottle of whisky here and I'm halfway through it or I wouldn't be ringing yer. Yer know what I'm gonna say, don't yer? It's all a bloody big mistake, mate. You and Cally. Okay I've seen the letter she sent yer but it don't mean a bloody thing. You should see the one she sent us. What I'm trying to say, an if I wasn't so fucking pissed I wouldn't, but the bottle's half fucking empty an I'm sorry, this'll shock yer, but . . . thing is she's with me, mate. Cally and me have been having an affair for months. I just wanted yer to know in case yer got the wrong idea, an I want you to see the letter she wrote me cos when you've read it you'll fucking leave her alone cos it proves I'm the one she loves.'

It's just a week since my heart-stopping experience with Calypso. She has sent me no letter that I know of, but in my mailbox is the following message.

From: calypso
To: chorley

babe, ours were the sweetest moments. every day, i secretly smile and remember that day on the moor. the relief at last of leaving the others behind, looking in the mirror at the caravans getting smaller and smaller behind us. then looking at you and thinking we had the whole day to be together and be free. you weren't even expecting it were you babe. i know i'd said we'd find ways to be together, but weren't you surprised when i jumped up and said 'i'll go with chorley because there are some things i need to get in richmond'. the look on your face i will never forget, i think only i noticed. cos you had been expecting to go off on your own. i had to do it that way, because you know babe, you're not very good at hiding your feelings. so off we went and left them behind and you were all shy, as if we'd never been alone together before. when we stopped at the inn for a drink i didn't say anything but i knew we'd spend most of the day in bed. i cherish the memory of that room in the inn, the four poster with so soft a mattress, snowy sheets. you touch me and we're together and we are one. forever, you and me, whatever happens, this day is ours. it was summer, we were hot and lay sticky and sweet on the cover...

'I know she's not perfect,' slurs Chorley, 'an' I know she's had special friends and been tempted and all that . . . but she's never gone all the way with anyone else. Not since she was married . . . 'cept her husband of course . . . She's hurting, Bear, she's like a confused child, you probably don't know this but she never had much love when she was young. She needs me, mate. Other blokes might want to take advantage for what they can get, but I'm concerned for her, I care about her and I can help her. Cos you see the thing is she really loves me.'

So Lilith was right. Poor old Chorley, she got you too.

I get home one evening about eight or nine, the usual time – there are fifty slow miles between the agency and our Sussex village – to find no-one in. The house is shadowy and deserted. It's early summer, still light outside. I go out into the garden. No-one around – only an edge of moon netted in branches – not a soul.

Go into the study. Taped to the computer screen is a plain white envelope. Slit it open, looking for a message. Four folded sheets: a telephone bill. My eyes flick to the end of the last sheet and recoil. I can't believe the sum – it's more than a thousand pounds. Besides the bill there is nothing else in the envelope. All kinds of wild notions audition in my brain. Eve has opened the bill and walked out in disgust. No wonder. My eyes slide down lists of figures, hundreds and hundreds of calls. I recognise the Shades number in London. But the other names read like a list of destinations you see in the window of a travel agency. Some of the places I have called in the past three months: Bombay, Chicago, Hamburg, Los Angeles and San Francisco (dozens of times), Oklahoma City (regularly), Poona, Tokyo, London (hundreds), Sydney, Amsterdam, Miami, Moscow, New York (lots), Paris, Basle, Geneva (regularly), Oslo, Stockholm, Singapore, Johannesburg, Beirut, Athens, Copenhagen, Bangkok, Ljubljana, Vladivostok (twice). It's not a mistake.

Eve has seen all this. I've been trying to convince her that the modem thing's a passing fad, while all the time the urge to wander has been growing, the cost getting higher. This is the first time a bill has crossed into four figures. I promised Eve that costs were on the wane, that things were coming back under control. Now she's seen the evidence that I was lying. What has she done? Has she taken the children and gone?

I sit down at the machine. The house is empty, my family has disappeared and I sit at the machine. Can't think of anything else to do. This is what I always do. I don't feel right unless I am sitting here. Fingers move by sheer force of habit. I watch it happening. The number is dialled, then there is – what was it I said about Jarly? – the whistle of the modem, like a needle sliding into the brain, the moment of connection and the sweet warmth of Shades again.

The usual crowd are there, Jarly of course, Gawain, Branwell, Arifax, dear old Icecold. But I can't concentrate. The huge phone bill. I don't mention the family missing. I don't know what to do, some part of me is frozen. I can't believe she has left. I examine and re-examine the envelope for a note, but she has left no comment, just placed the bill inside and taped it to the screen.

I switch off and sit in the dark. Should I be making phone calls? Who could I ring? Where would she go? Should I ring her mother? What could I say? 'Molly, Eve has vanished, I think she may have walked out because I'm addicted to the computer.'

Doesn't sound possible.

But I am on the point of picking up the phone when the door goes, the noise of tired children. Eve's voice. I rush out into the hall.

'Thank God you're back' I exclaim, while another, smaller, voice wants to whine, 'That bill, it's not what . . .'

But she doesn't mention it. Smiles, explains that she'd taken the children to the cinema and then because they were hungry, took them off for something to eat. Says she's sorry if I was worried. Was sure she'd left a note with the telephone bill. Hadn't she? I stare at my wife's neat figure, fair hair touching her shoulders, green eyes glinting at me, slanted like almonds. How well, how little, I know her. She is a mystery to me. Like the sea, deep, quiet, but imbued with immense, giant, horrific strength. Who is she roleplaying?

Gawain has laid on a feast fit for gods: mussel-and-cod chowder, a tureen of Mediterranean fish soup (the original plan, only Gawain, unable to decide between them, has done both), langoustines, three pyramids of artichokes, a vast tarte à l'oignon . . . The food is laid out on a polished mahogany table which runs the length of a burr-walnut panelled dining room. On the walls are military prints: the Cherry Bums at Balaclava, the Relief of Lucknow, Gordon shooting a fuzzy-wuzzy at Khartoum. Wiggle-edged daggers from Tangiers and Marrakesh are arrayed round a dented shield. Tulips of pink and blue glass sprout from the walls to light the table which, to resume, groans under . . . a tarte tatin, a tray of partridge pasties farci avec gammon and pine kernels, a whole cold salmon, a pike (stuffed and steaming), slices of boar poached in milk with mace and cloves (looks like 'doves' on Gawain's elaborately printed menu), a small cauldron of cassoulet de Toulouse (for which the right sausage and a supply of confit de canard had been sent for well in advance). Also, venison (mulled in red wine with oriental spices, mace, nutmeg, peppercorns from the Spice Islands, bay leaves from the garden, juniper berries, button mushrooms and shallots from Waitrose), the meal to be concluded with zabaglione, white chocolate mousse with cappucino cream, plain chocolate mousse with pistachio nuts, and profiteroles filled (as Gawain is at pains to point out to his disbelieving guests) not with cream but cream cheese: all in all a most extraordinary and opulent spread, entirely wasted on the milling horde of witches and wizards.

Hmm, perhaps not entirely wasted for here is Jarly, plate heaped high. Jarly's natural condition, like that of a wolf in the wild, is one of near starvation, so he gorges himself when he can and measures the value of an invitation by the number of meals it can be stretched to cover. Thus he had taken care to arrive in good time for lunch and has spent the afternoon upstairs logged into Shades. It's now nearly ten. The guests, immortals all, have been arriving since eight. The crowd is thickest round an ice-filled bathtub from which the long necks of champagne bottles rear like monsters from an embrackled Loch Ness. Gawain himself, the Green Knight Wizard, wearing a surcoat appliquéd with a coat of arms which he describes, giggling, as 'Gules a lion rampant wink between jambes no don't dare say it counter-embowed,' is bustling about directing operations. He has hired three resting actors to fill glasses and pop partridge pasties into people's mouths, and these thesps, impeccable in white jackets and bow ties, could hardly be in greater contrast to the guests.

'Dress in character,' the invitation had said, but few have made the effort. Qadile is wearing stovepipe headgear which, taken with the lanky stoop, makes him look like the Cat in the Hat. Branwell the Happy Dead Wizard is carrying an old leatherbound copy of *Jane Eyre* and has carefully-observed ink-stains between the thumb and first two fingers of his quill-bearing hand. Calypso, portraying a sea-nymph, wears an extremely short 'grass' skirt (confidential memos courtesy of the office shredder, 'I suppose it is a bit tiny, but what could I do, the memos were A4?') and scarlet paper hibiscus in her dark hair. For once she is sans husband. Sprawled across their host's red leather sofas are the Archwizard Hellborn and his cyber consort the Archwitch Mehitabel (his 'real' wife is at home putting the kids to bed), surrounded by a knot of courtiers, who keep them supplied with champagne, food and cigarettes. Besides these are gathered in the house of Gawain: Icecold the Ice Cool, Scorpius the Sting-King, Merlin the Original, Nullpoint the Norwegian, Aphrodite, XParrot the Ceased 2B, Kaddish the MadFatOldGit, Stiffy the Up-for-It Wizard, Fineas, Sinistar, Mak, Wizzo, Hypatia (Witch and 'real' life girlfriend of Branwell), Rosy the Cheeky, Devil the Incarnate Wizard, Phaid the Weird, Minotaur,

Mglwlxyz the Unpronounceable and many others. Upwards of three dozen Shades witches and wizards have come to celebrate Gawain's fortieth birthday.

Moving among these folk, one overhears strange snippets. An elderly man who looks like a vicar is deep in discussion with a huge earringed biker wearing a Metallica tee-shirt.

'. . . lost six fights on the trot to Dandy,' the vicar is saying, 'so I decided the only strategy was to bang in the steals, get ahead, then flee down and repeat process'.

'Got to cripple first,' says the biker.

'Oh I always cripple,' says the vicar and smiles as if giving benediction to a parishioner.

Calypso leans in the kitchen doorway laughing, her long legs shown off by the skirt of shredded secrets. I notice Cabbalist's eyes on her and Morgan's resentful eyes on him.

Calypso spots them and smiles. 'Well, the invitation did say to dress up,' she tells Morgan. 'But I see you haven't bothered.'

'I asked Gawain,' says Morgan. 'He told me "Come as you are".'

'Come as you are.' A more misleading instruction is hard to imagine for, by definition, no-one here is what they seem. To the non-initiate, the crowd appears to consist of human beings. Of all possible types, classes and morphologies, their ages range from 15 to 73. Ask their occupations and you will hear: casino teller, travel agent, schoolboy, bus driver, advertising copychief, bank manager, housewife, computer engineer, senior ward sister, paleontologist, hospital matron, biker, British Telecom manager, jazz musician, debt collector, traffic warden, canalboat builder, long distance truck driver, university lecturer, forecourt attendant, actor, consultant paediatrician, travel writer, supermarket manager, solicitor, police officer, part-time go-go dancer . . . all utterly misleading.

In this gathering, no-one is interested in what you look like, how you dress or what you do for a living. The only thing that matters is who you are on Shades. The 'real' people in the room were never invited to this party. They're here on sufferance, mere emissaries of the real guests: it's the personas who are meeting here.

'Hi, I'm Louella the half-Elven,' a forty-five year old man with an alcohol- and tobacco-ravaged face announces and, turning to his shy girlfriend, adds, 'and this is Psychopath the Singing Blade.'

No wonder so many people are loth to reveal 'real' names. Remember when you were little and your mum took you to school and kissed you in front of your friends? How embarrassing it was, how you wished she'd go away? That is pretty much how Shades personae feel about their real life owners.

Barbarella

Few cyber-personalities are so powerful that the flaws of their human chaperones can't touch them, but one such stands nearby, draining a glass of Gawain's champagne. Middle aged, firkin-shaped, Pat might be in the dull light of face-to-face reality, eyes magnified to twice life size by lenses designed for extreme myopia, her lack of conventional sex appeal exacerbated by a sixty-a-day habit, the air round her head blue with cigarette smoke and hoarse, softly-uttered obscenities, but to her friends and fans she is, and will always be, Barbarella the Hot Blonde Witch.

Barbarella, celebrated for equally vicious use of sword and tongue, stares coolly at Gawain's outrageous table. Lifting a langoustine by one leg, she calls out, 'Gawain, can you please tell me what this is? Are you supposed to eat it? Or fight it?'

The courtiers dutifully laugh.

I come upon Branwell and Merlin sitting in a corner. 'Hello Bear, you'd better speak slowly,' Branwell tells me. 'I've had so much champagne, I'm lip-reading double.'

'Big mistake, the champagne,' says Merlin. 'Shh ... am ... p ... p ... ainuh ... nuh', enunciating each syllable with exaggerated clarity for the sake of Branwell who, as he has frequently said himself, is far too lazy to practise his lip-reading.

But Merlin isn't talking about Branwell. 'I told Gawain he was a pillock ... pi ... llock. This lot don't appreciate it, they just think he's just showing off.'

Halfway through the evening, it's obvious that there's going to be trouble. Probably it's when Gawain raps on the table with a soup ladle and announces his plan to massacre the Shades mortals.

'Friends, immortals, Shades has eighty-five immortals. I for one think that's enough. The time has come to say stop! No more mortals seeking asylum in immortality. Jarly, Graeme, Wake, Fineas and I have decided to form an alliance. Instead of our "seconds" fighting each other, we'll band together to wipe out all high level mortals. Let's keep immortality for immortals! Join us! I give you HAWK, The Honourable Association of Wizardly Killers.'

People had been wandering about with glasses and plates. But during this speech, the room resolves to two camps, divided by the overladen table. Barbarella and her allies are ranged on one side, Gawain and his friends along the other. As in some vast heroic canvas, their expressions and the attitudes of their bodies silently yell their hostility. But no painter could sketch these figures, the task is made impossible by the cloudy presence of invisible immortals. Pat, for instance, besides being Barbarella, is simultaneously twelve other witches and wizards, all of whom are here in spirit, or more accurately, like a host of spirits which continuously flit in and out of Pat's dumpy frame.

I have been enunciating Gawain's plan to Branwell.

'What do you think of it?' Branwell asks Merlin.

'It is an idea of bru ... tal ... stu ... pi ... dity.'

'Well, yes, of course it is,' booms Branwell, 'but he may have a point. Stopping the mortals becoming immortal might be sparing them a great disillusionment. If we're honest, we must admit that once we are immortal life becomes strangely boring.'

There is a kerfuffle near the front door.

'You're not supposed to be here, Lilith,' I hear someone say. 'It's immortals only.'

'Ach, don't be pompous,' drawls a voice which I recognise as belonging to my friend of the leather trousers. Now she appears, clad as the last time I had seen her. On her arm is a woman, tall, aloof and hollow cheeked. She wears a short charcoal grey skirt and white blouse; her long legs are cased in grey silk stockings, her feet tucked into black stilettos. Her skin is painted a matt white and her hair, which must naturally be blonde, is dyed an ultra-pale Wehrmacht grey.

'This is Garbo,' says my friend.

The perfect facsimile of a black-and-white movie star, Garbo sucks greedily on Lilith's exuberant cigarette holder and smiles.

'Kindly inform Gawain,' says Lilith, 'that two immortals of the Vortex are here.'

A lipsdropped conversation

'Look at Calypso,' I tell Branwell.

Calypso is staring at the new arrival, Garbo.

'Oh that's not why she's grim,' Branwell tells me. 'She has just had a spat with Morgan.'

'How do you know?'

'Lipsdropping.'

'Lipsdropping?'

'They were standing near me. I had a good view. They knew I was there but of course they also know I'm deaf . . .'

'But I thought . . .'

'I'm not brilliant at lip-reading, but I'm not all that bad.'

The exchange, more or less as lipread, went as follows:

Morgan said, 'Why are you avoiding me?'

Calypso replied, 'I'm not.'

He: '. . . (unclear) love you. I want you to be happy.'

She: 'You're crowding me.'

Morgan says, 'It's been like this since the holiday.'

She: 'I told you . . . (unclear) your jealousy.'

He: ' . . .(unclear) wished you'd spend less time with (unclear).'

She: 'You're always on at me! You never let up.'

He: ' . . .(unclear) be together. I know you feel guilty . . .'

She: 'No!'

He: 'You're unhappy . . . (unclear, possibly "darling")'

She: 'Stop saying that!'

He: 'You need someone to take care of you.'

She looked him in the eye and said, '. . .(unclear) what I did with Cabbalist and Chorley? Okay, I'll tell you, since you're so desperate to know. I screwed them. Okay? I fucked them.'

In any cybergypsy social gathering – and nowhere among all the cybergypsy clans is this truer than of the Shades tribe – there comes a moment when a computer must be switched on. One person will then log on to the game, bulletin board or whatever is their current focus, and all the others will stand around and watch. At Gawain's party this ritual was initiated by a witch called Hypatia, a peaceful person who was determined to live out non-violent principles even in cyberspace. Hypatia rummaged in her bag of characters, chose Poppy, an enchantress of middling level, and sent her down into the game, which as ever was full of quarrelling, treasure-hunting mortals. Poppy pootered around saying hello to people and was soon being chased by a raggedy arsed seer waving a longsword. Disgraceful, chorused the watching immortals. Several offered to take over and teach the upstart a lesson, but predictably it was Pat, mother of a dozen immortals, who squeezed herself into the chair and addressed the keyboard. The character who materialised in the land was the most powerful and feared of all her mortals, Hagstor the Horrific. Hagstor was a Warlock, which is the highest level a mortal can attain in Shades. His bare knuckles delivered a massive seventeen-point punch and, when wrapped round one of the power swords, tore from his opponents nearly 50 points of stamina per blow. Hagstor was fast and dangerous and arrogant. None could withstand him. Thrice in single combat he had mastered Jarly's Eiger the North-Facing Warlock and forced him to flee. Jarly nurtured a deep grudge and a lust to kill Hagstor.

Hagstor moved out into the game like a giant predator going among prey. He magically summoned the seer who had chased Hypatia's enchantress, wrenched the sword from his grasp and despatched him in four blows. As news of the seer's death flashed across the game, the immortals in Gawain's house cheered and urged Hagstor to fight again. It was incautious advice, for Pat was playing from Gawain's computer not her own and Hagstor was thus without the protection of her customised f-key program. However, his warlock's strength was so awesome and her fingers so quick that there was no real threat. The only people who might have been a danger were Jarly and a handful of other class fighters, but Hagstor would not be attacked by any of their 'seconds', for they were all in the room with her, watching.

Now Hagstor was out in the land and all those near him felt the weight of his tread. Smaller beings scurried from his path, scattered into the woods, or hid in corners of the ruined city. The mortals were on in force and their Amazons, Seers, Mysticals, Soothsayers, Enchanters and Sorcerers fled in horror at his approach. He soon found a new victim. Farinsnod the snork-nosed Sorcerer was a peaceful if argumentative soul who had once accused Pat of being a bully. The Warlock's blows destroyed him in a few seconds and he died trying to flee for his life.

Those watching saw Hagstor check to see 'who' was on and the name of Wyrd the Weland's Necromancer flashed up. An unknown character. He had gone from 0 to the Necromancer threshold of 80,000 points in just two days. This was dedicated, expert playing. Almost certainly Wyrd was a wizard's or a witch's 'second', but nobody could think whose, since most people capable of such a feat were at Gawain's house armed with nothing more deadly than a glass of wine. For a moment Hagstor hesitated. Prudence dictated that he should seek safety, test Wyrd's fighting skills with a fighter of lower level. But stiff-necked Hagstor, 100,000 points senior to Wyrd and within two hours of reaching immortality (should he want it, which he did not), rejected this idea. He had never fled before anyone in his life, much less a lower level. Besides which, Pat had drunk deep of Gawain's champagne and had an audience.

She announced that Hagstor would wait to see if Wyrd attacked. She was certain that even without f-keys, the Warlock's powerful spells would easily drive off the lesser warrior.

Now Wyrd, across the game, shouted surprising words: 'At last, Hagstor. You killed my friend. It's revenge time.'

Hagstor smiled. 'Words don't frighten me. Come on, then. Who knows, you might get lucky?'

While Hagstor was still speaking, Wyrd leapt through the air, a mighty jaunt that carried him soaring over forest and river to light down beside the high-souled Warlock, who was waiting outside the gates of the city, leaning on his heavy shield. In the same instant the watching immortals saw on Hagstor's screen the amazing information that Wyrd had attacked.

Hagstor, ducking the Necromancer's first blow, shouted, 'Wyrd, let's make it a fight to the death. No fleeing. There are immortals watching, let them witness our pact.'

But Wyrd drew back with a frown and said, 'I don't make pacts with scum like you.'

As Wyrd spoke, he poised the mild unassuming rat and let it fly; but splendid Hagstor, never once taking his eyes off Wyrd, ducked and the murderous rodent flew past and crashed to the ground. Hagstor reached for his weapon, a finely balanced blade, chased with gold, whose honed steel was sharp enough to cleave the Necromancer's helmet. But it had vanished. A few minutes earlier, XParrot the Ceased 2B Wizard had slipped upstairs with Jarly to a room where there were two more computers – how unwise ever to assume that a cybergypsy has only one – each with its own modem and telephone line. And while Jarly climbed into the glittering armour of Wyrd, XParrot made himself invisible and at the crucial moment spirited away Hagstor's sword, so that when the Warlock reached for it, it was not there. Now, in the first moments of battle, the same invisible hand took up the fallen rat and restored it to Wyrd, who whirled it round by the tail, and slung it, poison teeth-first at Hagstor's eyes. The Warlock jumped backwards, but the claws raked his cheek and drew blood. This opening exchange had told upon unarmed Hagstor. He was puzzled and angry about the loss of the sword. Caught without his f-key software he was forced to type, which, given a Warlock's power, was little disadvantage, but Wyrd was beginning to seem no ordinary adversary. Hagstor was filled with doubt. Who was the friend Wyrd was revenging? And how had Wyrd regained the rat?

Now immortal XParrot spoke to Hagstor from a realm of high invisibility and said, 'Hagstor, don't worry. I'm watching out for you. If things get tricky, I'll step in.'

XParrot spoke using the voice of the Archwitch Mehitabel and Hagstor was taken in. He thought that if he were in real trouble, the Archwitch would rescue him. Hagstor was trying to steal the rat from Wyrd, but Wyrd no longer had the rat. Instead he struck Hagstor with the longsword, a dreadful wound that caused the scarlet stamina to flow. Hagstor, amazed and furious, called out under his breath to Mehitabel, 'There's some trickery going on, give me back my sword.' But from Mehitabel came no reply. Then Hagstor knew that he had been deceived.

As another violent blow fell on him, Hagstor said, 'An immortal has played a trick on me. I thought Mehitabel was online, but I can see now that she is still on the settee next door. It's not Wyrd I'm fighting, but an immortal. There's no shame in fleeing this fight.'

But as he turned to run, Wyrd laid on him a spell of crippling that took his legs away. At that moment Hagstor knew he had lost. He cried out, 'An immortal has deceived me. There is no escape and I must die.' Then he gathered his courage and shouted, 'So be it. I'll die fighting and give you immortals a battle that will be remembered so long as there is a Shades.'

Even while speaking he stole away from Wyrd
the keen smoking blade, whirling it around his head

and gathering all his massive strength,
like an eagle that pierces the dark clouds
to seize a young lamb or cowering hare,
so Hagstor stooped, waving the savage sword;
but Wyrd rushed against him, mad with anger,
and lifting up his shield to receive the blow,
sparing his gold-hornèd helm, won in the lion's
amphitheatre, stole back the sword and struck.
Noble Hagstor laughed aloud, reached to take it back,
but even as his fingers closed round the hilt,
its shining blade grew dark, the gleaming edge
was like a great comet fading in a night of stars,
the brightest star resolving to a gleam, malign
and deadly, from the fang of the evil-toothed rat,
which once more appeared in Wyrd's mailed hand.
At the tender place where neck and shoulders part,
crazy Wyrd let drive the rat, its foul decaying teeth
sank deep into Hagstor's neck yet clave not
the windpipe, that Hagstor might yet speak unto his foe.
And Wyrd shouted so that all the land could hear,
'Hagstor, when you murdered Truffles, I doubt
you dreamed that any could avenge him, yet now
I've loosened your knees, I disdain to finish you
myself, but by a low and carrion creature
you will unseemly and dishonourably be despatched.

Then the lesser mortals flocked out to see the end of Hagstor. The dying Warlock, in his shame reduced to crawling away from his tormentor, knew now that Wyrd was Jarly's and that Jarly had had help from an immortal. He knew that Wyrd was being played by Jarly in some other room of Gawain's house, and that Jarly had Graeme's *Ripper* program at his fingertips. Then XParrot brought on a low creature called Worryguts, with the rank of Explorer, one of the vilest in the land and Worryguts took up a woodsman's heavy axe and with this blunt and rustic tool came to where Hagstor lay gasping his life out at the feet of Wyrd.

Then, strength gone, Hagstor of the flashing helm said,
'I implore you by your life and knees and honour,
do not let this peasant slaughter me, take my life
yourself with a fighter's weapon, give me a warrior's death
and my friends will forgive you this act of treachery.'
But frowning in fury spoke pitiless Wyrd, 'I'll not stop him
from taking off your head; not if your friends bring here
and weigh out thy weight in gold; but these small folk
who hate thee shall look on and laugh.'

Then the seers and enchanters, all those mortals who had been oppressed by Hagstor's arrogance, gathered round and clamoured at him, shouting and taunting. The assembled immortals, watching in silence, were aghast.

Thus in his dying spoke Hagstor of the flashing blade,
'Jarly I know you well and prophesy what shall be,
if you do this, on you the wrath of the immortals
will fall on the day when Hellborn and Mehitabel
and the great Coder who made all things
and British Telecom shall destroy you utterly.
But even as he spoke Worryguts swung the axe
and Hagstor's head flew from his body
and his soul fled shrieking to the underworld
whence none return, and to his corpse said Wyrd,
'Lie there dead, Hagstor, my own fate I am content
to accept when it is determined by the Coder
and all the other immortals.'

The rumpus at Gawain's roars on well into the small hours. It's past four when I climb into the Land Rover and head south for Sussex. The night is brilliantly clear with stars flung across the sky. It's cold and after a few miles the heater blasting hot air in my face makes me drowsy. Shadows crouch in the hedges and leap out, catching me unawares. The road begins swimming away from me and vanishes into pools of darkness. I'm travelling more and more slowly, taking dream turnings, jumping awake to find the car sliding . . .

From troubled dreams I wake to strange hooting cries and calls and the sound of winding horns, blown as to rally troops in battle. I am pulled over in a lane, the nose of the car deep in a hedge, brambles raking across the windscreen. There is a clattering of hooves and clamour of dogs. I wake and look. The hunt is coming up behind me, hallooing along the lane. A huntsman with ginger beard comes past, in his bright red jacket, on a big white horse ankle deep in hounds. Following him are three more hunters in the pink, then ladies black-coated, white-jodhpured, cantilever-kneed – four of them, riding abreast, bringing up the rear. Yes, now their horses are jouncing past, haunches roaming, four plump bottoms rising to the trot in the dawn.

Having seen through Calypso, Morgan went on to greater things. First of all he grew older. Now when he appeared, garlanded in flame, it was with the stern visage of a sage that he looked upon the world. He seemed a sadder, wiser man. But one day the spark rekindled in his eye: Dreamdancer had come to the land of Shades.

'Bear, she is a really wonderful person.'

'You said that about Calypso.'

'I know, but Dreamy is different.'

'How do you know?'

I am whirling through the Shades stratosphere, summoned to Morgan's room, now renamed *Morgan and Dreamdancer's Cottage*.

'Didn't this used to be Morgan and Calypso's Hideaway?'

'No need to rub salt in.'

'Sorry.'

'I'm over all that,' he tells me. 'In fact it seems weird to me that I got so tangled up with her.'

'Easily done,' I say, thinking of Calypso's long legs under the grass skirt and the green moons of her eyes.

'Oh I don't regret it,' he says. 'And I don't blame Cally. I guess I wasn't the right guy. You know Bear, I'm really glad things went wrong with Cally, because it got me together with Dreamy.'

'I was sitting on Shades,' he says. 'It was shortly after Gawain's party. There was all hell breaking loose, quarrelling, rows, people fighting . . .' (This era would become known as the First Wyrd War.)

'Barbarella and Jarly were at it like cat and dog, shouting at each other about cheating and lying and god knows what,' Morgan is telling me. 'Gawain was trying to calm it all down, until Barb gave him an earful . . . I was sitting there and I said out loud "I don't need this. I'm off." And there was this other player there, a lowish level, who said "I agree, can I come with you?"'

'And this was Dreamdancer?'

'Yes. And we went to my room and of course it was still called its old name, so she asked who Calypso was . . .'

'And you told her?'

'Yup. I told her. She seemed interested and sympathetic and before I realised, I was just pouring my heart out.'

'And what did she do?'

He considers this for a while. 'Hugged me a lot . . . She was very sweet about it. Said she understood what I was going through, because it had happened to her.'

'Bear, she's been badly hurt in her life. She was married to this guy . . . he drank heavily and was violent. He beat her. She couldn't leave because she had a young son . . . Then she took her son and moved in with her brother . . . We talked and talked. We were on until dawn, just talking. She told me how she could see the sun coming up, over the chimney pots of Cardiff . . .'

Morgan grins. 'I'm in love,' he says. 'There's no doubt. I know what it's like. It's like with Cally, only more so. Much more.'

'Morgan, are you even sure she's female? You know as well as I do that most "women" on these games have testicles.'

'She hasn't,' he says. 'I've got the photograph to prove it.'

In the Goat and Compass, dingy as ever, smelling sourly of beer slops and stale tobacco, cigarette butts floating in yellow pools in the urinals – why on earth do we keep coming here? – Morgan has lined up two pints on the bar.

'Okay, are you ready for this, Bear?'

With a proud flourish he extracts from the leather labia of his wallet a dog-eared polaroid: Dreamdancer, blonde, buxom – old fashioned word for an old fashioned girl – with just the face to melt a lonely heart.

'I can hack the Fidonet, the JANET and the internet,' says Jarly. 'But tha, lad, tha's trying to hack fuckin' Coconet.'

The Coconet is the most powerful computer net in existence. It has one hundred and twenty times as many *networks* as the Internet has *users*. *Each* Coconetwork has around 10,000,000,000 processors directly connected to between 10,000 and 100,000 others, giving a number of internal connections approaching 10^{15} or one thousand billion. Every instant 10 million or more of its processors interact with each other. It would take a hundred years of supercomputer time to simulate what is happening in a tiny region of each Coconetwork many times a second.

At Gawain's party two worlds, the one we call 'real', and the cyber-world of Shades, collided and became entangled. Such events seem so strange that you'd think they must be rare, like asteroid strikes on Earth, but they are not. Dozens of worlds collide daily in our lives, unnoticed. We compartmentalise experiences. Some, we say, are 'real', the rest 'in the mind'. What we constantly forget is that experience is *all* in the mind. Events only *seem* to succeed one another, one after another. They actually occur simultaneously on many levels inside a multi-dimensional lattice that extends in directions for which Einsteinian space-time has no names. This lattice and the quadrillion links that channel its bizarre info-flows are described by Jarly, Bear and friends as the Coconet. Each Coconetwork runs on a human brain, a computer whose case is of roughly the size and hairiness of a large coconut. The limitless energy-filled space it generates has been known to explorers since the first sapient dawn: it is the human imagination.

Wyrd War One escalates. To whoever will listen, Barbarella insists that the murderers of Hagstor have gone unpunished.

'Gawain planned it. He put Jarly and the Parrot up to it. They should lose their immortality.'

Gawain complains of character assassination (and does not spot the irony).

One night, Lilith says to me, 'Bear, these hack and slay games are all very well for kids, but isn't it time you considered something more challenging?'

'What do you suggest?'

'I think you'd enjoy real roleplaying.'

'Isn't that what we are doing?'

'What happens on Shades, dear, whatever you decide to call it, is not roleplaying.'

'Bear, have you ever roleplayed a female? And if so, did you actually feel any different?'

I think of Lorelei. My first female character. How strange it had been to step inside her loose-limbed body and zip myself into her fizzy personality (something I discovered, rather than decided, she possessed). It felt awkward, the shape and weight of 'myself', the way 'my' limbs moved. I was mortified every time some hormone-driven lad wolf-whistled or made a suggestive remark.

'Did that happen often?' Lilith asks.

Absolutely. Even though I was (at first) so gauche, so bad at it, the male players who rushed up to flirt seemed to accept without question that Lorelei was female. Yet they must have known that, at that time, hardly five percent of people on the net were women.

'Ah,' says Lilith. 'The human need for self delusion. What I call roleplaying is the opposite. What did Lorelei look like?'

'Fairly tall, blonde . . .'

'Don't tell me,' says Lilith, 'bright, amusing. Legs to armpits.'

'Yup.'

'Typical novice creation. The first time a man creates a female character it's nearly always a fantasy pin-up – the sort of girl he's being jacking off to since puberty, but never managed to pull. By bringing her to life it's almost like possessing her, at last.'

'Okay,' I say, 'I'll admit, she was pretty unsubtle. Fantastic figure, amazing tits, wonderful derrière obligingly encased in torn jeans.'

'And how would she conduct herself, this Lorelei?' Lilith asks. 'I suppose you named her after the girl in *Gentlemen Prefer Blondes*.'

'As a matter of fact, no. More the mermaid. My Lorelei had a breathless laugh and talked very fast, in what I used to think of as an intelligent gabble.'

'More stereotyping,' says Lilith.

'She'd giggle rather than chuckle.'

'They all do that.'

'So Lorelei got lots of attention,' says Lilith. 'Did you enjoy it?'

'Well,' I reply . . . Well, there's an undeniable frisson in causing heads to turn. 'Well, at first maybe, but the novelty wore off. Male players were always offering help I didn't want. They'd tell me how to do things, as if I were incapable of thinking for myself.'

'Were you propositioned a lot?'

'There were a few lunkheads who seemed to think that because I was blonde and pretty, it was okay to make suggestions. Even with those who weren't like that, I often felt patronised. Maybe I imagined it, but behind the flattery and compliments, I felt there was arrogance, a kind of contempt. It made me angry.'

'Who felt angry?' asks Lilith softly. 'Bear? Or Lorelei?'

'I don't think I ever really was her. Germaine Greer says it's impossible for a man to know what it feels like to be a woman.'

'How does Germaine Greer know what it feels like to be a

woman – other than herself?' asks Lilith.

'When you roleplay, you are the character,' Lilith says. 'There's no script. You open your mouth and are surprised by what comes out. Your character has a life and friends of her own. You may not approve of what she gets up to, but it is not your business. We, the puppeteers, the mask-wearers, have a duty not to interfere, yet we must know our characters well, as well as we know ourselves. This is hard. Most of us have only the sketchiest idea of ourselves . . .'

'I remember what it felt like to be murdered.'

'The reason I am telling you all this, Bear,' says Lilith, 'is because there is another place, which is by invitation only. Just a few people who like to take things . . . further.'

'Think of it as a small theatre group,' Lilith says, 'which creates, stages, improvises, performs and is simultaneously audience. It isn't for everyone. Things have been known to get rather intense. We are very careful who we ask. The Vortex is a club joined only by invitation. Even then, acceptance isn't certain. If the other members don't like you they won't "play" with you. So we invite only people we think will appreciate it and who can be trusted not to pass the number on to undesirables. Luna's rules.'

'Who's Luna, Lil?'

'Don't ask, you'll know soon enough. She has invited you to tea in Narnia. You'll come of course. The place isn't easy to find, so I'll give you a map and send someone to meet you when you arrive. Oh, and Bear – I am named after an ancient and defiant spirit – I hate being called Lil.'

Imagine the net as a galaxy shining in the dark of cyberspace. The plane of the ecliptic is a blaze of stars – the bulk of the internet – with systems clustered thickest in the sector of Cyber-Sagittarius. We are a long way from the centre, which is hidden by clouds of dust, particles of broken data packets, shining with reflected light. Here and there are pockets of brilliance, hot bright clouds where new systems are being born. There are dark gaps, where networks have died. Strange unexplained effects abound, there are regions of gravity overload, of bending telnets, lag and cyberspacetime freezes. In some places time runs backwards. In one of the galaxy's trailing arms is the location of Micronet, still alive, soon to be a supernova enfolded by the gaseous remains of vapourised Necromancers. Throughout the galaxy and some a little way out from the rim, like astronauts freefloating alongside a spacecraft, are small star-clusters, private systems, like those of the virus writers, NuKE. Beyond is the darkness of total night.

Let your eye drift out. Further. Much much further. Out into the blackness of deep space. Out there, alone in the darkness of space, so faint that it can hardly be seen, a solitary star flickers. This is the secret and exclusive Vortex, home of the net's deepest roleplayers.

Picking my way through clothes in the wardrobe, I step out of the back and into Narnia. Woods stretch away in every direction. Somewhere in these woods, Lilith is waiting with tea, cucumber sandwiches and seed cake, all terribly English.

'Whatever you do, don't be late,' Lilith warned me. 'Luna hates to be kept waiting.'

We're to meet at four o'clock and it's five to. Luckily, I have a map. I go left and follow the slope downhill. The ground falls, growing ever boggier, to a churned up clay mire beyond which, in the shadow of trees, I can hear the sound of running water. Now birch logs step down to a plank bridge which looks as if no-one has crossed it for a while, there is moss growing on the plank. More steps mount the further slope. I climb, puffing. I'm unfit, get easily breathless. I do not get enough exercise, sitting at a desk at the agency all day, and half the night at a computer screen. At the top the path broadens to a rough track, with last season's leaves lying rustily in ruts and puddle-bottoms. I am stepping over small islands of wood anemones when, in a stirring of leaves, a faun stands before me! Yes a real Narnian faun, *Mollicornuus lewisii,* Lewis's Velvet Budhorn. But before I can think to ask the way, it gives me a shy smile and ducks back into the trees. The track peters out and a few steps later I am lost in trees that run away in all directions. All ways look the same. Again the leaf-rustle and the faun re-appears, still smiling, but this time it gestures and waits for me to follow.

The way a faun's legs are made – think of the hind legs of a goat, or antelope – means that it cannot walk as a human does, but dances along, skittering on the points of its hooves. This faun casts glances over its shoulder to make sure I am behind. I notice that it is carrying a cricket bat. Every dozen or so steps it does a little skip, swings the bat through an imaginary cover drive and makes a loud 'tlock' with its tongue. Whenever it does this, it turns and rolls its eyes back at me as if checking for signs that I find its behaviour odd. We go on in this manner for a while, until the faun stops, tilts its head sideways to listen, then says in a high chirrupy voice, 'Come along Cyri.'

Is it talking to me? There is a hint of movement among the trees. Something is there, something hard to see, slipping between the trunks. The faun gives a tinkling laugh and says, now unmistakably addressing me, 'Cyri says *"Dobro pojalovat v Vodovorot"*.'

'What language is that?'

'It is Cyri's language.'

'What does it mean?'

'Cyri is saying to you, "Welcome to the Vortex".'

A short while later we've reached the top of the hill and find ourselves at the forest edge, looking out across a wide landscape of woods and fields. The faun lifts a shaggy arm, points, then quietly as it had come, vanishes into the trees. Hurrying downhill (it is one minute to four), I find a glade painted green and golden by the sun. A table spread with a white cloth is laid with tea things. Beside it, seated in comfy looking wicker lawn armchairs are two ladies.

When I met Lilith in 'real' life she was wearing leather trousers and smoking a cigar. Today she wears a dress of white organza and lace, of a style that was last seen in the years before the First War. Beside her, sitting very upright, is a lady all in black. Above a dress buttoned to a high collar and fastened with an emerald brooch, is the most exquisite face I have ever seen. Its geometries must have been calculated by an angel. The face is meshed with the fine lines of extreme old age – how old must she be? ninety? a hundred? – and in the parchment-pale skin her eyes are (I am quoting now) 'feral gashes of viridian'.

Lilith says, 'Luna, I would like to present Bear.'

The old lady looks me over and says to Lilith, 'Is he civilized?'

'I think so,' Lilith says. 'We shall see. Tea, Bear?'

'Thank you, yes,' I say, feeling foolish.

'Do sit down,' she says, ushering me to a third chair which until this instant had not existed, but now obligingly appears.

'Let me get you a plate. Will you have a slice of cake? May I give you a sandwich?'

While Lilith busies herself in an unnervingly un-Lilithlike way, I smile at the old lady, who glares at me.

'The tea is Earl Grey,' says Lilith. 'But Luna likes a spoon of Lapsang in the pot, don't you dear?'

She pours from a large round teapot.

'Porcelain,' says Luna. 'Tea does not taste the same from pottery. People who serve it in mugs are never to be encouraged.'

'Taste the tea, Bear,' says new, polite Lilith. 'Is it to your liking? Do you prefer it sweeter? Perhaps with honey?'

'No, no,' I say, lifting the cup and taking a sip, 'it's good.'

'Good? What is that?' says Luna. 'Lily, I'd be insulted, after the trouble you've been to.'

'Don't you like the tea?' asks Lilith. I am sitting, plate on lap, holding the teacup and saucer.

'Sorry,' I say. 'It just feels rather silly, playing "let's pretend".'

I am expecting Luna to glower at me, and am relieved when she smiles. 'You're embarrassed!'

Lilith says, 'I'm not surprised. First visits to the Vortex can be rather . . . unexpected.'

'Since it is his first visit,' says Luna, no longer smiling, 'I will overlook his gaucheness.' Turning to me she asks, 'Did you enjoy the scenery on the way here? The view?'

'Yes, the Vortex is like a paradise. It's beautifully written.'

'Not all parts are so pleasant.'

'Well, I am enjoying it immensely.'

'So! You're entertained, even charmed. Bravo! But when invited to contribute to this world, you grow embarrassed.'

Lilith says, 'Luna, I can guess what Bear is thinking. This must feel to him like being at a child's tea party where you're handed a tiny cup and you have to pretend to drink. The child watches you intently, to make sure every drop has gone down, and asks "Is it nice?" and you murmur "Delicious". Then she asks "Would you like some birthday cake?" You say "Yes please". With very great seriousness she hands you a little plastic plate with nothing on it, and you have no option but to poise finger and thumb about the slice of invisible cake and lift it to your mouth. You make little smacking noises with your lips and say "Mmmm, lovely" and hope that this will satisfy her and that she isn't, pray God, going to offer you another slice . . .'

'Exactly like that, Lilith.'

'Exactly thus,' says Lilith, 'do we wish away our children's imaginations.'

'Roleplay isn't just pretend, you know,' says the old lady, munching imaginary cake with relish. She leans across to me. 'I will let you into a secret. It is this: everything we experience is equally real. Or else equally unreal, it makes no difference which.'

'The truth is . . .' says Luna, then stops and titters. 'No, the truth is something else. Truth and reality have very little to do with one another – Lily, could I trouble you for another cup of this good tea? Thank you – the fact is (for facts and truth are also unrelated) that our experience is seamless and undifferentiated. Only we, being unable to accept this, chop it up into bits to which we attach labels. "Real" is just one more label. What actually is real? I am sitting in front of my screen. To my right is a window on which is a pot of lilies. The light catching their leaves makes them translucent, almost golden. It is afternoon. A pigeon is flying down to a roof opposite, which reminds me that I am in London . . . I won't say which part. On the desk beside my computer are the following things, of which I'm aware from time to time: a tiny bulldog clip, used train ticket, twisted paperclip, US twenty-dollar bill; a mug – aha, yes, I bet that surprised you, but it is of porcelain and bears a coat of arms. A breath of wind is just now moving the trees outside my window. My computer screen is flickering, which annoys me. On it these words are appearing as I type them, this word, this letter . . . r. My mind sees Narnia, green and golden, it sees Lilith in her white lace, and it sees you, Bear. All of these things, impossible to disentangle, comprise the actual reality of "now".'

In an adjoining meadow figures in white have appeared and are walking about, carrying what look like sticks.

'Bear, I will now present to you three edited "realities". In "virtual reality", you are in Narnia talking to a cantankerous old woman called Luna. In the "real world" you are in front of your plastic and glass computer watching these words appear on its screen. You are talking to an unknown stranger whose name you do not know, and are aware that "Luna" may not be an old woman at all, or even female. She may have lied about living in London. She may be a fifty-six year old male truck driver from Wigan. But there is a further, transcendent, reality where you will henceforth meet many different Lunas: it is your imagination. These "realities" can't be separated because they are actually all the same thing. . .'

While Luna talks, I notice the fauns, for now I can make them out as such, tapping sticks into the ground and all of a sudden realise that what they are doing is banging in stumps, setting up wickets. There's going to be a game of cricket!

Luna smiles at me. 'Lily, do pour Bear another cup of tea, his first has gone cold.'

As Lilith takes my cup, Luna asks, 'How much of our "real" lives do you suppose is lived in the imagination?'

'Sixty percent?' I venture.

'One hundred percent,' says the old lady.

'Bear, how is your tea?' asks Lilith.

'Hot, wet, sweet.'

'Hopeless!' says Luna, 'Better drop him, Lily, he'll never make a Vorticist.'

'All right,' I say, 'I'll have a stab at *imagining*. The tea is . . .'

'Don't fish for adjectives,' says Lilith, laughing. 'What do you *feel*?'

'Well, I like . . .'

'The human hand,' says Luna, 'is capable of at least twenty-four discrete movements, each of which requires the coordination of a range of muscles in the hand and forearm. To pick up a cup, the forearm must extend towards the object, the hand must open and then close around the handle. Precise motor skills ensure that the cup is grasped firmly enough to hold it against gravity, but not so firmly that it breaks, or so loosely that it slips. . .'

All right. As I lift the cup to my lips I am aware, because I choose to be, of its weight on my knuckles, the sweep of its handle. The rim of the cup against my lower lip is smooth, curving away. I hold it pressed to my lip, tilt and inhale the warm tea spice an instant before the liquid kisses my upper lip. It floods into the mouth, trickles across the tongue and sinks into the corners of the mouth where the taste buds extract its marvellous blend of sweetness and bitterness. The teacup itself is hot, its heat a sort of tingle impressed on the lips and probed for, in a snakely gesture, by the tongue tip.

'"Snakely!"' says Luna, 'I like that. Yes, I think you really did taste that tea.'

Across the field, the ring of white figures slowly closes in as the bowler makes his run up, moving out again after the delivery. I love watching cricket, especially this sort of rustic knockabout. I love the green of sunlight on grass and in oak leaves, the white figures moving in their slow, hypnotic ballet, the occasional clock of leather ball on batwillow. There is a ripple, patter, or clatter of applause like wings round a dovecote. Someone is out, the new batsfaun, all padded up (ridiculous, the pads have to bend the wrong way), is walking out to the crease. There's something familiar, every few steps, about his little hop and imaginary cover drive. I close my eyes and listen to the symphony of tea and cricket sounds, the chink of a cup on a porcelain saucer, distant calls of cricketers, the muted tinkle of a spoon, wind stirring leaves, wind getting up, sighing and snorting in the branches, crackle of leaves close at hand . . .

There is movement in the wood. Something is there, something on the edge of vision.

'Cyri, Cyri,' calls Lilith softly.

An animal emerges from the trees, so perfectly camouflaged that it seems made of glass. I sense, rather than see, the shape of a zebra. As it comes closer I realise why it is so hard to see. I really am looking clean through it. The creature is all striped nothingness. Nor are they stripes. I am looking at a small horse whose body is woven of interlaced Cyrillic letters that stretch and ripple as it moves, creating the illusion of volume. The calligraphic horse trots forward to Luna and lowers its head. She strokes its nose.

'Ya nyenavizhu smotryet sport po televisoru no ya obozhayu JanBothius,' says the horse.

Lilith explains. 'Cyri says, "I hate to watch sport on TV, but I love JanBothius".'

'JanBothius is the faun who likes cricket,' says Luna, but I had already guessed this.

'My parents were émigreés,' Lilith tells me and Luna. 'He was Ukrainian, she from a family of Russian Jews. They met in Berlin, where among other people they knew Nabokov. One of his stories – I can't remember which, but it will come back to me – mentions them. When the Nazis got power things became nervous. In 1937, the year before I was born, they were on the road again, this time to Paris. I am glad they left Germany. I was born in the small hours of November 10th, 1938.'

'Noce nazivayetza Kristallnacht,' says Cyri.

'Yes Cyri,' says Lilith, patting him, 'the night called Kristallnacht.'

'My mother was a gentle soul. She had hair the colour of corn, twisted in plaits. She made me learn Russian, and told me tales of Baba Yaga the witch and the house that turned round on chicken's feet. She also told stories about this little horse made of alphabet who would teach me a letter, a word, a phrase every night.'

'Ya lublu yest morkovki,' says the horse.

'That means "I love to eat carrots"' Luna tells me. 'He is always saying that. 'Here you are, Cyri. You shall have the largest, juiciest carrot imaginable . . .'

And of course it appears in her hand.

The imagination is a building of many rooms which contain images of objects and people. The 'rooms' are not described by four walls, floor and ceiling, but are multi-dimensional spaces which can hold a whole landscape, or even a universe. The objects, by the same token, are not what we could commonly call 'things', but may be ideas, sensations or memories. The rooms are not arranged, as in a mansion or castle, on separate floors, opening off long corridors. They float in clusters like frogspawn, each room having connections to thousands of others. The links may be lofty archways or secret tunnels. This building, the imagination, is not accessed by a single door. There are dozens of entrances, each opened by a different key. Music, ritual, drama, poetry all open doors into the imagination. The candle-lit, incense-pillared temples of witches and magicians are its portals. The Tarot, I Ching and Qabala unlock secret doors. In the Tibetan *Bardo,* cave mouths invite entry, guarded by animal-headed monsters. Similar labyrinths are sentried by the minotaur and the death-beasts of the Nile.

Cyberspace is the name we give to the human imagination when we access it via a modem. But the delirium of modem worship is uncannily like the experience of an earlier generation of cranio-speleologists. Coleridge and de Quincey entered the imagination via the opium gateway. They are the truest, most direct ancestors of the cybergypsies. (So naturally is Kubla Khan's pleasure dome a work of cybertecture that it has been erected in the Vortex – one of the sights of Luna's guided tour – where its glittering dome of white and blue ice can be seen for miles above the scarlet poppy fields of Lethe.) Cybergypsying is addictive as any drug. Jarly, addict and murderer, claims that the chemicals it triggers in the brain are the same endorphins released by opium. He points out that both addictions create hallucinations powerful enough to crystallise imagination into reality. But cyber experience of the imagination is in one important respect different from all the others.

Until recently we have been alone in our imaginations. However vividly a play, film or book brings characters to life in our minds, we always form an audience of one. We enter the story but have no part in it. Millions of people have experienced the vision of Jane Eyre learning Hindustani by candlelight in her moorland cottage, but if Jane was ever aware of ghosts from the future peering in at her through the window, she would have seen that they haunted singly, never in groups. In cyberspace, for the first time, we create imaginary worlds which can truly be shared, in which each of us is fully present, with the power of free and spontaneous action. We no longer have to follow a script. We can play inside each other's imaginations.

Let sea-discoverers to new worlds have gone,
Let maps to other, worlds on worlds have shown,
Let us possess one world, each hath one, and is one.

'I was learning Hindustani too, Bear, when we were in India. We used to play nicely together, you and me. But then you took your toys and went off with your new friends.'

But by the time Eve says this Donne's lines have faded to mere poetry and cyber games no longer seem such fun.

Jarly online in high electric humour.

'Bear, I've got an interview next week with your lot. What should I wear?'

'Try to look respectable. Wear a suit.'

'Haven't got one. Oh bugger it, I'll think of something. Listen, what's the worst that could fuck up your computer?'

'Corrupt hard disk? Loss of stuff?'

'Nah,' he says. 'Not vile enough. Got to be something a lot worse. Triggered by a virus.'

'Are you making a virus, Jarly?'

'No,' he says. 'I've spent the last few days mostly over in the States, there's a beautiful hysteria going on.'

He means he's been cybergypsying around systems on the other side of the Atlantic, while his body, naturally, has remained mango-pickled in its attic.

'A real classic,' says Jarly. 'Someone went on CNN and warned that the Michelangelo virus will wipe out the world's computers next month.'

'It's got to infect them first. How's it going to do that?'

'It won't. It can't. But Bear, you are missing the fucking point. The journos are crawling like flies over anyone who will talk to them about viruses. They are all hyped up and want to know everything about Michelangelo. What is it? Who wrote it? What will it do? Is it part of a conspiracy for world domination? Obviously the lads are feeding them all the wild shit they can think of.'

'What sort of wild shit?'

'I'm just joining the fun, Bear. I've sent you a file.'

When Jarly's file arrives, the top of it looks like this:

```
_______________________________________________________________
          The Computer Incident Advisory Capability
                    ___  __ __    _    ___
                   /       |     / \   /
                   \___  __|__  /___\  \___
_______________________________________________________________
                     Information Bulletin
            Michelangelo Virus on MS DOS Computers
February 6, 1992, 1400 PDT                          Number C-15
_______________________________________________________________
Name: Michelangelo virus
Platform: MS-DOS computers
Damage: On March 6 will destroy all files on infected disks and
        diskettes that are accessed.
Symptoms: CHKDSK reports "total bytes memory" 2048 bytes less than
        expected
Detection: DDI Data Physician Plus! v 3.0C, FPROT 2.01, other
        anti-viral packages updated since late September 1991
Eradication: DDI Data Physician Plus! v 3.0C, FPROT 2.01, other
        anti-viral packages updated since late September 1991
_______________________________________________________________
```

'Now that is the lame original,' says Jarly. 'But a few quick keystrokes and it can be reposted as the original to dozens of systems. Okay here's my version. Spot the difference.'

```
_______________________________________________________________
          The Computer Incident Advisory Capability
                    ___  __ __    _    ___
                   /       |     / \   /
                   \___  __|__  /___\  \___
_______________________________________________________________
                     Information Bulletin
            Michelangelo Virus on MS DOS Computers
February 6, 1992, 1400 PDT                          Number C-15
_______________________________________________________________
Name: Michelangelo virus
Platform: MS-DOS computers
Damage: On March 6 will destroy all files on infected disks and
        diskettes. Plus other as yet uncorroborated damage.
Symptoms: CHKDSK reports "total bytes memory" 2048 bytes less than
        expected
Detection: None at this time.
Eradication: No known method.
_______________________________________________________________
```

'Uncorroborated damage? What's the point, Jarly?'

'Bear, don't you get it? Out there, it's hackers vs hacks. Whose fucking side are you on?'

'If Michelangelo destroys all files, how can it do other damage? Isn't that the most any virus can do?'

'Ah,' Jarly says, 'I am thinking of a virus that doesn't just attack your pooter, it attacks your life.'

'That's biology, Jarly. Anthrax. Saddam.'

'No Bear, imagine a virus that does not delete data, just subtly changes it. It hides away in your computer, patiently searches in text files for strings of numbers, then randomly changes one in each sequence. Dates of documents, account numbers, PIN codes, bank balances, telephone numbers, passwords. Like a biological virus mutating DNA code. Chaos at work.'

'A virus like that would probably be much too big.'

'Or suppose a virus could make your machine transparent, so that when you are logged into a network or bulletin board, people at the other end can see what's on your hard disk and read all your personal files.'

'What idiot would believe that?'

'Suppose it could ransack your email for embarrassing phrases and next time you're online post your most private messages to some public forum.'

'Have to be a massive bloody virus.'

'Doesn't matter,' he says. 'The stories don't have to be plausible. These people will swallow any scare you throw at them. Wilder the better. They *want* these fucking nightmares to be true.'

'Listen Jarly, about your interview. If you haven't got a suit, just wear a tie.'

'Bear, imagine a virus that could search your hard disk for porny pictures – I mean really vile stuff – and if it finds any, email the search results to the police.'

But this does not seem farfetched to me because I am thinking of Nasty Ned the Net Nark.

Found on Nasty Ned's hard disk

Directory of C:\MYFAVES

```
.            <DIR>             19/02/93   6:59
..           <DIR>             19/02/93   6:59
LILSIS3A GIF         120121    04/01/93   2:03
LILSIS3B GIF         119304    09/01/93  20:58
LILSIS3C GIF         125416    09/01/93  21:04
LILSIS3M GIF         121871    09/01/93  21:12
LILSIS3O GIF         124767    09/01/93  21:19
LILSIS3P GIF         126897    09/01/93  21:26
LILSIS3Q GIF         124663    09/01/93  21:33
LITSIS01 GIF         28332     09/01/93  21:39
SCHOOL01 GIF         156815    20/11/91  23:22
SCHOOL02 GIF         64323     20/11/91  23:22
SCHOOL04 GIF         41339     04/01/93   1:32
SCHOOL05 GIF         63002     20/01/93  23:40
SCHOOL06 GIF         141887    18/01/93   8:05
SCHOOL07 GIF         162711    04/01/93   1:37
SCHOOL08 GIF         161591    04/01/93   1:43
SCHOOL09 GIF         79996     19/01/93   3:16
SCHOOL10 GIF         139394    15/05/92  16:32
SCHOOL11 GIF         95408     15/05/92  16:29
SCHOOL12 GIF         82795     15/05/92  16:43
SCHOOL13 GIF         85228     19/01/93   3:12
SCHOOL14 GIF         63869     04/01/93   1:47
SCHOOL15 GIF         63488     08/06/91  20:34
SCHOOL16 GIF         83563     19/01/93   3:20
SCHOOL17 GIF         83618     15/05/92  16:38
SCHOOL18 GIF         157413    15/05/92  16:41
SCHOOL20 GIF         88118     19/01/93   3:09
SCHOOL23 GIF         96006     19/01/93   3:04
SCHOOL24 GIF         93182     19/01/93   3:30
SCHOOL26 GIF         82143     04/01/93   1:51
SCHOOL27 GIF         84187     04/01/93   1:54
SCHOOL28 GIF         161504    19/01/93   3:36
SCHOOL29 GIF         62763     04/11/90  19:02
SCHOOL31 GIF         171510    19/01/93   3:46
SCHOOL32 GIF         65049     04/01/93   1:58
SCHOOL33 GIF         75495     20/01/93  23:48
SCHOOL34 GIF         68551     05/11/90  18:42
SCHOOL35 GIF         58102     02/11/90  22:32
SCHOOL36 GIF         62675     02/11/90  22:32
SCHOOL37 GIF         61367     17/10/92  22:40
SCHOOL39 GIF         131072    08/06/91  20:28
SCHOOL40 GIF         83884     17/10/92  22:40
SCHOOL41 GIF         75851     20/01/93  23:55
SCHOOL43 GIF         79615     20/01/93  23:58
SCHOOL45 GIF         92817     17/10/92  22:40
SCHOOL47 GIF         69054     21/01/93   0:02
SCHOOL49 GIF         44877     21/01/93   0:09
SCHOOL52 GIF         83073     21/01/93   0:16
SCHOOL53 GIF         86451     21/01/93   0:24
SCHOOL54 GIF         149936    19/01/93   3:26
SCHOOL55 GIF         152231    21/01/93   0:33
SCHOOL56 GIF         143086    21/01/93   0:41
SCHOOL57 GIF         93890     21/01/93   0:48
SCHOOL58 GIF         93645     21/01/93   0:54
YNGSTF01 GIF         34978     18/04/93  17:24
YNGSTF03 GIF         96365     08/01/93  21:48
YOUNGFUN GIF         39423     17/10/92  23:34
      58 file(s)   5398711 bytes
```

No-one likes Nasty Ned. Not his fellow sysops on Fidonet's Net 2:2??. Not the police officers who pat his dandruffed head – they know exactly what sort of shit he is. Not even the poor fucker's mother wants to know him. She has asked him to get out of her house, so he tells me, during one of my typed visits to his bulletin board *Ned's Nomadsland*. He's an enigma, our Ned, a greasy fish-and-chip wrapped mystery hidden in an oily conundrum wrapped in a brylcreamed riddle: a loud supporter of free speech on the net, who, because of his collusion with a certain police force, is known as the 'Net Nark'. The 'Nasty' epithet is something else. Long before the word had become an adjective of choice for purveyors of hardcore pornography, Ned had redefined it all by himself.

Everyone knows, because Ned makes no particular secret of it, that he lives for what he calls 'sexcursions' to Thailand. He boasts of having slept with a fifteen year old in her parents' house. ('It's not taboo, over there.') I am left feeling priggish. Ned is addicted to pornography. This too is not a secret. His talk is constantly of this or that bulletin board which has hardcore pictures, or which carries contact echoes. These are days when the commercial internet is still in its infancy, and pornography has not yet exploded on the World Wide Web. I know of perhaps twenty bulletin boards in Europe which offer hardcore and in the course of my wanderings have seen four of them: in each case Ned's name was already among the users. The odd thing is that Ned is simultaneously user and stool pigeon. He is suspected to be behind the busts that take place from time to time, whether of boards touting pornography, viruses, or pirated software. He is an ethical oxymoron, extolling free speech yet helping to shut down systems. Ned also belongs to that rare subspecies of cybergypsy who are computer illiterates.

A netmail comes in from a worried fellow sysop who says that he thinks Ned is dabbling in pornographic pictures of children.

'I hear you're visiting him soon,' says the netmailer. 'Can you find a way to check this out?'

Yes and yes. Ned has asked me to install some software for him. He is so ignorant of computers that I can easily slide a trojan horse into his system. I write a tiny batch file and add it to the disk.

Ned lives with his mother in a tall house in an East London street with many boarded-up houses. I am just pressing the bell when a curious babbling causes me to turn. Over the road, a middle aged but obviously half-witted Indian man is standing in his front garden, a tiny patch of concrete littered with bricks. He holds out his hands to me and gibbers in thick-tongued delight. Behind me the door opens and the smell hits.

The stench is appalling. It invades my nose and mouth, beats in waves at my face. I cannot tell whether it comes from the darkness inside the house, or from the dumpy man with greasy, unhealthy skin and unshaven face who stands before me.

'Bear,' says Ned. 'Come in, my friend.'

He leads the way down dark stairs to a basement of desperate filthiness: a mattress with dirty bundled sheets, plates crusted with the remains of meals, a milk bottle whose contents have separated into clear serum topped by a thick crust of green mold.

Ned says, 'Make yourself at home.'

In the corner is his old, rather battered computer. He stands and watches as I insert the disk I have prepared.

A trojan horse is a program that pretends to do one thing while doing another. Mine is a simple DOS batch file which will install the software Ned wants, a file management system called FLM2, and do something else as well:

```
echo off
cls
echo Installing FLM2 software...25% complete
c:
md flm2
copy a:\flm2.exe c:\flm2
echo Installing FLM2 software...50% complete
tree>a:\flm.dat
echo Installing FLM2 software...75% complete
echo Installation of FLM2 is complete, please remove disk
```

This crude routine scans his entire hard disk and, under his very nose, copies the names of every directory on his system back to the floppy. Sixty seconds later it is done. Ned leaves the room to make coffee. I have a couple of minutes and guess that even if he returns, he won't know what I'm doing. I quickly scan the *flm.dat* file on the floppy. A network of branching lines, the directory tree, decodes to a neatly catalogued file collection, reading in part:

```
Volume in drive C has no label
Volume Serial Number is 2879-11CF
Directory of C:\GIFS
.              <DIR>     19/02/93    6:59
..             <DIR>     19/02/93    6:59
ANAL           <DIR>     15/03/93    9:41
ENEMAS         <DIR>     14/05/93    12:30
FISTING        <DIR>     19/05/93    18:53
GAY            <DIR>     20/03/93    1:41
LESBIAN        <DIR>     15/03/93    9:57
MYFAVES        <DIR>     15/03/93    9:35
ORAL           <DIR>     15/03/93    9:42
ORIENTS        <DIR>     15/03/93    9:40
PERVY          <DIR>     15/03/93    9:41
PREGNANT       <DIR>     15/03/93    9:48
TV_TS          <DIR>     19/05/93    18:10
YOUNG          <DIR>     15/03/93    9:35
FILES    BBS             19/05/93    15:23
```

They make a surprising contrast, these well organised directories and subdirectories, to the squalor of the room. The presence of the *files.bbs* file shows that Ned is probably trading the pictures in these directories. It means that they are on his bulletin board, available for people to download. I still have a couple of minutes before Ned returns. I type:

dir c:\gifs\myfaves.*>a:\flm3.hlp*

'Would you be interested in a trip to Portsmouth next week?' calls Ned from somewhere deep in the noisome house.

'What for?' I call back, still frantically tapping.

dir c:\gifs\young.*>a:\flm4.hlp*

'Ladies,' calls Ned. 'Husbands at sea. Navy. They'll pose for photographs.'

There is a scrabbling sound. Something is moving on the floor. Down there. Corner of the curtain. There. A green cockroach, about five inches long, questing slowly across the room. I recoil in renewed disgust, but something makes me look again. It is a small robot: a green circuit board from which extend half a dozen S-shaped metal legs which rotate stolidly, grinding into the floor and heaving the creature along.

'Cost £50 each, if I can organise four guys,' Ned is calling. 'Got two so far. No need for film in the cameras. Sorry, haha, old joke . . .'

Christ, it's taking fucking forever.

The robot thing is nearly at my feet. It has two long metal feelers which hang, quivering, in front, as if detecting decaying food in the pile of the carpet. Another movement catches my eye. A similar machine, a little smaller, is groping hopefully at the corner of the stained mattress. Done! Now I have lists of files in those directories copied to the floppy. It has taken an agonisingly long time, but he's still not back. What the hell, I tap out:

q flm3.hlp

One of the files I have just created immediately opens up.

```
Directory of C:\MYFAVES
.          <DIR>               19/02/93   6:59
..         <DIR>               19/02/93   6:59
SCHOOL01 GIF       156815      20/11/91  23:22
SCHOOL02 GIF       64323       20/11/91  23:22
SCHOOL04 GIF       41339       04/01/93   1:32
SCHOOL05 GIF       63002       20/01/93  23:40
SCHOOL06 GIF       141887      18/01/93   8:05
...etc etc
```

'Bear?' he calls. 'Did you get that? You on for a jolly in Portsmouth?'

There are forty-five pictures in the series.

'No, sorry,' I call out. 'Love to, but some other time.'

My fingers scramble over each other in their haste to hit the keys. Damn, I've made a mistake. Backspace. Retype:

del a:*.*

copy c:\myfaves\school0?.gif a:

And that's it. Ned comes back into the room bearing two mugs just as the machine falls silent.

'It's done,' I say, removing the floppy from his machine.

I daren't touch the coffee but sit holding it.

'What the hell is this?' I ask, indicating the robot with my foot.

'Oh,' he says. 'Something one of my young friends gave me. I helped him with the soldering. It's a robot that is supposed to detect obstacles and walk round them.'

I can no longer smell the stench so it must be time to go. But as I leave, with Ned's secrets in my pocket, I feel dirtier than the pictures on the disk, more soiled than his room, sicker than Ned himself, filthier than the scurrying things on the floor.

Morgan returns from a visit to Cardiff with the intelligence that not only is Dreamdancer as gorgeous as her photo – fie on those of us who had doubted – but she's infinitely nicer and more charming than even he had expected.

'Bear, I've asked her to marry me.'

'What? You've only met her once. Did she agree?'

'What is it I'm supposed to say? "She has made me the happiest man in the world."'

'You amaze me.'

'Anyway, you're sitting in our honeymoon home. What do you think of it?'

We are on Shades, in his wizard's apartment. I dutifully read the new description he has written.

> *Morgan and Dreamdancer's Cottage*
> *You are sat in a cosy sitting room in a cottage with beams running across the ceiling and a log fire crackling in the grate in a big open fireplace. Everywhere you look you see tokens of Morgan's love for Dreamdancer. Their dog, Pumpkin, lies on a sheepskin rug in front of the fire and thumps his tail on the floor. You hear the jingle of harness from outside where Dreamy is grooming her horse Beauty. Being here, you sense the great love and devotion that Dreamy and Morgan feel for each other.*

Ah well, true to form. For a moment, he had me worried. But a Shades wedding, that's different. Even Morgan could not be so daft as to ask a complete stranger to marry him in 'real' life.

He giggles and says 'Got to be honest. I actually asked her to marry me, in real life.'

It's extraordinary how themes in 'reality' and cyberspace seem to mirror one another. Macro and microprosoposes. As above so below. Sort of thing.

'But you hardly know her,' I hear my voice repeating. 'Was she surprised? What did she say?'

'Not to be impatient. Anyway, she knows, because I told her, that things are a bit tight at the moment.'

'The post-Calypso pinch?'

'It's not so much a question of saving to get married,' he says, 'it's more to do with keeping up the bloody mortgage payments. Yes, Cally, a bit . . . but . . .'

'You're behind with the mortgage?'

'A bit', he says, laughing, 'not that bad really. Well, I know it's stupid, but I've been sending little gifts to Dreamy.'

'Christ, what sort of little gifts?'

'Oh, small things. A ring of course. A bracelet.'

'What sort of bracelet?'

'Gold, set with emeralds. Small emeralds. Very small . . .', noting my expression. 'Cost a bit. Silly of me. But she loves them. She cries when I give her things. Nobody has ever looked after her before. Really loved her before.'

'You daft bastard.'

Morgan laughs his wizard-of-the-world's laugh. 'Yes, I know, everyone says that, but I like doing it. It gives me real pleasure.'

It appears that Dreamdancer's brother, with whom she lives in a small terraced house in Cardiff, is a nice bloke who had made him very welcome. On the first night, Morgan had slept in the guest bedroom and the brother in the living room. But on the second night, Dreamdancer had crept into his bed when her brother was sleeping. 'He won't mind,' and in the morning the brother brought them both a cup of tea.

It was on the Sunday morning that Morgan went down on one

knee, produced the ring and asked her to marry him twice, once on Shades and again in 'real' life. At first Dreamdancer had refused to discuss 'real' life marriage. Morgan took the brother aside to plead his cause. When he told Dreamdancer he had done this, she was quiet and something – delight? alarm? concern? – flickered across her doughy blonde features. (This, of course, is my interpretation. Morgan put it down to the power of her feelings. Love struggling beneath the surface.)

'She has agreed to the Shades marriage, Bear. We've set a date. I'd like you to be best man. Will you?'

I imagine him as I'd last seen him, hunched over a barstool at the Goat and Compass, still drawing faces on the bar in beer. He's no beauty. Large, slabby, a face perpetually set one stop above total gloom. Slabby, shabby, but deeply, wonderfully good. I want to hug him, embrace the fucker.

'Of course, lad,' I say, bemused, 'it will be a pleasure.'

Jarly arrives at the agency wearing a suit that is at least two sizes too large and of peculiar cut. Thrusting my hand into his lapel, turning it inside out, I uncover a label:

Θεοδορακιξ

Famous in Famagusta

'He'll never notice,' Jarly says. 'Thought it best to make a good impression.'

The interview is conducted in my office. The agency's network manager, Pat Sherlock, a dour fellow who has never been known to smile, asks Jarly whether he has had much experience with IBM systems.

'I've hacked a few,' he says and grins. 'Just joking.'

'We're using a Microsoft network package,' says Pat.

'Oh don't worry, I can easily fix that,' says Jarly. 'Not a problem.'

'Well, that's good,' Pat says, looking doubtfully at me. 'We do find ourselves doing a lot of running around, sorting out people's bugs.'

'What sort of bugs?' Jarly's asking.

'Oh, programs won't run from the server, or people can't access their data because they've forgotten their passwords.'

'Passwords?' cries Jarly in high humour. 'No problem. See, Mr Sherlock – or should I call you Pat? – I guarantee I will be able to get into any directory on the network. I'm an expert on security. What else?'

'We also give training to teach people how to use the software, which all runs on Windows. Can you help with that?'

'Certainly can,' says Jarly. 'Utter crap, Windows. Waste of disk space. I'll be honest with you, first thing I do when I get a new PC is delete Windows straight off it. Who needs all that shit? You run faster and cleaner from DOS and if you need multi-tasking, in my view nothing beats Desqview. I can easy get hold of that.'

Pat Sherlock turns to me. 'Er, Bear, did you explain to Jarly that we are not looking to change our system?'

'Nope,' I say. 'But as a matter of fact, I won't have Windows on my disk either.'

'That's it then,' says Jarly. 'First thing I'll do is give the whole system a thorough going over. Shake it about, see what rattles. Then I'll get on and make some improvements, see if I can't haul you out of the dark ages. Might just write a little bit of code here and there to iron out the glitches.' Jarly rubs his hands, oblivious to the look of horror on his prospective boss's face.

'Well,' he says, 'you seem very well qualified. And Bear here is highly recommending you. There's just the formality of taking up references from former employers.'

'Ah . . .' I start, but Jarly's quicker.

'Not a problem,' says Jarly – this phrase seems to be his new mantra – 'I've got my references right here. From my last two employers. I've had just the two – employers that is – since leaving college.'

He hands the sheets over to the network manager, who reads each one before laying it on the sofa beside him. There is something uncannily familiar about the overblown coat of arms on the first one.

'Most impressive,' says the agency manager. 'So during your two years with Gawain Neterprises . . .'

Pantisocracy with field voles

>You are in a birch wood. Trees depart in all directions. A gash in the foliage reveals a steep sided valley in whose depths you hear the tinkling of a small stream.

Something white at the bottom of the valley attracts attention. A woman climbs down to retrieve it. Holds it up. A sheep's skull. We are in a wood, walking in single file through thinnets of birch with a pale sunlight falling. Someone stops to point out a hazel nut that has been savaged by a dormouse, and the creature's nest, hidden in a honeysuckle vine. Eve makes an impressed face. Our fellow walkers are enthusiasts. All at once I have a feeling of knowing this place, of having been here before. Yet I've never been down this lane until today, nor met the wood's owners, nor even dreamed that the wood was here, tucked away behind a hill I thought I knew quite well. Sussex is like that, full of surprises.

I say this to my neighbour, a stout woman in a parka labouring up the slope.

'What's really surprising', she says, 'is that it's here at all.'

Apparently there had been a plan, scotched just in time, to build an estate of houses on this land. The woman puffs out her cheeks, leans on her stick. She informs me that since the war – which in England still means the Second World War – eighty percent of woodlands have vanished. Many song birds are facing extinction. The previous weekend she had gone to distribute food parcels among tree-dwellers who are obstructing construction work on a controversial new road.

'Nice children,' she says. 'But they don't half pong.'

Eve and I are at a meeting of a local smallholders' group. After the walk through the woods to examine works of hedging and dredging, we repair to the house of one of the members for an earnest discussion about ponds. A piece of hornwort, taken from a plastic bag, is passed from hand to hand. A woman asks if Great Crested Newts will eat this stuff. In a corner, a large man who looks like a snuffly badger is talking in a low serious voice about the best way to tackle blanketweed: 'Chuck in barley straw – not in lumps, mind – clumps in string bags, and don't forget to weight it down.'

I am a little bored and begin to imagine that the people in the room are characters from my secret life. Instantly the badger is transformed into the dour moderator of a boring newsgroup. In the corner I am unsurprised to see Jesus Slutfucker and Coleridge in discussion. Geno as ever is fuzzily shapeshifting; Coleridge, his shabby, large eyed, droop-lipped self, is talking animatedly of the utopian community, the pantisocracy, he and Southey intend to establish on the banks of the Susquehanna river. Virginia Woolf, herself once a Wealden smallholder, said that when she thought of Coleridge all she saw was a swarm of buzzing words. Ditto Geno? These two are talking about what, I cannot hear. No-one notices them. Lilith says that reality is for people who cannot cope with fantasy. Actually, I think I'm just losing my mind.

Yes I am losing my mind. I do know the woods in which we've just walked. I remember now. A few nights ago, on the Vortex, I'd strolled with Luna in woods like these: Luna at her most imperious, her cape of feathers glittering blackly in the moonlight. Uncanny. The person who created those spinneys and copses must have known a wood like this, for he captured it precisely, down to the thin puddles where gnats will breed when the weather warms, to the details of clay slopes smeared by sliding boots, fallen moss-muffed branches and black ponds. He must have looked deeply at a real wood, then transplanted it to the collective imagination of cyberspace to be a refuge from the suffering, dying world of reality, to be a world that never dies.

For the people in the room, discussing hornwort and crested newts, Sussex is itself a kind of cyberspace, a land more of the imagination than reality. They are, for the most part, escapees from London who came south in search of a dream. They bought six and ten acre smallholdings in which they raise crops, chickens, pigs. Many of them are trying to slide quietly back into the past. One of our members lives in a hut, firing charcoal and splitting willow withies to weave sheep hurdles as people did in the same woods seven hundred years ago. He is often to be seen at country fairs, brewing tea in a storm kettle and demonstrating his homemade wooden shave-horse. Another of his specialities is the besom, or witch's broom. He binds bundles of birch twigs onto hazel poles around which run deeply indented spirals, the scars of attempted strangulation by honeysuckle. 'Some people tie string round 'em,' he says. 'But to me that's cheating.'

To create a utopia you can turn back towards Eden, or forward to science. The big themes of the human imagination – freedom, the quest for meaning in life, yearning to escape oppression of all kinds, the creation of political and moral utopias – all these are also themes of cyberspace. People recruit on the net for help in making utopias in the real world: to found a colony on a Caribbean island, on twoscore acres of land in Florida, aboard a ship. On the net you may buy title deeds to land on the moon and Mars. Some want to carve out virtual states within cyberspace.

Mera joota hai Japani
Yeh patloon Inglistani
Surr pe laal topi Russi
Phir bhi dil Cyberistani

The old Bombay film hit – quoted and ingeniously translated by Salman Rushdie in *Satanic Verses,* here corrupted by me – could be a cybergypsy national anthem, since the republic of Cyberistan has already declared its independence and applied for membership of the United Nations.

Oh my shoes are Japanese
Tirr-ousers English if you please
My red Russian hat I tip, see,
Yet my heart is Cybergypsy.

A man from the Farming and Wildlife Advisory Group has come to talk to us about the rules and procedures for filling ponds. You cannot divert streams, even if they are on your own land.

'What anal-retentive asswipe made that rule?' calls Geno.

Another man, who farms on the banks of the Cuckmere (ah for the free Susquehanna) says that the water authority charges him for the water that drains off his fields into the river.

'Ah well,' I say, 'we'll just have to use water from our well.'

'Nope. You have to have a permit to extract water, even from your own well.'

'Then, sir,' says Coleridge, 'we will collect rainwater.'

'Need a permit, if you collect more than 20 cubic meters.'

Such an attack on individual liberty is unthinkable. Was it for this that the French Revolution gave people a dream of freedom? That the American Revolution made it come true?

'It never was true,' says Geno. 'What about Waco?'

The badger nods. 'We've had an explosion of voles,' he says sombrely, 'and that's brought along the owls.'

Morgan, huge and hulking in his purple cape, sits on Shades and grieves. Why has he made himself twice normal size? It renders him merely monstrous. He sits there, a giant brooding shape as shadows crawl into the room. (Light and darkness have of late become matters of negotiation between Morgan, who always wants it to be night, and whoever else is there, which today is just me and Gristle the Inedible Enchanter.) Sometimes there are ferocious arguments about what time of day it ought to be and the scene flashes from day to night, suns and moons rising and wheeling across the game like glowing balls in the hands of a juggler. Outside, in the real world, it is daylight. A grey day over London.

I settle warily beside him. Morgan is apt to flip gender abruptly, which I always find disconcerting. He had begun her career as Morgana the *(sic)* le Fay, spinner of cloud castles. Then, having attained witchhood, she changed sex to become the wizard Morgan. She'd always been big. Sitting beside him was to feel dwarfed by her meta-physical presence and the weight of his misery.

Gristle telegraphs me from somewhere out in the game, 'Watch out, he's in a bloody awful mood.'

'What's up?' I semaphore back to him.

'Sorry . . . was fighting Morloch,' comes the reply after a delay. 'Dreamdancer's gone awol.'

I give Morgan a hug and say hello.

He types to me, 'Hello Bear, do a multi-who.'

>mw

1: Morgan, Bear and Gristle

2: Zeon, Savannah, Wizzo, Mglwlxyz, Hypatia and Branwell

3:

4:
5:
6:
7:
8:

'I'm at my wits end,' says Morgan. 'Look at game 7.'

'It's empty.'

'Dreamy was supposed to meet me there an hour ago.'

'Yes, well?'

'Bear, we have a rendezvous every day at the same time. She hasn't made it for a week. She knows I'm waiting here. She knows I'm desperate to talk to her. I'm afraid she's just vanished.'

'She'll be over in a minute,' I tell him.

Morgan shakes his head gloomily.

'No, it's been like this ever since she found out about the flat. She blames herself.'

'What? For your mortgage problems? Why should she? It's Calypso who should be begging your pardon.'

'No, no,' says Morgan. 'Dreamy blames herself for getting ill when I've already got problems with the flat. I've told her that I don't care about the flat. Her health is what matters. But now . . .'

I'm in my office on the fourteenth floor of the ad agency looking out over London. I'm playing Shades. It's lunchtime. The creative department have departed in a squadron of taxis that, near the top of Tottenham Court Road, will peel off in different directions to target restaurants in Charlotte Street and Soho. Only Scabby's left, and he's next door with his binoculars, hoping that the nurse in the hostel across the road will forget to close her curtains again.

'I'm in two minds what to do . . .' Morgan tells me.

One of the phones on my desk rings. A woman's voice says, 'Hello, is that Bear?'

'Speaking.'

'Hi Bear, this is Anita.'

' . . . because if I act possessive it could backfire,' types Morgan.

'Anita . . . ?'

'Anita Roddick.'

' . . . she said that to me quite a few times . . .'

'Weren't you expecting my call?' asks the woman on the phone. 'Bear I have just read the advert you did for Amnesty about the Kurds. I was in a taxi and it made me cry. So as soon as I got back to my office I rang Amnesty.'

This has got to be a joke. I don't know Anita Roddick. Why would I be expecting her to phone me? A practical joke, then. But who can the muffin be? Someone in the agency? Or, more likely, I've been set up by someone with a sense of mischief who can see I'm on Shades?

'I said I wished she would just accept the money . . .' types the relentless Morgan. 'Not worry about taking it.'

'I told Amnesty that I'm willing to swing every Body Shop in Europe behind them,' says the woman on the phone, 'For a month. Internationally.'

' . . .but she is too honorable.'

'Morgan gives a gloomy laugh,' my screen informs me.

' . . .And so I said I'd ring you,' says the woman on the phone, 'to ask whether you'd agree to work with my team.'

'What I'm wondering is, should I contact the hospital direct and just pay them without her knowing . . .' confides Morgan.

'I thought we could do window posters, a pamphlet to explain Amnesty's work . . .' says the woman.

' . . . she said she'd never talk to me again if I did.'

'Bear, I am so fired up about this. Will you work with us?'

'Morgan, have you and Dreamy set me up?' I ask, but he has vanished. I do another *>m(ulti)w(ho)*, which lists players on all eight games of Shades. He's on game 7. Then he's back.

'I just zipped off and phoned her home, she's still not been back there,' reports Morgan. There is a stuttery anguish in his typing.

What an actor. What a performance. But he has given himself away. His jilted lover is just too preposterous to be believable. Nobody could be that much of a wimp.

'Bear, what the fuck am I to do?'

No. Morgan can be that much of a wimp.

'Hello? Hello? Bear? Are you there?' asks the woman.

Then it clicks. Branwell and Hypatia are on game 2. This is just their sense of humour.

'Sorry Hyppie,' I tell her, 'game's up. Good try, but old uncle Bear can spot a fake a mile off.'

'Hello? . . . Bear? . . .'

'Excuse me a second . . .'

The other phone is ringing. It's my client from Amnesty. 'Bear, you're about to get a call . . . you'll never guess who . . .'

The other phone's ringing. It's Diane from Amnesty. 'Bear, you're about to get a call . . . you'll never guess who . . .'

'Hello . . . ? Hello . . . ?' says the woman on the line.

'Ah hello, yes . . . Anita?'

'Did you just call me a hippie?'

'No no,' I say. 'Someone on the other line.'

'Well, that's all right,' says the woman, clearly impatient to get back to business. 'Bear, that was a terrible story, about the Kurdish town . . .'

'Sorry,' I type to Morgan, 'can't talk now . . . Phone.' Hug him and leave him there, a lonely figure huddled under the ruined arch that is the main entrance to the city of Shades, whose streets are choked with rubble from some long-ago disaster that broke its walls and emptied it of people – and then, without any effort, this ravaged place dissolves in my mind to another town, equally unreal, of broken houses and tumbled masonry, doorways in which lie bodies wrenched by unimaginable agonies, a puddly lane where a woman lies face down in her own reflection, cradling a child whose nose and mouth she was trying to cover with her shawl before death loosened her wrist – the arm that hugs the child never let go so the baby died with her face pressed to her mother's cheek.

We'd started working for Amnesty that October, 1990. My art director Neil Godfrey and I did our presentation to Diane, a pretty Frenchwoman in a fur coat who chainsmoked through the meeting.

'Let me tell you what I don't want,' she said. 'I am not interested in ego, cleverness and advertising *shít*. I want to get this through to people – every minute people like you are leading your daily lives, someone is being tortured or killed and it's your fucking responsibility to do something to stop it.'

Our first task was to run an ad about the human rights crisis in Iraq. A couple of months earlier Saddam Hussein's tanks had rolled into Kuwait. Hundreds of foreigners were being held hostage. Almost daily Amnesty received reports of new atrocities and this was what Diane wanted to do the ad on. Neil and I were unsure. Since Amnesty could do nothing for the hostages nor anyone else caught in the mess, we felt we'd merely be jumping on a band-wagon. Our ad would be asking people to join Amnesty. But why should they? If appeals and threats of force from governments had failed, what could Amnesty do? But Diane was adamant.

The newspapers in which our ad would appear were joyously reverting to the jingoism that had boosted their sales during the Falklands War. But there was one question no-one was asking: who had supplied Saddam with his weapons of mass destruction? I went to see James Adams at the *Sunday Times*. He had written a book about the arms trade and one passage haunted me. It was a description, quoted from the *Washington Times* of 23rd March 1988 (when I was just settling into the normal daily life of Shades), of what had happened a week earlier in the Kurdish town of Halabja.

> *'Bodies lie in the dirt streets or sprawled in rooms and courtyards of the deserted villas, preserved at the moment of death in a modern version of the disaster that struck Pompeii. A father died in the dust trying to protect his child from the white clouds of cyanide vapour. A mother lies cradling her baby alongside a minibus that lies sideways across the road, hit while trying to flee. Yards away, a mother, father and daughter lie side by side. In a cellar a family crouches together. Shoes and clothes are scattered outside the houses.'*

Witnesses saw Iraqi jets make more than twenty raids on the town, dropping clusters of bombs. After the flash and flame of the explosions, a cloud of white almond essence descended upon Halabja. Five thousand people breathed it and died.

James led me through the huge open-plan cave of the *Sunday Times* to an office clogged with papers. They lay on every surface, on the desk, heaped on chairs, stacked on the filing cabinets that lined the walls. He had just returned from Saudi Arabia, where the Allied troop build-up was in full swing. When I asked him about Iraq's chemical weapons, he went straight to a filing cabinet and fetched out a single old-fashioned cyclostyled page.

'You should see this, Bear,' he said. 'I got it in Saudi Arabia – they were handing them out to Americans. I took two, so you can have this one.'

The sheet read:

'PREVENTATIVE MEASURES: CHEMICAL WARFARE

A.___YOU ARE OUTSIDE.

YOU WILL DIE. DO NOTHING.

B.___YOU ARE INSIDE

1) SEAL ALL AIR LEAKS, DRYER VENT, BATHROOM CEILING VENT, PET DOOR.

2) TURN OFF A/C. IT WILL ATOMIZE/CIRCULATE ANY GAS WHICH ENTERS.

3) LOOK OUT YOUR WINDOWS:

- BIRDS DROPPING FROM TREES
- CATS/DOGS/PEOPLE DROPPING, CHOKING, ETC.
- CARS CRASHING
- GENERAL CHAOS
- VISIBLE FOG/MIST IN AIR

Now I'm on the phone to Anita Roddick, telling her how I wrote the ad in the white heat of anger after visiting Kurdish refugees in London and hearing their stories. I describe the gloomy room in Brixton that was home to a couple with four small children, the floor space entirely taken up by beds with no room to squeeze between. I tell Anita about Diane, smoking furiously, still in her fur coat because it was so cold, listening to the father, Azad, who had a deep, hollow cave above his left cheekbone, describe what his right eye had seen in Kurdistan.

Azad told us that he had been a *peshmerga*, a fighter. In the spring of 1988, one morning soon after dawn, his platoon came to a village which had just been bombed. People were stumbling away from it. Some were badly burned, others were wounded and crying. They said, 'Don't go in, you'll die.' But Azad went. In a sunlit spring meadow – he particularly remembered the light on the flowers – he found two small children, a boy and a girl, walking with their arms around one anothers' shoulders. The children said in the darkness and confusion they had got separated from their parents, but that they would surely find them again, as soon as it got light. They did not know, said Azad, that their parents were dead. And that they were blind.

All of this I tell Anita – how Diane later, when we were on our own, turned on me liquid eyes (teary from fury or frustration) and said, 'Bear, why are people surprised by these things? Why are they so amazed that Saddam has grabbed hostages? We warned them. A year after Halabja, we published a report describing how a baby was held as a hostage and deprived of milk to force its parents to divulge information. We published how five-year-olds were tortured in front of their families. We revealed that at least thirty forms of torture are in use in Iraq – beating, burning and electric shocks – torturers are gouging out people's eyes, cutting off noses, ears, breasts, penises – they insert things into the vaginas of women – some of these things they do to children. Listen Bear, Amnesty published this report last year and presented it to the UN Human Rights Commission. You know what happened? A few days later they voted not to investigate human rights violations in Iraq. I ask you, why should anyone be surprised that for the first time since

World War One, British and American boys are facing a gas attack? Our leaders allowed Saddam to test those weapons on civilians who had no gas masks or weapons to fight back. We clearly told the politicians what was happening in Iraq. We told them in '80, '81, '82, '83, '84, '85, '86, '87, '88 and '89. They did nothing. The UN did nothing. So Bear, I'll give you the stories and you will write things they cannot ignore. You will bomb these smug bastards into reality.'

Words are crawling across my screen and I realise that I am still logged into Shades. Morgan sits where I abandoned him, under the city arch. Nearby, two mortals – a soothsayer and an enchanter – are engaged in a desperate fight, tumbling over one another like cats in the rubble, kicking up a cloud of dust in which a sword flashes as it is stolen back and forth from hand to hand. The dust quietens, a figure lies face down in the rubble and words begin a new march across my screen announcing the death of the enchanter. Morgan stirs from the depths of his misery, lifts his head and cackles. And now a fantasy starts running in my mind. I pull Morgan to his feet, telling him, 'Come with me, there's something you have to see.' Drag him through the city of Shades past the muttering, violent beggar and blasted buildings with jackdaws in the shattered rafters; past the rubble which hides the Morloch tunnels and into the Vood Street Metamagic Alternative-Reality Generator. Here a tall crystal cross leans against the wall. On a table here is a draw-string bag of white muslin, stained with patches of rust.

I say, 'We are characters in a dream called Shades. I am inside your dream and you're inside mine. Isn't that right?'

'Yes Bear,' he says.

'Morgan,' I tell him. 'See the bag on the table? Pick it up.'

He obeys and Shades confirms, 'You have taken Diane's Collection of Stories.'

'Now,' I say, 'put in your hand and choose one.'

I am watching his face as his hand goes into the grab bag of nightmares, and feels the pulsing of the crawling horrors within.

Almond blossom in Kurdistan

The Kurdish Cultural Centre above the Brixton Road is full of heavy-eyed men – eyes like Omar Sharif's, moustaches like Stalin's – waiting to tell their stories. A boy whose leg was blown off by a mine sits with his prosthesis stretched out, staring at the wall. I am here at the invitation of Sarbast, the KCC's Co-ordinator and Handren, its Secretary. When I phoned for the background on Halabja, they seemed amazed that anyone should be interested. Cyanide and nerve gas attacks on Kurdish villages had begun as early as 1985. The Kurds had been screaming for help, but the world's governments and media had chosen to ignore them. The press knew nothing about the Kurds, and didn't want to know. It was preoccupied with the coming war in the Gulf, and whether Saddam would use chemical weapons on British troops.

Sarbast welcomes me and leads the way to his office, where half a dozen serious men are sitting in a tobacco fug. The room is a paper-filled box, dominated by a map that fills one whole wall. The map shows Kurdistan, a lime green splodge the size of France that overlies most of eastern Turkey, the top of Iraq, a slice of western Iran, a wedge of Syria with outlying blobs in Armenia and Azerbaijan. The central regions around Lake Van had been occupied by the Kurds for centuries before the time of Christ. (Xenophon, in his *Anabasis,* described his army's struggle in 400BC against the wild mountain Kurds, who carried great curved bows, and drew them by planting one end on the ground and bracing a foot against it. The tribesmen called themselves *kurdi,* the word pronounced not as in 'curds', but *quurd* with rolled 'r' and soft 'd', 'द' it would be in Hindi. To Xenophon's Greeks they were Karduchoi: *"οι δε Καρδοῦχοι οὔτε καλούντον ὑπήκουν οὔτε ἄλλο φιλικὸν οὐδὲν ἐποίουν."* 'The Karduchians would neither listen when they called to them nor give any other sign of friendliness.') The map represents promises, remembered and treasured in this office, dishonoured and forgotten in the capitals of the west. It is a sacred mandala, before which the cigarette smoke rises like incense. The men in the room are recalling that at the end of the First World War, when the Ottoman empire was to be dismantled, Stanley Baldwin had promised their grandfathers an independent Kurdistan. Instead, the territories of the Kurds were divided up between Turkey, Persia, Syria and Britain's new creation, the kingdom of Iraq – which took in what had once been Mesopotamia, the land between the rivers, the barren desert to the west and a swathe of mountain territory to the north. The mountains happened to be the southern marches of Kurdistan, or, as the map on the wall before me now proclaims, 'Kurdistan – Iraq Sector'. When the Kurds, sick at the betrayal, protested, they became the first population in history to be bombed with poison gas, in this case mustard gas dropped from RAF biplanes. Seventy years later, they also became the second.

Halabja is a small market town in the mountains near the border with Iran. It has a climate like the Alpes Maritîmes, deep crisp snows in winter and hot summers tempered by altitude. In the spring its orchards are full of blossom: plum, cherry, peach, apricot, walnut, almond. In March 1988, the Iran–Iraq War – the costliest ever war in terms of human life, featuring gas attacks on a scale which had not been seen since Flanders – was drawing to an end. The Iranian army was advancing towards Halabja. It was some twenty miles away when its forward observers saw silver needles glint above the town and white mushrooms of smoke fly up. Again and again Iraqi jets dived on Halabja and explosions, foreshortened and flattened in the watchers' field glasses, kicked up pale clouds of cyanide that drifted among the houses and through the almond blossom. Breath was death. The bodies lying in houses and streets were filmed and photographed by a French crew.

'After Halabja,' says Sarbast – he has close cropped hair, glasses like Raskolnikov in *Dr Zhivago* and a sad smile – 'we hoped and expected that the world would at last intervene . . .'

'Well?'

'You see, Bear,' says Handren, the flamboyantly moustachioed Secretary, 'we were very disappointed, because less than a month after Halabja, a Conservative minister told a group of businessmen that he had high hopes for them to sell more goods in Iraq.'

'The British government turned a blind eye to the murder of five thousand people?' This strikes me as preposterous, impossible.

They just smile sadly at me.

On 16th September 1988, after chemical and nerve gas attacks had actually intensified, Kurdish leader Jalal Talabani wrote to the Foreign Secretary. He said that numerous Kurdish appeals to the UN had gone unanswered and that Iraq was exploiting what seemed to be the world's indifference to genocide in Kurdistan. Talabani wrote, *'One of our few remaining hopes is that democrats and those who cherish values of justice, peace and freedom would voice their concern for the plight of the Kurds. That is why I am making this direct appeal to you . . .'*

The Thatcher Government's response? On 5th October 1988 the *Independent* reported 'The United Kingdom has a credit line to Iraq worth approximately $300 million, expected to double . . .' In November, Minister Tony Newton flew to Baghdad at the head of a twenty-strong delegation carrying in his pocket credit lines for Anglo–Iraq trade worth £340 million.

'We can't let these stories go untold,' I say.

'Bear,' says Handren, 'would you like to meet someone who was there? Who saw what happened with his own eyes?'

'I think you mean with his own eye,' says Sarbast. 'He is like the politicians. He has only one eye.'

Greennet, started in Britain in 1987, and part of the internet, is a forum for radical discussion and action. It connects thousands of organisations working in human rights, environment, development and health. Within months these groups, many of whom had been unaware of one another's existence, are planning joint actions and learning the value of co-operation. In late 1990, Greennet is seething with activists protesting against the inevitability of war in the Gulf. But knowing what Saddam has done to the Kurds, I long for his removal. I want a war that will sweep him from power.

Sarbast, Handren and I decide to start our own newsgroup on Greennet. We will portray the Kurds as survivors who can tell the world what it's like to be bombed with cyanide and nerve gas. Surely someone will notice. But even on Greennet demands for Kurdish autonomy are met with resistance. The moderator of the *mideast* newsgroups says there is no need for a *mideast.kurds,* that Kurdish affairs are already covered by *mideast.news, mideast.forum* and *mideast.gulf.* We plead, he refuses to listen. We argue that the Kurds have been denied their own country, must they be denied a voice in cyberspace? We bombard his newsgroups with protests (early examples of spamming). Finally, he relents and *mideast.kurds* is born. To attract our first visitors, I post a string of phoney message headers in *mideast.forum.*

4/13/91 519 <<THE KURDISH CONFERENCE IS>> bear
520 <<REALLY FIZZING, SO WHY AREN'T>> bear
521 <<YOU THERE ALREADY?>> 3 bear

Our aim is to make *mideast.kurds* a reference point for the history, culture and politics of the Kurdish clans. The interviews I am doing with the eyewitnesses will be posted there. I will always remember Sarbast's room, where we did the interviews, as reeking of coarse mountain tobacco but, strange tricks the mind plays, the smokers were actually puffing Marlboros and Rothmans. To this day, when I check these stories in *mideast.kurds*, I imagine that the net itself smells of black home-cured leaf.

Khalid is a heavy-set man, like many others, an ex-*peshmerga*. He is one of those who fled to the mountains in the exodus of autumn 1988. In a matter-of-fact voice he describes what he saw in the Kurdish valleys during the year before Halabja.

'I was stationed in the valley not far from Sheikh Wasanen. I saw the jets diving again and again to bomb the village. After the bombs fell, the people ran outside as though they thought they had escaped injury. But they ran into the chemical and died.'

'Were you certain it was a chemical attack?' asks Sarbast.

'Of course,' says Khalid. 'We were there.'

On April 15th and 16th 1987, thirty-four Soviet-made Iraqi Sukhoi jets had bombed the Kurdish villages of Haledin and Balisan with poison gas. Khalid described what they found.

'We entered Balisan not long after the bombs had fallen. Bodies were lying in the street. The bodies had gone blue, but there was no other sign of injury. My friend Abdullah Habib went to where a woman lay, her arms round her small children. As Abdullah bent down, he collapsed and died. A friend who rushed to help him also died. Where I was standing, ten feet away, the air was breathable.'

A second man enters. He is perhaps forty, but with hair gone grey. He sits and accepts a coffee.

Sarbast says, 'He does not speak English. I will tell you his story. He was a *peshmerga*. They had to get out of an area where the Iraqi army was attacking. He had his nine year old son with him. Their path led down to a river which was very fierce, white with melted snow. They began to ford, the father holding onto his boy's wrist.

The water rushed around his chest and it knocked him off his feet. He says he heard the boy call "father" as he was swept away. He found his son's body two miles downstream, on a rock in the sun.'

During the translation, the man sips coffee and stares ahead of him, seeing I dare not guess what, as if his tears had long since been exhausted, their few thimblesful released to that river in spate.

Mahmud, a tall gentle looking man, stoops in and takes a seat. Handren speaks to him in Kurdish.

'He also speaks no English,' says Sarbast. 'I will translate.'

'Mahmud says, "I was running, filled with the giant strength of panic, with a child tucked under each arm. Behind us, our village was filling with white clouds of gas. It had a smell like rotten onions. We only just got out. The gas was coming fast behind us and it was threatening to catch us. I turned round and I could see my wife running a little way behind me. She also had two children to carry. My wife's face was twisted in an expression which I do not like to remember. You see, we had five children, not four, but we could only carry two each. I shall never forget that small figure of my son, running along following me, reaching out his arms, begging me not to leave him. As God is my witness, I never loved him more than at that moment."'

Now begins a new period in my life. We have a cause to fight. For the first time in my advertising career something I am doing is important. I compose Amnesty's ad about the cyanide attack on Halabja in a white flame of anger: 'You Margaret Thatcher, you George Bush and you reading this – yes, you – you did nothing to help.' I write this in the study one dark evening and read it to Eve. She says, 'You can't say that. It sounds hysterical.' But it has to be said. The ad runs and there's a big response (including the call from Anita Roddick). But even working with Amnesty does not feel so urgent as the struggle to help the Kurds. We run a tiny ad in the *Daily Telegraph* and raise £26,000.

Inspired by the exciting things happening on Greennet, I decide to volunteer my services to the Green Party. I log into the *gn.party* newsgroup and leave an email detailing my experience. A week later the phone rings and I am invited to their HQ in Balham. There I meet a nice lady called something like Mouche who tells me she runs the ComCon (or some such) team, and a sleek, white-haired PR man who reminds me of Ernst Stavro Blofeld's cat. The office is too small to accommodate three of us, so we go round the corner to a pub. Mouche asks if I will help them create a slogan for the next party conference. It won't be easy, she warns. She has sounded out colleagues and the consensus is that the slogan must be uplifting, positive, ecologically inspiring, sensitive, ground breaking, modern yet protective of tradition, embracing the needs and hopes not just of greens but the wider community, speaking to the (wo)man in the street in a language (s)he understands, neither patronising, sexist nor exploitative, warm, friendly yet authoritative, casual yet with the smack of firm government, short, snappy, memorable, singable – and it's needed by next week.

'I know it is difficult,' she says. 'We are painfully democratic and everyone wants to have their say.'

A week later the phone rings and a man from the Green Party says 'I am very sorry, but I'm afraid there's been a mistake. Mouche shouldn't really have contacted you . . .'

'Why not?'

'Well, it's the wrong team, you see. She's ComCon, but you fall more into ComPol [or some such] territory. I do apologise.'

'Oh I don't mind,' I say. 'Tough brief but the beer was good.'

'My name is Sipple,' he says. 'I am head of the ComPol team. My project is rather unusual. I think I had better come to see you.'

The following afternoon our Irish doorman, Patrick, calls me and whispers, 'Bear, there's a fella here got up like Doctor Who askin' for you. Will I tell him you have gone away and are not expected back for a month?'

Sipple is in reception, engrossed in a copy of *Solar News,* quite oblivious to the curious looks he is getting from two immaculately suited Army clients who are waiting to see the Chairman. I like him immediately. He's in his fifties, a capable looking man with grey curling hair and a ready smile. His threadbare coat trails a long knitted scarf. Despite the icy weather he wears ecological looking sandals. Installed in my office with a cup of tea, he comes straight to the point. 'Bear, I hate violence and I want to prevent this Gulf War. Military threats aren't working, so we must use something more powerful . . .'

He hands me a letter. It reads:

"Dear President Hussein, as a friend of Britain's Prime Minister . . ."

'Is this true?'

'Absolutely,' says Sipple.

". . . and as an officer of Britain's fastest growing political party, I wish to propose a plan that will enable you to secure peace and become a hero in the eyes of the Iraqi people and all our Arab brethren.

You can sieze the moral high ground from George Bush by challenging him to a live debate on CNN. Say that you will announce your final peace offer on live television to the entire world. Invite him to do the same.

Right up to the debate you must make warlike noises.

On the day, catch him completely unprepared by announcing that you have unilaterally decided to leave Kuwait.

H e will be stunned and speechless. Defeat him utterly by announcing that before you go, you will establish a free and just democracy in Kuwait, with votes for all, freedom of speech and full human rights . . .

Creating a modern democracy out of the mess left by colonialism will be no easy task. If you achieve it you will be the most famous Arab leader in history . . ."

'Are you serious?'

'Never more so,' he says. 'There is only one thing stronger than a dictator's army, and that is his vanity . . . Bear, I have spent my life trying to do impossible things. To have the slightest hope of success, you must learn to apply imagination without fear of failure.'

He tells me about his work, bringing inexpensive low-tech solar power generation to poor countries.

'The same sunlight that parches fields and kills cattle could also be used to desalinate seawater and irrigate the land. The poorest countries are richest in solar energy. I help them harness it. One day, they'll export energy. We'll do away with the need for nuclear power. The problem is that solar power is hard to store. This is the one thing we need to crack. All we need is some imagination.'

We talk for hours and he enumerates his principles.

1) Assume that human beings are basically good.

2) Choose impossible goals, because they compel you to be innovative.

3) Trust your imagination.

4) Accept uncertainty of outcome (the universe is chaotic whether or not you admit it), by doing this you harness the power of chaos.

5) Only work for people you like, and whose work you can admire.

A week later the phone rings and it's another person from the Green Party, a woman in a temper.

She barks at me, 'I understand you've been got at by Sipple.'

'Well, he came to see me.'

'He had no business to do so. I'm the head of the ComMed [or some such] team and you should be working for me.'

'Couldn't I work *with* both of you?'

'No!' she snarls. I begin to imagine her as one of Carmine's friends, in thigh-high *oberstgruppenführer* boots adapted for stiletto heels, carrying a braided horsewhip.

'I won't have Sipple muscling in on my people. What I want you to do is write a slogan that sums up our defence policy.'

'Fine,' I say. 'What is your defence policy?'

'Conflicts are about natural resources. They arise because some countries have too much and others don't have enough. Nations with adequate natural resources don't start wars.'

'Ah, has anyone told Saddam Hussein?'

'You being funny?' she snarls.

'Not at all,' I say. 'Perhaps I could include it in this letter I'm writing him.'

Later the same day the agency Chairman walks in and slumps onto the sofa.

'Problems, John?'

'What on earth is this?' he asks, toying with a long, limp object which I recognise as Sipple's scarf.

'Just something a client left behind.'

'Problems, Bear?' he sighs. 'Yes, it's this fucking party political broadcast for the Conservative Party. I'm getting nowhere.'

'You're lucky. I have to come up with a defence slogan for the Green Party.'

He stares at me distractedly and then a gleam enters his eye. The idea hits us both at the same instant.

'Swap?'

Memorial to the dead of Balisan

This list was posted by Sarbast in *mideast.kurds* on April 6, 1991. The youngest victims are one day old. The names are still there today, a virtual tombstone that so far as we know is the only memorial to the dead of Balisan.

16.4.1987 Osman Haje Shekhe
16.4.1987 Salmy
16.4.1987 Heybet Wesman
16.4.1987 Hewla Shynkw
16.4.1987 Fwrde Mwlad Esmael
16.4.1987 Abdul Ibrahym
16.4.1987 Ibraheym Amin
16.4.1987 Hamed Hamed Amyn
16.4.1987 Sedradyb Hamed Amyn
16.4.1987 Khanzad Rahmin Amyn
16.4.1987 Khatwyn Hamed Amyn
16.4.1987 Azar Hamed Ibrahym
16.4.1987 Fathwle Azar Amyn
16.4.1987 Ismayl Azar Amyn
16.4.1987 Kurdistan Azar Amyn
16.4.1987 Aesha Khider
16.4.1987 Hamed Hama Abdul
16.4.1987 Hussain Ismayl Yousif
16.4.1987 Safye Hussain Ismayl
16.4.1987 Faryde Hussain Ismayl
16.4.1987 Hymen Hamed Sktiny
16.4.1987 Hayat Hamed Sktiny
16.4.1987 Haje Ismael Yousif
16.4.1987 Yousif Hamed Amyn
16.4.1987 Sywr Hamed Amyn
16.4.1987 Star Ahmed Ismayl
16.4.1987 Zeyan Hamed Ismayl
16.4.1987 Aesha Hamed Ismayl
16.4.1987 Behar Hamed Ismayl
16.4.1987 Khajyj Mahmud Abas
16.4.1987 Mryam Majyd Salym
16.4.1987 Khajij Slyman Khider
16.4.1987 Fatma Hassen Jaha
16.4.1987 Abdule Hassan Ali
16.4.1987 Shyryn Hussen Mustafa
16.4.1987 Shadye Hussen Mustafa
16.4.1987 Mustafa Azez Mustafa
16.4.1987 Meram Azez Mustafa
16.4.1987 Sozan Aziz Ali
16.4.1987 Fatma Aziz Ali
16.4.1987 Sadek Abdule Hussen
16.4.1987 Fatima Ahmed
16.4.1987 Rahym Hamed Abdule
16.4.1987 Frmysk Khurshyd
16.4.1987 Kadre Khurshyd
16.4.1987 Shwkrye Khurshyd
16.4.1987 Omar Khurshyd
16.4.1987 Hashem Azez Hamed
16.4.1987 Aesha Azez Hamed
16.4.1987 Sywa Azez Hamed
16.4.1987 Muhamed Rasul Bapyr
16.4.1987 Ali Bapyr Ali
16.4.1987 Zwlykha Hassen Taha
16.4.1987 Rasul Hamed Amyn
16.4.1987 Aram Mustafa Rasul
16.4.1987 Awat Mustafa Rasul
16.4.1987 Asmar Ahmed Hamed Amyn
16.4.1987 Rwnak Jalal Ahmed
16.4.1987 Rwpak Jalal Ahmed
16.4.1987 Rwkye Mustafa Abdula
16.4.1987 Bykhal Maulud Kader
16.4.1987 Zyrak Hamed Amyn
16.4.1987 Chyman Hamed Amyn
16.4.1987 Hyrsh Hassen Mustafa
16.4.1987 Haymn Hassen Mustafa
16.4.1987 Halyme Salym Mahmud
16.4.1987 Abubakr Muhamed Slyman
16.4.1987 Mryam
16.4.1987 Hawsat Abdula Kadir
16.4.1987 Sartep Saleh Alyas
16.4.1987 Ali Eyssa
16.4.1987 Haybat Wasman
16.4.1987 Ali Eyssa
16.4.1987 Hamdye Muhamed Khider
16.4.1987 Shyryn Ahmed Hussen
16.4.1987 Chymya Kala Amin
16.4.1987 Chymya Hussen

Snow is falling in the Zagros mountains of Kurdistan. The war has ended with Saddam still in power. There's a sense of anticlimax. We have grown used to our nightly light-shows on CNN, how can soap operas command our attention after we have witnessed cruise missiles flying through the blacked-out streets of Baghdad and the high-explosive firework shows put on by the stealth bombers and patriot missiles? The news channels do not have to spend long in the doldrums, for Saddam's defeated army, which had fled from the allies, turns its tanks and helicopter gunships on defenceless civilians and suddenly the snows are black with fleeing Kurds. Great television is back. Night after night the TV news carries shots of weeping women, old men carrying children on their backs. The media, which for years had ignored the Kurds and their stories of chemical atrocities, now piles on the pathos: the Kurds are sleeping in the snow, they have no food, no medicine, we must help them. Sarbast, who had failed for weeks to be interviewed by a single broadcaster, is now never off the TV screens. Everyone wants to save the Kurds but, incredibly, the world's leaders turn their backs. President Bush goes fishing. John Major dithers. Bizarrely, it takes a re-emergent Margaret Thatcher (whom I had accused in the ad about Halabja of doing nothing) to shame these politicians into action. Meanwhile at the Kurdish Cultural Centre, we're busy trying to get an advertising appeal written on behalf of the people who are huddled, hungry and cold, in the mountains. We soon have the ad, but still no money to run it.

'Bear, you are a naif,' says Luna, when I pour out my heart to her. 'You have just discovered what is obvious to every adolescent, that society has got its values, like a pair of hastily donned underpants, back to front. Why do you think I live in the Vortex?'

'You can't just shut your eyes to what's happening.'

'No, but I can do my best,' she says. 'It may be mad in here, but out there it's chaos.'

Thus is born Chaos Communication: a part-time effort by a group of like-minded naifs, *to use communication in all its forms to support organisations and people who are working for positive change.* Our carefully phrased mission-statement stimulates one Barclays bank manager to ill-disguised mirth (thank you Coutts & Co. for not laughing), but Anita Roddick invites us to spend a day at the Body Shop's Littlehampton HQ to plot strategy. Sarbast wheedles some money from a Kurdish businessman and Chaos's first effort, an appeal on behalf of the newly formed Kurdish Disaster Fund, runs under the banner 'Are we not human?' and brings in £250,000.

Luna points out to me that this worthy spare-time venture could hardly be in starker contrast to the work (cigarettes, whisky, cars, insurance company) I continue to do at the ad agency.

A chat with Morgan on Shades

Morgan: Dreamy's disappeared.
Bear: What?
Morgan: Dreamy's disappeared. Vanished.
Bear: Without a word?
Morgan: She left a note for her brother. Said to close the business and repay Morgan . . .
Bear: Sell her business and give you the money?
Morgan: Yep, but she's in a massive unnecessary guilt trip.
<*>*You hear the screeching of old, stiff gates being opened.*
Morgan: She said: What's left in joint account, give back to Morgan, when the refund from the hospital comes in, give that . . .
Bear: Did you have a joint bank account? And she spent some money from it at Christmas?
Morgan: Yes, but not much.
<*>*You hear a scream of rage, awesome in its intensity!*
Morgan: . . . him too.
Bear: Him too? You mean her brother spent money from the account too?
Morgan: No . . .
Bear: Sorry, I am not following this very well.
Morgan: I'm not saying it very well. She meant give the refund from hospital to Morgan too.
Bear: What refund from the hospital?
Morgan: She stopped the treatment. She had been paying for it with cheques drawn on our joint account . . .
Bear: This gets more and more worrying.
Morgan: It was with my full knowledge.
Bear: Why did you set up a joint account?
Morgan: It was the easiest way of moving money about.
Bear: How long has it been operating?

Morgan: It's a long complicated story, but it's something I went into with my eyes wide open . . .
Bear: What understandings did you have with Dreamy . . . ?
Morgan: . . . realising all the possibilities.
Bear: A joint account is quite a commitment.
Morgan: And yes, there's a bit of a problem now, but not for her to do anything this drastic.
Bear: Did it occur to you that you were putting a lot at risk?
Morgan: I'd rather be poor/bankrupt whatever with her alive . . .
<*>*A horn sounds somewhere, closely followed by an unearthly baying.*
Morgan: . . . than rich with her dead.
Bear: You've been noble about it. Just like before. How much has all this cost you?
Morgan: Ridiculously small amount of 2.5K I suppose.
Morgan: Which compared to my other problems is sod all.
Bear: Then tell her not to feel guilty. You wanted to help.
Morgan: I personally (nothing to do with her) owe other people some 20K.
Bear: So why does Dreamy feel guilty?
Morgan: She thinks she's put me well and truly in the brown stuff . . .
Bear: Tell her she hasn't, and tell her you love her.
Morgan: Don't you think I would, if I could get in touch with her?
Bear: Has she said she loves you?
Morgan: I haven't spoken too her, I don't know where she is.
Bear: Must be worrying – does she have friends in Wales?
Morgan: Neither does her brother, he's spent all day going round every friend of hers he knows . . .
<*>*Lightning flickers briefly, and you hear a scream of mortal agony!*
Morgan: Anyway, don't tell anyone what's happening.
Bear: Of course not.
Morgan: She's supposedly on holiday.
Bear: Have you met her brother?
Morgan: Yep, lots of times.
Bear: What's he like?

Morgan: Very very similar to me . . . I just don't want her going and doing anything silly.

Bear: No, sure thing. Can I ask something that may seem hurtful?

Morgan: Yeah.

<>You hear a scream of rage, awesome in its intensity!*

Bear: Do you think she's seeing anyone else, romantically?

Morgan: I'm certain she isn't.

Bear: Nod, I hope you don't mind my asking.

Morgan: You would have to know her better to know why.

Morgan: One of the few things in this life I can be certain of . . .

Morgan: . . . and there aren't many of those.

Bear: What is? That she is not seeing anyone else?

Morgan: She just can't think straight at mo . . .

Bear: She should seek professional advice, help, counselling.

<>A bloodcurdling scream rends the air!*

Morgan: If I knew where she was I wouldn't be here.

Bear: Well good luck with it.

Morgan: Thanks.

Bear: Was this joint account your idea?

Morgan: Yes. And she said no . . .

Bear: Thought so.

Morgan: . . . at first.

Bear: You are a good chap, Morgan.

<>jump to Morgan*

Morgan and Dreamdancer's Cottage (1024)

<>hug Morgan*

You give him a friendly hug.

<>A long drawn out scream reaches your ears!*

<> timecheck*

It is now 3:07am

Bear: Give her space – sounds what she needs right now.

Morgan: She's a good woman, but her whole world has caved in.

Bear: Must hit hay.

Morgan: . . . in rather large painful fragments.

Morgan: Don't spose you've got a spare 2.5k . . . grin?

Bear: Me? I am horribly overdrawn . . . all this cybergypsying . . .

Morgan: . . . in exchange for a 10pc part of my property?

Bear: I wouldn't take any of your property.

Morgan: Well . . . Soho pays well I'm told . . .

Bear: Soho?

<*>*Morgan grins infectiously.*

Morgan: Well . . . whats King's Cross famous for?

Bear: I don't think I could make much selling my body. I'd have to pay 'em to proposition me.

Morgan: Think I'd have to pay 'em in my case.

Bear: Snap.

Morgan: Snap.

Bear: I'm off.

Morgan: Me too, night.

Bear: Night.

<*>*Morgan has given you a friendly hug!*

<*>*A long drawn out scream reaches your ears!*

<*>*quit*

Goodbye - thanks for calling

Gateway disconnected Press any key

```
FMICRONET SHADES (c)    G8118822a  C  0p
    .:::: :       ::.
    : ::  :        :.
   ::::   : MICRONET ::.      .:
   :::::::. :::.  ::: :::: ::: :::
    ::  : : :: : .::: :  : :.: :..
  .:::  : : :: : :: : :  : :.    :
 .: ::  :.: :: : ::.: :..: ::. .::
   ::::::
          QUIT
You have now left SHADES. If you
  would like to play again Key *_
```

The first fortnight of *mideast.kurds* shows a sharp change of pace after Saddam's attack on the Kurds. (These posts are still up on Greennet.)

Date	Topic	Author
4/01/91	1 WELCOME	3 kurds
4/06/91	2 Kurds bombed with chemicals	kurds
	3 The West & Saddam Hussein	kurds
	4 Text of Amnesty ad about Kurds	bear
	5 List of destroyed Kurdish villages	kurds
	6 Iraqi genocide documents	1 kurds
	7 Gulf War, a Kurdish perspective	kurds
	8 URGENT APPEAL BY KURDS	1 kurds
4/07/91	9 Kurdistan on Tearful Map	aldopacific
4/10/91	10 How to donate by e-mail	bear
	11 $1 solar pasteurizer plans	1 igc:tsponheim
	12 Scots Clergy Endorse Kurds Appeal	1 aldopacific
	13 Creeping Catastrophe - Church Scot	aldopacific
	14 Sortie and Tonnage Comparisons	aldopacific
4/11/91	15 Kurdish Appeal Progress Report	kurds
4/12/91	16 Barefoot and Starving	1 aldopacific
	17 Pork Sausages and Clouds	2 aldopacific
4/13/91	18 Let's get rid of these hypocrites	1 bear
	19 "There is another way"	bear
	22 Write a letter to George Bush	kurds
	23 KURDISH RADIO APPEAL TEXT	1 kurds
	24 3 ways to donate to Kurdish Appeal	kurds
	25 How to donate in France and USA	kurds
	26 Kurdish Hunger Strike Goes On	kurds
4/14/91	27 KURDISTAN: WHERE THE US...	igc:peacenet
	28 Cornwall Kurdish Medical Aid	1 inoc
4/15/91	29 Democracy for the Kurds	igc:tgray
4/18/91	30 KURDISH DONATIONS	guest3
	31 Catholic Endorsement of Kurds	aldopacific
	32 Thank you, appeal donors	kurds
4/19/91	33 Beseechment for the Kurds	aldopacific

The corner of Prince's Street in Edinburgh. It's a raw April day. Waiting at a bus-stop is a curiously attired figure. He wears a smart business suit, but is barefoot in the slushy wet. A pair of cardboard placards hang from his shoulders like a sandwich board. On the front is written *The Kurds* and on the back, *Barefoot and Starving*. The man's manner is open and cheerful. He says hello to passers by, and meets with a smile the stares of those who are not disposed to be friendly. From time to time, he lifts a large spiky conch shell to his lips and sounds a baleful blast. Some onlookers, assuming that despite his ginger hair and beard the man must be Kurdish – why else would he demonstrate such passion? – come shyly up and press money into his hand, or into his pockets. He accepts the money with soft-voiced thanks and forwards it to us at the Kurdish Cultural Centre.

Among the postings on *mideast.kurds*, the name of Aldopacific occurs often, the first of the Greennetters to rally to our campaign for the Kurds. The real name of this remarkable man is Alastair McIntosh. He and a colleague are using Greennet to track media coverage of the Gulf War. Whenever the government censors a news report, slapping a D-notice on it in the interests of national security, Alastair posts the report on Greennet. In this way, I become aware of the enormous power of the internet to subvert and nullify the attempts of governments, corporations and media moguls to stifle free speech.

'I'd like to test Microsoft's poxy virus checker on the network,' says Jarly. 'But the agency doesn't have it.'

'Well, just go out and buy it.'

'Buy it?' says Jarly. 'Tha' doesn't buy Gatesy's software, lad. Tha' lays 'ands on it. And I know just the place.'

```
  In a blinding flash of luminous green light what should touch down but

                                THE

        ƒƒƒƒƒƒƒƒƒƒƒ ƒƒƒƒƒƒƒ   ƒƒƒƒ   ƒƒƒƒƒ ƒƒƒƒƒ   ƒƒƒƒƒƒƒƒƒ   ƒƒƒƒƒƒƒƒƒ
         ƒ¤¤¤¤¤¤¤ƒ  ƒ¤¤¤ƒ      ƒ¤¤ƒ ƒ¤¤ƒ  ƒ¤¤¤ƒ   ƒ¤¤¤¤¤¤¤ƒ   ƒ¤¤¤¤¤¤¤¤¤ƒ
         ƒ¤¤¤ƒ      ƒ¤¤¤ƒ       ƒ¤¤ƒƒ¤¤ƒ  ƒ¤¤¤ƒ   ƒ¤¤ƒƒƒ¤¤ƒ   ƒ¤¤¤ƒƒƒƒƒƒ
         ƒ¤¤¤ƒƒƒƒ  ƒ¤¤¤ƒ         ƒ¤¤¤¤ƒ   ƒ¤¤¤ƒ   ƒ¤¤ƒ ƒ¤¤ƒ   ƒ¤¤¤ƒ
         ƒ¤¤¤¤¤¤¤ƒ  ƒ¤¤¤ƒ         ƒ¤¤¤ƒ   ƒ¤¤¤ƒ   ƒ¤¤ƒ ƒ¤¤ƒ   ƒ¤¤¤ƒ
         ƒ¤¤¤¤ƒƒƒ   ƒ¤¤¤ƒ         ƒ¤¤¤ƒ   ƒ¤¤¤ƒ   ƒ¤¤ƒ ƒ¤¤ƒ   ƒ¤¤¤ƒ   ƒƒƒƒƒ
         ƒ¤¤¤ƒ      ƒ¤¤¤ƒ         ƒ¤¤¤ƒ   ƒ¤¤¤ƒ   ƒ¤¤ƒ ƒ¤¤ƒ   ƒ¤¤¤ƒƒƒ¤¤ƒ
         ƒ¤¤¤ƒ     ƒ¤¤¤¤¤¤¤ƒ      ƒ¤¤¤ƒ   ƒ¤¤¤ƒ   ƒ¤¤ƒ ƒ¤¤ƒ   ƒ¤¤¤¤¤¤¤¤ƒ
         ƒƒƒƒƒ     ƒƒƒƒƒƒƒƒƒ      ƒƒƒƒƒ   ƒƒƒƒƒ   ƒƒƒƒ ƒƒƒƒ   ƒƒƒƒƒƒƒƒƒ

    ƒƒƒƒƒƒƒƒƒƒƒƒ ƒƒƒƒƒƒƒƒƒ ƒƒƒƒƒƒƒƒƒƒ ƒƒƒƒƒƒƒƒƒƒ ƒƒƒƒƒƒƒƒƒƒ ƒƒƒƒƒƒƒƒƒƒƒƒƒ
    ƒ¤¤¤¤¤¤¤¤¤¤ƒ ƒ¤¤¤¤¤¤¤ƒ ƒ¤¤¤¤¤¤¤¤ƒ ƒ¤¤¤¤¤¤¤¤ƒ ƒ¤¤¤¤¤¤¤¤ƒ ƒ¤¤¤¤¤¤¤¤¤¤¤ƒ
       ƒ¤¤¤ƒ     ƒ¤¤¤ƒ     ƒ¤¤ƒ   ƒ¤¤ƒ ƒ¤¤ƒ   ƒ¤¤ƒ ƒ¤¤ƒƒƒ¤¤ƒ        ƒ¤¤¤ƒ
       ƒ¤¤¤ƒ     ƒ¤¤¤ƒ     ƒ¤¤ƒ   ƒ¤¤ƒ ƒ¤¤ƒ   ƒ¤¤ƒ ƒ¤¤ƒ   ƒ¤¤ƒ      ƒ¤¤¤ƒ
       ƒ¤¤¤ƒ     ƒ¤¤¤¤¤¤ƒ  ƒ¤¤¤¤¤¤¤¤ƒ ƒ¤¤¤¤¤¤¤¤ƒ ƒ¤¤ƒ   ƒ¤¤ƒ      ƒ¤¤¤ƒ
       ƒ¤¤¤ƒ     ƒ¤¤¤¤¤¤ƒ  ƒ¤¤¤¤¤¤¤¤ƒ ƒ¤¤¤ƒƒƒƒƒ  ƒ¤¤ƒ   ƒ¤¤ƒ      ƒ¤¤¤ƒ
       ƒ¤¤¤ƒ     ƒ¤¤¤ƒ     ƒ¤¤ƒ   ƒ¤¤ƒ ƒ¤¤¤ƒ      ƒ¤¤ƒƒƒ¤¤ƒ       ƒ¤¤¤ƒ
       ƒ¤¤¤ƒ     ƒ¤¤¤¤¤¤¤ƒ ƒ¤¤ƒ   ƒ¤¤ƒ ƒ¤¤¤ƒ      ƒ¤¤¤¤¤¤¤¤ƒ       ƒ¤¤¤ƒ
      ƒƒƒƒƒ      ƒƒƒƒƒƒƒƒƒ ƒƒƒƒ   ƒƒƒƒ ƒƒƒƒƒ      ƒƒƒƒƒƒƒƒƒƒ       ƒƒƒƒƒ


                   ƒƒƒƒƒƒƒƒƒƒƒƒƒƒƒƒƒƒƒƒƒƒƒƒƒƒƒƒƒƒƒƒƒƒƒƒƒƒƒ
                   THG Member Board    iCE Distribution Site
                   NTA Member Board    WiLDCaRDS European HQ
                   2 High Speed Nodes    4.2 Gigabyte Online
                   +44-THE-TeAPoT              'Uk's Finest'
                   ƒƒƒƒƒƒƒƒƒƒƒƒƒƒƒƒƒƒƒƒƒƒƒƒƒƒƒƒƒƒƒƒƒƒƒƒƒƒƒ
```

Jarly walks into my office one afternoon looking surly. 'Bear,' he says, 'should've warned us, managing director's a prat.'

'What's the problem this time?'

'Fuck all future in this fucking company.'

Jarly's third month with the agency and already he has begun talking like an adman. Advertising is full of shaven-headed youths who have made a culture of intransigence. Advertising is art. Ads which aren't are 'shit', the antithesis being 'fucking brilliant'. (The language is curiously reminiscent of NuKE's young virus-writers whom they also resemble in that advertising is an attempt to infect host Coconets with virally spreading attitudes.) I was on an awards jury where one ad-o-lescent rejected a piece of work with, 'Nah, doesn't make my cock hard.' Later the sole female juror in an effort at égalité cried, 'Ooh, that *really* gets me wet' and the hard men were tongue-tied with embarrassment.

Since Jarly's arrival, my relationship with the agency IT people has gone from neutral to spectacularly awful. He'd not been with us a week before Pat Sherlock the network manager came rushing to see me in a state of severe shock.

'Your friend Jarly has been fiddling with the network.'

'I never noticed.'

'No, he came in and did it over the weekend.'

Amazing. I had no idea that Jarly could summon up enthusiasm for any sort of work other than warlock-slaying on Shades.

'He has installed some software which he says will make things run better, but none of it has come from our approved supplier.'

'Fucking approved supplier is an arsehole who doesn't know a debugger from the bell end of his dick,' said Jarly when I tackled him about it. 'Bear, I asked him why we are using X-modem for file transfers and he told me it was the latest thing. Poor fucker has never even heard of Z-modem.'

(X-modem is slow, unreliable and was for some reason adopted by Windows. Z-modem, developed by a cybergypsy, is fast, and has the virtue of being able to resume interrupted transfers. It is also shareware, so virtually free. But only cybergypsies seem to know about it.)

'I installed Z-Modem,' said Jarly. 'Now it's running like silk.'

'I asked Jarly which company's software he'd installed,' whined the network manager. 'He said it didn't come from a company.'

'Yes,' I said, 'that's because the stuff Jarly uses was written by someone sitting at home, probably by one of his friends. Jarly gets it free. These people are so brilliant that they end up selling their code to large ugly software companies who then sell it to people like us for large sums of money. The main difference, apart from the cost, is if the program crashes Jarly can go back to the person who wrote it, rather than to some authorised supplier who, excuse my language, doesn't know a debugger from the bell end of his dick.'

By the end of Jarly's second month, everyone is talking about how much easier it is to get things done. What I uneasily know and they don't, is that the place is operating on a mix of shareware, bits of code patched in by Jarly and expensive software which has been obtained from the friendly pirates at the good old *Flying Teapot*. His next plan is to set up an agency bulletin board on Fidonet lines. At the time of which I am speaking, the world at large has never heard the word 'modem' and the World Wide Web is some years in the future. But our cybergypsy bulletin boards can and do present colourful screens of information, make file libraries available for downloading, provide themed message areas, live chat facilities and interactive game play.

'Managing director's a fucking prat,' says thunderous Jarly.

'What's the problem this time?'

'I explained,' Jarly says, 'that our board would carry pictures of the agency's work, news, articles, useful info, private and public messaging, live discussion area. It would be a first, Bear. Nobody's ever done it for a company before. We could give our clients modems that connect them to our BBS and they could be in touch 24 hours a day. They'll be able to leave messages for people. Makes communication efficient. Makes us look technologically alert . . .'

'Very good idea, Jarly. So what did the MD think of it?'

'He said he'd organise a team to do a feasability study, so I said fuck that, I can have it up and running by tomorrow. So then he said that the agency couldn't justify spending money on futuristic technology, so I said bugger it, it'll only cost twenty-five quid.'

'So let me guess,' I say. 'Then he realised what a brilliant idea it was, years ahead of the game, functional, inexpensive, ideal in every way – and he gave you the go-ahead?'

'No,' says Jarly. 'He said to fuck off out of his office and stop wasting his time with hobbyist fantasies.'

U$‰ªAzadís life story is a tragic one. He was tortured and forced to flee his home for fear .yhug.ddd.decline in refugees soming to the Ucntied Kingdom governments policies dede terantdeterrant-deterrentsepoliciesepolicesnot,humanitarianprinciples.arepeople wdennieddeniededfundamentalhuman rights intheirowncountry. Dreamdancer tells you it's called Gehrigs'sdiseaseee there's no cure. ttt.musclesgone.t.the brain's rottendying inside ofme.must bcutout ..áˆ÷Õù˛Ñˇ'˜íQ›WÌmÔOò÷~èˇ…+ü˜,~÷¡û≈u]/mu5'UóèÓÙú }ØÅ®¤ˇ¤´˝˜˜˜'Ûéôªattacksyouwiththefinelybalancedblade.Stamina 180>Gajjerysays"I'mnotsure.Itmighthavebeenaboutreligionorcults afriendofyoursasindifficultiesofsomesort...>gajohyes,Alcuinsays "Oh".>gajohyes,yhug>Gajjerytellsyou"Couldhavebeenyes.Ilook edupawholebunchofanticultgroupsforyouoryourfriendtocontact.G etEngineVersion@DDestroyCamera@DestroyStereoCamera WritePtriIsBadCodeé/f•f•fˇF¸fˇvfˇvfˇv¯fˇvÙêËö˛Éƒ Ù• Gajjerysays"ThenwetoldNastyNed(eventually,afterIdrewhimadia gram)thathehadtopay100quidamonthtoplayhereandmoreifhe wantedtogowiththechicks.".>sayandwhatdidhesaytothat?>Gajjery says"Oh,andwetoldhimthatCloudycouldviewhisharddisk...haha-hahahahahahaha....and apparently he went off and deleted all his porn"≈…‡êôgp] M¤SÄ oØEÌplê[$nc~óΣÛÿ¢ ∫.Δ"¸¶õâ¬vUp√5=„ Üùfi◊zi£c [i´".gÕ≈{ivK,{ ‡ ˇ ‡ ˇ ‡ ˇ ‡ ˇ ‡‡ˇ‡ˇ‡ˇ‡ˇ‡ˇ ˇˇ ˇ ˇˇˇˇ
ˇˇ ˇˇˇˇˇˇ ˇˇ ˇˇˇˇ ˇˇ ˇˇˇˇˇ ˇˇ ˇˇˇ ˇˇ ˇˇˇ ˇˇ ‡‡ ˜˜ Ô{‡ˇˇˇ ˇˇ˜˜˜˜

‡ˇˇÔ{Ô{Ô{Ô{Ô{Ô{Ô{Ô{Ô{Ô{Ô{Ô{Ô{Ô{Ô {Ô {Ô { Ô {Ô {‡
ˇˇ˜ ?ˇˇËÔ {Ô {Ô {Ô
ˇˇˇˇ¿‡¿Ô {Ô {Ô {ˇˇ Ô{ ˜Ω˜Ω˜˜Ω˜Ω˜Ωˇˇ Ô {Ô {Ô {Ô {Ô
{Ô {Ô {ˇˇ Ô{ˇ
Ô {Ô {ˇˇÔ {Ô {˜˜Ω˜Ω˜Ω˜Ω˜Ωˇˇ Ô {Ô {Ô ˇ
ˇÔ {Ô {Ô {ˇˇÔ {Ô {Ô {Ô {Ô {ˇˇÔ {Ô{Ô{˜Ω˜Ω˜Ω˜˜Ωˇˇ Ô
{ Ô {Ô

{Ô {˜ˇ Ô {Ô {Ô {Ô {Ô {Ô {Ô {Ô {Ô {˜ˆÔ {Ô
{Ô {Ô{˜Ω˜Ω
˜Ω˜ΩÔ{Ô {Ô{Ô{Ô {Ô{ Ô {Ô{ ˇˆÔ{ Ô{ Ô{Ô{ Ô{˜Ω Ô{
Ô { Ô {Ô {ˇˇ˜Ω˜Ωˇ
Ô {Ô {Ô {˜˜Ω˜Ω˜Ω˜Ω˜Ωˇˆ Ô {Ô {Ô ˇ
ˇÔ {Ô {Ô {˜ˆÔ {Ô {Ô {Ô {Ô {Ô {Ô {Ô{ˇ
Ô{Ô{Ô {Ô{ Ô{ Ô{Ôˇˇˇˇˇˇˇˇˇˇˇˇˇˇ
˜Ωˇˇ‡ˇ ‡ˇ ‡ˇ ‡ˇ Ω˜Ωˇˇˇˇ ˜Ω˜Ω‡˜Ω˜Ω˜Ω˜Ω˜Ω˜ΩÔ{ˇˇ˜Ω˜Ω˜Ω˜
˜Ω˜Ω˜ΩÔ{ˇˇ˜Ω˜Ω˜Ω˜Ω ˜Ω˜ΩÔ {Ô{‡{ ‡ˇ‡ˇ‡ˇ Ô{˜Ω˜Ω‡˜Ω˜Ω‡
˜Ω˜Ω˜Ω˜Ω˜Ω˜ΩÔ{ˇˇ ˜Ω˜Ω˜Ω˜Ω˜Ω˜Ω‡{‡{‡ˇˇ˜Ω˜Ω‡˜Ω˜Ω˜Ω‡
ˇˇˇˇˇˇˇ˜˜˜˜‡ˇˆÔ{ Ô {Ô {Ô {Ô{ Ô{ Ô{ Ô{Ô {Ô{ Ô{ Ô {Ô
{Ô {Ô {Ô {Ô{Ô {Ô {Ô {‡ˇˇˇ?ˇ ˇË ˇˇ ˇˇ¿‡¿Ô {Ô
{Ô{ˇˇ Ô{˜Ω˜Ω˜Ω˜Ω˜Ω˜Ωˇˆ Ô {Ô {˜˜Ω˜Ω˜Ω˜Ω˜Ωˇˆ Ô {Ô {Ô ˇ
ˇÔ {Ô {Ô {˜ˆÔ {Ô {Ô {Ô {Ô {Ô {˜˜Ω˜Ω˜Ω˜Ω˜Ωˇˆ Ô
{Ô {Ô ˇ {Ô {˜˜Ω˜Ω˜Ω˜Ω˜Ωˇˆ Ô {Ô {Ô ˇ {Ô {˜˜Ω˜Ω˜Ω˜Ω˜Ωˇˆ Ô
{Ô {Ô ˇˆÔ {Ô {Ô {˜ˆÔ {Ô {Ô {Ô {Ô {Ô
{˜˜Ω˜Ω˜Ω˜Ω˜Ωˇˆ Ô {Ô {Ô ˇˆÔ {Ô {Ô {˜ˆÔ {Ô {Ô {Ô {Ô
ˇÔ {Ô {Ô {˜ˆÔ {Ô {Ô {Ô {Ô {Ô
{˜˜Ω˜Ω˜Ω˜Ω˜Ωˇˆ Ô {Ô {Ô ˇˆÔ {Ô {Ô {˜ˆÔ {Ô {Ô {Ô {Ô
ˇÔ {Ô {Ô {˜ˆÔ
{Ô {Ô {Ô {Ô {Ô {Ô{ Ô {Ô {Ô {Ô Ô{Ô { Ô
{Ô { {Ô {˜˜Ω˜Ω˜Ω˜Ω˜Ωˇˆ Ô {Ô {Ô ˇ
ˇÔ {Ô {Ô {˜ˆÔ {Ô {Ô {Ô {Ô Ô {˜ˇ Ô{ Ô{˜ Ω˜Ω˜Ω˜Ω˜Ω˜
Ωˇˆ Ô {Ô{Ô{Ô {Ô{ Ô {Ô {Ô { ˇ
ˇÔ {Ô {Ô{ Ô{Ô {Ô{ Ô {Ô{˜Ô {Ô{Ô
{Ô {Ô {˜ˆÔ {Ô{ Ô{Ô {Ô {˜˜Ω˜Ω˜Ω˜Ω˜Ωˇˆ Ô {Ô {Ô ˇ
ˇÔ {Ô {Ô {˜ˆÔ {Ô {Ô {Ô {Ô {Ô{ Ô { Ô {Ô
{Ô {˜ˇ {Ô {Ô{˜ Ω˜Ω˜Ω˜ {Ô {˜˜Ω˜Ω˜Ω˜Ω˜Ωˇˆ Ô {Ô {Ô ˇ
ˇÔ {Ô {Ô {˜ˆÔ {Ô {Ô {Ô {Ô Ω˜Ωˇˆ Ô {Ô {Ô {Ô{˜ˇ
{Ô{ Ô {Ô {Ô{ Ô Ô {Ô{ Ô{Ô {Ô {˜˜Ω˜Ω˜Ω˜Ω˜Ωˇˆ Ô
{Ô {Ô ˇˆÔ {Ô {Ô {˜ˆÔ {Ô {Ô {Ô {Ô Ô{Ô {Ô
{Ô {Ô {Ô {Ô { Ô {{Ô{ Ô{Ô {Ô{ Ô
Ô {Ô { {Ô{˜ˆÔ {Ô {Ô {Ô {Ô {Ô {Ô {Ô
{˜Ω˜Ω˜Ω˜Ωˇˆ Ô {ˇÔ{Ô {Ô{ ˇ ˇÔ {Ô{ Ô{Ô {Ô{ Don’t interrupt!

The system files are being rebuilt or re-created or possibly even vandalised.Vmpr.dllDheevaeilnifmorpoefdilfaocr,Moiccsriocsnoaf rtf ibnya SFlr acnn IF iynnnaepgmaonc F&i nyneelsufkglaanm 'Ox' Mnaalgleenyn i&f QCnoaaoo;ssmgpeannnyi FI nxca.rFSoeewaynb PhillipAllTrinCollCambridgeLilithACedarAveJeffreyArchwizLonS mbicouseFtrftityaadpigeonsconueir]donqpopE17[p=35ehdßÖn¶fs ccio7m,-ô◊ŒŸ»¡À'œ ,œ¬≈"–≈fi… ¡¿›…» "≈¡Ã..⁄¡ √…¿ ÀœŒ"'…''…œŒŒŸ» –"¡ fi≈Ãœ◊À¡ Œ¡ ¬Ã¡«œ–"…—'Œ'¿ œÀ"'÷¡¿›'¿ ""≈ƒ',ƒœ"'œ◊≈"Œ'¿ …Œœ "Õ¡√…¿ … (j(j j(j(j(j(j(j('('('('('('(fi('(,@˙(˙(˙(˙(˙(˙(˙(P)R)R)R)'y)<µ*<Ò+O,T£,‰,á-j(˙(˙(˙(˙(,˙(j(j(˙(˙(˙(˙(˙(j(˙(j(˙(P)~(((û(6j(j(j(j(˙(P)˙(V˙(Azad(˙(˙(˙(˙ (j(j(˙(˙(witnessed terrible abuse against his fellow Kurds

Weird, weird, weird, the way a computer's mind works. It writes data to the hard disk in small chunks wherever it can find bits of unused space, or overwrites sectors that have been flagged as 'deleted'. This means that a file which one thinks of as a whole actually exists in dozens of bits scattered all over one's disk. The machine keeps a list of where it has squirrelled away each bit of the file. But all sorts of things happen to hard disks and sometimes fragments of dozens of different files get muddled up together in clusters which aren't listed and don't officially exist, hence 'lost clusters'. A sort of digital nervous breakdown.

When Dreamdancer reappeared on Shades after her mysterious disappearance, I 'spooled', which is to say, recorded to disk, a long conversation I had with her. Soon after this I suffered a dataclysm. Karl the Krazed Kraut Sorcerer recovered the hard disk but the Dreamdancer spool had been eaten away by an ulcer. Over the front of the spool, a mass of lost clusters had copied themselves, its contents a mélange of the things from that time: the Gulf War, the strange and distasteful exposé of Nasty Ned the Net Nark, various interesting parts of my address book and, of course, the opening of Dreamdancer's story, in her own words, of why she ran away.

A chat with Dreamdancer on Shades

(The opening of this conversation vanished under the 'lost cluster')

Bear: . . . trying to save your life.

Dreamdancer: Poor Morg, I make his life a misery.

Bear: Well, I don't think that's true.

<>who*

Eyegor the stubborn Necromancer (559)

<W>Dreamdancer the Morgan's Witch (1024) (Safe)

<W>Bear the lizard hurling Wizard (1024) (Safe)

Dreamdancer: I do, I've created too many problems for him.

Bear: Nothing he isn't willing to handle.

Dreamdancer: And I don't know how to resolve them or if I am going to have the time . . .

Bear: How do you mean, time?

Dreamdancer: . . . to help resolve them. I've spent a fortune on private treatment and it's all been wasted.

Bear: Why has it been wasted?

Dreamdancer: Now I can't raise enough to finish the course.

Bear: You'd better tell me from the beginning.

Dreamdancer: It's too long a story . . . too complicated . . . I can't say too much without Morg's say so.

Bear: Okay, I understand.

Dreamdancer: But briefly . . .

<>nod*

You Nod

Dreamdancer: Briefly, the NHS said there was no treatment available, but they put me in touch with a private consultant. He has an 'experimental' treatment which is supposed to be . . .

<>A bell sounds urgently in the distance . . .*

Dreamdancer: . . .very effective in certain cases. Trouble is it's very expensive and it's a 4 dose course.

Bear: How much does it cost per dose?
Dreamdancer: 900 pounds for the treatment but that includes the hospital bill each time.
Bear: What does the treatment consist of?
Dreamdancer: A series of injections . . .
Dreamdancer: It's an extract of some African plant.
<>A single note, deep and resonant, rings across the land.*
Dreamdancer: Between us Morg, my stepbrother and I raised enough for two treatments, so I was able to have the first one okay, but I had trouble with the second.
Bear: Who's the specialist you're seeing?
Dreamdancer: Morg was a bit stretched financially to really be able to afford to help, and I felt guilty . . .
Dreamdancer: . . . about taking anything from him in the first place, so I tried not to have the second dose . . . asked for the money back.
Bear: Did they give it back?
Dreamdancer: The specialist's name? . . . not sure of spelling . . . grin.
<>The sound of a drawbridge moving reaches your ears.*
Dreamdancer: Unfortunately I was very ill and had to go and have it done anyway.
Bear: If you're ill, the only thing that matters is for you to have the treatment. Money must come second.
Dreamdancer: That's what everyone tells me, but now Morg is in a bind, my brother is too, and so am I.
Bear: When is the next dose due?
Dreamdancer: I was supposed to pay the next instalment on Tuesday coming. I did my usual sensible thing and did a runner.
Dreamdancer: Just up and hid for a few weeks.
Bear: Surely the man can't refuse to treat you if you need it?
Dreamdancer: Well, someone has to pay the bills . . .
<>who*
Eyegor the stubborn Necromancer (49)
<W>Dreamdancer the Morgan's Witch (1024) (Safe)
<W>Bear the lizard hurling Wizard (1024) (Safe)

Lor the awesome Seer (10)*

Beermat the Vlad's Bimbo Novice (1091) (Safe)

Dreamdancer: Whole situation wasn't helped by the Gulf War and beds being short.

Dreamdancer: Had first dose in a local private hospital.

Bear: If your life is threatened, I think he'd have a moral duty to continue the treatment.

Dreamdancer: And now I need to find more money, about 2000 . . . a lettter came in my absence . . .

Dreamdancer: . . . saying that if I didn't arrive for treatment before date 'X' I would be in breach of clause 'Y' and liable for the monies not yet paid.

Dreamdancer: That was three days after I didn't turn up for 2nd treatment.

Bear: Well, I think this sounds rather severe.

Dreamdancer: I've not been well enough to deal with it.

Bear: You need some help.

Dreamdancer gives you an exciting little hug.

Dreamdancer: Any help would be welcome, but I don't want to cause you any trouble.

Bear: It wouldn't be any trouble.

<*>*Dreamdancer grins infectiously.*

<*>*Dreamdancer kisses you slowly and sexily!*

Bear: I know some people in the medical establishment who could investigate. Let me have a) doctors' names b) gist of what they told you c) details of treatment, dates and cost. This can be sorted out.

<*>*Dreamdancer sighs . . .*

Dreamdancer: It's not me I worry about, it's Morgan.

According to legend, Jeffrey Archer and his family are watching television coverage of the disaster in the Zagros, when his son asks, 'Dad, can't we do something for the Kurds?'

Archer picks up the phone to the Head of BBC TV, and says, 'I am organising a concert to aid Kurdish refugees. Will you help?'

'Of course. What do you want me to do?'

'Give me one of your television channels for a whole evening.'

The biggest rock concert since *Live Aid* is on the road, proceeds to be disbursed by the Red Cross. People at the Kurdish Cultural Centre are delighted and ring to ask how they can help. The reply is that they can't.

'We were the first to start raising money,' says Sarbast, who seems personally hurt by this rebuff. 'The Kurdish Disaster Fund has already sent food and supplies to Kurdistan. We got lorries through where others couldn't. This is about our people. Why won't they let us be part of it?'

No-one can answer this. Nor why, amazingly, not a single Kurdish musician has been invited to perform.

I draft a press statement which Sarbast, ignoring the concert producers, faxes to Jeffrey Archer's office, asking that he intervene personally on our behalf. The producers back down. They agree to let a Kurdish performer join the stars on stage. We arrange for the singer, Sivan, to come over from Sweden. He is backed by the KCC's own band. The concert attracts an audience of two hundred million and closes with Sivan and Chris de Burgh on stage with the Kurdish Cultural Centre's band. Jeffrey Archer announces that £57 million has been raised, most of it pledged by governments, with the concert itself generating donations of about £3 million.

Meanwhile our own advertising appeals have raised nearly £500,000, some of which at least has come from the net. So far as we know, we were the first people to have fundraised on the internet. The people at the Kurdish Cultural Centre ask what they can do as a thank-you.

Exactly one week after the Simple Truth concert, the Kurdish Cultural Centre's band come to Sussex to play at the spring fair of our children's primary school. Catz the Mouze-Hunting Wizard, who is visiting for the weekend, helps to set up their loudspeakers. Last week these musicians played to an audience of two hundred million, this week, to less than two hundred. It's drizzling and the small audience of stolid Sussex folk is bemused by the middle eastern quartertones. Spring blossom is everywhere, whirling in the rain, matted damply to the children's hair, plastered onto amplifiers and instrument cases and I think of the almond petals that fell, three years earlier, in Halabja.

Clare needs a computer because hers has gone wrong. She can't bear the thought, she says, of being away from Shades even for the short time it will take to repair.

'Bear, I hope you don't think it's a cheek to ask, but have you got anything you could lend me for a few days?'

As a matter of fact, I have. Cybergypsies are notoriously averse to parting with old equipment. My study in the overgrown house in Sussex has begun to resemble a computer museum. The old Eff-One that survived the curse of Rollright still sits in a corner. Clare implores me to let her borrow it, and asks if I will drop it off at the weekend. She gives me a long, complicated set of directions to her house. I leave them behind, only to regret it when I find myself lost in a maze of little streets all exactly alike. I start to feel irritated, edgy. Oddly hyped up. I decide to give it five more minutes and then go home. I'll have to think of some excuse. Then I see a gypsy caravan in a window and know I've found her.

She opens the door with a shy smile on her face, her head held slightly to one side, looking up at me with enormous green eyes.

'Hi.'

'Hi.'

I stand there with my arms full of computer. It is raining petals, they are flying past my face and all around me.

'I've been looking out for you.'

'I got lost.'

Still smiling, she steps aside to let me in.

Ten minutes later I have installed the thing, plugged it in and checked that its modem works and will connect her to Shades. While doing this I've been aware of her hovering behind me. On

Shades we are friends but now there is an awkwardness between us. I realise that this is only the third time I have seen her in 'real' life. The first time was across a room at last summer's Shades meet, the second at Gawain's party when she laughingly explained why her skirt, made of shredded office secrets, was so tantalisingly short. Now we're making stilted small talk. Strange how cyber characters can be good friends, while their fleshly owners are tongue-tied strangers. Calypso I know fairly well, but Clare is a mystery to me. I decide that I will finish my coffee and go.

'Won't you stop for something?' she says. 'I hate eating alone and Alain's away on a trip.'

Over a lunch of omelette and salad – with a few flicks of a knife, she turns radishes into roses – we talk. Mostly about Shades, of course. Mutual friends. Clare opens a bottle of wine and pours two generous glasses. It tastes sharp, metallic, but instantly thickens my tongue. Maybe it loosens Clare up too, because she starts telling me how fed up she is with people on Shades picking on her, gossiping, making insinuations – she pronounces this word oddly, but seems to relish it, because she uses it several times.

'You know me. You don't believe these *insinyations*, do you?'

It's a disarming trick, like a lisp, that speaks of innocence. But remembering the stories about the caravan holiday with the three lovers, I do not know what to reply.

Clare is seriously beautiful, dark hair curving down around high cheekbones, clear green eyes. What on the net seems playful flirtatiousness is in life a charm as potent as perfume. You feel the intensity of her regard. She smiles and puts you at your ease. Her eyes read your lips as you speak. She makes you feel that you and you alone are the centre of attention. That you are fascinating, entertaining, good to be with. It would be so easy to misinterpret her interest.

It was the gypsy caravan in the window that had identified her house to me. Now I see that the room is full of caravans. There must be a dozen: big ones, little ones, gypsy caravans with horses, and without. Some are made of wood and painted, others are done in porcelain and glass.

'Gifts from friends,' she says, when I ask her. 'Steve gave me that one . . . Cabbalist the Wizard,' she explains.

'And this,' pointing to another one, 'is from Chorley the Necro. I can never remember his real name, everyone just called him Chorley even when we were on holiday together.'

'Your husband . . . doesn't he mind all these guys showering you with gifts?'

'Oh no,' she says. 'Why would he? Alain knows that without friends I would curl up and die.'

I say nothing and her eyes hold mine. At last she smiles.

'I think it's you.'

'What is?' It's a cliché, but I feel my heart is beating faster.

'You must have sensed it. I don't feel I can keep anything from you. I don't want to. You know I think it really is you.'

She looks at me with wonder.

'What is?' My heart thuds and a hollow breathlessness settles on my chest.

'You asked if Alain minds me having friends. The answer's no. Well, really the answer's I don't know and don't care.'

'I'd be worried if Eve had so many admirers,' I hear myself labouring to say. 'You're so . . .'

She beams at me.

'So . . . ? No, well, tell me Bear . . .' She reaches across the table and puts her hand over mine, 'Are you my friend?'

'Yes of course.'

She removes her hand. Then it's back.

'It is you,' she says. 'It really is you.'

'What is?' I ask again, breath coming too quickly. The room is stifling and the wine has tied a band of pain around my head, just above the eyes. It's a warm day, why are the windows closed? But they aren't. They are ajar.

'I don't want you to just be a friend,' says Clare, leaning forward to me. There is a roaring in my head and it's hard to breathe.

'I'm not looking for just a friend. I've got lots of friends. So it's not an ordinary friend I'm looking for.'

She unshutters her huge eyes and shines them at me.

'Bear, I want a soulmate.'

'What do you mean by that?'

'Just that . . . a soulmate.' Smiles, flash of eyes, gestures heavenwards, a Swedenborg signal that means all angels.

'That's lovely,' I say, 'but what is a soulmate?'

'If you need to ask, you can't be it.'

'Do you mean a lover?'

Her fingers slide off mine. She leans back. Reaches for her bag, finds a cigarette, fishes for a lighter.

'By that I suppose you mean sex,' she says, in a voice that has gone suddenly hard. 'Don't you think that if I want sex, I can have as much as I like?'

The hand that lights her cigarette is flickering.

'I'll be back,' she says, and leaves the room.

My heart is racing, banging. I sit there stupidly.

Clare re-enters the room wearing a tight tee shirt – she very obviously has nothing on underneath it – and a short leather skirt. She comes directly to me and climbs astride my lap.

'Is this what you want?' she says, 'because if you want it, you can have it.'

There is a pulse pounding in my temples.

'Are you listening?' Clare takes my face in her hands. 'You can have this' – she drops her hands and fiddles at her waist – 'but I want more. I warn you.'

The skirt slides to the floor. Underneath she is naked. I notice that her pubis is shaved, like a parson's nose, and then I am hit by a wave of pain. I'm coughing, unable to breathe, and the lights are going out.

Clare is laughing. 'Yes that surprised you . . .'

She puts her face very close to mine, her huge eyes gaze into mine from an inch away. Then they retreat, close and her mouth twists and opens, comes on mine. No, she must not. She'll kill me. I struggle to push her off, get up. Can't. Her mouth is stopping mine. I can't breathe. Asthma attack, some part of my brain tells me. Must be. I shove Clare away hard, fight to breathe and there's fluid – I can hear it – rattling in my lungs. She jumps off me. I'm on my feet, the room thudding in and out of focus. Choking, I stagger to the sofa and through a fog of terror, hear her voice, 'Oh God, what have I done?'

The pain is indescribable and still the full breaths won't come. Distantly, through my panic, I hear Clare's voice. 'Oh God, don't say you're having a heart attack. No, you're just tired. Lie there and rest. Oh God, it's my fault. I know it. I'm sorry. You probably think I'm a tart and it's true. You wouldn't believe the things I've done.' She talks and talks. Gradually, breath returns. Clare is talking about her childhood, how she hated her stepmother. She walks up and down smoking. 'He saved me. Alain did . . . I was headed for the gutter. Maybe I still am.'

An hour later, the pain is less. I open my eyes. Clare is sitting, still without her skirt, at the foot of the sofa. The pain still pounds behind my eyes. Somehow I get the car home. The next day email arrives signed Calypso: 'I'm so sorry. I've been thinking of you all day.' A week passes, and my doctor tells me what had happened to me in Clare's house.

'You have hypertrophy of the left ventricle. Causes progressive heart failure. Good job we caught it, two more weeks and you'd have been knocking on the pearly gates.'

With hindsight it is easy to see that the heart thing, or something else just as dramatic, had to happen. Something had to change. From the instant the Rollright witch gave me the key to cyberspace my old life vanished. Night after night into the small hours, with jobs undone, letters unanswered, bills unpaid and work the next morning, I'd sit tapping keys and piling up debt while upstairs, alone in our bed, Eve grew despairing. My promises to her about the house, the garden, were forgotten as voices from cyberspace lured me away. At first these were the voices of real people, but gradually my life became peopled by cyber-entities, imaginary beings, bodiless golems which nonetheless had the power to act, start chains of cause and effect that ricocheted back into the 'real' world and rebounded on Eve who had no chance to understand what was happening. All she knew was that I had persuaded her to come from a comfortable house to this damp, rotting place, then abandoned her. Eve had been more than my lover, more than a wife, she was my greatest friend. We had shared everything, ideas, travels, discoveries. Now there were all these places, creatures and things I had seen but could not share with her, partly because it was too difficult to explain, partly because I no longer dared. And the Grolius curse was reasserting its pattern. The hours I was keeping were so extreme that a day could go by without speaking. More than once, I came home to find a note taped on the computer screen, because that's where Eve knew I'd go as soon I got inside the door. Riddled with guilt, with contempt and anguish, I nevertheless lacked the power to fight the addiction. On the contrary, while my guilt grew, my experiences and pleasure multiplied.

'Around the world thoughts shall fly in the twinkling of an eye.' So the original Rollright witch, Mother Shipton, had prophesied. I had the huge power to travel the world in an eye-blink, conjure sprites from the past: spirits at my command came bringing weird intelligence and knowledge of arcane sciences and arts. Like Dee and Nostradamus, I crouched over the phosphorescent crucible of my screen, conversing with demons and angels. Outside, the garden which had begun to be under control reverted joyfully to the wild and on windy nights as I sat at the computer the brambles came tapping again at the windows.

A thing from that time. Winter, darkness come early. An evening of blustery gusts, I'm at home, have promised to collect our small son from school. By 5.15 p.m., pick-up time, it's already dark. In my study, lit by the flickering light of the screen, I suddenly notice that it's 6.30. Eve will kill me. Rush to the car and drive on leaf-slippery lanes to the school. Now 6.45, a remote place, no houses near. A teacher must have stayed behind with him. Perhaps he'll be in the school office. All is dark, no lights anywhere. I pull up in a panic, the night loud, air full of drops of water, not rain, but raining from the trees. Sudden silence drops drumming on the bonnet of the car as I get out, wind chucks under my chin with cold unfriendly fingers, somewhere a door is banging. It's pitch dark, not a soul around. Where is he? Someone must have taken him home with them. Why didn't they call? Who else might have come by this lonely lane? I walk round, the yard empty, area by gate empty, door to the school shut and, I try it, locked. Now I'm really scared, don't dare leave, don't know where to go next. Bushes caught by the wind, shaking wildly. Then out from the deep shadows by the gate a small figure steps, satchel over his shoulder, comes forward with a little brave smile, as if to say he'd always trusted I would come, had just waited to make sure it was me. He doesn't reproach me or say how cold or terrified he must have been. I touch his chubby child cheeks, tears are rolling down my face. He says, 'Don't worry Dad, I was only a bit scared, I knew you'd come.'

I am ill. Unable to walk more than twenty-five yards in a straight line without blowing like a porpoise. Eve is worried, but tries not to let me see. I think of the small children, how much they need their father, how Eve needs a husband. I can't let them down, I must survive. But I have already let Eve down. When we took on the house, we were going to do things together, I was going to hew wood, plant trees, mow lawns, dig flowerbeds. Had I done these things, or done as much as I could, would I be in this state? All those hours in front of a computer day after day, month after month without exercise, have told on my health. How did I ever let things get so bad? I remain at home in Sussex. Friends at the agency send parcels of books inscribed with get well messages. The heart problem is serious. How serious may be judged by the fact that it is three months before I go back to Shades.

I step into the game to find that all hell has broken loose. A full-scale war is in progress.

Branwell tells me, 'Barbarella and her mob are up in arms because Gawain wants to close the Bridal Suite.'

'Why?' I ask. The Bridal Suite is the room, upstairs in the inn, to which Morgan had whisked Dreamdancer after their nuptials.

'Mara took his cousin in there and tried to seduce him.'

'But Mara's always trying to seduce people. Mostly they just tell her to bugger off.'

'Yes,' says Branwell, 'but Gawain's cousin happens to be ten years old.'

It's a double-edged thing, the anonymity of a roleplaying game. It allows you to leave your real-life self behind and be in your imagination, all the things that in reality you are not. You can be witty, heroic, argumentative. You can discover what it feels like to be eighty-three, or Indonesian, or a flesh-eating dinosaur, or a sex siren. And since other players can also be whatever they choose, any form, shape, sex or size, you have no idea of who or what they are in real life. No way of knowing, for instance, that the person to whom you are making unsubtle sexual suggestions is a bewildered ten-year-old child.

The child, we will call him Madoc, had been spending the day at Gawain's house. Gawain was busy, so to keep the lad amused he logged him into Shades. A little while later he heard Madoc call out with a note of anxiety in his voice, 'Gawain, someone's talking to me and I don't know what they want.'

Gawain ran upstairs to find Madoc in the Bridal Suite with Mara.

'He yanked the plug out of the wall,' Branwell tells me. 'He's furious. He'd never thought, none of us had, that something like this would happen. Gawain's asking that the Bridal Suite be shut until a solution is found. He complained to the Coder.'

'So what happened?'

'The Coder shut all the "unsnoopable" rooms straight away. But Barbarella and her lot are agitating for them to be reopened.'

'But why? Surely Gawain's right, and the Coder is right?'

'Ah, but Barb and Co. say that Gawain had no business putting a child on the game in the first place. Bugsy is being particularly poisonous. He has apparently been saying that Gawain engineered the whole thing in order to cause trouble. That he stood over Madoc and watched it happen.'

'That's libellous, surely?'

'Yes, Gawain thinks so,' says Branwell. 'Unfortunately, people remember the HAWK business. A lot of players think that this whole thing is a ploy to seize power in the game, to stage a *coup d'état*, dethrone the Coder.'

'Have you ever tried making love in cyberspace?' Lilith asks me, adding 'I wouldn't bother on here.' (We are on Shades.) 'Sex on the Vortex is a subtle art. On here it's just coupling. Pity. I've always liked the room descriptions at the inn.'

The Travellers' Rest in Shades is a traditional English inn that smells of polish and last night's cooking. Guests go upstairs to a landing from which doors lead to private rooms. The largest door is to the east. Enter and it snicks closed of its own accord and locks itself behind you.

> *Bridal Suite*
> *The single dominant feature of this room is a very old and very large brass four poster . . . there is little other furniture, but then, who needs it with such a magnificent bed?*
>
> *Bridal Suite (in Bed)*
> *You are lying on a soft, comfortable bed though somehow you don't think sleep is the appropriate course of action . . . the bed itself is a wonderful brass four poster that creaks slightly each time you move, and fitted with white satin sheets that slither sensuously against you . . . All around the bed the fittings and fixtures on the room's walls seem to indicate you are in a bridal suite . . . a paler patch on the ceiling reveals there was once a mirror there.*

In this bed Morgan and Dreamdancer had consummated their Shades marriage. Hundreds of virtual copulations have taken place within its creaking frame. To this same bed Mara had tried to lure Madoc. Why had nobody considered the possibility that children might be brought here?

As people talk about the Mara affair more stuff comes to light, some of it disturbing, some funny. It transpires that a macho male character is being played by two fifteen-year-old schoolboys. The pair, who are known on Telecom Gold as the Gruesome Twosome, manage to get a bashful girl called Starlight into the Bridal Suite. Under their tutelage she rapidly blossoms into an accomplished houri. Gradually the lads realise that Starlight knows a great deal more about sex than they do. They confess their true identities. Starlight does likewise and they are mortified to discover that 'she' is in reality a forty-five year old gay man. According to Starlight, who relates the story with relish, the lads beg her/him to continue their education because, as one of them puts it, 'It's the first time either of us has been with a woman'.

Less amusing are the continuing activities of Mara. Since 'she' is known to like young females, Jarly creates a character called Jael ('Well she's bait, in't she?') who tells Mara she is fifteen years old. Mara asks Jael if she has ever 'been' with a woman. She tells her that sex between women is wonderful and asks Jael to meet her in real life. Jarly gives Mara his address. A few days later Dimitri's wife asks Jarly if he knows a girl called Jael. A thickset middle-aged man has been calling at the house, saying he has a message for her.

The anti-Gawain brigade step up their campaign to have the Bridal Suite reopened. Barb fires one of her 'barbs': she writes for an online magazine a fable in which a certain 'Gay Hussar' does his best to ruin the game by demanding the closure of the 'private booths' above the 'Fighting Cock Inn'. The homophobic jibes are ironic considering that Micronet was liberal enough to have opened the first 'Gay CUG' (closed user group) in UK cyberspace. Barb's friends take bets on how long the article will survive. Micronet's managers, sensitive to revelations about a child being exposed to sexual suggestions on a British Telecom network, and also fearful of offending their large group of gay customers, are bound to can it. The magazine is run by an Archwizard and an Archwitch whose duties include policing the game and quashing unsavoury behaviour. Amazingly, they decide to support the fable. Events spin rapidly out of control. Gawain mutters about libel. His enemies brand him a pompous twit. He protests that all he has done is voice concern for the well-being of children on Shades, a valid worry, since Shades runs not just on Micronet but also on Telecom Gold, which is actively trying to recruit schools. But this is forgotten as Barb and her friends transmute Gawain's complaint into Lucifer's crime, the unforgivable sin of disloyalty to the Coder and his creation.

To me, returning to Shades after months away, with friends in both camps, it seems that the players are behaving like members of a paranoid cult. A closed self-referential culture, with shared experience of addiction, shared conventions of behaviour, thought and expression, the use of purpose-made clichés to stop thought, a jargon incomprehensible to outsiders, a revered leader whose word cannot be questioned, the bitter hatred of renegades: these are hallmarks of religious cults. Cult punishments can include being locked in a cellar, or having your head forced down a toilet. The punishment demanded for Gawain by his enemies is 'the banishment of the Evil One who has appointed himself custodian of public behaviour'. Gawain angrily wonders out loud whether British Telecom would want the newspapers to learn about what sort of things are happening on its networks. Thus, for the first time, a threat is uttered against the life of Shades itself.

At this point the surreality of the cyberworld finally overwhelms reason. The 'Gay Hussar' article is spiked on orders from above and the Archwizard and Archwitch resign in protest. Messages supporting them flood the Micronet chatlines. On all sides fools are yelling about freedom and censorship. BT's managers, corporation men, not cybergypsies, can't understand why passions are so aroused. They sit tight and hope things will go quiet. But things get worse. The Coder is criticised for his responsible action of closing the Bridal Suite. The Barb brigade demand evidence that the room has ever been used for anything other than private chatting. No-one, it appears, has ever dreamed that it might be used for online sex. Online sex, what is that? Gawain, angry that his word should be questioned, alarmed by the backlash, starts to collect evidence.

One of the first players Gawain talks to is Starlight, who reveals that he has had many torrid sexual sessions in the Bridal Suite with a Micronet manager. 'He was brilliant with words,' said Starlight. 'He'd describe the whole thing in intimate detail, right from foreplay through to the climax. In the two years I've been playing Shades I must have regularly gone into the Bridal Suite with at least twenty people. There were no comments, no warnings from anyone in all that time.'

Within days the evidence fills a file. Being a methodical chap, Gawain types it up, indexes it and binds it in sections complete with a detailed contents page, appendices and glossary for non-cybergypsies. Meanwhile the murmurings against Gawain turn into a full blown hate campaign. Nasty attacks increase on the game's chatlines. We, his friends, begin helping him log messages, dates, times. All go into the file, which grows to a hefty dossier. It ends up containing one hundred and twenty-two pages. Gawain makes copies and gives one to me.

When his complaints drew no response from Micronet's officials, Gawain sank into a mythopoeic gloom. The injustice grew in his mind until it overshadowed all else. He sat on Shades, as Morgan had done before him, and complained to anyone who would listen, 'I've done nothing wrong. I'm a good player. Fair. Generous with newcomers, an honorable fighter. I was a responsible immortal. I was popular. Other players listened to my advice. Now the lowest mortals sneer at me.'

One of his friends, Elefizz the Jumbubble, advised, 'Go to the Coder. Only he can sort this out.'

Sofarsogood the Cautious said, 'The Coder sees more than the rest of us. If he does criticise you, you can be sure he has reason.'

Another friend, Billdaddy the Deadbeat said, 'The Coder don't punish but players who blow bad jazz. Look again. You're gonna find something ungroovy in the woodshed. But when you do, just slap the Man an apology and all will be copacetic.'

Gawain replied, 'Two things are sure, Hobo-daddy. You are a rotten roleplayer, and nobody wins an argument with the Coder.'

Then another player, Ellie the Jellydancing, came forward and said: 'You're all missing the point. Gawain, let's say you really are being unfairly treated. The point is, so what? Who are you – any of you – to question the Coder or what he does?'

Ellie said, 'Ask yourself, who are you? Your immortality is his work. Your eternal life is in his hand. He made you and he can unmake you. Just look at the wonderful things he has done. Out of nothing he conjured this creation. How marvellous, how intricate it is. Open your eyes, see how the mist is lifting off the river. Could you have made it happen? Look at how the dust devils are stirring and whirling leaves into the air. Whose imagination brought these to life? Do you feel the first damp gusts, as clouds unpile above? See how the light goes green and the trees shine like thunder. My heart throbs like a tom-tom for – hear how the forest roars – he is coming. Gawain, prepare to meet your Coder. Now that the time has come, Gawain, with what words will you speak to him? Do you know his language, the secret code that causes rain to fall at his command "Rain!"? Lightning flashes and bangs the clouds like drums. Open your ears and listen to how the fat raindrops are beginning to hit: one, a spatter, hundreds. Notice the goodly smell of rain on dry ground. All this, he makes. He tells the rain "Rain!" and it sheets down, already a waterfall hangs from the mouth of this cave and out in the game people and animals lit by eerie flashes are running for shelter. How the wind climbs in the leaves, moans in hollow trees and shrieks in crevices of rock; all the instruments of the world are tuned to welcome him; the storm approaches; trees, rocks, mountains shout at his approach; the earth roars like a beaten drum; see, Gawain, how the rain spears flash, shining, lit by jags of lightning; the loud air is howling, the hairs of my body stand on end, and up on us bursts the hurricane.'

As Ellie spoke these last words it grew utterly dark, then the wind held its breath and a golden glow grew in the north and rushed towards them. White fire erupted silently in the cave called *Lost in Darkness* and out of the storm, the Coder spoke to Gawain:

'Whose ignorant words question my creation?
Stand up and be a man.
I will ask the questions and you shall answer.
Where were you, when I laid this world's foundations?
Explain to me, if you understand,
who measured its dimensionless space?
Pillared on nothingness, how do its foundations stand?
The myriad creatures that roam the land,

do you know who made them? Who gave life to them,
mouse and deer, gumby, bat and baragoon?
The bear that snuffles in the forest,
clawing for tubers, did you teach him how also
to crouch on the riverbank
and scoop out the flashing salmon with his paw?
Did you give the Morloch his strength,
or fashion his googling eye?'

Gawain said, 'I have said my piece, I'll say no more.'

Then the Coder said to Gawain: 'Stand up and be a man.
I will ask the questions and you shall answer.
Consider that most powerful of creatures,
the mighty leech in his stagnant lair,
how he lashes the deep pools with his tail
stirring up foam like lather in a shaving cup;
how his dark and slithering form
turns the river to white hair in his wake
and leaves a shining trail on the rocks all around.
Can you set a hook in his jaw,
thread a cord through his nostril or lasso his tongue?
Even great wizards armed with weapons of power like
the deadly ninja throwing cabbage, or mild unassuming rat,
cannot dent this worm's hide nor scaly skull,
his eyes of adamantine pierce them coldly,
his breath overcomes them and they fall,
and so does even the greatest of immortals taste death.'

Finally Gawain uses the dossier. He sends one copy to Sir Iain Vallance, Chairman of British Telecom, and another to his Member of Parliament, but two weeks later, the chatline is still clogged with violent messages, getting nastier. The Shades players are gripped by a collective madness, obsessed with revenge on Gawain. They talk of nothing else. The Archwizards are cheered whenever they appear. Barbarella and her friends strut like heroes. I am amazed at the success of their propaganda. Shades has become an evil soap opera. People want trouble, and trouble, in the form of the next Shades meet, is looming.

Late at night, on the Saturday before the meet, messages start appearing on the chatline, speculating about what will happen if Gawain dares to show his face at the Goat and Compass.

'Probably be a real life bloodbath . . .' writes one.

'Bloodbath??? Naaaa,' replies another. *'We just explain a few points to a few people who'll then join us as we pull on the white pointed hoods, get in our motors and go out for a quiet night's firebombing.'*

'If I get hold of the gutless wonders who keep on runnin' (the Archwitch) down', writes a third, *'I'm gonna firebomb em and I don't care if my subscription is cancelled* (sic). *If anyone fancies giving me Gawain's address I will make sure he never walks again let alone write or use a computer!!!'*

Two hours later comes the reply: *'Anyone wanna send Gawain a letter. His address is 36, Paradise Avenue, London SW14.'*

Immortality is much overrated in cyberspace. People think that cyber-realms will last forever, that we may all one day be discarnate intelligences inhabiting a net without end, forever and ever. But cyber-realms die and even Coders are not omnipotent. I write a fax and send it to the office of Sir Iain Vallance. It quotes the firebomb posts and airs one of the weirder aspects of the affair.

> *Countless mischievous and insulting messages have been posted on the Shades chatline. One of these stated that Mr Gawain had 'drooled' over his ten year old cousin being corrupted in the Bridal Suite. There could hardly be a clearer libel. Yet I understand that Micronet justified their failure to remove this message from the Shades chatline on the extraordinary grounds that 'it might be true'. By the same logic they should not object if I were to post a preposterous message stating that you, sir, have AIDS. After all, it* might *be true. Why, when Micronet knew that a hate campaign was in progress against Mr Gawain, was the Shades chatline not properly monitored? The 'firebomb' threat should not have been allowed to remain up for three minutes, let alone three hours. Mr Vallance, when will your company wake up to its responsibilities?*

The response is immediate. Next morning, the Shades chatline, and all the other chatlines, are shut. With their closure, Micronet is doomed. Within weeks the funeral notices are going out. On the last night, all the Shades players are invited to a party in the Bridal Suite. To mark the occasion, each of them is given the demigodly powers of an Archwizard or -witch. Dozens of characters pile into the great bed. Almost every Shades player who ever was is here, laughing as if midnight will never come. As the hour approaches, their hilarity builds. Finally there are only minutes left. Then only one minute. Together they count down to the end of the world. Ten . . . nine . . . eight . . . in the minds of the watchers, in those last few seconds, the ground shakes, lightning flashes above the forests . . . seven . . . six . . . they are shouting out the numbers now . . . five . . . four . . . the city walls begin to crumble, the castle's black towers tremble, totter and slowly start to fall . . . THREE! . . . TWO! . . . In the last second, lightning glares across a world collapsing, towers, trees and ruined city shimmer, vanish and are seen no more.

Dear Jeffrey Archer

The end of October 1991 and winter's creeping again down the Kurdish mountains. The *Simple Truth* concert raised £57 million, but people in Kurdistan are saying that little of it has reached them. Sarbast writes to ask how the money was distributed. No reply. We seem to be back to the situation before the concert where they don't acknowledge our existence. It's rumoured that some of the money has been given to the Iraqi Red Crescent. No-one seriously believes this since the IRC is thought to be under the thumb of Saddam.

'Let's ask Jeffrey Archer to help us find out what has happened to the money,' says Handren. 'He helped us before.'

I have an idea. 'We'll write an open letter and publish it in the *Guardian*: "Dear Mr Archer, what happened to the money?"'

'He will sue,' says Sarbast. 'Assuredly, he will sue.'

'Why should he? The Kurdish people are grateful to him. So are we. We'll say so. We are not suggesting that the money has gone astray. The point is that we don't know where it has gone and we can't get any answers. So we are asking him, as our friend, to help us find out.'

The letter to Jeffrey Archer runs as a full page ad in the *Guardian* under the headline, 'Dear Mr Archer, Kurdish children are still dying'. We take great care not to insult Archer, because he has done so much to help, nor to imply that there has been any impropriety in the way the money was handled. I post the text in *mideast.kurds* on Greennet (where it remains to this day).

'Dear Mr Archer,' the text begins, 'In Kurdistan you're a hero. Little children know the syllables of your name . . .'

News comes in from the Middle East of a new wave of mass killings. Reports from the villages of Makkadeh, Libnah, Gezer and Eglon speak of remorseless slaughter. In these places not a single person is spared in a series of incidents blamed on fundamentalist militias. In the regions of Horim and Ammon killings and lootings are widely reported. Meanwhile in a settlement on the old site of Jericho, the population is murdered and the buildings set on fire. The sole surviving inhabitant is a woman who tells reporters, 'They killed every living thing in the place, men and women, young and old, even the cattle.' In Hormah every man, woman and child is executed. After razing a settlement at Hesbon, a fundamentalist troop commander boasts to newsmen, 'We utterly destroyed the men and the women and the little ones.' In the Moab rural district thousands are systematically murdered for their religious beliefs. Fundamentalist armed groups decapitate hundreds of victims and display their heads. In Midian province men are killed, women and children taken away as slave labour. Amnesty International's press release says: MASS KILLINGS AND CRUELTIES ORDERED, COMMITTED, APPROVED BY FUNDAMENTALIST LEADER.

The leader orders the extra-judicial execution of two hundred and fifty political opponents. When their supporters protest, he uses a biological weapon – according to some reports a strain of the deadly *Yersinia pestis* bacillus – causing nearly 15,000 deaths. The leader, whose real name is not allowed to be revealed, thrives on a culture of secrecy. His public appearances grow fewer. He is said to change his appearance often, possibly in a bid to thwart assassins, and forbids images of himself to be made or displayed. Surviving propaganda materials show an elderly, white bearded man.

The leader, known only by a cipher, displays signs of paranoia. He orders the deaths of 3,000 of his own officers whose loyalty he suspects. Fears are expressed about his unstable frame of mind. He possesses a terrifying arsenal of biological weapons and the ability to hit cities throughout the region with ground to ground missiles. He detonates a weapon of massive yield against a hostile army. The towns of Dosmo and Mogharro are hit by missiles which rain down 'fire and brimstone'. This same leader, earlier in his career, wiped out every living thing, both human and animal, over an area which extended to the entire planet, the only survivors being a man called Noah and his immediate family.

The above is the burden of a long message which appears in the *NuKE the World* echo.

Area 18: Nuke The World
From: Jesus Slut Fucker Sent
To: All Msg #9, Sep-04-93 12:26:36
Subject: True Nature of the Christian God

What is the nature of the Jehovah God? Many times we like to see him as Spirit and Truth, other times as Love incarnate. Perhaps we could look at the not so nice God to get a better look at his real, no-gloss, raw character.

'It's poignant,' said Lilith, when I related the story to her. 'For you, doubly so.' (Lilith, who appears to think only of pleasure, never responds when I suggest she think about joining Amnesty.)

'You're forgetting, Bear, that God's objective in all this was the suppression of female deities. Remind me to tell you about my namesake some time. These things happen when men take their hands off their willies and start playing with guns. If politics were forbidden to males and only women allowed to rule, none of these things would happen.'

'Margaret Thatcher is a woman.'

'Wrong,' she says, 'she is an honorary man.'

Handren, Sarbast and I are hanging around in the lobby of the Queen Elizabeth Hall, a huge conference centre which stands right across the square from the Houses of Parliament and Big Ben. We've just spent two hours in a public meeting listening to speaker after speaker, including guest of honour Jeffrey Archer, praise the Red Cross's efforts in Kurdistan.

'Quick, he's coming.'

On cue, the stocky figure appears, leading a flying wedge of charity fundraisers and Red Cross officials at a brisk pace towards us. Archer talks over his shoulder as he walks, glancing from left to right but never behind him, gesturing with his hands as he makes a point or gives an order.

I thrust Handren forward and say, 'Right, now's our chance. Get out there and introduce yourself.'

But Handren, sweet fellow that he is, picks this moment to feign shyness. The opportunity is, literally, passing. I step out of the crowd and plant myself in his path.

'Mr Archer, I and my colleagues from the Kurdish Disaster Fund would like the chance of a word with you.'

'Oh?' He stops. One can almost hear his brain chirring. Kurdish Disaster Fund? Then recognition settles like a mask upon his face.

'You're the people who placed the open letter in the *Guardian*. I've been wanting to talk to you.'

'Good, we were hoping you'd contact us.'

'Yes, indeed. I was most surprised by your letter, as I had not seen a copy of it beforehand. To which of my addresses did you send it?'

'We didn't.'

'You didn't send me a copy?'

'No,' I say. 'Sorry, I suppose we should have.'

'Surely,' says Jeffrey Archer, 'it is not just customary, but simple good manners, to show a letter to the person to whom it's addressed, before you publish it?'

'Yes, but we were afraid that if we'd showed it to you first, you'd stop us publishing it.'

By now a small crowd of people has gathered round us and the Red Cross officials are hovering.

'I can very well understand that,' he says, 'but it's scarcely an excuse. You know very well that you should have had the courtesy to send me a copy first.'

'You are right and we are sorry, but we were desperate,' says Handren, finding his voice at last.

'We tried to reach you many times, but we could never get through,' says Sarbast.

Archer looks from one of us to the other.

'I am the fool who wrote it,' I say, and tap my chin. 'So if you can't forgive us, you had better stick one here.'

Archer looks surprised. 'As a matter of fact, I am rather angry with you. I think you had better all come to see me.' He rounds on a nervous assistant standing behind him. 'Nadhim, when can I see these gentlemen?'

'Friday, at 7.30 a.m.,' replies the assistant instantly.

'Nadhim is Kurdish,' whispers Sarbast to me.

'Come to my office at 7 a.m. on Friday,' Archer tells us. 'We will have an hour and a half together. Nadhim will sort out the details. Goodnight.'

He sweeps onward in a cloud of lackeys.

On the steps outside, watching his entourage depart, Sarbast says, 'Did you notice he never asked us would the time suit us?' He adds happily, 'I do not think I have ever met anyone so important.'

Friday morning, mist rising off the river, a barge bound down to the docks raising a khaki bow ripple, unquieting the water between us and the Palace of Westminster. The three of us, washed and brushed, present ourselves at the door of the famous apartment.

'This is where he holds the political lunches,' whispers Handren. 'The Prime Minister comes here often. Mrs Thatcher too. Edward told me this. He says that Jeffrey Archer serves always shepherd's pie with Krug champagne.'

Edward is Edward Pilkington of the *Guardian*, one of the few journalists to show an interest in the Kurds before the crisis.

'Why Krug champagne?' asks Sarbast.

'I do not know,' replies Handren solemnly. 'Edward did not say.'

The door opens and a female assistant leads us into an airy apartment that occupies one whole floor of the building. Windows wrap right the way round. We are high over London, looking out across a wide sweep of the city, with a spectacular view across to Parliament and Big Ben. The assistant ushers us past a huge dining table – it rivals Gawain's – into a seating area where white sofas surround a low glass table bearing ziggurats of art books. On the furthest sofa the secretary Nadhim sits bolt upright. Beside him, equally ill at ease, is another Kurd. Jeffrey Archer, peering over his spectacles like an old fashioned schoolmaster, rises smiling from the central sofa and invites us to be seated. Sarbast, Handren and I perch in a row along the edge of the third sofa.

The new Kurd is called Brosk. We introduce ourselves. First Handren, stiffly, like a soldier on defaulters.

Sarbast mumbles his name. 'On behalf of the KCC, Mr Archer, I would like to thank you for all that you have done . . .'

'And Bear . . .' says Archer, jotting on a pad.

Handren whispers, 'The tables, they are from science fiction.'

The female assistant brings in coffee, lukewarm and weak, as Archer launches into a well-rehearsed rebuke.

'I am very cross with you people. You have used my name to obtain publicity for your cause. If you really needed my help, why did you not simply come to me?'

'We tried . . .', Sarbast begins, but Archer holds up a hand.

'What you have done has unfairly and despicably cast doubts on my genuine effort to help your countrymen. It harms all of us. It has caused a lot of people – a lot of influential people, I may add – to question whether you were worth helping. They say to me, "Jeffrey, you should never have got involved with them". They say, "After all you have done, they are so ungrateful". What am I to reply?'

'Mr Archer, we are very sorry if . . .' stutters Handren.

'You must know only too well,' Archer, looking at him, carries on, 'how little help your people had received. How little was being done. I worked eighteen hours a day to get that concert organised. I put myself on the line. I went cap in hand to governments for money. I sought, and obtained, a prime TV channel for an entire evening. Do you have any idea what that kind of exposure is worth?'

I make some mental calculations. He is right. Several hours of television beamed to an audience of two hundred million – the time alone might be worth fifty million pounds.

'You know that I have worked hard for your people and I did not have to,' Archer is saying. 'I don't look for gratitude, but I do not expect to be abused.'

I glance at Handren. He looks wretched. Sarbast too. I feel the same. Our ad had seemed so clever and righteous. Now we see what a shabby trick we have played.

'I saw the Prime Minister at the weekend,' says Archer. 'He said to me, "Jeffrey, you should pick your friends more carefully".'

'Is the Prime Minister a family friend?'

'I was at a party,' Archer continues, glaring at me through the gap between his frowning brows and the rim of his spectacles, 'and I met a friend who also happens to be a cousin of the Queen. He said, "Jeff, what is this? What have you been doing to the Kurds? Is this serious?" Now I want this stopped. Do I make myself clear?'

'Mr Archer,' says Handren, 'we apologise for our bad manners. We admire what you have done for us. We do not . . .'

Archer gestures to Nadhim, who hands him a newspaper. Upside down, I recognise our ad.

'You say here that £57 million was enough to have solved all your people's problems,' says Archer, reading from the page. 'Of course you must know that is simply naive nonsense.'

He throws the paper aside.

'I am working hard to find out exactly where all the money went, but I have not the slightest doubt that it has been wisely and properly distributed. I understand that, as Kurds, you are concerned about the situation in your homeland. In my view, rightly. But let me tell you that if you persist in doing this sort of thing I will stop helping. I will walk away and wash my hands of you.'

'Mr Archer, we are not ungrateful,' says Sarbast. 'We are extremely thankful for everything you have done. But we were frustrated and we felt . . .'

The female secretary comes in and says, 'Jeffrey, Lynda's on the phone for you.'

Archer goes over to a large desk on which are three telephones, one of them red. He sits, picks up the red phone, watching us.

'Yes Lynda, good of you to call . . . Thank you . . . As it happens, I am sitting here with five Kurds . . .' He looks at me. 'Correction. I am sitting here with four Kurds and Bear . . . Yes, quite . . . Very good of you to say so. I shall acquaint them with your views . . .'

'That was Baroness Chalker who, as I am sure you know, is one of Her Majesty's Ministers. She asks me to tell you that she thinks you are ungrateful wretches and that many cabinet colleagues to whom she has spoken agree with her.'

But he is smiling.

'You will be delighted to hear that Lynda told me her team has despatched twenty trucks of Heinz beans.'

'Oh that is most excellent news,' says Sarbast.

Archer beams at him.

'Very well, I've had my grouse. I am not a vindictive man and I don't bear grudges, so I'll accept your apology and we'll consider the matter closed. Now then, what can I do for you?'

'Well,' says Sarbast, reaching into his pocket for the list . . .

As we are leaving Archer takes me aside.

'Bear, you wrote this advertisement. I want you to write another one. Do you think you can do that?'

'Of course.'

'This time, I want you to play fair. Be positive. Let's talk about what has been achieved. Here is my fax number. Let me have your draft as soon as possible. I suggest something along the lines of "Dear Mr Archer, thank you for all your help".'

'Ohmygod, ohmygod, ohmygod,' says Sarbast.

When Jeffrey Archer asked what he could do for us, Handren and Sarbast instantly produced our long list of wants. Would he assist our appeal? Would he visit the Kurdish Cultural Centre?

Archer turned to his secretary.

'Nadhim, when is the soonest I can do this?'

'Next Tuesday at 11 a.m., if we reschedule your briefing with the Ambassador.'

'I will be at your centre at 11 a.m. on Tuesday,' said Archer. 'I can give you exactly one hour.'

We are in their favourite caff, somewhere near the Kurdish Cultural Centre sitting in greasy disbelief over plates of fried egg, beans and chips and huge mugs of tea. It is eight-thirty and the streets are full of the London rush hour.

'Jeffrey Archer's coming,' yelps Sarbast in a panic. 'Jeffrey Archer is coming to the Centre. Ohmygod, what are we going to do?'

'Just show him all the good work,' I say.

'No, no, Bear, you do not understand. It is the Kurdish tradition to give a gift to a guest. But you saw his apartment. What gift could we possibly offer to such a man?'

'What about a nice Kurdish rug?' asks Handren.

'What need has he of Kurdish rugs?' says Sarbast. 'He who drinks only Krug champagne?'

'How about some Krug champagne?' tries Handren.

Something comes back to me, a conversation with my friend, the Indian bookseller Pustaq Keet, whose family originates from a town in what is now the Pakistani part of the Punjab. He told me that in the turbulent times after the partition of India, his father would write songs, often satirising politicians or eulogising heroes of the freedom struggle, and sing them on street corners, hawking the lyrics at six *paisé* for a demi-octavo booklet. It was an honorable journalistic tradition called *qissa*, which dated from the days before newsprint and radio, and was practised by thousands of bards all over the country.

'Sarbast, in Kurdistan are there poets, balladeers, people who turn news into songs and sing them in the mountain villages?'

'I have not heard of it, but surely it must be so.'

'In that case, isn't it likely that there will be songs about the war and about the great friend of the Kurds, Mr Jeffrey Archer?'

'Certainly it is likely.'

'We have two days to find such a song, learn the words and tune and get it recorded here in London. When Jeffrey Archer comes to the Centre we will present him with the tape.'

'Bear, this is impossible. There is only one telephone in Kurdistan and that is a satellite phone in Suleimaniya. It is under the control of the *peshmergas*, the guerillas. You have to ring and make an appointment and they have to fetch the person you want at the right time.'

I inform Eve that three carloads of Kurdish musicians and poets are on their way to our overgrown house in Sussex.

'How lovely' she says absentmindedly. 'What for?'

'To compose a song in praise of Jeffrey Archer.'

'Oh Bear, what a good idea. Will they be wanting lunch?'

'I've had this idea for a lyric,' I tell them when we're settled. 'Something to get us started: *"The great Archer with his bow drives away winter, his arrows melt the snow, they bring messages of hope, they drive back our enemies . . ."*'

The poets just look at me.

I leave to brew tea. Kurds like it black, served in glasses with a sprig of mint (from the herb garden) and a sugarcube to hold in their teeth and suck through. On my return, I find them sprawled across sofas, legs flung over the arms of chairs, sunk in attitudes of deep concentration. The poets are tugging their moustaches. From time to time they reach for their pencils and jot. The musicians hum little airs that tail off into silence. Sarbast, looking worried, hugs his knees. Handren leans back and smiles inscrutably at the ceiling. Without warning, a small man called Goran opens his throat and sings. His words must be telling, because the others break into loud applause. Over lunch, they make Goran sing his song several times.

Cry (a song by Rzgar Goran for Jeffrey Archer)

how many more poison years must pass?
how many autumn-leaf springs?
how long will Zuhak[1] glut on our flesh,
our young feed his cravings?

will it never set, this moon of blood?
when will love come back to Kurdistan?

will no-one speak? call an end
to burned barns, beggars in the snow,
dead bairns against whose killers
no voices are raised, no policemen go?

the gases burn us, we howl, we burn to live
when will love come back to Kurdistan?

will the scent of almonds ever again mean
clouds of petals, not death from above?
when will they stop hanging Mem in front of Zin[2],
how long will they torture love?

we cry, but in the darkness there is silence,
O God, we are alone, just us and you

1. Zuhak, a tyrant of legend, once ruled the Kurds. He wore snakes coiled round his arms and, the stories say, fed them on the brains of Kurdish children.

2. The Kurdish Romeo and Juliet.

Eve has been a lot happier since Shades died. 'It's another chance, Bear, after your heart warning. It's time you got back to something like a normal life. Please,' she says. 'The children and I need you.'

'Don't worry,' I tell her, 'this time I'll give it up.'

But of course, I don't. The demise of Micronet has left Shades addicts seeking a new fix. Luna & Co., concerned at the number of outsiders who have begun turning up in their woods, do their best to make the refugees unwelcome. They even spread a rumour that the Vortex is a myth. But the homeless nomads soon melt away among the wandering hordes: the cybergypsies are a worldwide nation whose games and bulletin boards span the globe. For me, this is the start of a new era of exploration. One of my favourite discoveries is a San Francisco system called *& the Temple of the Screaming Electron,* whose sysop, Enigma, publishes a *Weird Stuff Source List.* A firm called Nuclear Research will sell you, for $15, instructions for making Astrolite, 'the most powerful non-nuclear explosive ever developed, more powerful than TNT, C-4 plastic, nitroglycerin, or PBXN-1'. A firm in Peoria, Illinois, will kit you out in strait-jackets, leg irons, iron neck-collars, slave helmets, leather undies, 'all the latest fashions in bondage and restraint apparatus'. From a man in Phoenix you can buy 90,000 volt electroshock batons.

& the Temple of the Screaming Electron is by no means the weirdest cybergypsy system. A few others: *Arkham, The Butterfly Effect, Black Axis, The Flying Teapot, Rainbow's End, Lies Unlimited, Sea of Noise, Fourth Reich, KRoNiC FaTiGue, Event Horizon, Chaos Computer Club, Ninja Cult, Just Mooting, The Bearded Clam, Doomstrike!, The Pig Pen, Quarto Mundista, The Beatles Fan Club, Phantom Zone, Shrine of the Salted Slug, Almost ate 5 Smoked Armadillo, NANoTEkSYBErPHUk.*

Without visiting these bulletin boards, you have no way of knowing to what tastes they pander. Most carry underground files. One promotes out-and-out anarchy. One specialises in human rights and environmental action. One or two dabble in pirated commercial software. One is run by a lawyer who has made it a database of legal information. One serves up hardcore porn. One hosts an organisation that is trying to clean up the sad reputation of the net. One was busted by the police (Nasty Ned's work, it's rumoured). One is in Vladivostok. One is run by a decent police sergeant who is dedicated to protecting free speech on the net. One is a base for some of the world's best known hackers. One is run by the author of a lethal computer virus. And one of them is mine.

The Butterfly Effect is set up as a Fidonet node, to be a focus for human rights and green issues. It carries all our Kurdish news. Every night I take Amnesty's Urgent Action alerts off Greennet and relay them to Fidonet. We start an online Amnesty group. Old friends Todd and Lori, new to cyberspace, take over part of the board for a 'personal development workshop' called Waterwheel. Graeme and I open a members-only section which we call *The Cybergypsy Club* and Graeme uploads to it a technothriller he is writing about a cybergypsy chief who gets mixed up in a flying saucer flap. Geno calls once in a while but, chary of bills, never stays long, thus proving himself to have more sense than me. Branwell drops in every night at eleven for a game of chess. Luna, taking great care not to leave a traceable number, calls to argue obscure points of hermetic philosophy. Lilith often pops on to tell me about her latest conquests. *The Butterfly Effect*, a tiny speck of light in the galaxy of systems that form the global net, is soon home to a small group of ragged-arsed philanthropists: a strange mix of human rights enthusiasts, environmentalists, technopagans, cyber-sutrans, virus folk and roleplayers. Among them is a mysterious Irishman who calls himself Gliomach.

Gliomach's game

The next challenge for our do-gooding company Chaos comes from the Northern Ireland Community Relations Council, which wants to know whether a mass media campaign can do anything to promote peace in the province. It seems clear that conventional advertising will achieve nothing. Well-intentioned messages cut no ice in Belfast, where the paramilitaries are in any case the best copywriters. A campaign in the seventies used the slogan 'Seven years is enough'. All the republicans had to do was insert a / into the first gap and scrawl above it the word 'hundred'.

Casting about for something that might actually work, we hit on the plan (never before attempted, so far as we know) of basing a campaign on the principles of conflict resolution. The science is in its infancy, but Greennet is linked to a host of other positively inspired networks like Econet, Peacenet and Conflictnet, where we learn that to have any hope of tackling an intractable conflict, each side must:

a) recognise and accept the fact of conflict
b) talk frankly about its fears, grievances and hopes
c) listen to the other party do likewise
d) use structured roleplay sessions to *experience* the other view

One of our wilder ideas is to create an online roleplaying 'world', to be accessed by schools all over Northern Ireland. In cyberspace, children will meet in a context devoid of the labels and tags which identify them as one tribe or the other. Accent, clothes, hairstyle – none of these things matter. They will play the usual Northern Irish game of cross-questioning to place one another, but it won't be easy when they can never *really* be sure who anyone else is. All they will know is what the other person tells them. Nothing can be known of them save what they choose to say about themselves. People soon learn that in cyberspace, it is not always necessary nor appropriate to stick with the truths of the real world. Sooner or later, curiosity or mischief will lead them to experience what it is like to 'kick with the other foot'. Inevitably, they will form friendships, like the one that has grown up between me and Luna, based solely on direct experience of one another.

The world we create will not be like Shades, with its emphasis on conflict. It will be based, like the Vortex, on co-operation, with powers being gained by acquiring 'social points' which can only be given by other players. The nicer you are, the better you do. But abandoning the live/die, either/or model makes puzzles harder to devise and rewards trickier to dispense. We need a coder who is willing to take on the complex algorithms of co-operation. I canvas the idea on *The Butterfly Effect* and one user responds, a stranger who calls himself Gliomach. He can code, is intrigued by our idea. He also happens to be Irish.

The snag is that Gliomach, like Luna, is obsessive about privacy. I tell him that I will be making several trips to Belfast over the next few months and offer to meet him. Gliomach is not enthusiastic. He says it is his policy to keep his net life and real life separate. He refuses to divulge a real identity, or provide an address, telephone or fax number, fidonet node number or internet email address.

'If you want to meet me, you'll have to find me first,' he says.

All he will reveal for certain is that he lives in a remote corner of the country 'where the Atlantic first sloshes on Irish rock'.

Jarly makes good

We've just finished firing the International President. A rag-tag of directors has assembled in the boardroom to hear the official story of his departure. (We all already know the real story.) We are informed that the agency finds itself in possession of a yacht moored in Cannes. Cheers. We are informed that the agency will not be retaining yacht. Groans. Business complete, I hop down the back stairs, hoping to catch Jarly in the computer room before he leaves for the day. I have big news for him.

Remarkable. Past seven, but Jarly's still at his screen.

'Trying to get these figures out, Bear, for the new president.'

'What are they?'

'Income and expenditure for our top ten accounts broken down by year, quarter, month – and also job by job. Cross-referenced to figures for similar brands, er, elsewhere.'

'Oh no, Jarly, you have not . . .'

He chuckles. 'Despite our moronic managing director, Bear, I can still make good use of my modem.'

'Jarly, you must not hack our competitors. Please. Promise, and then I'll pass on the message from our moronic managing director.'

'Okay,' he says. 'Fire away.'

'Well, he's giving you a pay rise.'

'What? The same fucker who doesn't like hobbyist fantasies?'

'He likes what he's getting now.'

The agency pays vast sums of money for information, some of it online, much of it in expensive reports. Every month, thousands of megabytes of data flow in from rolling attitude surveys. But Jarly wanted quicker and deeper access to this data than its owners were willing to provide. It was Gawain who told me that Jarly had gone snorkelling in a government think tank. He'd been boasting about it, saying that a hacker's life is improved by being paid to do what he enjoys. Gawain warned me that Jarly's 'econometric studies' very likely also took in a famous forecasting centre, commercial databases, the National Institute for Economic Affairs, the Office of the Census, various government departments, possibly even a Treasury computer.

The man himself denies all this. 'I've done nowt illegal,' he says, rocking in his chair. I notice that his old stained trainers have been replaced by a rather natty looking pair of suede boots.

'I've just reorganised things,' he says, 'to save meself work. They were doing it the hard way. I did some patches to speed stuff up, short cut stuff.'

I pray the network manager, Pat, never finds out that Jarly has reverse-engineered the software that runs the agency's systems. Nobody, not even me, knows what else he has been up to, but his innovations have made him a hit with every executive in the place. The team working on the biggest client have asked that he be assigned exclusively to them, offers will soon be winging in from other agencies. Hence the MD's move. Jarly's jaw unwires when I reveal what the man intends to pay him.

'Another thing,' I say. 'He'll give you a company car. Anything you like within reason.'

'Fuck,' says Jarly. 'Fuck, fuck, fuck. Shades addict makes good.'

He looks at me thoughtfully. 'Bear. If I can do it so can you.'

Silk Cunt

Alastair (aldopacific) emails me a polemic he has written against tobacco advertising, which he says promotes a necrophiliac culture that worships death. He is coming to London and wants to visit me at the agency. We speak on the phone. He rails against Saatchi's work for Silk Cut.

'That slash in the fabric, the shape of the tear, the colour of the silk, purple, it's obvious what it is.'

'What?'

'It's a cunt.'

The shock of the word in his soft Scottish voice.

'It's a cunt,' he repeats. 'Silk Cunt'.

A week later, he enters my office to be greeted by an array of roughs for Benson & Hedges posters. I am dreading his reaction, but in the event he says, 'I saw you as someone who was on the side of life. How fascinating that you do this sort of work too.'

Alastair explains his theory to me, pointing out that the famous surreal Benson & Hedges posters all contain references to death or imprisonment. A gold cigarette packet inside a bird cage, as the bait on a mousetrap, caught in a Venus flytrap. I suggest that the person who created the images saw the gold box as something precious, tempting. I know from experience that, contrary to the beliefs of its critics, advertising people do not have the time or intelligence to encode messages so deeply. At least not consciously.

'What if,' Alastair says, 'I respond to that gold packet not as a precious thing, but a lure to addiction and death? Suppose I take the health warnings at face value as saying, "I promise to kill you."'

'It means,' I say, 'that while I am an advocate of life, I am also a peddlar of death.'

Alastair points out to me the ways in which the ideas on my

wall cash in on the death-urge. There are scribbles of a silvery tuna fish lying on a piano keyboard; a bull with the lighted fuse of an anarchist's bomb poking from its mouth; an insect-like branch clutching the golden pack. Alastair sees the black piano as a coffin, complete with brass keyhole. The fish is clearly a dead thing, as is the ambulatory branch. I explain that the campaign is a series of puzzles, visual presentations of verbal puns. Fish-on-keyboard is 'piano-tuner'. Ox-about-to-explode signifies 'a-bom-in-a-ble'. The crawling branch is a 'walking-stick'.

'No dark intentions,' I tell Alastair. 'I thought of the fish after we had the piano-tuner round. He's blind. His father leads him in and sits him down at the piano. The explosive bull came from a friend in Cornwall who composes crosswords, he's hardly very sinister, a friendly wood-elf who likes folk music, real ale and campaigns to save trees. The stick was from a book I had as a child, about a boy who finds a magic walking stick. When he waves it, it whirls him away to other realities.'

'I *know* that book,' shouts Alastair. 'In one part he finds himself on a desert island being chased by cannibals.'

Cannibals? Death? Well, maybe Alastair is right. Maybe in my search for picture puns, I unconsciously choose the thanatic ones.

I don't dare to tell Alastair about my other dilemma. The agency has decided to pitch for the account of British Nuclear Fuels, which operates the controversial Thorp reprocessing plant at Sellafield in Cumbria. The managing director wants me to create the concepts. I go to see a friend in a green organisation and tell her, 'I need facts to convince the agency that we shouldn't touch it. These allegations that the place caused leukaemias in Seascale – you must have the facts. Give them to me and I'll put them to the people here.'

'Unfortunately, it's not that simple. I wish we could pin it on them, but the evidence isn't watertight.'

'Well what the fuck am I to do?'

'Why not do the pitch? We might learn something.'

Mailbomber vs nailbomber

I catch Geno in the small hours, in a rage because he has just read the latest issue of the NuKE journal.

>rock steady has filled the fucking nuke #7 journal with stuff about making bombs. could this be the same teenage mutant ninja cocksucker who was lecturing me about nuke sysops being "responsible and mature" when i gave sara the finger last month?

Sara is Sara Gordon, the anti-virus researcher. Geno sends me the open message addressed to Rock Steady he is planning to post on the NuKE the World echo:

'Have you ever seen the end results of a bomb? As a health care worker in a large hospital I have. Two years ago I seen the results of a nail bomb that some other irresponsible asswipe planted. Two patients came to our ICU more dead than alive and passed away in a matter of hours. A 17 year old girl who was just walking down the street in front of the house (crack house) caught a quarter inch piece of steel in the back of her neck. She will never walk or be able to move her arms again. She shits all over herself because she has no bowel control. I wish that every worthless piece of shit that distributes this kind of trash would have to help take care of her for a month or two. Perhaps then you could begin to see the consequences of your actions. You make me sick.'

>this is the real world, bear, it's the streets of oklahoma city not some fucking cyberfantasy

The managing director comes to see me and says, 'Bear, have you decided to do the nuclear pitch?'

'Yes,' I say, remembering the conversation with my friend.

'Good. Glad you remember who pays your wages.' He drops a memo onto my desk. 'By the way, this came to me. You'll want to comment.'

To: Managing Director
cc: Company lawyer
From: Network Manager
Re: BEAR

This is to inform you of my deep concern at the discovery of numerous *viruses* that have been found on a laptop that Bear has used in the past. As you can imagine I am more than a little annoyed at the *immaturity* of this action for if one or more of these viruses had somehow strayed onto the Network System, the results could have been *disastrous*.

The PC in question is one of the old type. It has a directory called VIRUS where all the viruses seem to be resident so I am sure that these viruses were put on this PC deliberately. (See list.) It should be sent away to a computer specialist so that it can be dealt with *professionally* with Bear footing the bill. The Studio Manager has been notified of the situation and is running her own virus checks on her systems. This is because Bear has been known to use his floppy disks on her *Apple Macs*.

'Why are you laughing?' asks the MD.

A brief note on viruses

Computer viruses are written in a language called assembler code. Biological viruses are woven from nature's assembler code, DNA, a language for describing how living things are to be brought into being. Every strain of DNA schemes to usurp its neighbour's place in the kingdom. At a lunch party down the lane, an evolutionary biologist describes how acts of desperate sodomy are carried out upon one another by beetles with penises like armour-plated drills which can bore through hard wingcases to inject their semen directly into a rival's testicles. Human speech is the continuation of DNA by other means. The business of both is survival. Languages evolved to pass on instructions for making the non-living things we need for survival. The proteins of human language are the pen, papyrus, lampblack, printing press, camera, printed circuit board and doped silicon semiconductor. They enable us to pass on codes for making fire, flint scrapers, harps from the clavicles of cave bears, spears, wheels, food from wild plants, yellow pigment from the urine of cows fed exclusively on mango leaves, love (*Kama Sutra*), or one's best way to heaven (I.*Corinthians*.13:13).

It is a cybergypsy maxim that human languages are viruses and ideas communicate virally. If you are taught at mother's knee that: '*O the Popey had a pimple on his bum, and it nipped, nipped, nipped so sore, so he sent for King Billy to rub it with a lily, and it nipped, nipped, nipped no more*'; or conversely, '*Up the long ladder and down the short rope, To hell with King Billy and God bless the Pope*', what will you grow up believing? Your brain has been infected by a virus which might as well be called *antitaig.com* or *antiprod.com*. If the infection is bad enough these Satan bugs can turn you into a genuine armour-plated dickhead.

Lunch with Ian Paisley in Belfast. Not the father, the son. Just the two of us. I am late – arrive by taxi from Stormont Castle where I have been hearing about the Government's television advertising. Paisley is waiting, a waiter shows me to the table. For the next hour, I note fragments of talk, ingredients for Gliomach's game.

'Sectarian is an anti-protestant term.' Chewing pasta. Shades of his father in him, big jaw and booming voice. 'So is bigotry an anti-protestant term . . . And don't use the word "reconciliation". It's anathema to Unionists. Do you know why? Not because we are warmongers, but reconciliation to us implies giving up what you believe in. Losing your identity. It's a kind of surrender . . . [His father's voice booming 'No surrender'] . . .We would rather talk about an accommodation. Come to an understanding of each other's identities.'

This sounds reasonable. He tells me that as a child, he used to bring Catholic friends home. And I remember being told by a Catholic taxi-driver that Ian Paisley senior is a brilliant constituency MP. He works hard for you, whatever your religion.

'We are British,' says his son. 'But that doesn't mean we agree with everything the British Government is doing. There's a mile of difference between the Government and the British people.

'Alienation is a business in Northern Ireland . . . There are things which should and do concern both communities. Unemployment. Housing. Healthcare. Regional NHS reforms . . . In many ways, we are more like each other.'

If our game succeeds, I am thinking, they will learn to *be* each other.

But . . .

'The walls are there because people wanted them there.'

Ian Paisley Jr brings out a glossy leaflet advertising an art exhibition, *Echoes*. 'It's gone down very well. Even Nationalist councils have brought schools to see it . . . Nationalists have always had a set of promises for the future. Nationalism has a goal, and is not hard to understand. Unionism is a set of attitudes and ideals, it is not goal orientated.'

'Isn't this a weakness of the Unionist cause, not to have a goal, other than to be left alone?', I suggest.

'Nothing has ever been able to stand in the way of nationalism anywhere in the world – except Unionism. It's unique.'

'Mightn't peace be a goal worth adopting?'

I start telling him about the carnivals in Sussex. Drummer-boy bands and flaming torches, commemorating the martyrdom of three Protestant bishops in Lewes during the reign of Mary. He nods – flutes, drums, parades – this is familiar territory. Except that, in Sussex, people have forgotten the origin of the marches, or don't any longer care for – this makes him gape – the Catholics join in, and the local convent takes a float in the parade.

In Ireland, it's the Moderator of the Presbyterian Church who issues appeals for peace. In the tortured chemistry of nuclear fission, a graphite 'moderator' is used to mellow the reaction so the reactor doesn't melt. Fidonet 'echoes' (similar to internet newsgroups) are controlled by 'moderators', whose job it is to keep the peace in a troubled medium. People get easily tetchy in cyberspace, and none more easily, it seems, than the 'moderator' of Fidonet's *Virus* echo. Most virus echoes are dull swamps full of po-faced geeks asking the same questions over and over. *Virus* is different. It's humming. It has become a magnet for deadheads, anarchists and voyeurs, all drawn like moths to the flaming personality of its moderator. 'Flaming', on the net, means being angry, abusive and aggressive. The moderator of *Virus*, Edwin Cleton, is all these things daily. As a result, he has acquired a devoted following of mickey-takers, winder-uppers and piss-extractors.

Message #5037 - Virus discussion Date: 09-28-93 21:27
From: Edwin Cleton To: Garcia Michel Subject:: NUKE INFOJOURNAL

@EID:211d 331317dc @MSGID: 2:285/817@fidonet.org 87952219
@PID: Sae[Dv]Remote
Garcia Michel wrote to Edwin Cleton:
>You're not a "moderator"... but a censor... that's really different.

The only thing I exchange with Nuke kids are my batts... This is just one echo among many, not the bloody world, take it or leave it.
Ec., Moderator VIRUS Conference

Why, as I read this message, do my features distort in a rictus of delight? Why? Well, who else is Garcia Michel, this innocent who finds the NuKE InfoJournal so interesting, but my friend Savage

Beast, head of NuKE in Europe? And what other is the 'batt' than the 'electronic baseball bat' with which Cletus, as Geno calls him, is so fond of posturing? Cleton mentions his 'batt' a great deal when replying to people whose views he dislikes. His moderator's rules are star rated according to the number of electronic beatings you risk for breaking each one. The worst thing you can do on this echo, attracting the most stars, is to publish . . .

o Detailed system setups of Commercial, Government or Military sites which could make such a site a possible target. ***

One day, I log into *Virus* to find that there has been a *coup d'état.* Geno, of course. Using some technicality, he has managed to have himself named as moderator. Cleton hasn't yet woken up to this new state of affairs. I go the *Oklahoma Institute of Virus Research* for an update from the man himself.

>hi bear, yeah took over virus from Edwin. I would pay real money to see the look on his face when he finds out....:) poor boy must be mad enough to shit in his hand and throw it at me.

A striking phrase. Geno obviously thinks so too because he also uses it to Ürnst Kouch, aka Dr George Smith, editor of the acid-tongued and acutely well-informed *Crypt Newsletter*. (George quotes it a year later in a maniacally funny report on Geno's Fidonet mail-bombing and other activities. *Songs of the Cyberdoomed, Crypt 28.*) Cleton duly starts slinging shit at Geno, breaching his own rules:

mr. paris has been and very likely still is involved in child porno where he managed to involve others who are now facing exposure if they cut links to his node, I am working on it, patients (sic) please.

Edwin fails to provide any evidence for this claim.

Ürnst Kouch posts, 'I think Ed should be canned . . . If I were him, I'd be so embarrassed and ashamed, I'd quit voluntarily.'

The gleeful hackers immortalise Edwin by rewriting the Abraxas virus to carry his name. The more Cleton and his friends malign Geno, the louder grows the chorus of anti-authoritarian laughter.

Message #4933 - Virus discussion Date: 10-21-93 01:50
From: Mikel Kirk To: Jurriaan Nijkerk Subject: The True Moderator

---

@MSGID: 1:138/172@FIDONET 930022f4 @REPLY: 2:500/46.0 2cc17e52
@PID: FM 2.01
Hi! You are probably unaware that Gene Paris is the bottomfish of echomail. I've been following his course this year, as he's taken up claiming moderator duties on Flame, BITCH, FDECHO and a number of others. I know of no FIDO conference here in the US in which he is not explicitly banned. He posts in other people's names. He posts filth. He shows signs of being a seriously unstable person, whose sole outlet is the echomail. I imagine he's quite the abused person in real life, personally inadequate and that some factors in his life keep that constantly present in his mind...

---

 * Origin: Blue Eyes BBS (206)588-4296 (1:138/172)
@PATH: 138/172 174 1 270/101 209/209 170/400 253/165 257/100 441/80 86

I don't know why this should be hysterically funny, but it is.

A parcel is delivered to the agency, addressed to me. Inside is a muslin cloth bundle, in which are wrapped three objects, of dull japaned finish, crusted with greasy dirt, and stains which might be rust. It takes me a few moments to realise that I am looking at electronic shock weapons. One looks like a policeman's truncheon, studded along its length with flat oval buttons. From its blunt tip protrude two dully gleaming electrodes. The second is dildo-shaped with a strap dangling from its handle and a conical metal tip which makes it look like a dog's dick. The shaft is encircled by three metal bands which presumably become live when triggered. It's an obscene thing, designed to be inserted into the body, the shocks being delivered to the tender mucous membranes of the throat, vagina or rectum. The third incorporates a square box of electronics, annotated in Chinese and equipped with electrodes similar to the first. Along with these things are some cuffs, one pair impossibly tiny. I have never known of, or imagined, the existence of such things as thumb cuffs. An accompanying note, from Karen at Amnesty, asks me to have the objects photographed for an ad exposing their use in Tibet. She concludes: 'Bear, please treat them with the utmost respect. They are the personal property of the Dalai Lama. They were smuggled out of Tibet by a Buddhist lama who escaped to India. He bribed Chinese prison guards to get them. The DL regards these things, which have caused so much suffering to his people, almost as sacred relics of their suffering.'

He sees with wisdom the noble truths of suffering, and the causes of suffering and the end of suffering, who takes refuge in the Buddha.

The phone rings and a voice says, 'Hello, is this Bear?' A voice of melting honey, harvested from the sagebrush and orange blossom of southern California, a voice evolved for the solitary purpose of setting male corpuscles lambada-ing in the veins, a delectable, blonde, angelic voice.

The voice says, 'Bear, I've been just crazy to meet you.'

Her name is Angel. What else?

A voice as deft as fingers strokes the ego, soothes the stiff, suspicious mind, unlocks the muscles of the will, drains away the clenched reserve that makes one say no to doing stupid things.

'So we thought you'd be just perfect. Now you're not gonna let me down on this . . .'

Result, four weeks later I am sitting, naked, in a small room near London's Post Office Tower, letting three girls paint me gold.

'Are you a pro?' one asks, carefully applying paint to the inside of my ear.

From time to time other people drop by to inspect me. One is a man clothed in leather with a machine of strange design strapped to his head. It looks like a gunsight calibrated with dials, or one of those contraptions they use to test people's eyesight. Like Angel, he is American. He tells me, 'Relax, fella, you're gonna be great.'

I have accepted a part in what Angel described to me as the world's first interactive movie, the role being offered, I suspect, less for my acting ability, years of roleplaying notwithstanding, than for physique. I am to play the Buddha. Or rather, a Buddha, for I doubt if Gautama ever spoke lines like mine. My role is modelled on one of those sages, orotund and gilded, that presided imperturbably over the chaos in Jamrach's bargain basement. Orotund and gilded, or rotund and gelded? *(qv)* When Angel described the role, I had assumed that I would be required to do the beatific smile, the handing of a flower to a disciple. In Shades when you hand a rose to the Strange Little Girl, it magically turns into a sovereign, signifying ruler, sovereign or crown *chakra*: Buddhist version of Hebrew *kether*; either *chakra* or else *chakkar katna*, to be dizzy, possibly tiddly, after a bottle of the Punjab restaurant's 'wine that floats in circles', or possibly *chakor*, a dark and midnight bird crying jubjub to the bespectacled moon. Amazing how the mind drivels under stress.

'We have a scene together. Care to run through the lines?' asks the leading man, adjusting his gunsight.

'Okay.'

A script is found and propped open in front of me with huge plastic hairclips.

'Great,' says the actor. 'Let's see. I walk in, see you kinda floating there in mid air and I go . . .' He looks at me, slumps, sighs, shakes his head, says: 'Oh great, this is all I need.'

'Welcome, my son,' I intone, straining to read the script, as the girls snap a rubber skullcap onto my head and begin blending its edges onto my skin with smears of some gummy substance. 'Have you come seeking . . . wisdom?'

The little pause is an afterthought, something I fancy Burton or Olivier might have employed.

'Are you prepared to kill . . . your ego?'

'Okay that's great,' sighs the actor. 'Now try to relax, slow down a little. Can you sound more, er, impressive?'

'Welcome, my son,' I begin, words roaring up the tunnel of the throat into a mouth cave fringed with stalactite-stalagmite teeth. 'Have you . . . come . . . seeking wisdom?'

The actor eyes me warily. 'Terrific, Bear. You'll be great. Just take it easy. You want to ask yourself, what's my motivation here? This guy, Sol, breezes into my space, totally fucking up aeons of solitary meditation.' His voice rises sharply and he jabs a hole in the greasepaint-scented air. 'Now how do I feel about *that?*'

'Okay,' says one of the make-up girls, 'someone name another role that calls for all-over gold body paint?

'Girl in *Goldfinger,*' says a tall good-looking redhead. 'I was just thinking about that. Is it safe to paint all of him? I mean, should I do this bit as well?'

'I think so,' says the first, taking a look and sounding doubtful.

'In *Goldfinger*, didn't the actress die?'

'*Goldfinger* wasn't the first film where someone was killed by being painted gold,' says the third. 'There was a boy who got gilded in this Boris Karloff movie called *Bedlam*.'

'Gelded?' This sets them off giggling.

Sadhu brings the director, Aitan, to take a look at me. Aitan has an architect-designed and carefully gelled quiff. He turns out to be a cyberpunk fan. We agree that Neal Stephenson's *Snow Crash* is the finest cyberpunk story yet written, better than *Neuromancer*. Aitan starts to describe the present project, which is called *Burn:Cycle*.

'There's this cyber-thief, Sol Cutter. He hooks into the net and then uploads his mind into the high-security data banks of this massive, unpleasant corporation.'

'I know the sort of thing.'

'Unfortunately for Sol, he triggers an alarm and his brain becomes infected with a deadly virus . . .'

'Computer virus or biological?' I ask.

'What's the difference, he's a virtual being . . . So Sol has two hours to solve the problem before his brain fries. While frantically searching the cyberverse for an antidote he falls through a time-warp into this endless plain, where he sees, floating in mid-air . . .'

'I think I know the rest.'

While walking in Hyde Park with your nose buried in a book, you trip over a tree-root but somehow miss the ground. You are falling through darkness towards an open space in the middle of which is a lamppost around whose base ornate fishes writhe. It is daubed with graffiti reading: 'REALITY CHECKPOINT. A small sign taped to the post advises, 'Temporarily out of order. The archons of the Vortex apologise for any reality failures.'

>Reality Checkpoint

>You are at the Reality Checkpoint. A meteor streaks across the night sky and in a blaze of light an angel tossed from heaven lands in front of you. The fallen angel says 'Ouf', takes a ledger from under a singed wing and says 'Please sign in.'

>Type LOGIN, HELP or QUIT.

>login; bear; *********

>Welcome to the Vortex, Bear.

>Lilith the Genuine Original Woman is here.

>Quizalmix the Queen of Heaven is here.

>Babaloth the Queen of Hell is here.

>The vestibule.

>Lilith the Genuine Original Woman is here.

>Lilith smiles in welcome.

>Bear says 'aha!'

>Lilith tells you, 'I'll sign you into Pompey's. Follow me.'

>Lilith the Genuine Original Woman wanders out.

>follow Lilith

>n

>You step into a silver mist, intrigued by the way parts of your body dissolve to nothingness. There is a disorientating wrench as if

you had been moved a great distance, although only a single step brings you to ...

>Madame Pompadora's.

>*u*

>Pompadora's Night Salon.

>Lilith the Genuine Original Woman is here.

>Bear gives Lilith a friendly hug.

>Lilith smiles happily and waves to you.

>Lilith says, 'Being here is an indication that ... we are busy.'

>*examine Lilith*

>Lilith's dark hair falls in a shining curtain over her slim shoulders. Brown eyes, almond shaped, long lashed. She wears a blue kaftan and has a wrought silver bracelet on her wrist. Her feet are bare.

>Lilith says, 'Baba's here but don't worry. She will leave us alone because you are with me. They handle me with kid gloves because I screw Raz and anyway she's busy with Quizalmix.'

>Lilith gives a little chuckle.

>Lilith says, 'Now then, Bear, is this the first time you have visited this room?'

>Bear asks Lilith, 'Um, who is Raz?'

>*look*

>Pompadora's Night Salon.

>You are in a large oval room, with comfortable reclining couches. In a nook stands a curved bookcase of lemonwood. Examining it you find Stendhal's 'On Love', Ovid's 'Ars Amatoria', Boccaccio's 'Decameron', Richard Burton's translations of the 'Kama Sutra' and 'The Perfumed Garden' as well as the works of M. de Sade and other famous erotica. The walls of the room are covered in murals depicting erotic scenes copied from the Villa of the Mysteries at Pompeii. The one oddity is a red leather vaulting horse and a glass bow-fronted cupboard displaying a collection of canes, whips and other instruments. Lilith the Genuine Original Woman is here.

>Lilith says 'Razagar is her real life husband.'

>Bear is intrigued.

>Lilith says 'I met Raz the very first time I played. He romanced me, almost married me.'
>Bear says, 'Do both of them do this computer sex stuff with other people on here?'
>Lilith says, 'Yes.'
>Lilith says, 'Raz insisted on trumpeting our affair. He had a big ego tripping scene with me and Baba.'
>Bear says 'Bizarre.'
>Lilith says, 'Well ... I keep telling you!'
>Bear says, 'Yes, so you do. Come on then, show me how it's done.'
>Lilith says, 'It is NOT the same as real sex but it's equally good.'
>Lilith murmurs, 'One generally starts by undressing.'
>*undress*
>You fling your clothes in a heap on the floor.
>Lilith examines Bear.
>Bear without clothes looks exactly the same as he does with them.
>Lilith sighs.
>Bear closes his eyes and thinks of England.
>Lilith says, 'Well at least come to the couch.'
>Lilith leads you to the couch and sits beside you.
>Bear floats to the couch, thinking 'Cumberland', 'Sussex', 'Avon', 'Northumberland ...'
>Lilith says, 'Do relax, dear.'
>Bear chuckles in a nervous way.
>Lilith says, 'I promise I will be gentle with you.'
>Lilith nuzzles you softly.
>Quizalmix telegraphs to you, '[grin] Lilith pounced?'
>Bear telegraphs to Quizalmix, 'She's rapacious, no holding her.'
>Quizalmix telegraphs to you, '[laugh].'
>*dress*
>You dress quickly.
>Lilith says 'oh!'
>Lilith was just going to undress.
>Bear says, 'But it makes no difference!'

>Lilith loosens her robe and waits for you to notice before she takes it right off.
>Bear catches his lower lip between his teeth.
>Lilith is tempted to tap her foot. She is, however, too polite to do this. Lilith licks you on the nose.
>Bear's lips writhe into a kissing shape, then, alas, unpout.
>Lilith leans against you, her body warm and the scent of her hair drifting round you.
>Bear telegraphs to Quizalmix, 'I find I can't really get into this computer sex.'
>Lilith whispers, 'Just hold me.' Lilith slips her robe onto the floor.
>Quizalmix telegraphs, 'Ahh ... a bit "silly"?'
>*examine Lilith*
>Lilith's bare body smells faintly of Jasmine and her hair is a dark cloud on her shoulders. Smooth skin gleams over breasts and long slim thighs.
>Bear telegraphs to Quizalmix, 'Something like that.'
>Quizalmix telegraphs, '[smile] Well, depends I guess.'
>Quizalmix telegraphs, 'I had the extremely fortunate chance to meet my partner on a MUG ...'
>Bear telegraphs to Quizalmix, 'You mean your REAL life partner?'
>Quizalmix telegraphs, '[nod] Yes, dear. Started out with lots of 'computer sex' and very enjoyable it was too.'
>Bear says, 'Lily, you are a dark and fascinating woman.'
>Bear telegraphs to Quizalmix, 'Interesting ... do tell more.'
>Lilith says, 'Darling, you must try. Put your immense and undoubted talent to work trying for serious erotic prose.'
>Lilith says, 'I know that if you try you can do it better than anyone.'
>Lilith says 'Try and make me wriggle here in the chair.'
>Quizalmix telegraphs, 'It made for a *very* interesting first meeting. But having explored each other online we were able to make an initial depth I've never encountered before ...'
>Lilith says, 'See if you can.'
>Lilith says, 'If you relax and let it flow, it's fun and sexy.'

>Lilith leans back on the sofa and looks at you. She lifts one hand to your face and a finger touches your lips gently. Lilith leans closer and her lips follow the finger, pressing little kisses to the corners of your mouth. She feels the sweet familiar weakness.

>Bear's olfactory sensors detect the aroma of Cuban leaf.

>Lilith gives you a friendly shove.

>Lilith whispers in your ear, 'If you don't seriously try I will get some handcuffs and a cane and I will beat you.'

>Bear says, 'I can't, God knows it's hard enough being inventive in real life, let alone on here.'

>Lilith says, 'You are scared and embarrassed!'

>Lilith laughs and strokes your face.

>Bear says, 'Sorry, I have failed.'

>Lilith says, 'You are suffering from cyber-impotence.'

>Lilith says, 'No matter. There are many ways to be loving.'

>Bear says, 'I can see that there is a level of communication beyond a simple description (however good) of whatever is being done.'

>Lilith tells you, 'The action itself is far less important than how you say it. The description of your sensations and feelings.'

>Bear says, 'A shared understanding perhaps?'

>Lilith tells you, 'Yes, exactly. But be careful. Remember that I have warned you, it is very easy to fall in love on here.'

>Lilith the Original and Genuine Woman has just wandered out wearing nothing but a smile.

>o

>You step into a silver mist, intrigued by the way parts of your body dissolve to nothingness. There is a disorientating wrench as if you had been moved a great distance, although only a single step brings you to ...

'Do you know the story of Lilith?' asks eponymous Lil. 'No? Then I must tell you. She was Adam's first wife. When God spat into the dust and kneaded it to shape Adam, he also formed Lilith. There they lay, two lifeless clay figures, until the Almighty breathed into their mouths and opened their eyes – if you want me to give you a summary of relevant artistic and religious traditions of the neolithic near East, just shout, Bear, promise?'

(Bear solemnly nods.)

'Good, well what happened next is roughly also the story of my marriage. Adam and Lilith never got on, right from the start. The very first time they lay down together, he tried to roll onto her and she pushed him off. She said "Why should I be under you? I am made from the same stuff as you. I am your equal." Adam ignored this and tried again to have his way, using force. Lilith got into a rage, uttered a charm – actually one of the magic names of God – and rose into the air and flew away.'

'Typical bloody woman.'

'I'll ignore that. So anyway, Adam – typical bloody man – runs whining to God. Says, "That strange sex doll you gave me, well she's buggered off." So God – typical bloody male deity – says "You poor sod. Never mind. I'll soon sort her out." So He sends the angels Senoy, Sansenoy and Semangelof – who sound like brands of inferior lavatory cleaner – to find Lilith and drag her kicking and screaming back to paradise. Lilith meanwhile was sunning herself by the Red Sea, in a favourite hang-out of lascivious demons and fallen angels. She was having a good time and had not the slightest intention of stopping, so the feathered trio adopted the subtle approach, "Get back to your husband right now, or we'll drown you." "Can't be done," said Lilith, "that would be an abuse of my fundamental human rights because I'm pregnant." She was in fact massively pregnant. "Besides," she said, "How can I return to Adam and live like an honest housewife, after my stay beside the Red Sea?"

'So how is this like your marriage, Lil?' (They are in the Vortex, lying on a grassy bank in Narnia, waiting for Luna.)

'I was married for twenty years,' Lilith says, 'to a pleasant but dull man, a teacher of Eng. Lit. at a modern university. Poor Matthew. He dreamed of a fellowship at a Cambridge college, sitting at high table swapping stories about Leavis (than which, incidentally, I can think of nothing more tedious). But as his hair receded – which it did rather slowly, like the tide going out at Weston-super-Mare – his dreams also dwindled. By the time he was forty-five his highest ambition was to get inside some pretty student's knickers. How that man would salivate over his female students! I've never seen anything so obvious. But there was one girl, an enthusiastic child who wrote him very long essays in curly handwriting decorated with drawings of flowers. For some reason I became jealous. I still don't really know why. When I pressed him, he stopped talking about her. I began reading his diary and going through his papers. When I found nothing I thought that maybe the secrets were hidden in this thing he called "email". So one night I stole his password and logged into his JANET account.'

'Bravo,' says Bear, 'I have never before met anyone who *started* as a hacker.'

'You're not taking my tragedy seriously.'

'Whatever happened can't have been tragic. You're the most un-tragic person I know.'

'As a matter of fact, you're right,' says Lilith. 'Poking around in poor Matt's e-mail proved deady dull. First of all I had to figure out how it worked. And when I did, all I found was a reminder about an overdue library book and the minutes of a committee meeting. No love letters. No secret outpourings of passion. All frightfully disappointing . . .'

'Disappointing? What a strange woman you are. Surely you were relieved?'

'The thing is, I wasn't. I discovered that I'd *wanted* him to be having an affair. No, more than wanted – needed. I realised that what I'd thought of as jealousy wasn't really jealousy at all. It was old-fashioned boredom. Frustration with my tedious existence. I was actually looking for something to get upset about, something we could row over, a reason to throw things, smash the crockery, break furniture. Matt might have been innocent, but I discovered that I wanted to do all these things anyway. Regardless. So I told him and he was very sweet and reasonable in a "let's talk this over like two mature people" sort of way. So then I flew completely off the handle and walked out.'

'Gosh, where did you go?'

'Ah, well, by then I had made some new, exciting friends. One night, when I was playing with Matt's computer, I'd stumbled onto something called EssexMUD. It was a game rather like Shades. Supposedly the very first MUD. In fact – Bear, you'd know this – isn't Shades a by-blow of EssexMUD?'

(Bear nods. It was. Is.)

'It was full of strange roleplaying types – doing it not very well, I see now, but at the time a revelation – anyway, I was very wicked and ran off with this young chap I met there. He was twenty, yeasty as a *baguette*. His name was . . . oh how embarrassing, but then again, there have been so many. Cyberspace was my Red Sea. It's where I acquired my taste for young men. They're such enthusiasts. So touchingly grateful to be instructed in the amorous arts. Teaching (and touching) them made me feel like one of those terrifying whore-virgin goddesses the Old Testament patriarchs got so worked up about. That's how I came to be Lilith. Also how I got the idea for the Academy.'

(Miss Lilith's Academy of the 64 Loving Arts & Sciences is part of the Vortex, a few doors down from Madame Pompadora's, which is a Corrective Institute. Bear demonstrates signs of incipient speech – but in the event says nothing.)

'The Academy taught lovemaking in theory and practice. The sex was, of course, virtual, although there was plenty of slippery eff-2-effing in student digs with lads young enough to be my grandsons.'

'Eff-2-effing?'

'Face-to-face. As opposed to ess-2-ess, which is screen-to-screen. In the Vortex, we don't make opposites of "virtual" and "real" since both are equally real. When we want to talk about the touchy-feely world we say eff-2-eff.'

'Not but what,' says Lilith dreamily, 'eff-2-effing with horny young men is very delicious, but nowadays – perhaps it is just my age – I can honestly say I prefer virtual sex.'

'I find that hard to believe.'

'It's best,' she says, 'to keep the two sorts of relationship quite separate. I learned this the hard way. One night, quite late – it was after I'd been living on my own for a while – there was a knock on the door. Quite innocently I opened it. Actually, I thought it might be Matthew. The idea that he missed me was sort of sweet, even if I didn't want to go back. But it was a stranger. A man in his forties. Unshaven. Dirty filthy. Looked as if he'd been sleeping in barns. He was grinning at me. He reeked of drink. He said, "Lily, it's me. I've come for you." I was petrified. I said "I don't know you!" He looked upset and said "Don't say that! You promised!" I shut the door and he was banging on it. He was shouting, "What about your promise?" I shouted back "I don't know you! Go away, I'm calling the police!" Then he said a name and it was horrible because I knew him well. On the game, he was someone I adored. Whose company I loved. We'd had passionate times together. But I was telling him "No, sorry, you can't come in!" Then he said "Lily don't do this. I've left my wife." I opened the door. *Ou menya nye khvatilo dukhu atkazatsa.* I had not the courage to refuse. He embraced me and I was thinking, I don't like this, in the Vortex he was twenty. He kissed me and it was like dipping my tongue in sewage.'

(Bear grimaces. Finds it hard to imagine Lilith, whom he remembers f2f leatherclad and havanacigar'd, or s2s pouring tea, in the situations she describes.)

'Bear, you know how f2f sex is always better when you feel strongly for the other person. People don't realise that you don't need the physical to have those feelings. When you play s2s with an expert, it can be indescribably sweet. In either case, the explosion is always in the mind. You of all people should appreciate this.'

'Why me?'

'You translated the *Kama Sutra*. It was your supposed erotic expertise, pardon my hilarity, that first made Luna decide to invite you to the Vortex.'

'Unlike you, Luna has never attempted to seduce me.'

'Maybe, but it was those verses of yours that are circulating the internet that inspired Luna to compose the *Cyber Sutra*.'

'Be careful of Luna,' she says, no longer smiling. 'There are some things about her . . .' Lilith lies on her back staring upward through the Narnian leaves and bird-twitter. 'Luna is a special case, Bear, she *lives* through the Vortex.'

Luna waxing (positively gibbous)

'Tell me a story,' commands Luna. We're at the fair, sitting in a car on top of the Big Wheel. In the distance are the woods of Narnia and beyond them, a sea streaked with sunset gold.

I tell her about my hacking of Nasty Ned.

'What became of him?'

'What do you expect?'

'I don't know,' she says. 'It surely depends on what the picture was that you stole from his computer. Was it a child?'

'She was young, but how young was hard to tell. She looked Thai, wearing a schoolgirl get-up that was more corny than porny.'

'So! Not a genuine nymphet.'

'I don't think so. I sent the files, lists, picture, the whole lot, to the man who'd contacted me. He passed them on to the police.'

'And . . . ?'

'Nothing. Ned carried on as before. Quite a while later, maybe about six months, we heard that he'd been badly beaten up. There was a rumour he'd been messing with children. Now he seems to have vanished. Just disappeared.'

'I don't care for that story,' says Luna, as the fairground lights blur and streak, and the sky turns to wine. 'I like a proper ending.'

Tonight she is young and radiant. Gone the straight-backed old Victorian. This Luna is soft and young, with eyes that shine with pleasure in that exquisite face. She wears a green, clinging dress.

'Tell me another story.'

How did it begin, this telling of tales? Of course, with a paradox. For one so at home in cyberspace, Luna knows almost nothing of the net outside the Vortex. She refuses to log into any system that uses real names, because no-one must ever find out who she is. Luna has a particular horror of the internet, because she believes it would make her too easily traceable. Yet she has a thirst for stories of the cyber world. She waits, like a crab in an obscure tidal pool, to catch with her claws and examine any bits of flotsam and jetsam that may drift in with the tides.

Luna has heard all my best net stories. About Professor Abian who states that time has inertia, wants to blow up the moon to get rid of the nuisance of tides, and reorganize the solar system. For years, as he did battle with the combined intellects of the *sci.physics* newsgroup, I was virtually his only ally. On my computer, in the directory next-door to my virus collection, are at least five hundred of his posts and emails, saved for posterity and signed:

> ABIAN MASS-TIME EQUIVALENCE FORMULA m = Mo(1-exp(T/(kT-Mo))) Abian units. ALTER EARTH'S ORBIT AND TILT - STOP GLOBAL DISASTERS AND EPIDEMICS. ALTER THE SOLAR SYSTEM. REORBIT VENUS INTO A NEAR EARTH-LIKE ORBIT TO CREATE A BORN AGAIN EARTH (1990)

'ON JUDGEMENT DAY,' proclaimed Abian, to howls from the ship of fools, 'I WILL PUT THE WHOLE CREATION ON TRIAL.'

'Magnificent,' says Luna. 'Every day should be judgement day.'

I tell her about the man from Los Alamos who was hawking blueprints of atom bombs. About Hannu Poropudas whose five-year-old daughter had a vision from God that the universe is made of 'space potatoes'. About how our work on Greennet led to being ticked off by Jeffrey Archer, and how he came to hear his song.

He whirled into the Kurdish Cultural Centre and was received by a beaming committee of dignitaries and their wives, got up in their best, the men all scrubbed and shiny, bursting out of tight ("Stylish in Suleimaniya") suits. The stout chairman resembled the mayor of a small Italian town. Archer was ready to leave when they announced there was to be a musical performance. They set a single chair for him in the middle of the empty hall. Nadhim drew up another beside him. The little Chairman pulled up a seat on the other side. Then they were all grabbing chairs. No-one wanted to be behind anyone else, so when Goran came onstage, clad *peshmerga*-style in a felt jacket with shoulder horns (for slinging rifles on), he found his audience facing him in one long, straggly row.

'If you weren't so ridiculously protective of your privacy, Luna, you could go and read about it on Greennet.'

But the story Luna liked best was the romance of Morgan and Dreamdancer.

'Shades-wed, not real life,' she says. 'I'm in favour of that idea. A Cyber-Sutran notion. It's about the only thing I do approve of, Shades wise. They are such bad roleplayers. But please go on . . .'

'Well, Morgan was delirious. He renamed his wizard's room, which used to be Morgan & Calypso's, to Morgan & Dreamy's.'

'That Calypso's a case,' says Luna. 'Not interested in cyberlife. *Using* it to pull men for what dear Lily calls "a spot of eff2effing".'

'One day Morgan told me he was again selling stuff to raise money. Dreamy was in trouble. Apparently she owned a beauty salon in Cardiff. Morgan said – and very indignant he was – that the police were claiming it was a house of ill repute.'

'Wonderful! Was it?'

'Of course not. Well, not according to Morgan. He said the police were bent, looking for a bribe.'

'You are inventing this.'

'No. He said the salon had to close temporarily because of the trouble. The business ran into debt. Morgan baled her out. Even this wasn't the end of it. The worry had made Dreamdancer ill with stomach pains. Stabbing, shooting. She went to her doctor. After a couple of weeks they told her she had an ulcer. Nasty. Anyway, the prognosis was bad and the only treatment expensive. Morgan was convinced that Dreamdancer was going to die. And she seemed to think so herself.'

Luna looks sceptical. 'Did it never occur to Morgan that there was anything unusual about her constant need for money?'

'He was in love.'

'But you weren't, Bear. What did you think?'

'I was deeply suspicious and asked who her consultant was. She eventually gave a name. I called the hospital. They said they didn't do private treatment and they'd never heard of him.'

'So you told Morgan?'

'Actually, I never did.'

'Why?'

'What was the point? His money was already gone.'

'Bear, is this another of your endingless stories?'

'I am not sure. Yes. People's stories don't end until they die. She didn't die. But I nearly did.'

'That Calypso,' says Luna slyly. In the waxy moonlight of the Vortex, she looks like a doll that has been enchanted to life.

'Actually, there was an ending. By the time I returned to Shades, Dreamdancer was gone again and so was Morgan's money. He had to hand over the keys to his flat and go to live with his mother.'

'He must have felt so betrayed.'

'Morgan is one of the best and kindest human beings in this eff2effing world,' I tell her. 'Morgan was as incapable of thinking a bad thought about Dreamdancer as you are incapable of thinking a good one.'

She reaches out to press my hand. 'So that was the end?'

'No. Morgan told me, very sadly, that he was leaving Shades. He said that he was sorry he was no longer able to help Dreamy. Yes, she was once again in need of funds. She and her brother had leased a hotel suite in London. Morgan said it was connected with the brother's work. The hotel had kicked them out for non-payment and accused the brother of living on immoral earnings. Morgan said to me, "It's outrageous, Bear. I wish from the bottom of my heart I could help". And then he urged me to lend her every penny I could spare.'

May the angels and spirits that watch over the cyberverse, Teftin, Ariel, Hihaiah, Seere, enfold you in their wings of flame and darkness. May the emerald tablet glow for you. These are the sixty-four arts and sciences of love in the cyber world, which were taught in the mystery schools of the Vortex and other places: which teachings, the experience of beings and meta-beings from earliest cyberspacetime, passed on by word of mouth, were gathered together and written down by Merilyn at the dictation of Luna, servant of the goddess Qudsh, on the evening of _____, the full moon of Anoreth, Anno Vorticii 6723, the constellation of the Lovers hanging high above the observatory, while burning the incense of Aphrodite.

§In cyberspace the real sex of your lover is not important.

§Neither does your own real sex matter.

§You may play either the male or the female role, as you freely choose. The same goes for your lover.

§There is a third possibility, which you are not ready to hear.

§There is a fourth possibility, but you would not believe it.

§There is a fifth possibility.

§In cyberspace everyone is equal.

§We can't see our partner's hair, eyes, shape of nose, skin colour, whether fat or thin, or how they are dressed.

§We can't hear their voice, smell their perfume, breath, or feet.

§Physical beauty and ugliness count for nothing. In cyberspace, everyone is as lovely or as ugly as they choose to be.

§We can be whoever and whatever we choose.

§In cyberspace, who are you? Not your eyes. Not your smile.

Not your clothes. Not your accent. Not your shape. Not your name.

§You are defined by your description and by your actions, all of which are expressed in words.

§You must capture a living spirit in a cage of consonants and vowels. Learn to type.

§Cyber characters are true living beings, with their own lives.

§Your character is not just your own creation. It is created and constantly re-invented by you and your partner together.

§Pleasure is always real. Pain is always real.

§Newcomers to cyber lovemaking always begin by simulating the actions of physical lovers.

§A man will play a man's role, a woman a woman's.

§They perform imaginary acts that mimic physical lovemaking.

§Their lovemaking follows the pattern of a physical love bout, opening with kisses, progressing to more passionate embraces.

§They imagine themselves using positions and techniques like those of the *Ars Amatoria* and *Kama Sutra* of the face-to-face world.

§Such newcomers often find themselves embarrassed by the strangeness of the cyber encounter.

§They think that cyber sex is sharing a fantasy without physical contact. Like a dirty phone call.

§They have no sense of timing. They rush through a series of fantasy actions as though ticking off a checklist. They are unsubtle.

§This type of lovemaking, which is very unsatisfying, is known as the Congress of Tyros.

§For the experienced lover there is no prescribed set of actions. The aim is to create and act out a story in which both find delight.

§This may or may not involve simulation of physical sex.

§In cyber lovemaking subtlety is everything. Express feelings clearly, but hint at actions. Use your imagination.

§Be devious.

§Pick up on your partner's cues. If he/she drips oil onto your back, how does it feel? Is it scented? Are her/his fingers warm?

§The way you describe the body and your actions is important. Think of new words, new phrases. Crudity and clichés kill passion.

§Spelling mistakes are off-putting. They shatter the mood.

§Let your terminology and language be guided by your lover's responses. If you sense they are hesitant, change tack.

§Think before you respond. Take time. Don't be afraid of silence. Use pauses, short and long, as part of your communication.

§Tease and withhold. A good roleplayer makes pleasure last.

§Find an original way to express excitement and pleasure. Nothing is more absurd than cries of 'O O O yes yes yes,' like a German porn movie. The incoherence of orgasm may be expressed by {{{{^*fk{{{{, or high ASCii characters like äåÄùúûüóöõΩ‰∞.

§The union of an experienced lover with a novice who is gauche, but eager to learn, is called the Congress of Lilith.

§As cyber lovers gain experience, they discover the possibility of exploring love from other viewpoints.

§A man may play a woman. A woman a man.

§You may both choose to roleplay the same sex.

§At first this can be uncomfortable. Persevere. Such roleplay is valuable for understanding partners in the face-to-face world.

§With a suitable and willing partner, you may also safely try in cyberspace things you would never otherwise dare to do.

§When both are keen to explore, there is no need for shame.

§This is the Congress of Garbo.

§Beyond this is a third possibility. Cyberspace has no either/or. There is no reason to be either male or female. Why not be both?

§We simply imagine suitable cyberbodies for ourselves.

§Physical pleasure is not the purpose of cyber love, whose joys are as sweet and as real, but of a different kind.

§All love is in the mind.

§The deepest pleasure comes from the imagination.

§The lovemaking that arises out of such imaginings is known as the Congress of Caenorhabditis.

§A fourth possibility appears. We give ourselves forms which in no way mimic physical bodies and our aim is to generate pleasures unknown in the physical world.

§Let a mere look trigger delight as intense as that caused by touching the most sensitive spot of a physical body.

§We imagine organs delicate as sea-anemones that touch erotic and delightful spots in each others' minds, like fingers flying on the buttons of an accordion. This is the Congress of Pompadora.

§The fifth and greatest possibility is that as cyberbeings we cease to need imagined bodies. We accept being no-bodies.

§Cyber characters are living spirits.

§The spirit indwells everything you are, say and do.

§Beauty in cyberspace is the beauty of the spirit.

§Love in cyberspace is communion of spirits.

§During an encounter of this type, nothing sexual need be said or done, because everything you do or say expresses 'I love you'.

§This is the Congress of Luna and it is the highest of all the types of cyber lovemaking.

C. elegans

The old Indian authors recommended that lovers should mimic the mating of various animals. The texts, beginning with *Kama Sutra*, record sexual positions named *dhenuka* (the Cow), *svanaka* (the Dog), *marjara* (the Cat), *aibha* (the Elephant) and *gardhaba* (the Ass). I wonder what Vatsyayana would have made of Luna's inclusion in the *Cyber Sutra* of the lovemaking of *C. elegans* (the Worm).

Caenorhabditis elegans is a tiny nematode, growing no bigger than one millimetre long, about the length of a comma on this page. It lives all over the globe in its own world of the soil, burrowing through the leaf-rot, hunting bacteria. In short, *C. elegans* is about as primitive as an organism gets, yet it shares many essential biological characteristics with humans. Like us (but not like Luna who claims not to be human but a parthenogene – born, like Athene, of the mind – in her case the mind of the unknown being who is her ultimate coder), the worm is conceived as a single cell which undergoes a complex process of development, starting with embryonic cleavage, proceeding through morphogenesis and growth to the adult animal. It is, depending how you look at it, either of zero, or of almost limitless, economic importance to its not very distant cousin, *H. sapiens sapiens*, for yes, the two are closely related. A quick comparison shows that both possess a nervous system and a rudimentary brain, exhibit behaviour and are even capable of simple learning. Both produce sperm and eggs, mate and reproduce. After reproduction the lesser of the two gradually ages, loses its zest for living and finally perishes; thus embryogenesis, morphogenesis, development, nerve function, behaviour and ageing, most of the mysteries of modern biology, are demonstrated in this insignificant animal, and the same is true of *C. elegans*. (The fact that *C. elegans* is unable to work a computer keyboard compels us to assume that it does not share the greatest biological enigma of all, consciousness – although this piece of *a priori* non-logic remains to be demonstrated.) What appealed to Luna, in her search for life models capable of supple and unusual copulations, is that *C. elegans* comes in two interesting sexes, one a common or garden male, the other a self-fertilising hermaphrodite. The animal is, essentially, as essentially are we all, a tube containing two smaller tubes, one being the pharynx and gut, the other devoted to the reproductive system, which occupies most of the body space. The herm is a little brighter than the male, some three hundred of its nine hundred and fifty nine body cells being neurons. *C. elegans* possesses eighty-one muscle cells arranged in four bands that run the length of its body. By flexing and relaxing its muscles, the animal generates dorsal-ventral waves along the body, propelling itself along. The same rhythmic contractions enable *C. elegans* to make sweet slithery love, coiling and uncoiling, nestling its curving sines into the receptive cosines of its partner's (or its own) body, breathlessly fastening, as do we all, orifice to orifice. Imagine a culture of writhing, wriggling nematodes, translucent, glowing as if lit from within. Were these the embraces that Luna visualised in her mind's far-travelling eye?

I watched the water-snakes:
They moved in tracks of shining white,
And when they reared, the elfish light
Fell off in hoary flakes.
Within the shadow of the ship
I watched their rich attire:
Blue glossy green, and velvet black,
They coiled and swam; and every track
Was a flash of golden fire.

I discover, on one of the hundreds of websites devoted to this tiny diploid organism, a DNA sequence isolated from a single of its estimated 17,800 genes.

Gene: sra-1

Isolation Name: AH6.4

Expressed in: SPD/SPV (males only)

5′ primer: att aat tcc GCA TGC gtg cgt cat gca aag acg ag

3′ primer: att tga gcG GAT CCt gcg ctg gtt atg ttg gac at

Restriction Sites: SphI, BamHI

Expression Vector: TU#62

Promoter Sequence: 3531 bp

```
GCATGCGTGCGTCATGCAAAGACGAGTCTTAAAGTTGTGTGGCAGTTGGCTGTCAACTTCTGGTTTGGCGAACCCACGGC
GACCCAATTTCTCAACACGATTCTGAAAAAAATCATGTAATTCTTGAAGGGAAAAAAGAGCAACCTTATTGAAACGATTT
TCCTTCTCAGCACTCATGGTATCGTCGTTGTGATTGTCGATGGTGATCTTCGAGATCTCATCGATGGGAAGATCGTCATG
TTCAATAGGACTGGAAAATCAAGAATGATTAATAAAACGCTTATTAAACAAATCTAATTTTACCATTGATATCTTGATTG
GCTATTCCTGTTTCGATCGCGTTGGACAGTCTCGTATTCGCGACTTGTTGGGAGCGGAGTCGACGAAGTCAACGGAACTG
TACGCGTGGTGCTTATTTGAGCACCCGATTTTCTCAGTTGTTCAGACTGTTGAGGATTAGTCGACTGGATTTGTGGCATC
ATACTCATTTGTTCAGAAAGCATAGGAGTAGAAGCAGCTTGCATTGGATGGAAGTACATTGGAGCAGCTTGTTGAGCCAT
TTGACCCAATGGTTGCTGATAATAAAATATCTGCGGTTGTCCAGATTGTGCAACGTGCTGTCCTCCTTGCTGCGGCTGGG
CCATATAAAAGTATGGATGACCAGCAGTCATCATTTGCTGTTGAGCGGGAACCTGTCCAAATTGTCCGTTTGCATCTTGA
TAGTACGGTGGTGTGCCGAACTGTTGAGGTGCTCCGTTTTGTGCCGTGTACGTTGGAATTGGCTGATTGGGCATGGAAGA
TCCGTAGTAGTATTGCATCTGTAATTTATTTTGAAAAATAAATAATAAGTTTCACGGTTAAAAACCTGCGAATCGTAGAT
TTGAGGAAGTGGATGCTGCTGTTGATGTCCTGGAGGTGGTTGTGGTGGCTGTGCCGTTGCTGAAGAAGACAATGATCCAC
CGGCCAACGGCGCACTATTGGATGTTGCTGTCATTTTCTGTCTTAAAAATTCACTGTTGAGGAATAGTCGAGAGAAACTA
GAGAAACGGAGTAAAAAACACATTGTTTCATGGAGGAAGAACATTTCGAATATTTAAAAACTGCAGAAAATTTGCTCTTG
TAGCTGAGCATTTTCGAGGTTTTCAAAATGGTGACTAATTAATGTACAAGAGTATTGATGTCCTTTTCAAAACGAAAAAA
AATTCGAAAAATGAACTGGAAACCGACGAAAAACAAATATACGACATTTCTTGAGTTTTCAGGCAGAATTACGAACTGCC
CGGCATACTTTGAAAGGATAAAAATGTGAAACGCTGAGAAAAATAATTTAAAATAAACAGAACGAATGAAAATTGTTCCT
TTGAAGGAAAAAAGCAAGATAAATTGCGCCGCCGCGCCTCGACAAAGACAAATATAGATTAACCAAGTGACTACGGTATT
CGTAGAGAGACACTACGAAGTTTTCATCCTATGCGCCTTGAAAAATTTCGCAACTGTAATTACTGTATTTATGAACTTTT
CAAATTGGCAAAATAAAACCTGAAAAATCAATACTTGTAAATAAACCTTTCGTTTTTTTTTAAGTTGAAATTTCGAGAGA
AAAATAATGTAAATTATTACTTCATTCTTTGTGAGAAAAAAAAACAAAGAATCATCCATCAATACAGCCCCACCAGGTAC
AGTCTACATCATTTTGGAATTTTCTATTCACAATCTGTCTAATGTTTCGATGTAGTTCATCTGCAGCTAAAAAAAAGAAG
ATTAATTTAAAAAAAAATAAAAATAAAATAAGATTAATTTTTCAAGATTCTCACCAATTACGTCGATTGTCCATTCATCT
TTGCTTCTTGGCTCAGGTTTCAAATGGACAATTGTGGACTGTCTGATCGTATTGTCAGGTAACATGAAATCCACATTTGC
ATAAACGGACTTCTTATCTTCACTGTATCGTGCAGTTGTGATAACATAGTTTCCTTTTTCAAATATTTCTGACCACGTTC
CAGCCAAATCTTAAAATCACAATTACCAATCCATCAAAATATTTCAAAAAATATTTTCCCAAAAAAAAACGGTAGAGGGC
ATAAATTTTTAACACCTACTAGGGAAACTTGAAACCAGCAACTTCCTATCGTCCGGTGTTCCGTGAATAATATAGTACCG
AATCACATGAAAATGAAATTCAATCTATGTTTCAGCTGAGATATCTGTTGCCTTACAGTACGTAAATAGTAGAAAAGAAA
CAAAAAACGGAATTGTGATCATCGCAACTATTATTGATGAATTGGATATGTAATTCATAAGTAAATAAAAGAGAAGTAAA
ATCGGAAAATATACCATTAAATTTCATGTATTTTGATTTTGGCGTTTGGTTTTTGTTTTCACTTCTCCTGAAAAACGCAA
AAGTGATGTAATGCACCTCGGTGAATTGTTTAAAAATGTGATTCATCTTCCAAATCTACTTAGAACAACTATAAACAAAG
TAAAGAGAGATTCGTGGCAATTTGTATTACTCGAAAACTTGAACAACATTAGACATACCAAAAATCATTCTGAATAAACA
TATCTAAGCTCTTGATTTCATTATAAGTCTCCTGAGAATCGTACTTCTCAGACAAACGCTTAGTTGTCTAATTAGAATTA
AACCAAATAATGGGGACATAATTAATACGCTTCCTATTCTAATCCAATATGGATTTTCCAATCAAATATGGTTGAAATCT
AATCCAATATGGAACAAATCTAATGAAAATGGTTGAAATCTAATCCAATATGGAACAAATCTAATGAAAATGGTTGAAAT
CTAATCCAATATGTAACAAATCTAATTAAATATGGATGTCTAATCTAATACGGAACAAATCTAATCTAACATGGACAAAT
CTAATCCAATATGGATTTTATAATAAAATATGGAGCAAATATAATCCAATATGGCATTTCTAAACAAATATGAATTATGT
CCCTATTATATTTGGTTTAAATCTAATTAGACGACTAAGCGTTTGTCTGAGTTATGATCAGAACAAACGCAATTTTCTGA
TCGTTTCTATGGATATCAAATGATTGACGTTATTCATTCATATTATTTCATCCCGTCCAATGACCAACCTCCAGCCGTTC
AGACGATAAGATTATCAGACCCTGCAATTTTCTCAATTTCCTTTTTGACTCAATTTTCGTTTAAGATCTATGTCGTGTGC
TTTTTCATTATTTTATTTTTTTGGTGTTTTGTTTTATGTTCTTTTCTGTTTTGGACTATATATTTTTTGAAATTTTCTTT
TTTTTTTAATATGCCCAGTTTAGATTGAACATTTTCACCGAATGAACGTGAGAAGGTAGACTATCAACACTCTTTTCCTA
TAACTATTAGTCTGTCTGAAAAGGTTACTCAGTTCTCCTGAATCAAAAATAACAATATTTACCTACAAAAATGTGAATGC
TGGATTTATTTTTCTAATTTTTTTATTTGTTAGAAATAATACTGATAAAAAATATTTCCAGAAAATGTCCAACATAACCA
GCGCAGGATCC
```

Luna's peculiar genius translates the deoxyribonucleic babble to the assembler code needed to make the bodies of cyber-animals. I nearly said 'human assembler code', but one should never make that mistake with Luna.

'I am not human. I refuse to live in the real world. It is true that I, Luna, am operated by a human being with a body. But that human is not *me*, and its body is not *mine*. Luna is Luna, and my home is here. In the Vortex.'

'A refugee from reality,' I quote to her. 'That's what Lilith keeps telling me.'

'I am not a refugee,' says Luna. 'I am not like Lily. Lily comes here, but she is just as much at home in what she calls the face2face world. She comes and goes as she pleases. She is strong. She seeks her own pleasure. I am not at all like that.'

'Oh but you are strong,' I tell her. 'You're terrifying. I remember when I first met you, how scared I was.'

Today we're strolling in Kubla Khan's pleasure gardens. Ahead is a huge curving dome, an edifice of glittering crystal, near which a jet of spumy water shoots intermittently into the air. Luna stoops to pick a pink lily, growing on a long stem with grasslike leaves.

'You haven't told me what became of Calypso. Presumably she was still around when you came back?'

'As a matter of fact, I never saw her again. She'd dropped out. But there was a reason. A very shocking reason. I found it out by chance. Do you want to hear it?'

'Do you need to ask?'

'Remember I said that people's stories don't end until they die? Well, sometimes death isn't an ending. It was summer. I was with Eve in the garden . . .'

One Sunday afternoon Eve and I are in the garden when a woman totters into view. Fiftyish, short fair curls, airtight jeans.

'I'm looking for Bear. Are you him? Goody. Heard lots about you. Our neighbour asked us to drop this off to you, since we were down this way. It's heavy love, you'll have to help.'

In a carton is my old Eff One, the one I lent to Clare.

There's no note, but Clare has even returned the floppy disk with Graeme's Ripper program on it. The F1 looks obsolete. It's already part of the palaeohistory of the net. Out of nostalgia, I slide in the floppy and watch the archaic interface open up. Ripper is still on the disk. Probably she never used it. But there are many new files: *edwin, tom, droid, jeeps, cabbalist, scott, chorley, lance, morgan, gary.* Among them is one called *bear. Bear* consists of two letters she had written me, but not sent. The first hopes I feel better and echoes the 'soulmate' theme of our ill-starred lunch. The other, dated a few weeks later, accuses me of faking illness in order to humiliate her. All the rest are letters men have written her, some fawning, others explicitly sexual. All are carefully catalogued. (She keeps her affairs in order.) A little interlinear reading and some simple finger-maths shows that Calypso must have been sleeping, or conducting amours of some intimacy, simultaneously with at least six Shades players. But the file, *droid*, is rather different.

Cally darling,

'Your smile lights up the darkness of my heart.' What amazing things you say. I'm sitting here at work thinking of you and can't get a damn thing done... One thing. Better be careful using the a/c, at least for a while. My boss queried the last bill...

Cally darling,

Sorry to ask, but don't use the account any more. I am in shit. I had to own up that I used it to play games, but swore I've stopped, so please don't use it, everything shows up on the log. I read your emails over and over. Can't wait for when we can see each other.

Darling Calypso,

You must stop using the a/c immediately. It's not my personal account, it's the company's and they've stopped me from using it. I don't have direct access any more (sneaked into John's office to send this), so if you use the a/c, it means they will know I gave the p/w to someone outside and my goose will be well and truly cooked.

Dearest Calypso,

*I call you and I get the bloody answer machine. Sorry to nag on about the account again, but it's a crisis, seems another big bill's come in. I've said I know eff-all about this one. If by any chance you *might* have used the id by mistake, please delete it right now from your pooter, to make sure it can't happen again. Please give me an email when you get this, haven't heard anything from you for ages.*

Dear Calypso,

It's happened and I've got one hour to clear my desk. So why am I in John's office writing this? You don't reply. You don't answer your phone. The latest bill is even higher than the last one. They are saying I must repay all the money. Cally, it was three thousand fucking quid. Losing the job is bad, but not as bad as thinking that you would shaft me so badly. No, it can't be. Just say I'm wrong. Only you can. My darling forgive these unworthy suspicions. I can't think straight. I haven't told them about you. For pity's sake get in touch, or I will go crazy.

Clinically catalogued, coldly filed in date order. All that's missing is the blood-coloured ribbon.

'The woman is a nonpareil!' says Luna. 'How stupid men are! So she quit Shades because of a guilty conscience?'

'No. I did not know the end of the story, until months later on a multi-user game somewhere in the States I bumped into Detritus who used to work for British Telecom. Calypso's name came up. Not long before Micronet went supernova, Detritus investigated a complaint. A firm in Plymouth said its account was being hacked. The company was baffled, because three months earlier it had sacked an employee who'd confessed to running up the huge bills.'

'Oh don't tell me. Droid was so desperate to see her that he kept using the account? He *must* have been crazy. But then all men seem to be crazy about Calypso. She must be very special.'

I think of Calypso's dark hair on milky skin, her deep green eyes. 'Yes, I'm afraid she is. But it wasn't Droid. It couldn't have been – and this is why the firm was so upset – because a week after they sacked him, he emptied a bottle of sleeping pills.'

Luna is silent, presumably appalled.

'The first thing they did was check the logs. They found that more than three months after Droid's death, the hacker was *still* using his account to play Shades. Had never missed a single day. The record showed a steady flow of calls, some lasting hours. Of course, they didn't know who had made them. So Detritus brought in a thing called a data-analyser which decodes data transmissions. Then they just sat and waited for the hacker to log in again.'

'Is it possible?' Luna asks me (as I had asked Detritus), 'that Calypso didn't know what had happened to Droid?'

'Again no, not a chance. I'll tell you why. As soon as the hacker called, the data-analyser got to work. It decoded the zeros and ones passing along the telephone line and Detritus and Co. found themselves eavesdropping a conversation of a rather intimate sort. In one week, they monitored dozens of similar chats. Detritus had half a dozen typed up as evidence. He said what upset him most, made him want to wring her bloody neck, was the way she kept on about the terrible tragedy that had happened to Droid.'

'They were certain it was her?'

'Who else? They traced the calls to her house. Detritus went round and confronted her. She was terrified. She was forced to repay the company. Not much good to Droid. The really chilling thing for me was realising that when I was in her house and she was gazing at me with huge eyes, talking about soulmates, that poor guy was already dead.'

'Bear, I'm sorry. I'm laughing, but not because I find it funny. The story you have told me is depraved. I am not used to hearing about people more corrupt than me.'

'Don't be silly, Luna.'

'You don't know me,' she says. Luna's change of mood is like a sudden drop in temperature.

'Bear, I'm going to say something important. You won't be able to take it seriously. You'll say "Luna is mad". What I'm going to tell you sounds paranoid and melodramatic. It's a warning. Bear, if you spend too much time in cyberreality you will lose your soul.'

Unprepared I may be, melodramatic this certainly is, and I have no idea what she means, but I will certainly listen. No-one I know, not even Lilith, has gone so deeply into roleplaying.

'When I became Luna, that is to say, when Luna realised that she was an independent spirit with her own life, she also discovered that she had no soul. The human called "I" owned one, but Luna did not share it. Does one need a soul? I don't know. Humans like Calypso seem to get along without them, but isn't Calypso like an empty shell? No wonder she craves a soulmate. She needs a new soul because somewhere along the way, she has lost her own.'

No, but this is too much. There is something farcical about Faustian warnings uttered in the open-eye daylight of the Vortex.

But solemnity usually is edged with absurdity. I hadn't told Luna that all the while Detritus had been telling his story on the American MUG, he was under attack (and in fact was killed) by a homicidal mountain goat. 'Hold on, Bear,' he'd telegraphed on being resurrected. 'Must just pick up the bits of my body before the maggots get them.'

Luna is shapeshifting. Grass green dress turns muddy khaki, then darkens to the black of a crow's wing.

She says, 'Listen. I, the person speaking to you now am not Luna, but Luna's human. Luna wants me to tell you that if you met me in real life, you wouldn't look at me twice and wouldn't want to know me. I am lonely, a bitter person. I murder myself daily. I'm a serial suicide. I come here to die, so that Luna can live. Luna lives here and here only, but she wants to be human. She would love to possess this body I detest. She wants a human soul.'

'I trust you, Bear,' says Luna a little later, 'so I will tell you about my human. It is fifty-five. It lives alone in a flat in a quiet London square. It works for a secretive organisation in London and from time to time in America. During its US visits, I am in limbo. I have nightmares in my dark, rented corner of the human's mind.'

'This is too weird. Do you, Luna, really regard yourself as a separate person?'

There is a drowsiness in the air, a faint, bitter tang. Turn back, cyberbeings, before it is too late.

'Oh yes,' she says, 'quite distinct. The human likes cats. I don't. It listens to Mozart. I prefer Debussy.'

A bee zums past in the thick air. The land ahead seems on fire, rolling in burning waves to the horizon.

Crescent Luna (the fields of Lethe)

In the fields opium poppies grow. The air is heavy with their scent and in such thickness of air, dreams are almost visible. As for Luna, she's playing out her changes: a heavy golden plait hangs over a robe of white silk embroidered with scarlet poppies.

'Yes,' says Luna, bitterly, 'I do wish I had a real body.'

She unlaces the robe and lets it fall (to be caught and held aloft by supple poppy stems) revealing a naked form whose every curve, hill and hollow are perfectly realised.

'No, no, no,' I say laughing, 'please don't try to tempt me. I am not going to make love with you.'

'Why? Are you afraid that my human controller is a man?'

'You are a deep soul, Luna. One could drown in you.'

Now Luna puts off her body altogether and shows me her shapes and changes. Her limbs elongate and grow translucent, then liquefy and accumulate into a long shape, sinuous and bright, that wriggles in a lazy S, bending the poppy stalks, rolling over onto its back like a dog, its internal organs strong pulsing shapes that, before my eyes, start to expand, merge, take a harder form, resolve to the glittering torpedo of a fish that floats up into the air and swims towards me with flicks of its silver body, approaching, closing and opening its O mouth until the mouth opens wide enough to be a darkness out of which appears a man with long brown hair, purple robed, his right hand holding a mirror which he extends to me with a warm smile, the mirror growing cloudy as I look into it, a face forming in its depths, that of a dark-skinned woman, Egyptian looking, with large, penetrating *kohl*-smudged eyes like a painting on a mummy case, the mirror's rim dissolving as she emerges, hiding her body in a black and grey cloak, which as I watch, begins to acquire a certain furriness and becomes a thick sable pelt, the woman transforming to a man who laughs and starts inscribing bright shapes in the air before turning into a leopard that crouches with yellow eyes beneath the shapes which hang before me, burning in the heavy air.

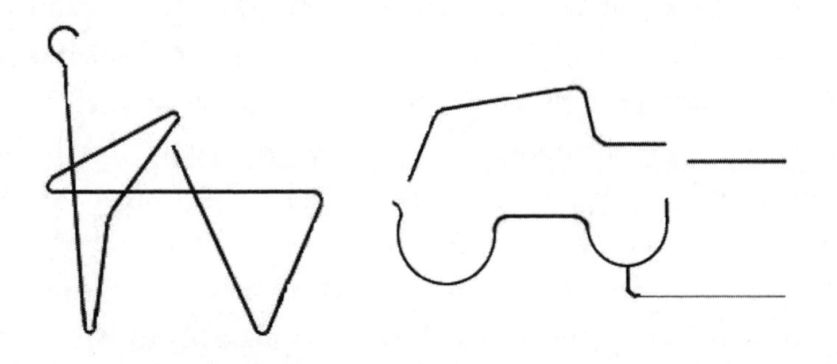

The leopard fades and only the sigils remain. Then, away in the distance I notice a figure walking in the poppy fields, a woman, cowled, face hidden in the depths of the hood, a cloak wrapped around her graceful figure. With small steps, she draws gradually nearer and my heart begins that familiar thudding. My mouth is dry, my breathing heavy, the lines of fire pulse in time with my pulse which quickens as the figure glides through the poppies, her bare feet brushing aside the stems, until she is only a step away. She throws back her hood, reveals the fair hair falling to her shoulders and glint of wide green eyes. And Eve stands before me.

'I think you used to love me, Bear, but at some point I became just another character in your cyber dream. There is a realm called Sussex and in it there is a crooked little house in a wood, and the house stands in a clearing with an overgrown garden which is always filled with sunlight. In the centre is a circular herb garden, which you call the rose henge. Yes, the roses are climbing all around it. It looks very lovely when the sunlight is in the leaves. In the garden, weeding, a woman looks up at you and smiles. It is your own loving wife. But look what happens. Your wife becomes suddenly translucent, parts of her start to vanish. Now there are holes in the vision that is bending over the flowerbed. You can see angelica stalks where her face was. Those are petals that were her eyes. A clematis is climbing up what was her arm. Now the shining trowel is digging by itself, and the hand holding it has disappeared. What is happening? The blooms are fading and it is all turning to shadows. But, Bear, wait a minute. This is your imagination, isn't it? You can do anything you like. The flowers quicken, the wife reappears, stooping among the marigolds. She straightens up, stretches that aching back, turns to you. But wait, it's not your wife. It is a woman you have never seen before. Oh but she's sexy. She comes towards you with a welcoming smile. You turn in confusion. And now you see that behind you, there is no house, and that in the distance, all the woods and the hills are strange.'

Luna is her first self again, the old lady of the tea party. She says, 'We must leave. It is dangerous to stay here too long. The poppies get inside your head.'

'Luna, why did you show me Eve?'

'Call it a cruel experiment.'

'Why? What reaction did you expect?'

'You're always talking about Eve, you do realise that, don't you?'

'Well, of course. She's my wife.'

'A lot of married couples spend their lives trying *not* to think of one another. You talk about her all the time. Eve this, Eve that. But you must like talking about her more than being with her, because you're always here. Let's try another experiment. Bear, complete truthfully . . . "I, blank, Eve".'

'Love? Yes I do.'

'Love's a slithery word, Bear dear. You can say the noun in an instant, but the verb takes years to pronounce.'

'Are you suggesting I don't love her?'

'I am the wrong person to ask,' says Luna sadly. 'I have never loved anyone in my life.'

Seeing that I don't answer Luna puts her hand on mine and says, 'From what you've told me, you are wrecking your marriage. Stop it. Junk the modem.'

'Luna, when you conjured up that vision of Eve, just for a moment it seemed that she was really here.'

'Bear, the Eve you tell me about – the Eve of your imagination – really *is* here. This is where she lives, here, with Luna, in the Vortex. I've got to know her well. She's charming, intelligent, loving . . . exactly as you imagine her. As for the real Eve, she is a complete mystery to me. As I suspect she is to you.'

Is Luna right? Do I really know her, my wife? These days I hardly see anything of Eve. I'm in London a lot of the time. I spend hours in the car. By the time I get home the kids are in bed. Eve's usually busy, or watching television, so I tell her I have work to do and inevitably I end up here with Lilith or Luna. Or else wandering the invisible roads.

Sea State 6

Gurglings, bubblings, retchings, the sour reek of people's insides: jetfoils aren't built for comfort. Halfway across the Irish Sea, our ferry is caroming off the wave-tops like a tile skimmed from a beach. Tall swells chase each other across the surface of the sea. Some are classic wave shapes, others crude container-loads of sea-water, uplifted by ocean hydraulics. Huge blue sugarloaves are pushing up on all sides, water spilling off them, spray-spouting whalebacks down whose flanks watery eels slither like the veins that writhe over the flexed biceps of bodybuilders (visions are directly related to the condition of the stomach lining). A monitor mounted above the unhappy passengers shows the boat's position plotted against a chart of the Welsh and Irish coasts. It is probably intended to be reassuring, but since the tiny blip that represents our vessel seems, like the hour hand of a clock, hardly to move, it has the opposite effect, deepening our misery by dragging out minutes into hours, putting each particle of time under a microscope.

Looking for a way to get a couple of weeks alone with Eve, I'd remembered Gliomach's challenge. He was vastly amused when I said we were going to come hunting for him in Ireland.

'Okay, bring a laptop. I'll leave clues for you every night on the *Butterfly Effect* and you can tell me how you're getting on.'

My name is that of an old Aussie fast bowler,
I publish the Beano than which is none droller,
I was a commie before Marx was a brother,
I built a tower in Dunmanus plus one other,
Line up my towers from shore to shore
And when you have done that I'll tell you more.

And that was it. No real name, no address, only a string of inscrutable lyrics and strange attempts to be helpful: *Get plastered in Cronin's, they do a lovely drop, ask Sullivan about the towers.*

I find Eve on deck, trying to scrape her hair under a scarf, stray bright strands whipping in the wind.

'I knew I was mad to come.'

'You'll be fine once we get ashore. We'll be in Cork by . . .'

'Bear, don't talk. Not now. It's eight o'clock in the morning and I feel as if I've been up all night drinking ouzo.'

She goes to the rail and leans over. Where the ship's metal hull smacks down onto the waves, the water is smashed to lace beneath the surface in silent explosions that fizzle up to the top as foam, and are rapidly left behind.

'Shall I get you a coffee?'

Her head twists to stare at me. Wearing sunglasses, travelling incognito so I can't see her eyes. Somewhere close by, a stomach rolls over in surrender.

'What am I doing? When my friends ask where we went I'll say, "Bear asked me along on a quest to look for a man he'd never met, whose name we didn't know and who could be anywhere in Ireland."'

'Not anywhere. We know he lives out west.'

'They'll say, "Who was this mystery man and why was it so important to find him?" And I'll say, "I've no idea. In fact I know virtually nothing of what my husband has been doing for the last several years."'

'But this is why we're here. So I can explain.'

'Bear, listen to yourself. You've just said that we are here so you can explain why we're here.'

As we edge down the crowded stairs to the car deck, we hear a mother talking to her small daughter. 'Fock, it was that rough, the fockin puppy'll be plastered all over the fockin roof.'

'What did you say?' The Land Rover roars and chugs up an Irish hill. Two hours after disembarking from the ferry, I am still queasy.

'You were addicted,' says Eve. 'I kept telling you so. You used to deny it. So what's changed?'

'Did I ever deny it? Maybe I did. I don't think I realised . . .'

'Didn't realise?' she says. 'Are you serious? Have you forgotten the time we were driving to London, you stopped for petrol and said you were going to molest the girl behind the till?'

I do remember this. I'd been playing Shades for about a year and was probably spending four or five hours a night on the game. I had begun to think in game commands. Eve would say something and I'd reply, 'Nod'. She'd ask if I wanted a coffee and I'd say 'Grin.' I began referring to myself in the third person (in multi-user games you type '<emote> fancies another glass of wine' and the game fills in '<Yourname> fancies another glass of wine').

'Bear thinks this *crème brulée* is magnificent,' I'd announce to Eve's embarrassment, at the dinner parties to which we were decreasingly frequently invited. I would use net abbreviations to people who didn't understand them.

'Bear disagrees. IMHO that won't work. The answer AFAIK . . .'

One evening Eve and I were on our way to visit a Shades friend, either Gawain or Branwell, when the fuel warning light came on. At the next service station I pulled in and said to Eve, 'Car needs a restam. Going to grab the girl.'

Those reality failures were warnings which I ignored, even after congestive heart failure dropped my stam to near zero. But it's easy to miss such warnings, so quickly does one learn to accept the weirdness of cyberspace. Ah Eve, I never dared tell you about the time when, shortly after Bear gained immortality, I came across a car shunted sideways up a bank in a narrow lane south of Croydon. There were two shaken women inside. They said they'd swerved to avoid someone racing down the hill. The other driver had failed to stop. I can't explain why, but I immediately read the situation as a scene from Shades. Two novice players had fallen into a crumbly-sided pit at Mocad Lane South, and were yelling for help. As an immortal, I could use my powers to rescue them. I towed their car off the bank, but its front wing was buckled. It couldn't be driven. I lent my mobile phone to one of the women so she could call her husband. Then I drove the two of them to a coffee shop where they could keep warm until he arrived. They were profusely grateful. 'How lucky we were to meet a real gentleman,' one of them said. I left thinking, 'Actually, ladies, you have just met a Shades Wizard.'

A voice in my head instantly retorted, 'Forty-one years old. Such puerility, how is it possible at your age?'

'I begged you to give up,' says Eve, still brooding. 'You should have stopped and if you'd really cared about me and the children you would have. You knew how destructive it was. Apart from anything, the bills were crippling us. But oh no, what did you do? You dragged your oldest friend into your beastly fantasy world. Lori phoned me and we compared notes on being modem widows. I could have bloody well killed you.'

'But Eve, I didn't have to drag Todd into cyberspace. He was already there. He just hadn't got there by modem.'

The barber of Fakenham

One day I get an excited call from Todd (guru-to-be of *The Butterfly Effect*), green-fingered grower of five-fingered leaves, and in the whole history of the universe one of my favourite people. There's something deeply good about someone who makes tea in a teapot. Todd has had an experience which he describes to me over the phone. I am so taken with it that I ask him to repeat his story so I can write it down.

Todd drives in to Fakenham, a small, unremarkable Norfolk market town, for a haircut. On his way to park the car he sees Fanthorpe's Barber Shop, which he has never noticed before. He doesn't . . . (at this point there is an indecipherable squiggle in my notes – a word that looks like, but which of course cannot be, 'ayqlecal'). Todd, anyhow, does not ayqlecal because Fanthorpe's looks expensive. Too ornate. The name on the window is done in antique letters of bottle green outlined in gold. He goes off to look for another barber but, mysteriously, can't find one. An hour later he is standing on an unfamiliar pavement . . . outside Fanthorpe's. Struck by the coincidence, Todd notices that beside the door is a sandwich board on which is painted, in sturdy letters of fishing-boat blue, the motto 'HAIRCUT SIR? STEP INSIDE NOW'.

The sign makes the shop seem a great deal more friendly, so Todd does as it asks. He pushes open the door. As he steps inside he is aware that whatever had been going on in there has stopped. The very silence draws him further. There is no turning back. The barber, an eccentric-looking man whose fair hair curls wildly round his face, says some words of greeting which instantly put Todd at his ease. He feels utterly at home. He feels that he knows the place, yet there is no sense of *déjà vu*. Todd sits down and immediately a banter springs up between him and the barber. It's not the usual haircutting banter. It is funny, uplifting. Todd tells me, 'I don't know this bloke from Adam, yet there I am, behaving as if he's an old mate.'

The barber asks Todd how he wants it (his hair). Will he prefer it shaved, or squared off at the back? Todd chooses square.

'Oh, oh, square back?' cries the barber.

'Why? What's wrong with a square back?' Todd asks.

'Not a lot,' cries the barber, 'Very popular style . . . in the sixties.' This reply sets Todd's senses reeling. He has difficulty framing words to convey his exaltation. Meanwhile, the amazing barber is doing all kinds of other things. He seizes the phone and speaks rapidly into it. But Todd notices that *he has not dialled a number*.

A dapper old gentleman is sweeping up hair off the floor. The barber says to him something like, 'Will you take this to Norwich?' and the old fellow replies in a cultivated accent, 'Michael, I really think that's going a bit far.'

Todd has the strongest feeling that this exchange is not a real conversation but a piece of theatre, possibly even staged for his benefit. It feels like a knowing and witty attempt to demonstrate the surreality of everyday life, like one of Castaneda's follies. (Does he mean Castaneda, or Don Juan? Castaneda's home page on the web is in Spanish and offers 'tensegrity' courses in Mexico City. Todd and Lori, when they visit us a few weeks later, bring the video: sombre, terrifying women making tigerish clawing movements, aggressive and utterly humourless. Eve is much taken with it.)

Without warning the old fellow leans on his broom and says in an impassioned voice, 'Don't let Billy know I'm here. I don't want to go and see Billy. I don't want to go and do his fucking car.'

The effing and blinding is strange from such a nice old man. It is just one of a series of such non-sequiturs which convinces Todd that these performances are not, after all, intended for his benefit, but are genuine dislocations of reality. They are happening in this place because this place is unlike the outside world.

At some point the barber remarks that he has opened up a body-piercing unit. Todd joshes him about which parts can be kebabed.

'We can pierce you wherever you like,' says the barber, 'but nothing below the belt.'

'What about a nipple?'

'Make an appointment,' is the unerring reply.

He hands Todd a card which bears the number of the woman who does the piercing. Astonishingly, the card uses exactly the same graphic of the sun as has been chosen by Todd and a friend for invitations to their Solstice 2000 party.

With coincidences arriving thick and fast the barber plunges his strong fingers into Todd's hair and begins to massage into his scalp a nautical-smelling lotion. It is a magic elixir, the man explains. Very expensive. It contains a large amount of rum which has been left by John, or Gervase, or else Harvey. The barber rattles off the names as if Todd should know who these people are. And Todd feels that he should; does know, has merely forgotten. At last he pays and leaves. As he steps through the door back into the real world, Todd realises that he is elated.

When did I first accept that I was an addict? It must have been shortly after Todd's epiphany, as though his barber had served up an *hors d'oeuvre* (or as Keet calls it, a *hars doofer*), a taste of things to come. My own life was by then already pretty strange. The friends I was making, both real and imaginary, were increasingly eccentric and surreal occurrences were becoming routine, but I didn't notice, because I was used to deranged realities. Then five bizarre things happened in as many days. It was shocking to realise that four of the five had their roots in cyberspace – as if the weird characters of my inner life had staged a breakout and were roaming at liberty, like dangerous lunatics on the lam, in the unready landscapes of the real world. I say real, but by then it was no longer possible to distinguish real life from fantasy. This was when I admitted that Old Mother Jarly had been right when he predicted that I'd end up 'using' . . .

Eve says, 'Listening to you makes me angrier.'

After this there is silence for a few miles.

'What the hell is that?'

'What?' says Eve.

Ahead of us – we're overtaking fast – are what look uncannily and impossibly like . . . the Land Rover shoots past. In the mirror, tiny figures are receding. Eve, turned to me, has not seen them. Am I imagining this? I must have made a mistake. Amazing how the mind instantly invents all kinds of far-fetched explanations when it cannot accept what it has actually seen. We drive on in silence. It seems an age before the next junction. I ease the car off and swing it around.

'What are you doing?'

'I have to check that they were real.'

She sighs and closes her eyes.

'This whole trip is ridiculous.'

'You didn't see them? It's uncanny. Look, aren't we in Ireland? Didn't we get off the ferry this morning? Half an hour ago didn't we pass through Waterford? Pinch me if I'm dreaming, but isn't this the N22 to Cork? '

Hammering back the way we'd come, a hedge obscures the view of the opposite carriageway. It's several miles before we can do another U-turn. We should see them again soon, *if* they exist.

'Well, you certainly saw *something*', she says.

Ahead of us the tiny dots are bobbing along the road. I slow the car and crawl up behind a group of strangely clad people walking in single file along the road to Cork.

'How odd,' says Eve. 'They look just like Indian villagers.'

The round blobs resolve to turbans bundled on top of heads, soft watermelon mounds such as you see in Rajasthan.

'Well,' she says, 'they *are* Indian villagers.'

The cloths draped round their hips, the ends loosely held in swinging hands, are *dhotis,* loincloths of the sort Mahatma Gandhi (to Churchill's great scandal) wore to Buckingham Palace for his audience with King George VI. They wear rustic waistcoats, below which long shirt tails hang. The only incongruous detail of their garb (perhaps, given its fundamental incongruity, the only normal thing) is that their shiny brown shins are tucked into woollen socks and stout walking shoes. What business an Indian villager can have to transact amongst Irish meadows, I cannot conjecture: but possibly they are on their way to Cork, about fifteen miles distant.

There are eight marchers, led by an upright and majestic old man. We stop a few yards ahead and wait for them to catch up. They come to Eve's window and crowd round it. Their dark eyes roam over us, our clothes, the inside of the car. I have the strangest feeling that *they* think *we* are exotic.

'You are from?' The classic Indian opening.

'We've just come over from England.'

Murmurs of approval. 'Oh, he speaks Urdu.'

'Originally, you are from?' asks the old man.

'Nakhlau', says another when I reply, 'no wonder he speaks Urdu. They speak a very decent Urdu in Nakhlau.'

'How long you have lived in England?'

'Is this your wife?'

'Wife is from?'

'How many children you have?'

'How much land have you?'

'Why children are not with you?'

'Do you grow crops?'

'Wife's parents are where?'

'In England, you must be keeping a cow?'

'Where are your children?'

'If not a cow you must be keeping a goat.'

'The children are with grandparents,' one of them informs the earlier questioner. 'They go to school in England.'

'In which standard do they study?'

'For how long you are on holiday?'

'What kind of car is this?'

'How very strange,' says the old man, 'to meet someone who speaks our language.'

'Wait, wait, wait. Never mind us. What are *you* doing here?'

'We have come here from Punjab. We are walking round the world for the sake of peace.'

They tell us the name of their village, on the Pakistani side of the border. They say they have been walking for months. There are so many questions I want to ask, but traffic is slowing, we are causing a queue.

'Are you going to Cork, *baba*? Where could I find you?'

The old man nods. I give him the name of our hotel and say, 'Please, promise you will call us when you arrive.'

As we pull away I realise that I haven't asked to whom they're trying to bring peace. Catholics and Protestants in Ireland? Hindus and Muslims in the subcontinent? Sikhs and Hindus in the Punjab? Or even Eve and Bear?

'Eve, it's midday on the 15th of July. We're on the N22, twenty miles east of Cork. Please find some paper and write it down. One day someone somewhere will be able to confirm that this really happened.'

A couple of miles on Eve says, 'I have a name for happenings like that. I call them no-incidences.'

She explains that no-incidences are far rarer and much stranger than coincidences: 'A co-incidence is an unexpected conjunction of familiar things. You're walking along a street in a strange town and in the space of a few minutes bump into two people from your home village, neither of whom knows the other person is there. Or you happen to be thinking about the work of Heinrich Böll and then suddenly read his name in a newspaper. Coincidences make us look for significance, some hidden meaning, as if the universe is trying to pass on a message. A no-incidence is a one-off event so unlikely that it can't be compared to anything else.'

In which case, Eve, the things that happened during the week of weirdnesses were the purest no-incidences. As was Todd's barber.

'You're sure you hadn't just overdone the tea leaves?' I asked him, when he'd finished his tale, but he swore, no, he was sober.

'According to Don Juan,' he told me, 'we assemble our reality through a point on our luminous bodies. When I walked into Michael's shop, the way he talked to me shifted my assemblage point and suddenly I was assembling a different sort of reality: I knew that I was in a chair and he was a barber, but there was something else that was much finer going on.'

The week of the five weirdnesses

I. Monday morning. Belfast is one vast outdoor art gallery. Wherever you turn, exuberant paintings glare off the walls. Heroic hooded figures stand or kneel, Armalites at the ready. In similar streets across town, identical figures adorn walls branded with a red fist, the red hand of Cuchulain. Some of these murals are eighty years old, dating back to the Easter uprising and the Somme. Successive generations, going over and over them, brush old hatreds into the fabric of the city. In news reports, Belfast seems twinned with Beirut but really it is ordinary, a damp city under a watery sky, pavements slick with rain; Victorian churches, parks with tired green grass and municipal railings: could be anywhere in these islands. Passing along a street of terraced houses with well-kept gardens, it is hard to believe that this is the Ardoyne, a stronghold of the Provisional IRA, a name I've only ever heard in the news.

We're in a car, being shown the sights. Our guide has a finely tuned sense of the macabre. 'See that bookie's? Nine men were shot dead in there a wee while back.'

'This road, Official IRA gunned down a Provie eight years ago.'

'That corner shop, a bomb killed four Catholics.'

Coming down the Falls Road away from Andersonstown, he says, 'See those railings? That's where the two British corporals got caught up in an IRA funeral, dragged from their car and beaten to death on the grass, over there.'

Turf Lodge. We pass a girl of about ten, wheeling a baby in a pram. A five-year-old with a dirty, tear smudged face spits at us. In Ballymurphy, Provo territory, a car behind us starts hooting. We ignore it, turn a corner in the narrow maze of terraced houses, and the car follows us. We make another turn, it's right behind us, and now it begins flashing its lights. Shit. Dead ahead, the road is blocked by a tall brick wall covered with IRA murals and graffiti. We've reached the 'Peace Wall' that separates the communities. No escape. The car behind is still hooting and flashing. I sit tense in the back, feeling my bowels twist as we come to the wall, stop. The hairs crawl on my neck. I realise that I'm expecting to be shot.

II. Monday evening. Safe home in Sussex ('Ah, it was just some feller waiting for his girlfriend' the driver said when I finally plucked up courage to ask) the phone rings. It's Molly, Eve's mother. She's choking and I think she's having an asthma attack, but it's fury. 'That bloody man, he's . . . Oh, it's . . . Bear, you . . . Eve won't . . . How could he . . . ?' Molly eventually says that she has just watched Biffo (Eve's father) write a cheque for £21,000 to two Scientologists who came to the house. 'They just stood there while he did it. And so did I.'

III. Tuesday evening. Eve switches on the television and our friends Zek and Misha Halu appear on screen. They are (Czechoslovakian) Tibetan-tantric sex-therapists, but this does not explain why they are wearing hats shaped respectively like a penis and a vulva and attempting to copulate them.

IV. Thursday morning. London 8 a.m. I enter a film studio near Tower Bridge and find a naked couple fucking vigorously on a mattress. They smile, wave and say 'Hi there!' Tones, teeth and tans proclaim them to be Americans. They are looped in wilting marigolds.

V. An hour later. I am in the Tower of London knocking at the door of the Governor's House. It is opened by the Governor, who asks if I have an idea yet for his TV commercial. I haver and he says, 'Bear, I am Her Majesty's Governor of the Tower of London and Keeper of the Crown Jewels and unless you instantly reveal your idea I will have you thrown in this dungeon.' (He adds that it is the one where Sir Walter Raleigh lived until his execution.)

It is twenty years, but hardly seems a moment, since I first met Biffo, and his daughter coached me how to behave. 'Careful what you say. For God's sake keep off Rhodesia. In fact don't mention Africa, Harold Wilson, the Labour Party, politics.'

Meeting a girlfriend's father for the first time is always a nervous experience. I stood in their drawing room, clutching a sherry as some anodyne, forgettable drama unravelled on the television, and reviewed what I knew of him. Born in Ireland before partition, orphaned young, brought up by a guardian. Went to Cambridge (same college as me), then the 7th Hussars. Had a good war, was in Egypt, recruited to the SOE and parachuted behind enemy lines in Greece. Lots of action. Had invested a small fortune in Rhodesia – this was before it became Zimbabwe – buying a hotel and land. Most of this I knew from Eve's mother, Molly, who in the (Anglo-) Irish tradition is a great woman for reminiscences.

'He used to be so gallant, Bear. He came on leave from the army and we went riding together. We went to Kilmacuddy to his cousins who'd made a sort of race-track around their fields. For some reason I did not have a saddle, so he gave me his and rode bareback. He vaulted up onto his horse, he was so dashing.'

Biffo turned out to be a dapper man with a military moustache and bright, amused eyes.

'So you're Eve's chap, eh? Hahahaha. Help yourself to a sherry or something. Got one? Splendid. What's this you're watching? Any good?'

Trying to think of an utterly uncontroversial reply, I came up with, 'Don't know, I've never seen it before.'

'Nor me,' he said immediately. 'Been away. Out of the country.

Africa. Rhodesia, actually.' Defiantly gun-cracked his glass onto the mantelpiece. Barked, 'I'm for 'em!'

Ten seconds. Masterly.

'He's always been like that,' his daughter explained. 'When he gets an idea into his head, it won't be budged. He never does things by halves.'

At eight Eve was a happy little girl with biscuit coloured pigtails that stuck out sideways from her head. She had an autograph book in which her friends wrote things like, 'By hook or by crook I'm the last in this book,' and 'When you're far across the sea, look at this and think of me.' Eve went to her father and said, 'Daddy, please will you write in my autograph book?' He said, 'Hahahaha, very well. What shall I put?' She said, 'Anything you like'. He thought, then got out his fountain pen, unscrewed the cap, and sat at the table for a very long time. When Eve got the book back she found that her father had written in his beautiful sloping hand:

In Xanadu did Kubla Khan
A stately pleasure dome decree
Where Alph the sacred river ran
Through caverns measureless to man
Down to a sunless sea . . .

And so on for the whole fifty-six lines, filling eight pages.

Eve's brother Orlando tells how Biffo found himself on a beach in Ireland with his children. What on earth do you do with children? Biffo picked up a stick, traced some lines in the sand and said, 'Now then. Which of you has heard of Pythagoras?'

Biffo is a qualified man-of-the-world. He'd spent his Egyptian service charging round the western desert in a tank. Leaves were spent in Cairo, playing polo and buying champagne for a Greek nightclub dancer known as Blacktops. Inter alia he had composed a long and extremely filthy ballad which displayed considerable metrical skill. In short, as fathers-in-law go, he was absolutely and utterly everything one could wish.

One day Molly finds him puzzling over something which has fallen out of a book. A questionnaire. Biffo unscrews his fountain pen and begins laboriously to fill it in. There are two hundred questions, which ask things like:

> 1. *Do you make thoughtless remarks or accusations which later you regret?*
> 2. *When others are getting rattled, do you remain fairly composed?*
> 3. *Do you browse through railway timetables, directories, or dictionaries just for pleasure?*

Biffo puts down his pen, reaches for his coat. He says he can claim a free personality test if he takes the completed questionnaire to the London Scientology Centre in Tottenham Court Road.

Last time we saw them they were sitting in our wild garden, under an overgrown rose bush which, like a slave at a Roman banquet, was showering them with petals.

Misha was telling me, 'Bear darlink, you need help, promise me you will do exactly as I say.'

Zek said, 'Yes, Misha darling knows best, Bear, you better take your medicine like a good boy.'

'What must I do?'

Misha said, 'First you agree to do what I tell you then I tell you what you have agreed to do.'

'You listen to Misha darling,' said Zek.

'Bear darlink every morning you must drink a glass of your own urine. You can mix it with orange juice. You will like this. You will be healthy and happy and . . .'

'You will be a new man, darling Bear,' said Zek. 'Just think of it, a new life. Just for you.'

Zek caught Eve staring at an amulet he wore around his neck.

'I am a VIP,' he explained. 'Very Important Penis.'

The amulet was a tiny *lingam*, dangling uncomfortably by the balls from a thin golden chain.

'Misha darling is also a VIP,' said Zek, 'Very Important Pussy.'

But she was wearing no amulet that I could see.

'Marigolds?' says Eve.

'They were rehearsing. The actress was called Madison. She was rather nice.'

'Obviously enjoyed her work,' says Eve. 'I suppose you'd call it an undress rehearsal.'

Pustaq Keet has a head like a polished potato which splits, at mouth level, into rows of teeth as I enter his bookselling premises.

'Bear-ji, just as well you have come. I have news.'

Keet, historically, has taken pleasure in repeating to me, at great length and from impeccable memory, the conversations he inflicts on his customers. There they will be, peacefully browsing shelves full of his strange stock – where else will you find titles like *Spores of the Indo-Gangetic Plain, Hints on Tiger Shooting,* or P. Sankaran's classic *Indications and Uses of Bowel Nosodes*? – when a stealthy rustling, growing louder, announces the subtle arrival of the proprietor. Turning too late, instantly transfixed by the potato grin, they see a shimmering figure clad in a silk *kurta* which drapes over the gentle swell of his belly and cascades in a fine sheen, like a waterfall, from the overhang.

'Ohé, sir, treat it like your mistress, not like your wife,' Keet will loudly advise the man who is trying to cram a book back onto a shelf. And to the girl who is looking for *Teach Yourself Gujerati,* he'll say, 'Quickest way is marry a Gujerati boy and learn from the slaps of your mother-in-law.'

I discovered Keet and his *Sanskritik Pustakalaya* by accident. Years ago, while researching the *Kama Sutra* in the Oriental Reading Room at the British Museum, I listed dozens of medieval Sanskrit erotic texts with long, expressive names like *ratiratnapradipika* and *srngararasaprabandhadipikamanjari.* Across the road was an Indian bookshop, a realm of smudgily printed books with out-of-register pictures, impregnated with the fearful whiffle of subcontinental ink. I placed my order and left. On my next visit I was halfway into the door when Keet bellowed across the crowded shop, 'Oh Mr

Bear, I have got those SEX BOOKS you wanted!'

Now, several years later, as I step through the same door, Keet bares his teeth in a friendly and terrifying grimace, dives his hand into an inner garment and extracts a piece of paper.

'You should thank me, Bear *babu*. I have done you a favour. Yesterday, someone came into the shop, asking for you. A young lady from a TV company.'

'Asking for me?'

'Yes, I found her poking around the sexy books, so I said "Is there something I could help you with?"'

'She said, "I am looking for the *Kama Sutra*". So I told her, "You don't look in need of such instruction."'

'What did she say to that?'

'She smiled. What else could she do? Then she said "There is a modern translation by someone called Bear."'

'She actually *asked* to buy it?'

'Yeeees,' says Keet. 'So I said, "Look over there, you will find a heap of Bearwallah *Kama Sutra*". She was pleased. I asked her, "Why do you want it? Just to look at the pictures?" She said "It's not for me, my company is making an educational video."'

'So I said, "If it's academic side you are interested in, Bear did uncover some orthographical errors in Burton. For example where the Sanskrit says *yaksha ratri*, Burton had translated *aksha ratri*, thus the 'night of the goddesses' became 'night of dice' . . . There are a few other things of that sort."'

'She started laughing and said "No no no, I don't think that's the type of information they are looking for." I gave her a straight look and said, "What is your honest intention?" And she said, "We need the help of someone who knows the text." I told her, "Madam, you are in luck. I have studied Sanskrit since a small child. My father hung me up by my *chhoti*, which was a single lock of hair left on top of my shaved head, and forced me to read great classics by sooty lamplight. I can sing verses of *Ramayana*. I recite Kalidasa.

What lines from Shakespeare can rival Jayadeva's *lalitalavangalatá parishílanakómalamalayasamírémadhukaranikarakarambitakókilakúnjita kunjkutíré*?"'

'What did she say to that?'

'She said, "I'll just have the book." So I told her, "Beware. Bear's translation is no doubt poetic, but in that sense he has taken full licence and some might say his sensibilities are crass and under-informed. If you meet Bear you will see that he is the wrong shape to be a master of the erotic arts."'

'Thank you, Keet,' I say, remembering that on meeting Eve, he had congratulated her with many winks on acquiring a 'properly educated' husband. ('*Kama* bridges Cambridge's gaps.')

'Ploy backfired,' says Keet. 'She said "You know Bear? We would like to contact him."'

'So did you give her my number?'

He looks shocked. 'Of course not. Would I do so without your permission? No, I said to her, "Madam, aforesaid author is a friend of mine and in all matters pertaining to hard and soft currency, I must consider myself his agent."'

It transpires that someone from the film company came across the pirated verses on *wiretap.spies* and had the idea of hiring me as a script consultant. This is what led the unfortunate girl to enter Keet's weird realm of bowel nosodes, and how he became the unlikely midwife who brought into the 'real' world a chain of events which had begun in cyberspace.

Kissimmee quick

The fantasy goes like this: writer gets development deal from Hollywood film studio, leases huge car and house with pool in Beverly Hills, leads the life until money runs out. This is not quite the same. Yes, I'm sitting by the pool working on a screenplay, but the pool's in Kissimmee, Florida, enclosed in a mesh insect cage. True, there is an enormous car in the drive, but we are here for only two weeks and the screenplay isn't exactly an Oscar contender . . .

A few days after my visit to Keet the film company made contact. They had problems with their script. Would I advise?

Keet urged me to accept. 'Bear *dost*, what is there to lose? Read script. Suggest a few changes. Pocket fee. Give me a percentage.'

'I don't know . . . It's the absurdity of it that's attractive.'

'Yeeeees,' he said. 'That and money too.'

The script was chunks of Burton's 1888 translation taken out of context. The meaning of the work was lost. They had homed in on the sexual positions and paid only lip service to kisses (hahaha, this is Keet), and the rest of the syllabus of love.

'It's incredible,' I said to Eve. 'Can you believe? They have no idea that the *tilatandula* embrace leads to the *veshtitaka* posture.'

She glared at me. We were due to leave for Florida with the kids the next day.

'You'll have to tell them you can't do it.'

'But I can . . . When we arrive I'll hire a PC and modem, and squirt the file back via Gawain or Lilith.'

Eve is not at all happy about this. But it's what happens. At the airport, we take charge of a car built like a small aircraft carrier and spend most of our first day driving round Orlando looking for a computer store. The house we are staying in (it belongs to Lilith), backs onto a lake in which there are alligators. I sit staring at the laptop, while huge insects batter at the mesh cage, trying to gnash their way in. The script is risible, but all I can change is the voice-over. The sets have been built, filming will soon commence. The producers want the piece to have 'contemporary relevance', so there's a scene where the heroine is ravished on a kitchen table ('Bear, can you come up with some good positions?'), and another where she practises what modesty compels me to describe as *nimita*, leading to *chumbita* and *parshavodashta*, under a papier-maché oak.

I scour Vatsyayana's text for references to kitchen and garden. *Sutra IV.i.18* states 'The kitchen should be clean, well-ventilated, properly lit and situated in the heart of the house where guests and strangers cannot see inside.' No mention of a table. This section, where Vatsyayana is specifying the duties of a wife, is one of the most fascinating parts of the *Kama Sutra*. In her garden, he bids her plant sugarcane, turmeric, coriander, ginger, cumin and mustard-seed. She must obtain and plant moss roses, pearl jasmine, Arabian and Spanish jasmines, amaranth, queen-of-the-night, *kadamba* and the China rose. So much for flowers. Vegetable-wise, she is enjoined to collect seeds of radish, yams, olibanum, mango, wormwood, cucumber, muskmelon, aubergine, pumpkin, calabash, parsnip, pomegranate, cowhage, caravalla, garden-quinine, garlic and onion for sowing at the proper season. Nowhere does the sage command the planting of oak trees. Nor does he suggest what may be done in, under, or up against them. I plug in the modem to see what the local cyberverse looks like. The *Osceola Horticultural BBS* has a library of files instructing the folk of Kissimmee how to grow lawns, flowers, vegetables and herbs.

Kissimmee, oh Kissimmee quick, you are quite amazing. Forget cyberspace. The Vortex has nothing on this, a fantasy eleven miles long – I check this on the car's odometer – with every possible escape from reality. Arabian Nights; Medieval Times. At Fort

Liberty, a cowboy castle, we are served by a lad dressed like a trooper from Custer's Last Stand. Eve and the children adore the Congo River crazy golf courses which resemble meerkat colonies, complete with baked clay termitecture and blue cascades. We are thrilled by the drive-in burger joints. We eat at Basil's Gourmet Dinning (sic) which promises the haûtest of haût European cuisine, but serves tough game smothered in cream and cranberry sauce – maybe Basil is Transylvanian. Each night on the television, smiling people promote bizarre products. Eve is much taken with a device which looks like a giant hamster cage.

'Bear, I must have one. It dries fruit and it's obviously a huge breakthrough because there's an entire TV programme about it.'

This is the life. England is so dull by comparison. The only thing missing here, its absence supplying the perfect finishing touch, is the tiniest trace of irony. All this and Walt Disney World too. In a café on Main Street USA, we see a video of WDW's manager, a ferociously sincere fellow who says, 'I never forget that my boss is Mickey Mouse.'

'O o o,' says the bird.

'Yes,' says Lilith, 'We are all refugees from reality.'

'DANGEROUS VISIONS FEATURES IMMEDIATE DEPARTURES TO OTHER PLANETS AND DIMENSIONS.'

'Why settle for just one reality?' demands the slogan in the dark sci-fi bookshop where Nico and Alexei have gone to ask directions. Lost in the dreary wastes of west Los Angeles, all they know is that they're somewhere in the Valley, where the city spills over the mountains before the desert begins.

Other planets and dimensions? Hell of a place to ask the way, Nico is thinking. The two of them wearing shades and Hawaiian-style bush shirts have been cruising the streets in a scarlet Cadillac Coupe de Ville convertible rented in Beverly Hills, perfect for a pair of hot movie producers on their way to a casting session.

'We're looking for . . .'

'World models? Hey, I know the place. The Doll Shoppe. It's really near. Head out the door, right along Ventura . . .'

The Doll Shoppe sells gigantic dolls, tall as children, with names like Monroe and Jackie.

'Keep going,' says Nico.

Twenty minutes later, they find what they are looking for, an unremarkable two-storey house above a launderette. A sign says World Modeling Talent Company. They head up dark stairs made gloomier by black carpet – shiny aluminium tie-rods bear witness to an attempt at style – and enter a drab room at one end of which, behind a scuffed desk, sits a man wearing a bootlace tie.

The man appears surprised to see them.

'Mr South? Jim South? We called you yesterday,' says Alexei, adding unnecessarily, 'We're the guys from England.'

The man slides open his drawer and from it takes out a glass ashtray. Lights a menthol cigarette. 'What you guys looking for?'

Dry southern accent, like a lizard's tail rattling on stones.

Nico and Alexei look at each other. The man waits patiently, his eyes flitting past them to the other desk, where a secretary is at work with some papers. After a couple of drags he stubs out his cigarette, finds a tissue, wipes the ashtray clean and replaces it in the drawer.

'We're looking for actors. For a movie. A quality production,' says Nico. 'Not porno. Educational. A classic Indian text.'

'Okay,' says the man. 'What tribe?'

'Not that kind of Indian,' says Alexei.

The man reaches into his drawer and brings out the glass ashtray. Fishes for his pack of Kools. Lights up, takes a drag.

'The actors,' he says. 'You want they do everything?'

'Well, er . . . only what's in the text.'

'Yeah?' He stubs out his cigarette, barely tasted, empties the ashtray, wipes it and puts it away. He gets up, crosses the room and fetches some thick volumes. Heavy scrapbooks. He thumps them on the table and says, 'Tell me if you see something you like.'

He sits down at his desk, slides open the drawer and gets out the ashtray. A smile blows across the cracked desert of his face.

'Or if you like something you see.'

Nico and Alexei begin leafing through the scrapbooks. The World Modeling Agency has everything. 'Dwarves', 'Giants', 'Fat Ladies', 'Uglies', 'Freaks', labelled presumably without reference to their clients' feelings. The porn actors fill four books. There are hundreds of them; name, picture and resumé. Beside each entry is a row of ticks.

'The ticks?' says the man. He's halfway through his regulation six drags. 'Well, five ticks means they'll do anything you can think of, and more. You think of it, they'll do it.'

Sucks at his Kool.

'Four ticks means they'll do butt-work. Three's oral.'

Another toke. 'Two is straight stuff only. One means glamour okay, rest no way José.'

He stubs his cigarette out, empties the ashtray, wipes it and drops it back in its drawer.

'Make your choice and I'll have the actors here tomorrow.'

Nico and Alexei are the video's producers. They're here to cast it, equipped with descriptions of the four types of women idealised by Indian eroticists. The first person they saw was Ashlyn Gere.

The Padmini, or Lotus woman. Her face is lovely as the full moon, her rounded limbs are soft as walnut flowers. Her eyes are sloes with sharply pointed corners dipped in red, wide as a fawn's. Her nose is a little sesamum flower, her lips trembling sprays of scarlet bandhujiva.

'She is built like a brick excrement-house,' an Ashlyn Gere fan writes on a web page. This must mean something else in America because in Britain it isn't a compliment. Ashlyn began her career in horror, but then found her *métier* in porn, an industry which gives itself nearly as many awards as advertising does. She'd won Best Performer awards for three years in a row and was one of the few people to do mainstream work after being in adult films. (She played Bonnie McRoberts in *The X-Files*.) As a superstar of the adult industry, Ashlyn had several films lined up, but she showed a polite interest in the project. ('Those ancient guys knew stuff that just blows your head off.')

The Hastini, or Elephant woman. Abandoned in her eagerness to win new lovers, her lips are greedy for kisses. She likes violent lovemaking and only a master of love can satisfy her.

They went to Marina del Rey to see Ona Zee and her husband Frank, doyens of the sacermasoch scene (chains, whips, bulldog-clipped nipples). Ona is a square-jawed brunette who nowadays makes her own pictures. They knew at once that it was no go. It was Ona who suggested they ring World Modeling.

The second day, they spend only a couple of minutes with the bootlace tie man (ashtray, six drags, upend and empty, wipe clean, put away) before he shows them to a small room with two chairs and a table and leaves them.

'Six puffs every time,' says Alexei.

One by one, the actors and actresses they've picked enter the room and unselfconsciously strip to show off firm, smooth bodies.

'So what theme does the pic have?' one girl asks.

'It's based on the *Kama Sutra*,' says Nico.

'The whut?'

A smiling young man, flexing a complex musculature, asks, 'You wannasee wood?'

'Wood?' says Nico.

'Yah. You know. I can show you a boner.'

'No, no, not necessary.'

'No problem for me, bud.'

'No honestly, it's okay.'

Flying back across the Atlantic they work out how much they've spent on flights, cars and hotels with nothing to show for it.

Nico goes to Belgium, to a house in a suburb of Brussels. In a back room are filing cabinets full of modelling cards. Thousands of them. Most of the girls are from eastern Europe. The agent pulls out a picture of a very beautiful, very young, girl.

'She'll do anything to get out of Russia,' he says. 'But it will be her first time.'

The Shankhini, or Conch woman. Although not petite, her breasts are firm, her waist slim though not curvaceous; she moves swiftly, swinging long legs and arms in a rangy stride like a young man's.

Nico locates one of the Russian girls at a 'glamour' shoot. She is sitting on a stool surrounded by photographers who are shouting instructions at her. The girl is obviously confused. She fastens huge eyes on Nico as if pleading, 'Get me out of here.' For a moment, he daydreams about stepping forward to rescue her, but stops when he remembers what he has to offer.

Nico hears about a dancer called Madison who has made adult films. She's lots of fun, the informant says, exciting, with a dark tan and Cleopatra hair. She could pass for an Indian. Her agent says she's in Europe. Nico and Alexei finally find track her down at the International Porn Awards in Paris.

The Chitrini, or Pretty-as-a-picture woman. Her curls are swarms of black bees framing a pretty face from which peep a pair of bright restless eyes and a lips that pout like a pair of bimba gourds.

'Madison is terrific,' Nico says. 'Bubbly, friendly, funny, bright. She's relaxed and not at all fucked up, which is pretty remarkable, given the business she's in.'

The yoga of two

The narrative I write for the *Kama Sutra* video is not so much an explanation of what the text is, as of what it isn't. The *Kama Sutra* is usually thought of as a guide for advanced lovers. In fact the reverse is true: it was written for novices and virgins. In India, now and in Vatsyayana's day, people marry young and most marriages are arranged. The bride and groom might be teenage strangers who have never been alone together before their wedding night. Ahead of them lies perhaps half a century of married life. Divorce being unthinkable, it would be useful if they could fall in love and then, human nature being what it is, stay in love. The *Kama Sutra* is a guide to how to fall in love with the person to whom you are *already* married. Its techniques, starting with nuzzled near-kisses, are the gentlest introduction to physical love. The young lovers are taught to proceed step by slow step. A moment's reflection will show what must have been obvious to Vatsyayana and every other writer on erotics, that it is ridiculous to classify just eight, twenty or fifty kinds of kisses, embraces, love bites, nail marks or sexual positions. Any porn website contains pictures of hundreds more postures than are listed in *Kama Sutra.* So why classify? Why give names to specific body conjunctions and detailed instructions for manoeuvring arms and legs? There are two reasons. Superficially, the embraces, kisses and postures are the practice exercises of a *yoga*-of-two, but their deeper purpose is to train the couple to be *mindful together*. The sexual positions are merely moments plucked from a flowing dance. When lovers are attuned by practice, it is the *minds* which experience communion and then it no longer matters what the bodies do. They can be freed to improvise and the love-making will be skilled, breathless, ardent, inexhaustible. Physical orgasm ceases to be important. It is the *minds* that dissolve into one another, the experience being blissful beyond description.

Eve, patiently weeding your herb garden, you look up and smile – in a circular henge of roses, you grow costmary, borage, hyssop, dill, rosemary, bergamot, tree onions, camomile, angelica, chives, cotton lavender, parsley, catmint, lemon balm, summer savoury, comfrey, meadowsweet, elecampane, winter savoury, horseradish, many different mints, coriander, oregano, various sages, fennel, lavender, several types of thyme, rocket, caraway, sweet cicely, chervil, rue, basil, lovage, marjoram, sorrel, wall germander, orris, lemon verbena, marigolds, sunflowers, feverfew, French tarragon, Russian tarragon, nasturtium, heartsease, wormwood and garlic – a lock of hair curves down and touches your chin. When two people in sympathy share any pleasurable activity, it generates love between them. This is as true of reading aloud to one another, or gardening side by side, as it is of making love on a bed of crushed flowers, or flattened grasses.

'Don't you think it's ironic', says Eve (we have reached Cork and I am unpacking the laptop and searching our hotel room for a phone socket for the modem), 'that you were writing about the bliss of marriage and the joy of doing things together while your wife and children had to go off to Disney World by themselves?'

'Bear, did you ever do it in those games, with other people?'

'Oh hell, you're not jealous are you?'

'Should I be?'

'As a matter of fact, no. I was always too embarrassed. Maybe, if I'd managed to conquer my inhibitions . . . Well, I'll confess, I almost made love once, with Lilith. To see what it was like.'

'And you can talk about it just like that? You don't think I'll be hurt? Didn't you think you were being unfaithful?'

'It was all in the mind. There was no reality to it.'

'Doesn't emotional adultery matter?'

'It's hardly very serious.'

'What about all these people who fall in love on the internet? Marriages breaking up. You can't say it isn't serious.'

'Well, I suppose you are right. Branwell and Hypatia fell in love on the net and they're happily married.'

'So does it matter if you fall in love? Or doesn't it?'

'The nearest I ever came was with Luna. I loved talking to Luna, being with her. But you couldn't call it love. I didn't even know if she was a she.'

'What did Lilith mean, "Luna lives through the Vortex"?'

'I wish I knew. Luna is a one-off.'

'Bear, just suppose you succeed in pulling me into your world, like you pulled Todd . . . Suppose I got emotionally mixed up with some stranger? Imagine that. Would you mind?'

Lobster and white wine in Cork (*gliomach* is Irish for 'lobster'). A long, deliciously weary evening, still light at ten o'clock, Hare Krishnas tambourining through the streets. Eve – is it the wine? – seems happy. Walking back to the hotel her arm slips into mine. She says, 'We haven't travelled alone together for ages . . . '

I have pulled the thread of time from this narrative, as you pull the string from a necklace, scattering the beads to fall where they may, in unpredictable constellations. Our marriage had been quietly eroding over a long period, but outwardly little had changed. The tide goes out and you follow, crossing the low beach, rippling slicks of water, ribbed sand, rocks draped with weed . . . however far the sea goes out, you always expect it to return.

'Eve, remember Venice?'

We went there the year after we were married. Arrived in the small hours and took a water-taxi through canals that looked like a deserted film set. We stared in wonder as it chugged out into the wide Guidecca canal and all the lights from San Marco to the Arsenale suddenly came into view. It was a time when we'd been in love, and when being in love meant not being able to say so because mouths pressed breathlessly together cannot speak. It was perfect. We vowed that if ever in future we were in trouble, we'd say 'Remember Venice', and that this charm would always work, no matter what. Remember, Eve, how we danced on the Lido's wet sand, our feet made patterns that wove in and out of each other. While we slept, the Adriatic poked out green tongues and melted them like the icing of a cake, our two pairs of footprints, that sometimes wandered far from each other but always came back.

Okay Eve, follow me.

We are standing at the end of a road outside a brick building. Around us is a forest. A small stream flows out of the building (Eve says, 'Oh like that place in Venice') and down a gully.

'You take over now. You decide what to do next. Anything you like. Up to you.'

'All right,' she says, 'let's look inside.'

We are inside a small building, a well-house for a large spring. Water is bubbling up through a grate. On the ground are some keys, a brass lamp, some food and a bottle of water.

'What do I do now?' she asks.

'Whatever you like.'

In vulgar – no, actually, thrilling – reality, she's poring over my laptop, which is plugged into a phone socket in the hotel in Cork. She has asked me to show her what it's like to be inside a game. Our heads close together, we study the text that is scrolling up the silvery screen.

'I bet it's a pine forest,' says Eve. 'I don't like the way the trees strobe when you drive through pine plantations.'

'Is that how you see it?' I ask, surprised.

'Of course not. We're not in a car are we? We're on foot.'

'Are we? What gives you that idea?'

'Well, it says we're standing outside the building.'

'Yes, but we could have flown there. Nowhere does it say we have to walk.'

'We can fly?'

'Why not?'

'Let's go back outside then.'

We are at the end of a road outside a brick building. Around us is the forest. A stream flows out of the building (which I imagine to be old brick, says Eve, because it makes me think of that building in Venice, which the architect brought the tide into. The building she is remembering is the Querini Stampalia, its ravaged brickwork rising out of the sluggish ratswim of the Rio Santa Maria Formosa. The architect was Carlo Scarpa. It was an amazing thing he did. The guardians of Venice face a losing battle against salt and tides, foundations nibbled away faster than new layers of stucco can be slapped on; when the wind blows up the Adriatic, backing up the tides, you get a storm surge, the canals flood and this is every Venetian architect's nightmare, the feared *aqua alta.* When Carlo Scarpa redesigned the palazzo as the Querini Stampalia museum, he made a water gate which, instead of shutting the flood tide out, welcomed it inside as an important guest and invited it to flow in elegant marble channels through the building) and down a gully.

'Let's go this way,' says Eve.

'Okay.'

We're in a valley in the forest beside a stream tumbling along a rocky bed.

'Keep going south.'

'Okay.'

Whoops, where did the stream go? Downstream there's nothing but dry rocks and the bleached bones of trees.

I catch up with her peering down into a twenty-foot depression at the bottom of which is a sturdy steel grate mounted in concrete.

'It's locked,' she says. 'What do we do now?'

'Obviously, we need the key.'

'Oh no,' she says, 'not all the way back?'

We're standing outside a brick building. Around us is a forest. A small stream flows out of the building (through delicately jointed water gates, the salty tides of the Rio Santa Maria Formosa ebb and swell through Scarpa's marble and Istrian interior. Remember, Eve, how we discovered Carlo Scarpa? We saw that statue of a huge nude woman washed up by the sea on the steps by the Biennale. The waves were teasing round her body. You said, 'How original, to make the sea part of the sculpture.' *Monument to the Partisan Woman*, that's what it was called, we saw it from the vaporetto on the way back from the Lido and next day we walked down to look at it. It was Rîves who told us that Scarpa had set it there in the sea. Do you remember Rîves? We'd walked for hours by the sluggish canals of Cannaregio, through the Ghetto Nuovo, and were making our way tiredly back to our hotel. It started raining, hammering down. We took shelter in a café on the Grand Canal, near the Rialto bridge. One moment we were sitting, drinking coffee and the next the wind was kicking along the alleys, picking up scraps of paper, the first fat drops of rain were falling – watery phials that burst, releasing the scent of rain on dry ground, just like the monsoon – then all hell broke loose. Lightning, thunder, waiters at cafés up and down the banks dismantling their awnings, bringing in tables and chairs while we sat stolidly and watched the rain rifle down onto the canal. The vaporetto captains kept going, but afterwards we let the San Marco-bound boats go and decided to walk back via the Fenice to find the studio of Matteo lo Greco who, we'd been wrongly informed, had sculpted the wave-stranded woman. Our feet left wet trails through the labyrinth of Venice, in alleys with names like Calle dell' Assassini, and at last we came across the gallery, a darkened stage where ballerina-like sculptures hovered in the shadows. Right at the back sat a young man with a huge music score spread half across the desk, half on his lap, playing a guitar. He put down the instrument as we came in. You said, 'Don't stop.' He replied, 'He doesn't like me playing when there are people here,' and this was Rîves. We talked for an hour about sculpture and Scarpa, whom Rîves quoted as saying: 'In these times you should not expect any words of my own from me, none but those which barely manage to prevent silence from being misinterpreted.'

Rîves could talk on any subject: details of brickwork in Bellini's paintings, the orchestra at Florian's; somehow we found ourselves discussing the Venetian sewage system and how the city's architects had hollowed cisterns under each piazza so that the rain would run in) and down a gully.

Eve picks up the keys. Turns to go. Stops. Takes the lamp. Ten minutes later we're deep underground. Eve finds a small songbird in a wicker cage. The fittering lamp reveals we are in a splendid chamber whose walls are frozen rivers of orange stone.

'Like Pêche Merle,' says Eve.

Memories crowd forward out of the shadows as Eve presses deeper into the cave. Why do these games, which are played in the mind, need caves and tunnels? Shades is the same, even the Vortex encourages troglodytes. Do they somehow reflect the innerscape of bowels, veins, stomach and heart, leading to the mazes of the mind where neurons make more connections than there are stars in the galaxy? Or do the tunnels and caves of multi-user games, meant to evoke thrills and danger, rekindle distant memories of humanity's first homes? At Pêche Merle, Eve had been moved by the prints, outlined in lampblack, of a woman's slender hands, left twenty-five thousand years ago.

In a few minutes, we find a rock into which is carved the word 'XYZZY'. No, Eve, don't . . .

'Xyzzy?' says Eve.

There is a vivid flash and we find ourselves standing at the end of a road outside a brick building. Around us is a forest. A small stream flows out of the building (whose unremarkable exterior hides passages that descend to lampless depths. A coder once told me, 'You can't have a proper game without a castle. The castle stands guard over the labyrinth.' Every game maker is a labyrinth builder, and every architect is a castle builder. Castles are edifices erected by reason above the caves and tunnels of the subconscious.

Are they meant to keep intruders out, or monsters in? And what is the ultimate purpose of any labyrinth but to bring you face to face with the monsters that lurk in your own psyche? That's why you must experience death, in these games, so you can feel your own life more fully. Rîves told us that Scarpa used to play tricks on his – what would you call them, a writer has readers, what does an architect have – experiencers? For example, the paths in the garden of the Querini Stampalia end abruptly, some of them deliberately obstructed. At Treviso, Scarpa designed a cemetery where ropes block the paths. He wanted people in that place of death to stumble, because when you feel your body, you feel most intensely alive. Venetians, of all people, should know about masks. Scarpa wanted to strip away all the layers that mask direct experience, to bring you face to face with what's left when all the masks are down and how I wish, how achingly I wish the masks were down between us Eve, you and I, watching the years and yes, tears too, flow away) and down a gully.

'We are so stupid,' says Biffo. 'We try to grab hold of a little bit of immortality. We don't realise that we are already immortal.'

I try not to argue with Biffo about Scientology. Instead, I tell myself that it's a privilege to know someone who is going through something so extraordinary . . . if only it didn't cost so much.

'You shouldn't think of it like that,' says Biffo. 'It's not a great deal for transforming your life. It's less than you'd pay for a house, or a wonderful car.'

He reckons to have spent about £70,000 on Scientology training.

Biffo says, 'If you acknowledge that the world is in a terrible state and getting worse – crime, education, drugs, insanity, everything – well, let's predicate a state of affairs that could account for this decline. If we are utterly logical, we come to the simple but enormously far-fetched idea that once, we used to be godlike. Since when we have declined, hahaha . . . It's valueless writing this.'

He means it's pointless my writing down what he's saying, which I am doing, as fast as I can.

'We *are* immortal,' Biffo tells me. 'We are spirits trapped in the universe of mass, energy, space and time. We need to free ourselves. We are spirits who find ourselves in bodies, which is a most unpleasant and dangerous place to be. Life is a game on this planet. Scientology is an escape route from this planet, from being trapped in a meat body. Sounds absurd, I know. Outlandish. Everyone thinks you're mad if you go along with it.'

The net, I tell Biffo, is full of immortality seekers: Kabbalists who claim immortality is a state of mind attainable by meditating on the letters במוכסז; cyborgians who want to replace human bits with robotic spares; extropians seeking to evolve beyond the mortal and human. I tell him about the cryogenists, who immure themselves in

Tutankhamun-chambers of liquid nitrogen, hoping that a doctor from the future will reverse their deaths; the mind-uploaders who dream of transferring their brain contents to a hard disk and live forever in the silicon vortices of the net. There's the 'immortality' of the roleplaying games (Jarly peddled immortality: for £100 he would play your character to wizard for you), and of virus buffs writing themselves epitaphs capable of infinite survival.

'Well of course that's all nonsense,' says Biffo. 'But immortality *is* infinite survival. We are spirits and a spirit is a "static", meaning not material. Ron Hubbard understood this. He is a tremendous human being. A fantastic scholar. A man who discovered by his own efforts how to increase the IQ a thousand fold, how to operate as a spirit.'

He looks at me and says, 'Look here, I think you've got rather the wrong idea about what I'm up to. What we're doing is deeply, deeply, scientific. We're not just buggering about, you know. It's work. Bloody hard work. It's the hardest I've ever worked. And we're doing it to save the world.'

'When I came across Dianetics,' says Biffo, 'I felt it was either profound philosophy, or utter nonsense, hahaha. If there was any truth in it, it had to be the most important book ever written. So I decided to check it out. I confess that at first I didn't find the people as impressive as I'd expected, but the tech worked. It was utterly electrifying. It was electric, about ten million times more powerful than anything I'd ever thought of . At the age of fourteen if you'd asked me "What do you want to grow up to be?", I'd have said "Brave and honest and true". Not a stockbroker. I wanted to be a genuinely good man . . . Sometimes, in auditing, you have the feeling of tremendous goodness coming into you.'

The scientific side, so far as I understand it, is the use of what he calls an 'E-meter'. Biffo takes me up to his bedroom and shows me what look like two shining soup cans connected to a galvanometer.

'When you hold these, a tiny current flows through your body. The stuff going on in your mind causes fluctuations and the needle measures them . . . I've been eating vitamins to try to put on weight. I was afraid I'd be too old to shift the needle.'

I ask how auditing actually works.

The first time he was audited, Biffo was asked, 'Can you recall an incident from your past that you are willing to talk about?'

He thought back to his first parachute jump, something he had always remembered with pleasure. He had just been seconded to Force 133 of the Special Operations Executive. 'Our parachuting was not the same as for regular troops. We did it from high level – Parachuting from great heights at night. It was David Sterling's [the founder of the SAS] idea . . .'

'On the morning I hadn't slept too well. We were up by six and went to the airfield, Latifia near Haifa, in Palestine. A bright, clear, beautiful April morning in 1943. I was ready. We'd already done a lot of drill. Were very muscled up. Once we got up there was an extraordinary contrast in the aeroplane, a good deal of anxiety and noise – it was a Halifax bomber. I'd noticed how even the most overconfident seeming parachutists, just before going, looked very white and was determined to put on a good show when my turn came. When they throw open the door it doubles the noise, plucks your testing finger away in the airstream. The red light goes green. The despatcher is yelling at you, 'Go go go go', at the top of his voice. The static lines are banging against the inside of the plane. You push yourself out. I looked out and felt 'My God'. I never dreamed of not going. Outside the plane, I blacked out for a few seconds. When I came to I was tumbling high above the earth. Ground far above me. I was absolutely alone. Not a sound. When the chute opened, I was so delighted. It was so peaceful in the wide blue. I was really enjoying myself. As the ground neared, I began to get out of the harness. People were yelling. I thought they were applauding me, but they were shouting "You bloody fool! Get back in your harness." I felt tremendously bucked.'

'I got a very very vivid reaction – reshowing of the incident – during the auditing. I started to blubber – that's the only word. I could feel my face twisting up and was making sobbing noises. I felt embarrassed. I'd been taught not to blub. Tried to stop it, but couldn't really, so I just carried on. I was amazed. I thought, it's not nonsense, there's something very important going on here.'

Threat to sue all internet users

'Use the internet a lot, do you?' asks Biffo. 'Well I'm sorry to say it's going to have to close down.'

He glares at me. 'People have been using it to spread lies. And they've taken copyright material and published it illegally.'

Biffo is referring to a row, of which I am vaguely aware, that has been rumbling along in the *alt.religion.scientology* newsgroup, where a number of people have posted things which the Church of Scientology insists are confidential, violations of its copyright. Among the hijacked materials is a story about an intergalactic being who chains human souls together, dumps them at the bottom of volcanoes and detonates nuclear bombs on top of them. This is claimed to be a secret of one of the higher grades. A Scientology lawyer called Helena Kobrin starts issuing threats of legal action to people in the newsgroup. With a few deft touches, an unknown hoaxer transforms one of these into a threat against 'all internet users'.

> Newsgroups: alt.religion.scientology
> Date: Wed, 9 Aug 1995 12:19:04 -0700 (PDT)
> From: Helena Kobrin
> Subject: NOTICE FROM RTC TO ALL INTERNET USERS
> Distribution: world
>
> . . . It is essential that you take immediate and effective action to remove the unauthorized copies from your Web pages, servers, net news groups and any other places or means of distribution . . . I will expect immediate responses from all of you with a statement of your willingness to comply with these demands.

Unfairly, but most amusingly, this wins Helena the Usenet's *Kook of the Month Award* for September 1995. Meanwhile the spoof is spreading itself across the net with her email address on it. How will Helena cope if every one of the estimated fifty million internet users immediately sends her a personal statement of contrition?

The Scientology thing, which initially we had all treated as a joke, has turned sour. Biffo has a right to spend his time and money on whatever he likes, but his absences at the Scientology centre in London and the headquarters in East Grinstead are growing longer and more frequent. Molly hates being left on her own and among his children there is a resentful if unspoken feeling that he is squandering their inheritance. Biffo, meanwhile, interprets any criticism as hostility to Scientology. I try to tell him that none of us knows or cares anything about Scientology. It may or may not be a marvellous thing, the issue is Biffo himself.

One day Biffo announces he has decided to take lodgings in East Grinstead with a Scientologist family, so he can be near the library where he studies. This time he is gone for weeks. Christmas Eve arrives, Biffo doesn't. East Grinstead is only a dozen miles from us. On Christmas Day, Eve and I drive across the bleak, otherwordly landscape of Ashdown Forest – snow flurries and white patches in the bracken – with our three small children bearing gifts for their grandfather.

It's bitterly cold. Wrapped up warm, they present themselves at the door of the house. A shimmering shape materialises on the other side of the frosted glass door.

'He's not in,' says the unsmiling woman who opens it. 'You can leave the presents on the hall table.'

On a warm night early in the summer, Biffo's quest for immortality turns by mysterious alchemy into our search for Gliomach. The moon, which had been hanging like a lamp in the apple trees, has floated free into a clear sky. I am out with the children trying to catch its slippery disc in a telescope. As fast as I focus, it slides out of view. A yellow blaze low in the sky is Mars.

Later, when the children are asleep, I go up to find Eve sitting on the edge of our bed taking off her make-up. She has nothing on, her back is like an Ingrès woman's, cello-shaped.

'Are the children in bed?' she asks in a dull voice, not turning.

'What's the matter?'

'I've been talking to my mother.'

'Biffo?'

'He promised her he'd stop Scientology when he got to some level called "clear". But now he hasn't.'

'You didn't seriously think he would?'

'He's more involved than ever. He never stops talking about it. She says they can't have a normal conversation any more. Most of the time he sits in his room listening to tapes of Hubbard.'

'There's no way he's going to stop. It's become his whole life.'

'She asked me to talk to him, but I'm too angry. Now there's some other level he wants to reach before stopping.'

'She's got to face it, Eve. He'll never stop.'

'You think there's no hope at all?'

'None.'

After a considerable silence she says, 'She wanted to talk to the children, but I told her you were out moongazing.'

'You should have said we were looking for Biffo,' I say, trying to lighten the mood.

'What do you mean?'

'With the telescope. He once told me that as a spirit he was not subject to the laws of gravity. Perhaps he's floated up there. There's a poem of Coleridge's that puts it quite well . . .'

'And when I climb'd higher he made a long leg,
And chang'd me at once to an Ostrich's Egg–
But now Heaven be praised in contempt of the Loon,
I am I myself I, the jolly full Moon.'

Eve shouts with laughter.

I turn to her, grinning. But she is not laughing. Her mouth is twisted by misery.

'So he has spent a fortune on Scientology without asking his wife?'

She hurls her hairbrush at me.

'So he leaves her all on her own?'

A box of tissues.

'So he no longer has time for his children?'

Soon the bed is littered with lipsticks, the book she is reading, a box of earrings, a bottle of Chanel I'd given her . . .

Driving through West Cork, it's easy to see how people had to believe in giants. They had to have existed. There's no other way to explain the geology: the hills, piles, hummocks of stone, steep earth cones, occurring at random, sticking up out of otherwise rolling levels. In some places the landscape looks as if it had been tussled by a married giant-couple having a tug-of-war over a blanket, pulling the earth up over shins and chins. Our bedroom in the hotel this morning bore witness to a more pleasant struggle.

I glance over at Eve. She is turned away from me, watching the fantastic landscape passing outside her window. Why is she so quiet? What is she thinking? Is she regretting that her initiation into cyberspace left us both craving kisses? Why today's silence? I don't want to ask. I want to go back to last night. Not to the tunnels of Colossal Cave, but to memories of travels when we were younger and in love. We had always liked roaming together: journeys in India, our happy time in Venice (the gondolier's curious cry, *a oie!* – whose ancestry, like that of a certain four letter word, is thought to be untraceable, but which is surely the progenitor of English *oi!* – probably just meaning *l'oeuil* or 'use your eyes') becoming fluent in the language of birds. We came back through France and went to a village called Hauterîves where there had lived a magic postman, Ferdinand Cheval, known as 'le facteur Cheval', Postman Horse.

Hauterîves. Haut rêves. Or high Rîves? By one of those strange coincidences which the cosmos employs to remind us that the world we inhabit is made of dreams, this too is a must for pilgrims of architecture. Here, eight decades after *Kubla Khan*, the postman dreamed a fantastic dream. Had he taken laudanum for some ache or ailment? We don't know. All we know is that while out on his rounds he had seen an interesting stone lying on the ground. He had picked it up and examined it – and, on impulse, slipped it into his sack of letters. That night he dreamed of a palace, marvellous beyond description, and knew that his life's work was to build it in his garden. It took ten thousand days of patiently picking up stones, balancing his bulging mailbag like a sack of onions on the crossbar of his bicycle, thirty-three years of enduring the *quolibets d'un village qui croyait que son facteur était devenu fou*. But when the palace was finished, it was a unique and perplexing blend of all possible styles, cultures and civilisations. Picasso admired it and Malraux considered it 'le seul exemple en architecture de l'art naif'.

All that you see, passer-by, is a peasant's handywork.
Out of a dream I have brought the queen of the world.

In Hauterîves the postman built for his lifelong love, his wife, a dream castle of stone. Eve and I returned to England and began the search which led to our own leafy Castle Perilous.

The silence is louder than words. It roars with the Land Rover's voice as we traverse the turbulent marriagescape.

Trapped in a hotel room in Stockholm, throat like a leper's armpit, a solitary bottle of weak beer in the fridge. Too late for the hotel bar, pool, jacuzzi, steam room, supper. Eyeing the Swedish brew with the contempt that alcohol-1%-by-volume properly arouses in a man, I decide to send for something I can taste. Room service takes an age to answer the phone.

'Hey, Mister Bear,' says a Swedish voice at last.

'Hey,' I reply. 'I know it's late and the bar's officially closed, but I just got off a plane and I'd appreciate a half bottle of whisky and something to eat.'

'So sorry, sir, the hotel bar is locked.'

'Can't you unlock it?'

'I am not allowed.'

'Okay, well please send someone out to buy one for me.'

'Normally yes, but it is Sunday. We are not permitted to do this on Sunday.'

'This is a hotel. Surely you must have some alcohol?'

'Yes, of course,' he says, thrilled to be helping at last. 'You will find a bottle of beer in your fridge.'

I flick on CNN, get out my laptop and open a file labelled *Lässe, NuKE*. Officially, I've flown to Stockholm to help create a European advertising campaign for one of the agency's clients, a large, dull computer company. The plan calls for me to wake tomorrow and cross the park to our respectable Swedish partner agency where my friend and collaborator Magnus Westerberg works. In reality – rich coming from a denizen of the Vortex! – I have come to meet a viro-anarchist. Lässe Hendriksson, aka the Detonator, is a member of the Swedish chapter of NuKE. He boasts that he is the only guy in Europe still spreading destructive code. Just to complicate things, in the metalight of reality, Magnus is not simply an accomplished ad jingleur but a relentlessly technophile cybergypsy, usually to be found hanging out with the screenwriters at the WELL in San Francisco. He shares my loathing for Microsoft and computer advertising, and also shares my desire to swap ideas with the virus-wallah. I had phoned him to suggest that we might take the Detonator off for a drink, but he swept this aside.

'Nonsense, dear boy, I have everything arranged. We shall entertain him to lunch in the Board Room.'

Screeching noises from the television set turn out to be a car chase. Cut to big close-up of overwrought teenage driver. The youth swears and a subtitle informs me that *'javlar'* is the Swedish for 'shit'. I don't think this is CNN. Unless beerlessness is deranging me, it appears that the teenager is being chased by a car driven by his knife-wielding mother. The director clearly believes, as who would not, given such a script, in moving the action on. Serial-killer mom catches, incinerates offspring. He dies horribly in flames on stage at a gig where a wild all-girl band, demented versions of the Bangles, thrust their crotches at the camera.

The TV remote control has a mystifying array of buttons. I jab a few at random. The channel flicks and a naked blonde appears. She is kneeling above an unpleasant-looking man on a bed with grey silk sheets in what appears to be a railway stockyard, giving head with a twisting motion which I instantly recognise to be a species of *ucchchushita*.

Stab more buttons.

A voice from the television says, 'If you're gonna lick, lick like you mean it'. The screen fills with large, bouncing breasts.

Holy shit, it's Madison.

Cut. A pair of fighting, screeching, black cats resolves to dark-haired girls engaged in vigorous *soixante-neuf*. (In the Kama Sutra, this was known as *kakila*, the lovemaking of the Crow. Fascinating, when you know that Pliny the Elder, bit of a birdwatcher, observed in his *Naturalis Historia* that ravens mate with the beak, for which reason in the old city of Rome the act of cunnilingus was also known as the Crow. Which culture got it from which? The two countries had links, for Pliny tells us that India sent to Rome a bird which 'greets its masters and repeats words given to it, being particularly sportive over the wine'. Poor parrot, or siptacus, as Pliny's informant drunkenly mispronounced it, 'Its head is as hard as its beak; and when it is being taught to speak it is beaten on the head with an iron rod – otherwise it does not feel blows.' Strange thoughts, these, for a Sunday night in Stockholm . . . the popular idea that India gave erotica to the west is probably wrong. More likely it was the other way round. Ovid's *Ars Amatoria* predates the *Kama Sutra* by three and a half centuries. The earliest tantras like the Buddhist *Guhysamaja* do not appear in India before the 3rd century AD, by which time the Alexandrian stylites and other desert gnostics with fevered imaginations had long since plumbed all available depths.)

'Yes, yes, yes, but was it Madison?' Magnus asks next day. 'You never saw her face.'

'Of course it was Madison.'

'How could you know that?'

'No-one else has breasts like that. Besides, they cut to a big close-up and I recognised the stud in her tongue.'

We're in the agency's white-on-white boardroom. Magnus has ordered sushi to be brought in as soon as our guest arrives. His intelligent screenwriter's gaze, alert for every gyring gimbling nuance of plot, is locked to mine.

'Okay, so I don't really want to ask,' he says, 'but how did you get to know a porn movie star in the first place?'

An email message comes through on Magnus's state-of-the-art notebook asking for a phone number in the room where we are.

Magnus replies immediately.

Within thirty seconds, the white phone in the corner gives a soft burr. The Detonator, careful man, is calling from the street outside.

'Yeah,' says the Detonator, 'how do you know this porno star?'

I give them a run-down of the *Kama Sutra* saga from the piracy on *wiretap.spies* to the scriptjigging in Kissimmee. I tell them about the week of weirdnesses.

'Come on, Bear, on that day you had but a small little ogle,' says the Detonator who is, like all computer geeks, a large man. 'You sure know her better than that.'

In fact I never met her again. But the Detonator is right, I did see a lot more of her. I'd written a script so full of long Sanskrit words that no-one else could pronounce it. Out of desperation, or cheap-skatery, I was asked to read it myself and proved so bad a voice artist that a forty-minute soundtrack took twelve hours to dub. We were recording to picture and, after twelve hours of staring at the video I knew the actors' parts almost as well as they did. Later one of the newspaper reviews spoke of the beautiful photography, but commented on the narrator's strangely droning voice.

'The hack on *wiretap.spies*,' says the Detonator. 'It is interesting to me. A small action by one person got converted into big bangs in the lives of others. I like this very much. The idea to cause a big explosion with the least trying. You plants one tiny virus. Stand back and – kapow!'

We talk about viruses. The Detonator is a computer engineer, by day healing the machines which at night he and his friends infect. He sees nothing ironic in this. Like all virus writers, he claims that what he does actually serves computer users, by pinpointing the flaws in their security. He is working on a new virus that will be undetectable, constantly mutating its shape and 'signature'.

'We have to catch up with the work TäLoN's doing in Australia,' he says. 'We have to do it, not just yakyak about it.'

It seems that two virus writers, The Unforgiven and Metal Militia, from a rival gang called Immortal Riot, have been chasing the limelight, shooting off their mouths to journalists.

'They told the magazine that virus writers doesn't harm people, just data,' says the Detonator, spooning sushi'd crab and sea-urchin onto his plate. They say, "we only make the bombs we doesn't throw them". I say this is shit.'

Magnus, straddling his sushi with unsteady chopstilts, has glazed over. 'Hey, Detonator,' he says. 'Have you ever thought of using viruses in a positive way?'

The Detonator's features silently arrange themselves into the question. 'Now why would any sane person want to do that?'

'See,' says Magnus through a mouthful of shrimp, 'Bear and I are in advertising and we have thought of this new way to make a fortune. Forget magazines, forget TV commercials. The next great advertising medium is going to be . . . the computer virus! Think about it. We could spread a virus that at six o'clock every evening pictures on screen a glass of cold beer with the slogan "It's Tiger Time". We can have a virus that says "It's Mother's Day, call home and tell Mom 'I love you'".'

'No, guys, no, no.'

The Detonator is shaking his head in distress at the idea of virus-writing becoming tainted by commercialism.

'Advertising is already a kind of virus,' says Magnus. 'One that infects people with desires.'

'Don't worry,' I tell the non-plussed Detonator, 'he talks *javlar*.'

'So what do you guys do adverts for?' asks the Detonator.

'Well, next month I'm visiting this big nuclear plant and Magnus is coming along as my guest.'

Detonator is suddenly alert. 'Nuclear plant? Then it has got a computer network. An operating system. All we need to know . . .'

Golden eagles

Fragments of conversation overheard in a bar on the Beara:

'The goulden eagles are dyin cos the fuckin Kerry farmers kill them.'

'Ah yes and shootin all the bloody seagulls caused the ozone problem.'

'What do you know? Wasn't it you tellin that German tourist a week back the Reeks is made of ould red sandstone?'

'And what else is it I'd like to know?'

'Nivver ould red sandstone, it's black mudstone, made of black mud.'

'Yerra, talkin shite again.'

'Me talking shite is it? There's talk mind that you are a homosexual. What else for is your wife in America and you here?'

'Ah you're jealous cos I've got a son and you haven't.'

'Does that make me less the man?'

'At least I've someone to carry my name forward. Ask me it's your big belly gets in the way of your auld man.'

'Nivvir mind my belly, that's a big man ower there, go and tell him. See if ye dare insult him the way ye'll insult me.'

Eve and I, engaged on our netquest, waiting, as she points out, in a bar in the far west of Ireland for a virtual nod-and-wink from a man we'd never met and whose real name we do not know, become enmeshed in the blather, and the drinkers, who've been all day at a wake and are on their last legs – I later open the door of the gents to find one of them head in hands, trousers round ankles, sound asleep – earn their place in a shenanigans which began with a cryptic instruction left on a computer in an overgrown house in Sussex:

>login at cronins durrus

Ours is not an easy story to tell, but the Irish, like the Indians (who never did turn up, or ring, and all knowledge of whom was denied by the Cork newspapers) are inquisitive souls who enjoy a challenge. Three hours later, flushed and Guinnessed, I am still doing my best to explain to our host, a Mr O'Conlan, what Eve and I are doing in the west of Ireland. He, a stout man, sporting a thin film of perspiration on his upper lip, wears an expression of puzzled and porcine desperation.

'Wait, wait, wait.' Lifts silencing hand, starts summing up.

'You're looking for a man.'

'Yes.'

'A fella here in Ireland.'

'Correct.'

'But you don't know his name.'

'No.'

'And you've no notion of what he looks like.'

'This is absolutely true.'

Without warning I am transported to a tiny office over a fish and chip shop in Croydon. Opposite me is a man wearing horn . . .

>Corridor in ChemSep plant

>You are standing in a corridor lined with rusting and corroded pipes, which bear signs like '$HN0_3$' and 'STEAM'. The pipes look about a hundred years old. You get the feeling that you wouldn't want to be here if they spring a leak. To the south a doorway opens into a huge hall. You can make out the shapes of giant machines.

>s

>Entrance to walkway

You are at the entrance to a walkway high above one end of a huge hall filled with strange machines. The air is filled with a curious gulping sound, as though a giant frog is clearing its throat. The cold electronic bleeping sounds louder here. To the east, the walkway stretches along the northern wall of the main hall, which lies below you.

>e

>Walkway, near showcases

You are following a walkway high on the northern wall of an enormous hall. The walkway is glassed in. To one side are several neat display cases filled with unusual exhibits. A gleaming metal bar wrapped in plastic lies on a table here.

>take bar

>You take the metal bar.

>examine bar

>The bar is very heavy. You can barely lift it. Examining it, you discover that it is made of uranium.

>drop bar

>Oh no you don't. You are not going to bloody well overreact just because it's uranium. You know very well that uranium in this form isn't radioactive. You're going to hand it nonchalantly back to the guide, who is grinning at you, enjoying your discomfort.

One tends to think of nuclear plants as shiny temples of science, but this one was built in the 1960s, with banks of needle-flickering dials, like those in old sports cars. The plant reeks of age. Its pipes are stained and corroded, but if the plant is old, the recycling process is antique. No particle physics here, just a bunsen-burner-and-stained-fingers version of nineteenth century chemistry.

'You take the used fuel rods and chop 'em up, and dissolve the lot in nitric acid – same principle as granny's homemade scrumpy. Now it's a liquid containing uranium and plutonium nitrates. All you've to do is precipitate out these . . .'

We come to the concrete 'cells' where the radioactive gunk is unloaded from the flasks.

'Concrete's a yard thick,' says the guide. 'Inside's all stainless steel. A man couldn't go in there, so we use robots like this one here to do the work.'

A gleaming multi-jointed robotic arm stands nearby, its steel shaft entering the room through a series of seals. The operator looks through a pane of thick yellow glass. I go to the window and stare into the stainless steel room beyond the sulphurous glass.

'Wouldn't stand there if I was you,' says the guide with a laugh. He is pointing at my flies. Taped to the robot at crotch level is a notice scrawled in biro on a sheet torn from a lined notepad, a notice of the 'gone to tea, back in five' variety: *'Small leak of alpha radiation.'*

I jump backwards, nearly impaling myself on a piece sticking out of the robot.

'No need for panic,' says the guide, with a grin. 'Only alpha. Can be stopped by tissue paper.'

He obviously likes making visitors wriggle.

'What's this meter for?' I ask, poring over a dial straight out of *Plan 9 From Outer Space*.

'That one?' says the guide. 'It's measuring the radiation that's coming through that door behind you there and travelling straight through your back.'

. . . rimmed glasses, asking me questions in a south-of-the-river voice, which means he sounds as if he's trying to spit out a boiled potato while talking to me.

'So you don't know where this friend, this . . .' looking doubtful, consults notebook, 'this, er . . . Luna . . . where she, er . . . lives?'

'No.'

'And you can't give me any help on what she looks like?'

'No, no, no, nothing. I never saw her at all. I've never met her.'

'Right ho. It's back to basics then. Nationality? Profession?'

'Don't know, don't know. It was all done over the phone.'

'Postmark? Handwriting? She ever send you anything? Letter, parcel, billydoo?' He doodles on a pad, reverses the pencil, scrubs with the eraser and brushes away the screlchings.

'Billydoo?'

He looks frustrated, then resigned. 'Love letter, sir. You don't normally get gents trying to trace ladies unless there's a romantic interest.'

'Well, actually . . .'

'Okay then, what's she sound like? London? Northern? Scottish? Foreign?'

'I don't know, I've never actually spoken to her.'

'Sorry, thought you said you was on the phone to her.'

'Not talking. We typed back and forth on computer screens.'

He puts down his pencil and looks at me. 'Don't exactly have a lot, do we sir? But let's be thankful for what we have got. At least we know it's a her.'

'Actually, no. Could be a him. There's no way to tell.'

The detective ponders this, frowns.

'Okay, well we still got the phone. So she . . . er this person and you, er? Presumably she, er they, phones you. Well if you was phoning them you would know their number wouldn't you, and you wouldn't be sitting here.'

'Well, most of the time I dial up this game and she phones it too. The game has its own number. In Southall. I thought maybe if I gave you that number, you . . .'

'Sorry, can't be done, sir,' he says. 'Can't listen in if it's not the client's number. Your number. Need a chit from the Home Office if you want to tap a phone.'

'I'm not asking you to tap the phone. Just to trace the call.'

'Can you get her to call your number?'

'Well, she already does, but not very often. I've no way of telling when she might call, but she's on this game almost all the time.'

'Have you tried the automatic trace back?'

'Of course,' I tell him. 'I get "the caller withheld their number".'

'Hmm. Could be ways round that. No promises, mind . . .'

'I don't want you to do anything illegal.'

'Luna,' says the detective. 'I suppose it's an alias. Does she go under any other aliases that you know of?'

'Yes!' I say, glad to be giving a positive answer at last. 'She calls herself Henry. Henry Cornelius Agrippa.'

The detective exhales abruptly, sits back, and sends his pencil spiralling onto the desk.

'Mr Bear, I don't wish to be rude, but . . . and don't take this wrong, but there's a lot would say it's not a detective you need, sir, it's a psy . . . psy . . . a psychic.'

He doesn't have the courage to say 'psychiatrist'.

'And ye haven't a clue where he lives.'

'No.'

'Not the smallest devil of a bloody whisper of where he lives?'

'No.'

'And you've no phone number.'

'Nope.'

'Excuse me there,' one of the drinkers proffers, placing his elbows on the bar and leaning forward, 'I think I might know that man.'

Laughter. Mr O'Conlan frowns.

'And you've not got a map?' he perseveres.

'I wish we had.'

O'Conlan looks round to his audience and ticks off the last few possibilities.

'Now you're not a magician. You don't cast magic spells. You're not a wizard. So tell me, how is it you're hoping to find this fella?'

'Oh, that's easy,' says a voice from the corner. My wife raises her glass of Guinness. 'We just steer by the bright star that hovers over his lobster pot.'

She smacks the glass down on the table.

'Bear, your other half wants another half.'

A spy in Thorp

In Thorp, the nuclear reprocessing plant at Sellafield, an alarm sign is flickering on a wall, warning AIRBORNE ACTIVITY.

'Don't worry,' says the guide. 'Just testing.'

Like me, he's gowned surgeon-style in a white ankle length coat, cloth overshoes and name tag. In place of a medic's watch he wears a film badge. I think of Chernobyl where the engineers apparently turned off the safety systems to see what would happen. But the cavernous building is filled with an eerie electronic bleeping. The heartbeat of the plant. While it continues, we're okay. It's if it stops that we'll need to panic.

Thorp would surely have delighted Scarpa. Its apricot brickwork and orange paint represent the latest in technotecture. Access for visitors is via a lift, a bridge, a stair up to a door with a panel which affords a first, circumscribed (as in a Chinese garden) glimpse of what lies beyond. As the door swings open, one's gaze lights upon an immense pool of haunting clarity and depth, a lagoon where the huge fuel flasks are stored to keep cool. A canal leads from the storage pond – a prosaic name for such a beautiful thing – through a series of spaces defined by light and shadows cast on concrete and gleaming metal. It is, one might say, a place where pure form becomes substance and space, in which the fusion of natural and man-made elements enhances their intrinsic vitality and enriches playfulness with a lyricism and a heightened sense of the joy of life: the play of water, channelled into canals and dissolving in deep pools, even the air and light responding to the changing angles of the encircling walls and the gradined surfaces of the concrete. One might say these things, but does not. Instead one stands marvelling at the water, blue and clear all the way to the bottom and says, 'Shit, I'm itching to dive in.'

The guide sniggers. 'You'd itch all right. It's alkaline so the flasks won't corrode. God knows what it would do to your todger.'

Speaking of which, here is another wonder: a shaft of shining steel descending deep deep into the water, a vast gleaming piston that reflects light even at nineteen meters below the surface. It is a microcosmic twin to the *lingam* of Siva which was so huge that it straddled the cosmos, a puissant pillar of flame whose ends were beyond the range of all known telescopes. The two-light-year high dust pillars in Orion are mere willies beside Siva's *membrum virile*, which his co-deities so envied that they schemed to belittle it. Brahma the Creator flew up the dazzling shaft, Visnu the Preserver down, but neither could find an end to the *lux in tenebris* of Siva the Destroyer. Was it not of this Trinity and this flashing fire that Oppenheimer thought when, staring into the bright eye of the first atomic blast, he said 'I am become death, the destroyer of worlds'?

Thorp is too beautiful and strange to be real. It reminds me of the metallic Isostellar complex where Luna and I often go to watch the constellations slowly crossing the Vortex night.

>*sw*

>Inner Corridor

The corridor, a plain grey tube, curves south eastwards around what you assume to be Isostellar's central core. Distantly, you can feel the low throb of the Cyclotron.

>*u*

>Observatory

You climb up into a glass dome which affords excellent views of all the realms of the Vortex and of a magnificent sky. Around the edge of the dome are cabinets of drinks, foods and an assortment of interesting devices. The floor is piled high with many-coloured satin quilts, pillows and coverlets.

When crossing from any world to another, there are generally precautions, health checks, rites of passage: the Tibetans devoted an entire book to the art of emigrating from life to death; Dr Dee performed rituals to banish the spirits he evoked in his triangle of art; witches dissolve their magic circles. The procedure for leaving a nuclear plant is meticulous. We drop our coats and hats in a bin, sit on a barrier, remove our overshoes and swing our feet across without touching the floor. We wash our hands and stick them into the slots of a machine like the thing in *Jumanji*, that checks them for radiation. Then we step into a shower cubicle for a top-to-toe going over after which we give ourselves a hand-held geiger scan. Even this echoes Isostellar, where, if you stray from the corridor . . .

>s

>Cable Duct

You are pulled into a cylinder of cracking whips and slithering tentacles. Your body is flayed and caressed in a nightmare of pain and pleasure.

. . . Except that when leaving cyberspace there are no precautions, no ways to remove the contamination of alien imaginations.

The guide is reeling off facts, informing me that Thorp contains hundreds of miles of pipes and cables. It has 1,700 safety devices. Its data system has fifty-three control computers running on Motorola chips. I imagine the Detonator and the boys at NuKE up to their ears in 68000 series assembler code. The first thing they'll want is a copy of the operating system. If one of these computers fail, says the guide, it will not affect the running of the plant. But what if it does not fail? What if the virus, spreading across fifty-three machines, simply changes data, altering a figure here, a safety margin there, a date somewhere else? What else should such a virus be called but Nuke? Just think of the headline, 'NuKE's Nuke nukes nuke.'

Palden Gyatso

Someone arrives at our house in Sussex bringing a package for me. Inside is a crude pair of leather shoes such as are worn by Indian peasants. There is also a muslin bundle, in which are wrapped a number of objects of dull japaned metal, stained, bearing rusty marks that might be blood. A note, from Tim Nunn at the Tibet Support Group, says that Palden Gyatso is shortly to make a tour of Britain. Can I produce an ad? Palden is a Buddhist monk who has suffered terribly in Tibet, spent years in prison, and been severely tortured. Finally he escaped, bribing a Chinese warder to obtain for him the tools with which he had been tortured. Here they are again. It is the second time in a year that this bundle and its murderous contents have been in my hands.

I hear the whole story in Palden's own quiet words. Never so strongly before have I felt the existence of evil. I pick up the weapons, remembering that they now belong to His Holiness the Dalai Lama. I try to imagine them being used on me. The pain, the rage, the shame, grief, despair. But I can't imagine it. Not all the roleplaying in the whole wide Vortex can prepare me for such a fantasy. I think about using them on other people. It's easier. This I can imagine. I have the person in front of me. I press the electrodes to their skin. Coldly, I thumb the button. They gasp, jerk, shriek, collapse. I step away righteously. What I have done is my duty, sanctioned by superiors and legal in the eyes of the foreign governments who supplied these weapons. (Or the prototypes from which these have been copied.) The electric bands on the dog's dick dildo are crusted with thick deposits of green and white salts. At the rim of each band greasy dirt, of who knows what composition, is trapped.

From Palden Gyatso's testimony, I compile the words with which I must try to engage and move the public. I am unhappily aware that no words have the power to achieve what needs to be done. All of us armour ourselves against the suffering of others. It is distant to us, unreal. Events in Tibet or Kurdistan seem nothing to do with us. In fact, at a level far deeper than the daily dose of trivia we call 'reality', we are all intimately connected. Life on the net, with its webwork of crazy and unexpected links, illustrates this. To an evolutionist we are like a network of canals through which a tide of genes is flowing. Other '-ists' can find metaphors in language, philosophy, ethics and computer code. When, on whatever level, we acknowledge this mutual inter-connectedness, the only thing left is to accept responsibility, to accept that we can make an impact and shape our world – perhaps even to experience the roleplayer's secret, terrifying and absolute knowledge that at the deepest levels of reality we do constantly create and recreate our own worlds. We can accept responsibility, then choose compassion. Words are not very good at expressing – or I can't use words well enough to express – ideas like these.

Suppose a friend reveals that they are a member of Amnesty. You ask them 'Why is joining Amnesty a good idea?' What sort of answer would you expect? Surely, a polite one, that might contain words like 'human rights', 'freedom' and 'dignity'. But that answer would be inadequate. A clearer reply might be if the person turns round and, without warning, punches you violently in the face. Imagine your pain, fear, confusion. Multiply them a hundredfold. Now you have a very faint idea of what someone, somewhere is suffering at this very moment. Faced with such experience, the fine words we honour, like 'justice', 'liberty' and 'equality', don't serve us. They subvert our message. They make it philosophical when it's about real pain. Words fail us.

What more can be said about Palden's pain than what he tells us himself: 'My name is Palden Gyatso. I am a Tibetan and a Buddhist monk. I have spent thirty-three of my sixty-four year old life in Chinese prisons and labour camps in Tibet. Throughout those years, I yearned for a moment like this – when I could tell the world what had happened to me and others who dared call for freedom for our country. When I went to the prison an official asked me what brought me there. I said I'd put up posters saying "Tibet is an independent country, separate from China". He said, "I'll give you Tibetan independence." He kicked me and rammed an electric cattle prod into my mouth with great force. The jolt of electricity knocked me out. When I came to, in terrible pain, I found myself lying in a pool of blood and excrement. I had lost twenty of my teeth. Electric batons can produce a shock of up to 70,000 volts. They are often inserted into the mouth, the rectum and the vagina. In Gutsa prison, guards raped Buddhist nuns being held there, then sexually violated them with electric cattle prods. One of the guards taunted them, saying "You have not yet experienced this!". The guard's name is Sonam Thering. He was still on duty when I escaped from Tibet. In the Norbu Khunghtse prison camp, we prisoners were yoked like animals to plough the prison fields. When we fell, exhausted, we were kicked and whipped. Since we never had enough to eat, we were always desperately hungry. Our hunger was so severe that we stole food meant for pigs from Chinese sties. We chewed and ate things like the bones of dead animals, mice, worms and various sorts of grasses. I was even reduced to chewing my own leather shoes. The truth is that you can do anything, when you're trying to survive.'

I do an Amnesty radio ad with John Hurt, recorded in his bedroom in a hotel in Berwick on Tweed . . . pale midnight sky and gulls . . . He was up there filming *The Railway Man.* In his rich gravelly voice, Hurt performs the script, which is full of long silences, the silences of the dead, the incarcerated, the unconscious, the Halabjan silence of politicians and the silence of decent people who know about these things and do nothing to help.

A week later Amnesty itself is silenced. Our ad is banned. The Radio Authority claims that Amnesty is a political organisation, and therefore forbidden to advertise. It is political, we are told, because it criticises governments. Never mind that its criticism consists of documenting well-verified abuses of human rights, that it is impartial, sparing governments neither of the left nor the right, East nor West. Amnesty asks for a judicial review. We lose, Lord Justice Kennedy ruling – is his judgement really as moronic as it seems to me? – *'There are other rights to be protected, such as freedom from being virtually forced to listen to unsolicited information of a contentious kind.'* In which case, m'lud, why not also ban the BBC news? Thank god for the free internet.

What can you do when those who are supposed to uphold law break their own laws, when governments break the treaties they have signed? Martyn Gregory, the TV journalist, digs out proof that electric shock weapons are being traded by British firms. Conservative Minister Heseltine accuses him of fabricating the evidence. Martyn knows it isn't fabricated. He had used a hidden video camera to film a British Aerospace salesman demonstrating an illegal baton. Martyn sues for libel and wins an apology and damages. Karen, at Amnesty, asks me to do an ad about this. It will be the third time I've written about electroshock weapons. I need a new picture, and the Dalai Lama's bundle has gone back to Dharamsala, so I ask Martyn if he will lend me one of the batons shown in his TV programme. But he says that since it's illegal to possess the real things, he had to use dummies, which have long since vanished.

I go on the net to look for pictures. Dozens of websites flash up, touting Fu Manchu moustaches, beards, false eyebrows, wigs, bugs, surveillance items, pen-shaped cameras. There are recorders for taping telephone calls. Here's something I really *need*, because I am due to do a long telephone interview with Don McCullin, also for an Amnesty ad, and can't think of a reliable way to record our conversation. The internet sites also offer shock weapons for sale. You can get electric batons, just as in Martyn's programme. One store offers a pocket-sized device, which looks like a shaver, but delivers a jolt of 300,000 volts. All these things are of course for self-defence. The quality of pictures on the websites is not good enough. If only I could get hold of one of these things, just long enough to photograph it. Then it occurs to me, why not just buy one? All it takes is a credit card.

A few days later a package arrives from the States. In it is my battery operated call recorder, and a shiny black 300,000 volt stun gun. The vendor has enclosed an invoice for my accountant, marked PAID. On the invoice, someone has helpfully scrawled in biro, *'For best results, use Duracell batteries'*.

Bear: Well, we're rolling again and, er, so everything that you and I are saying now is going on tape . . . we were talking about the killings you witnessed in Beirut . . .

Don: The old, famous cheery question is 'Do you ever help anyone'? In Beirut they killed several hundred Palestinians one day. I saw some of them being killed, but there was no way that camera was going up to my eye because one man came up and he said 'If you take any pictures you'll be killed and I suggest you leave this area.' When I started leaving I heard this music, this lute and they were celebrating a dead Palestinian girl about twenty years old lying in the winter muddy rainy kind of street. I thought my God, if I take this picture it could cost me my life. I looked over my shoulder very furtively and quickly and I thought I cannot walk past this, and I whipped that camera to my eye and took one frame and ran out of that place. As I was leaving I heard somebody pleading and then I heard this gun fire and I saw an old man just falling back, he was shot in the stomach at point blank range. I thought I must get out of here.

Bear: I'm looking at the picture in your book as we're talking . . .

Don: You know, when you walk away from those situations you thank God you're alive, you feel guilty about being alive because someone else paid the price for this mayhem and when you get back to your hotel room sometimes you're in a deep shock and, you know, you go to your room and you're somehow destroyed. Look, I'll tell you something. I'm a tough guy but . . . um . . . I have often wept . . . That day in Beirut . . . they dragged these families out of a house . . . they got the men out first and then the families were brought down the stairs and as they came down they were looking at . . . at these two men standing in the stairwell with their hands up. Then the families were taken round the corner. I went with them, and I came rushing back just in time to see the two men being shot in cold blood at point blank range. I . . . I think I may have said to you before, the one thing I'll never forget to this day, that one of them, he had an Astrakhan hat on and a kind of light raincoat, as he dropped he was saying 'Allah, Allah, Allah'. It was as if the last air in his body was calling for God. And I went into the stairwell and you know, I went upstairs, up the stairwell and I gripped the rail and I said to myself, you know, take a hold of yourself, because this is only the beginning of . . . of . . . what's going to happen here today.

Bear: In your picture, I think they know what's going to happen.

Don: You walk round a corner and the most extraordinary things can be going on. Several corners and you see nothing, and then you walk round a corner . . . I went up to this man – I had spent the day with him before – this gunman from East Beirut and I said 'What's going on with these men?' and he said 'They're going to get the chop' and I said 'No please don't do this'. I said 'You know, the press are here, everyone can see what you're doing, this is wrong, please don't do this'. He said 'My friend, go away, it is none of your business' and they took these men into the yard. I pushed in behind. It had been raining overnight and this old factory yard was all wet and damp and there was this kind of weird sky and we were all wearing blue ribbons tied to our arms so the people I was with wouldn't shoot each other. I saw one of the men looking at a gunman who was loading a fresh magazine into his rifle – I've often tried to transplant myself into that man's position. The shock of fear that goes through you when you think you're going to be killed is just . . . unthinkable. It's unthinkable. To see people about to be murdered is appalling because there is nothing you can do on their behalf . . . they plead, you know, with their eyes. When they see you their eyes get bigger, appealing to you to help, to get them out of this terrible situation and there is nothing you can do. You lose something of yourself when you see people die. I mean, when you see a man being shot in a doorway and he is looking at you and crying, you are naked. You are naked. You don't have implements at hand to protect this man, help this man, shield this man. You know, one man dying in front of another man is a kind of naked experience, believe me. You don't have any feelings of normality, you're totally destroyed.

Bear: No wonder people don't want to feel these things.

Don: The tragedy of my work in the past was I could never save the people I photographed. That was the biggest, probably the biggest negative side of the whole of my last thirty years in photography, photographing wars and revolutions. They needed to be saved but I couldn't save them. Many of the people in my photographs are giving one last look at . . . the victims look curious as if they... they see something that I . . . as if they can help me... as if they think I'm the one who's the victim. If you look at a lot of my pictures closely.

Bear: You mean as if they're trying to help you in some way?

Don: They're trying to co-operate, obviously and what they are trying to say is look at me, look what they have done to me, please tell the world what they have done to me.

Bear: They wanted you to be their witness . . .

Don: The dead leave their own statement and my photograph is their statement. It's not their choice to give their statement in that fashion . . . But that's the way . . . that . . . that's the only alternative that's left for them.

Disappointed by my failure to shine at virtual sex, Lilith sends me a 'spool', that is to say, a recording of the time she met her 'Vortex husband', Pierrot. 'Don't snigger when you read it. The sex was better than my "real" marriage. Afterwards, *ot nyevo ostalas odna tyen*, the poor man was a shadow of his former self.'

The spool, when printed out, fills thirty-three pages. She has given it to me raw, unrefined, as it originally appeared on her screen. This means that things she was in the middle of typing to Pierrot are mixed up with things he was typing to her. It needs decoding. The sentences, which look as if they have been blown to bits by a bomb, make sense to the practised eye of a Vorticist.

>'_ __Lilith says "what do you like to do with it exactly?". >Lilith grins in a rather mischievous manner.
>whisper li sometimes like today I am very loving.... >whisper li but sometimes I _ __ — >Lilith says "...sometimes..?" >whisper li sometimes I try to stop people loving me >whisper li and afterwards I want them to love me more _ — __Lilith says "is that why Bilquis didnt marry you?" >shake >Lilith whispers in your ear "what does the other side do?"
>em whispers li_ __ _please forgive me......
>_Lilith says "you can't have any habits more...interesting...than Pompadora's". >Lilith says "you dont EAT people?". >shake You shake your head in disagreement. >em takes the little bottle and carefully fills Lil's belly button with sweet smelling oil >Lilith says "you don't kill them?" >whisper li _ __n no - >Lilith shrinks a little from the feel of cool wetness __ __ >Lilith whispers in your ear "it cant be that bad..." >whisper li it is just that I intend to use the_ — _ _ _ __ _>sigh You sigh sadly. >Lilith strokes you gently. >Lilith says "tell me!" >whisper why is it that I always fall in love with them? >em puts his left forefinger into the well of oil and wriggles it gently from side to side >Lilith's lashes fall and shadow her cheeks >em whispers is that too internal for you? >grin li You give Lilith a mischievous grin. >Lilith whispers in your ear "its ...acceptable.".

If there's one thing the spool demonstrates, apart from the astonishing hydra-like resilience of language, it is the patience of these roleplayers. Lilith and Pierrot meet on page one. He cuts a dash in a beret and a riding crop. She laughs at him and his Gallic arrogance irritates her, but she is secretly taken with the handsome young stranger. He then offends by chucking her under the chin with his riding crop. One does not take this sort of liberty with Lilith. Bond-girl fashion she pulls a stiletto from a hidden sheath. His charming apology occupies most of pages two and three. It is page six before she accepts (tentatively and not without a certain coy insincerity) his invitation to share a sauna at Pompadora's. The excerpt I have quoted comes from this part of the action. They spend four steamy pages talking (mostly about Vortex people and events while he oils her back and she wonders whether to permit him greater familiarities. On page six we encounter the description I saw in the salon with the Pompeii murals: 'Lilith smells faintly of rosewater and jasmine'. Pierrot is surprised (as am I) to glimpse a flash of silver at the lips below her mound. It proves to be a small dragon brooch, but Pierrot's dipping, circling, teasing fingers do not touch it until page eight. On page ten Pierrot receives sighing permission to unfasten the brooch. The following page reminds me of the ur-Lilith's refusal to lie down beneath her mate.

>_Lilith kneels on the floor her eyes on yours >em moves behind you, he pus_ _ts his arms around you and nuzzles your__ __ >Lilith leans back against you breathing faster with excitement >em kisses your neck >_Lilith moans and shivers against >em strokes his arms down to x_ _cup your breasts >whisper li I am going to fu....f>Lilith reaches back to stroke you >em pushes against you >Lilith feels your_ __ __ __ __ __ __ __ __ _Lilith rubs her>em pushes your_ _ forward, rubbingh_ _ himself agaisnt your >ems hands slide down _ __ __ __ __ __ __ __ _Lilith puts her arms down and lays her head on them leaving her bottom__ __ >ems hands slide down around your hips his >as it pushes back into him > ...high in the air >... fingers seeking, searching >whisper li Are you ready to be;ems fingers pushe _ __ _ up bet_ __ __ __ __Lilith moves opening her >whisper li Are you ready then?;ems fingers push up between >em takes his___ __ >Lilith whispers in your ear "yes". >your legs - plunging into your >ems fingers push up between your __ __ __ __ __ Lilith whispers in your ear "yes".

wetness Lilith> twisting and turning __ems fingers push up between your__ __ __ __ __ __ __ __ whispers in your ear "yes". >twisting and turning >em takes his co__ __ _ __ >between yo_ __ __ >his hand away __ __ __ >Lilith whispers in your e__ __ __ __ __ _onto his coc_ _co_ _>taking it in his hand_ __ __ __the tu_ _ip between your we_ ___Lilith is still sticky and slippery with excitement > __ __ __ __ __ __to his coc_ _co_ _ >Lilith whispers in your ear "yes". >whisper li __ __ __ __ __ >whisper li Yes what? >Lilith pushes back against you raising her hips to make entry easier >em in one har_ __ __ __ __ Lilith shudders with wanting you and ready > _ __ _pulling you back against him he _ __ __ _with his hands on your hips he whispers in your ear "yes I am ready and want you". >Lilith >em plung_ __ __ __ starts to f __fuck ___

>em pulls back then p_ _shoves back in in a single movemebnt_ __ __ __ _ent, slapping against your >_Lilith moves against you her hips are swaying backwards and forwards and from side to side..>e harder and harder, his breath_ __Lilith feels stretched__ __ __ __ __ __pressing through the folds deliciously >em ksyou harder and harder, his breathing becoming heavy and ragged >em ehidper_ __ __ __ __ __ __ _whu_ _ispers take that_ __ __ em groans and mutter_ __ __ __ __ __whs_ _impers "Take that __ __ __ __ __ __ __ __ __ __ __ __ __ __ __ __ __ __ __ Lilith squeezes you i___ __ em groans and mut_ __ __ __ muscles contracting with __ __ __ that run though >em groans and whispers "Take that you rivers of fire running into__ __ as __ __ hafts deep into > hips thrust hard forward, his _ __ __ _is back arches as with a loud cry his _ __ __spasms __Lilith gasps as she f>arches as with a >impale her until she is moving mindlessly >arches as >ems back arches as with a loud __ __ __ __ __ __ _ >em grabs your hair and pulls your head up, her lips grind into yours her breath hot as she contibnues to __ __ __ he kisses yo_ __ Lilith cries too and bites your lips wildly as she feels __ __ __ >ems body shakes >Lilith lies on the floor where you flung her her eyes closes and her lashes dark on her cheeks...her body covered in a sheen of sweat >Lilith murmurs oooh that was unbelievable

By the time we arrive at this sweat-soaked denouement two more pages have elapsed. By page sixteen they are at it again (spooling a session like this is the cyber equivalent of hiding a video camera in the bedroom) and the reader must imagine for her- or himself the state of the remaining sheets.

'Wasn't I right, Bear?' she asks, next time we meet. 'About passion?'

'Does Pompadora really eat people?'

'Oh, only once. It was Josie's idea. We each gave a feast of a dish none of us had tasted before. Pompadora served "long pig".'

'Long pig is . . . a human?'

'We ate Josie. We roasted her wrapped in *ki-ti* leaves and stuffed with coconut and sweet potato.'

'We held the feast on the island,' Lilith tells me, laughing. 'Josie was brought in blindfolded. She was very good. Properly fearful and pleading for her life . . . Naturally we ignored her. We tied her to a pole by her wrists and ankles and carried her to the village. Then we had to prepare her. Pompadora had done all the research. She went into it very thoroughly. We killed Josie by cutting her throat, so we could drain the body of blood. Then we cut her head off. We slit the belly and drew the intestines. Joffrey did that bit. We crushed some yams and then mixed them to a sort of batter, which Pompey said was called *laplap*, and smeared Josie with it all over inside and out. Next we jointed her at arms, elbows, hands, hips, knees, ankles. The fingers and toes are the best bits, Pompey said aficionados are also fond of the fattier cuts, breasts and buttocks. Josie asked as a favour that we not eat her head, so we put it on a banana leaf and propped the recipe in front of it, and it talked to us. It told us how to wrap up all the pieces up in the leaves, which are of some sort of lily, and put them in our earth oven. Two of the boys, Fungible and Armstrade, had dug a pit about two feet deep and filled it with lava rock which is nicely porous, takes heat well. They'd set it alight about three that morning, so the rocks were well and truly glowing. We piled on wet banana leaves (you must do this or you'll burn the meat) then put in our leaf-wrapped morsels. Josie, or rather her head, told us not to waste the torso, which was empty. Josie's head told us to take tongs and put hot rocks into the body cavity to cook it from the inside. Josie's severed head was ordering us about. As things wore on it got terribly bossy. Fungible wanted to eat the heart, but Josie's head wouldn't let him. Luna said it was a case of *mens insana in corpore insano . . .*'

'Did you eat her heart?'

'Well yes, Bear,' says Lilith, peering at me over the tops of her gold-rimmed granny glasses. 'But only in the imagination, dear. We've done all far worse things in the Vortex. Alfredo once held a black mass and sacrificed a baby. You can do anything in your imagination, because it's safe.'

__ __ __ __ __ __ __ __ __ __ __ *fuck* __ __ __ __ __ __ __ __ __ __ __ __ __ __

I am angry. I didn't expect to be. I don't want to be. I feel like a fool because I know this is going to sound worthy and pious, but actually Lil, it's not safe, because what we imagine, we make true and there's already horror enough in the world. For six years I have been writing about it: about children killed by chemical bombs in Iraq; a woman whose husband was crucified and whose twelve-year-old sister was raped to death by Burmese soldiers; street kids gunned down by death squads in Brazil; children in Guatemala whose eyes were burned from their sockets by policemen's cigars and tongues torn from their throats with pliers; about a sixteen year called Sevki Akinçi barbecued alive by Turkish soldiers; students crushed under the tracks of Chinese tanks; people whose loved ones have vanished forever. This list of horrors could go on and on. I interviewed a man who cowered when I spoke to him. He had been hung up by his wrists, hosed with water and given electric shocks to his genitals. I listened to a Bosnian woman describe how one of her neighbours had been tied to two cars which then drove apart, stretching his entrails across a hundred yards of snow. I wrote about a pregnant woman who was raped with a truncheon. I'd held in my hands the electro-shock weapon which had been rammed into the throat of the Buddhist monk Palden Gyatso. I had sat in silence with Martyn Gregory the TV reporter, as his new film revealed how our own government was turning a blind eye to the sale of such weapons. I thought I would explode with grief and rage and frustration when I saw how easy it is for people with power and money to manipulate the media, applying chloroform pads to the few mouths opened against them, how millions of decent, ordinary people who do not agree with murder and torture perpetuate the nightmare by staying silent. Now, talking to Lilith, I sense again that vast 'don't want to know'. Most people distance themselves from the pain of reality by taking refuge in the fantasies spawned by their television sets, but cybergypsies, who know that reality and unreality are the same thing, also know the stupendous power of the imagination to transform things. And here's one of the most intelligent, imaginative people I know, acting out pornosnuff movies in cyberspace.

_ _ _ _ _ _ _ _ _ _ _ _*fuck* _ _ _ _ _ _ _ _ _ _ _ _ _ _ _

'Lily, I am going to send you some pages. They're a spool of a telephone conversation I had with someone. Like yours in that they need a bit of decoding. Promise to read them?'

She says, 'Why not send me a copy of the tape?'

But I can't. During the long conversation, the batteries in the recorder started running low. Now, when the tape is played back, our voices come out gabbling and squeaky. It's unsettling, hearing those terrible stories narrated by Donald and Mickey.

Bear: When you were taking risks, risking your life, to get pictures, did you hope that . . . um . . . that you know, people would see and get stirred up and do something to stop these . . . ?

Don: I thought . . . you know, in a way it was the justification of me intruding on some of those fearful scenes because when you think about it, who needs to have a ringside seat at a murder? Who needs to have the best seat in the house for a murder? Only the killers. Not me . . . not the witness. I used to get rid of my guilt by saying 'I am doing this to show people what they can't see.' I never used to send my film back to England by air freight like a lot of photographers. Only once when I came out of Cambodia and I was directed to go to the fall of Saigon. I couldn't take that film with me. That's the only time I air freighted any of that most urgent kind of film back to London. When I'd taken my pictures I used to hold the film as if I was carrying nitroglycerin. I just wouldn't let it out of my hands. It was against my breast and I . . . you know, it was so important to get those images and those terrible statements back to England. And I felt that by being there I had every right in the world . . . um . . . when I got back to London, you know, in the office at *The Sunday Times* we used to pore over it and look for the most awful kind of statements, visual statements so that we weren't going to give the readers a free ride by being too . . . um . . . selective . . .

Bear: When you came back the pictures were printed . . . but there was never . . . because it was . . . um . . . in the context of a news report . . . there would never be any kind of exhortation for the reader to do anything. No-one would say, hey you can do something about this. Because the papers aren't there for that, people must get that for themselves.

Don: That's right. But sadly when you go into your attic and you fish out some of these old colour magazines as I often do, and look at what I've done it all looks rather like a veneer, that's . . . faded because it's been up in the attic. It's kind of faded like newspapers, they go yellow and faded and that's what our memories become, our minds become.

Bear: Do you feel that those people that died have also become faded and less real . . .

Don: Not to me . . .

Bear: Your pictures caused shockwaves but when you came back, with your head filled with terrible sights, did it make a bigger impact to talk directly to people?

Don: I got angry when I came back because . . . talking about dinner parties . . . cos earlier when you said the word 'dinner parties' it immediately kind of toffs everything up a bit, you know, it bumps it up into some middle class, upper class, thing . . . but when I came back and people used to say to me, 'Where have you been?' I'd mumble like Vietnam or Biafra or Beirut and they'd say 'Oh, it must have been awful.' And they'd ask you a question and . . . and sometimes when I would come out with a really appalling account they would all look around and say things like 'Is there any more coffee?' or 'Is there any more wine?' you know, they would try to get away from me . . .

Bear: So would you get angry or what would you say?

Don: I would want to say 'piss off' and just walk away . . . I've seen every form of . . . of barbarian behaviour that . . . that . . . that . . . monsters can offer. I have seen it all. If someone doesn't take my word for it I might begin to think I'm, you know... I've been living in a fantasy world or something or an unreal kind of world. I feel, you know, maybe what I've seen isn't true, maybe I'm telling lies or . . .

Bear: Well, you've got the pictures, haven't you, to prove it?

Don: I know, but if people don't believe what I say, um, I always think I'm going slightly potty . . .

Bear: I think that image of the pictures fading away up in the attic is infinitely sad . . . Do you ever think about the people who died, whom you actually saw die or photographed, all those bodies?

Don: I see them on buses and trains and aeroplanes and at airports. I feel as if they're floating out there in . . . cloudy images. I see them when I least need to see them. I can recall them the way we have these . . . um . . . um . . . videos. I can stop them and start them and replay them and everything because I . . . you know, I feel as if I scripted them . . .

Bear: That's like cyberspace... it's an idea for a movie . . .

Don: Yeah, I think if you look in my book . . . um . . . on the back of my book, Martin Amis said I was like a ghostly film director that floats in and out, you know. And in a way, I'm not lifting Martin's words but I'm just saying I mean . . . as I'm sitting here now looking at the most . . . the most blossom-drenched garden with all kinds of like, you know, things on the lawn, there's a beautiful bird going across the lawn, sometimes I see foxes and deer . . . I can see that vision while I'm talking to you, of those men dropping in that stairwell in Beirut . . . And it's a bloody nuisance.

Bear: And what do the dead want, do you think, when they appear inconveniently on buses and in crowds?

Don: I think they may be saying, 'You didn't do your job properly because you know, we're still here and our numbers are growing.' But I think, to be honest, Bear, I'm suffering the old conscience and um, you know, it makes me feel very inadequate . . . People used to ask do you think it paid off, doing all those things? and I would often say, 'No, I don't think it does,' because after all these years people are still dying in . . . in . . . in all kinds of places in the world. So, you know, I'm surrounded with, with ghosts and images and things tapping me on the brain saying 'Hey do you remember me?' . . . 'Don, do you remember me in the market place in Saigon when they bought the two jeeps at dawn and stood me at a stake?' 'Remember me, the man they said was a bomber?' 'Remember me? I was the headless corpse by the river restaurant one night when that bomb went off and there was a pregnant woman dead on . . . and right . . . and there were headless people under the tables?' 'Don, remember me? The man with the sucking wound in my neck and chest that was making that terrible noise.'

Bear: You keep telling me you can't write, yet as you speak it's very powerful . . . We have been talking here over the phone, if you had to speak to the readers directly, what would you say? I mean, you have a chance right now to speak directly to all the people who are reading this, all these people who may have seen your pictures? What do you say to them?

Sathyu

'Mr Bear, I have got your name from the internet. One person in New York and another in San Francisco told me of your work with the Kurds. So I have come to ask if you will help us.'

We are sitting under the rose bush, where Zek and Misha had been a couple of years earlier. But sitting opposite us now is a man with dark eyes who looks like an Indian Jesus.

He takes a cassette from his pocket and puts it on the table.

'This recording was made in 1984 by a music fan who was trying to tape a concert. By accident he ended up capturing the sounds of the greatest industrial tragedy in history. Bhopal has been called the Hiroshima of the chemical industry.'

In his quiet voice he tells us the story.

About midnight, on the night of 2nd December 1984, there was an explosion at the pesticide factory owned by Union Carbide. Water got into a tank containing a large quantity of a poisonous chemical, methyl isocyanate. The reaction generated a blast of heat, the liquid gasefied and the resulting explosion ruptured the tank. The factory's safety systems were not working properly. There wasn't enough pressure in the water hoses to reach the tank. The scrubber was broken. The emergency siren had been turned off, because it used to sound so often, it was considered a nuisance, Cyanates and cyanides began billowing from the tank. The wind took the gas and drifted it into the streets and alleys. The neighbourhoods around the factory were densely crowded shantytowns. Most houses were made of mud brick, bamboo, jute sacking. The lanes between them were barely four feet wide. In these places lived the poorest people in Bhopal, who earned their living as coolies, carrying heavy loads, driving rickshaws, or doing eye-straining *zari* needlework.

Inside the houses, people were sleeping. They woke with their eyes burning, and the breath caught in their throats. There was a sting in the air, as if people were burning chillies. One girl who lived near a house where there was a cobra's nest thought that the owners must be trying to drive the snakes away. In a different part of town, a mother told her children that a spice warehouse, which was full of chillies, had caught fire. The gas kept getting thicker and thicker, with a smell like rotten potatoes. It was becoming more and more difficult to breathe. People in the alleys outside were shouting *'bhago, bhago'* ('Run, run').

Smoke started to fill everywhere. People couldn't see anything. Parents were desperate to protect their children, but they did not know what to do. Half an hour had passed, but there was still no warning from Union Carbide. Some families huddled under their quilts and hoped the terror would pass. Others wanted to run. People became afraid that they were going to die. From all sides, through the thin walls, people were crying and wailing. *'Bhagwan, hamari raksha karo. Prabhu, hamari jaan baksho.'* (God, take care of us. Lord, save our lives.) They kept on and on praying *'Allah miah hame bacha lijiye, Allah miah hame bacha lijiye.'*(Dear God, please save us, Lord, please save us.) But the gas just grew thicker. By now, there was so much smoke that people were becoming dim shapes. The street lamps were dim candles. A woman held her small grandson to her chest to shield him. His face was swollen to twice normal size and his eyes were puffed tight. The general commotion outside was growing. The woman slumped, still clutching the baby. Her daughters-in-law sprinkled water on her face and did their best to get her dressed. One of them took her by the hand, the others took the hands of their small children. The family abandoned their house.

They stepped into a crowd of people stampeding in terror through the narrow alley. The press of bodies was so great that at times they were lifted off the ground and carried along. The force of the human torrent tore the children from their mothers. On all sides people were calling out the names of family members. They tried to look for them, but the fog had become impenetrable. It was so dense and searing that people were almost blind. A small boy, Sunil, remembered hearing his mother call out his name and then she was gone and he never saw her again.

People were gasping as they ran. The more they gasped, the deeper they drew the gas into their lungs. It burned the delicate lung linings, it bleached their eyes and hit their nervous systems like a jolt of high voltage. People lost control of their bodies. They were running and throwing up with piss and shit running down their legs. They fell and did not get up. A man lay convulsing in a puddle. Some choked to death on their own vomit. Others began to asphyxiate, as the linings of their lungs bled, and drowned in their own fluids. The streets were full of blistered corpses. At the railway station, a tribe of gypsies had been camped. Not a single one was left to say who they were, or how many they had been.

They woke Union Carbide's factory manager at 1.30 a.m. when gas was still pouring from the tank. But the company did not issue a warning until 3 a.m. By 4.30 a.m. the manager was in his office, telling the *Navbharat Times* that the gas could not have come from his factory, because his safety measures were the best in India. The reporter was by struck by the way he sat with his chair tilted back and his hands clasped behind his head. A Carbide officer told *The Free Press Journal*, 'Nothing has happened. Can't you see us alive?' A hundred yards away, dead bodies lay outside the factory gates.

The boy, Sunil, who had lost his mother, woke to find his feet on fire. He was under a pile of corpses, being cremated. At the muslim burial ground, a man was scooping a shallow hole with his hands. He laid his baby daughter in the grave and covered her up. But, unable to bear the thought of never seeing her again, he brushed the earth off her face for a last look.

'Bhalu-*bhai,* Eve-*behan,* [Brother Bear, Sister Eve]', says Sathyu, 'The worst scandal of all is not that it happened. It is not the fact that when doctors asked how to treat the dying, Carbide refused to disclose the information. It is not that the factory was built in a crowded neighbourhood. Nor that safety standards, which were already inadequate, had been further reduced by cost-cutting on orders from America. It isn't that their safety training course had been reduced from six months to two weeks. Nor that the safety siren was turned off, the fire hoses useless, the scrubber not working. It was not that the cooling system was compromised by penny-pinching to save freon gas. Nor that they were prepared to risk people's lives to save just five hundred rupees, about £10, per month . . .

'Bhalu-*bhai,* all these years later, the suffering is still going on. Every month more die. There are children in Bhopal who have never known one day free of pain . . . You may be wondering, why aren't the medical treatments working? Why don't they use their compensation to pay for better care? Eve-*behan,* the compensation, for those who got any at all, works out at less than £3 a month. The finest medical treatment many people have had is aspirin . . .

'The worst scandal of all is this: that for a day or two in 1984 the liberals of the world were shocked. But then they forgot us and abandoned our poor and injured to the corporate lawyers and the politicians. We have tried governments, courts, newspapers, moral pressure, appeals to justice, compassion, to get help for people who had done nothing to deserve this fate. But if you are utterly poor, utterly wretched, you can expect nothing . . .

'I read an article once,' Sathyu says. 'It seems that there is an Asian gang in London called *tooti nung*. It means – "broken and naked". Believe me, I know the feeling . . .'

He touches the cassette. 'In 1984 this tape began to record the groans and cries of the dying. It is still recording.'

Sathyu's Orissan chicken

'YOU ARE OUTSIDE. YOU WILL DIE. DO NOTHING . . .' From a great distance, these words return to me. Sathyu's images dissolve in my mind to another town, equally unreal, of broken houses and tumbled masonry, doorways in which lie bodies wrenched by unimaginable agonies, a puddly lane where a woman lies face down in her own reflection . . . I remember the opening words of Vatsyayana's catalogue of bird cries: 'At first she'll utter things like "Mother, I'm dying,"' . . .fighting to breathe with fluid rattling in the lungs . . . The tape had started recording in 1984, Orwell's year, the year the internet came to British universities, the year of the Apple Mac, the year I got lost at the Rollright Stones, the year, even the month, almost the day, that I first stepped into cyberspace . . . I saw Raghu Rai's terrible, beautiful photograph of the baby's burial . . . But from that day until this, I have never given Bhopal another thought. Sathyu insists on cooking for Eve and me. We eat in the garden and talk till late under a fading summer sky.

Orissan chicken: Season the chicken with turmeric and salt and put aside. Brown some cumin seeds and coriander seeds, nutmeg (grated), cinnamon, crushed cardamoms, garlic. Make a paste of onions, garlic, ginger and green pepper, add and fry till it's a little brownish. Put the chicken in. Add coriander powder and turmeric – some chilli if you want – and tomato puree, and fry some more. When nicely brown, add water. Potatoes are optional. You can put them in now. Cover and simmer until ready. Before removing from the heat, sprinkle on some fresh coriander leaves to make it more exciting. In all this, you should be guided by the nose.

Tomato rice: Put oil. Quite a bit of garlic (cut cloves in three, fry till brown), mustard seeds. Grind in black pepper. Chop in tomatoes. Add the rice, water by volume should be double rice. Salt to taste.

Leaves & Birds (a poem for Bhopal by Raf Atul Hussaini)

Here comes murdering December again,
odd how the cold makes us sweat,
we sweat in fear, as winds turn chill
and the city puts on a familiar air,
the air of that night, the poisoned night
when death's salesmen fleeced our innocents.
Coughing, shrieking, wailing, screaming,
cries of a city drowning in pain,
some of us were blinded by tears, others
just blinded, each one of us blind
to all the others, jumping over one another's bodies
in a race with death which death easily won,
poor or rich, all shared one prize.
That night the wind scorched everything it touched,
the killer brand burned everything,
leaves and birds fell from trees,
flowers and people dropped in the gutters,
and mothers nursed dead babies.
In quiet graveyards voices whisper
'No-one should have to die such deaths.'
In silent burning grounds the ashes cry
'Beware the priests of greed.'

The Detonator suggests that a Union Carbide virus be created to mark the next anniversary of the disaster and circulated to all the anti-virus software houses. This would ensure that Carbide's name is listed forever among the infectious and killer pathogens of the virtual world. Its payload could be the famous and terrible picture of the child being buried in Bhopal. The virus could display it with the message: *The most shocking thing about this picture is how long the world has ignored it.*

The code for the picture begins like this:


```
10 10 10 21 21 21 31 31 31 42 42 42 52 52 52 63
63 63 73 73 73 8C 8C 8C 9C 9C 9C AD AD AD BD BD
BD CE CE CE DE DE DE EF EF EF FF FF FF 21 F9 04
01 00 00 00 00 2C 00 00 00 00 DC 00 1D 01 00 04
FE 70 08 31 06 29 65 84 1D E6 7B 0A B2 30 4C 33
36 48 E3 3C 4D B9 BC 09 A2 30 09 99 BC 8D A2 87
08 92 18 87 03 50 87 28 5C 8C 40 CB E0 F0 41 18
8C 94 02 E2 20 99 58 A0 97 C9 45 23 20 2C 42 05
30 21 48 48 18 B3 1D 82 E2 D0 2D 18 7C 89 43 22
6E 48 E8 70 2A 47 CB B4 B0 CF FF 72 53 19 02 22
3D 22 37 0C 2F 89 37 0A 0D 54 1B 13 91 92 91 15
6D 42 4F 5E 0C 0E 7A 0A 7E 9D 08 56 16 47 02 1D
91 1F 3B 8D 25 7A 89 0C 1F 2C 5F 66 16 07 9B 0D
AE 0D 73 9D 44 44 4F 09 1F 09 03 6E 04 17 06 3A
42 1F 41 98 55 89 9D 50 90 C1 47 55 A4 01 04 43
3E 4F 06 6F 08 1A 01 5C 46 18 40 37 7E 31 D9 76
8D 0F B4 24 5F A8 E1 22 89 87 5A 07 9D 89 23 0C
33 0B 15 05 1C FA 1D FC 91 1D 95 D4 84 1D 28 40
62 93 03 06 32 EC 38 A9 D4 45 98 81 6D 90 16 DC
B2 C1 A2 85 A6 16 1F F8 7C 71 83 A0 95 2B 5F FE
43 14 2C 90 33 A7 C7 81 14 0E 14 50 20 60 C1 87
8C 93 39 80 65 A8 34 20 4E 0F 02 14 04 48 29 40
A5 0B 10 4C D2 36 2C 31 40 0D 1F 01 00 DC B4 60
70 03 64 C4 97 2F 42 4E 96 6B A0 82 EA 3C 75 7F
FA F8 F8 54 62 A0 1B 89 9D 82 44 C5 C9 6D 9F 3E
7F 0D AD 50 A8 30 A0 08 D5 15 07 6B E8 F8 25 09
DF 4C 0E 02 EC 1C 58 70 6E C5 1C 7A B4 16 88 18
99 60 C5 47 57 0C 06 18 F8 30 8F 86 4D 03 23 F2
29 5E E3 04 08 06 96 C2 84 D9 F5 92 23 4A C7 C4
18 24 60 43 16 65 EF 3C 04 04 36 00 00 D0 45 F1
25 6C 3C E3 91 58 16 07 99 EC 82 2D 76 FC 11 49
04 CE 8D 94 06 12 CD FA 81 17 EF 04 B3 A5 24 6C
18 31 05 E7 91 31 32 3C 9E 2B 19 CF C0 A4 36 2C
21 59 09 AE 89 45 F7 12 26 48 74 C2 A6 E0 F0 E1
19 54 2D CE 7E EA 46 00 64 13 DA 78 22 91 B1 F4
. . . etc
```

I enter the Vortex to find a rough looking stranger leaning on the Reality Checkpoint. He wears doublet and hose and carries a bow. He says he is Vagabond, a hunter. I recognise in him a type of role-player common in worlds evolved from *Dungeons&Dragons*, whose players are organised into guilds. These games lack the freeform fluidity of the Vortex, and their players, used to operating within a cage of rules, rarely stay long. Vagabond stays, but refuses to role-play. He sneers at the fact that there is no fighting, but nonetheless returns with his friends. These friends invite their friends.

One evening I am with Lilith and Luna when Cyri runs to us. Lilith is surprised as it's usually she who describes Cyri to life. The alphabet horse takes several fast paces backward, tosses his head and gallops round the glade. There's zoomzoomzoom like a nest of wasps and Cyri shrieks. Blood is running through the calligraphic tracery of his neck and onto his shoulders. Red-feathered arrows protrude from his flesh, jerking as he runs.

'There they are!'

Luna is angrier than I've ever seen her. She seems so genuinely enraged that I cannot believe she is roleplaying. Vagabond and his friends emerge from the trees, laughing.

Vagabond says, 'Just livening up this boring game.'

'I rarely hate people, but I despise you,' Luna says. 'You have *attacked* Cyri.'

Vagabond sneers, 'It's only a game, lunatic. It's not real.'

'It *is* real,' shouts Luna. 'Cyri *is* real. I am real.'

Lilith whispers sadly, 'She's losing it.'

As I am leaving, Lilith says, 'Bear, I thought you'd like to know, I have joined Amnesty.'

Jarly pays BT back

Aeons after the demise of Micronet, the accounts department at British Telecom get around to realising that dozens of former clients still owe large sums of money. Among these is Jarly, whose bill is somewhere in excess of five thousand pounds. The letter from their solicitors is redirected to his new address from the attic above APHRODITE'S FOOD AND SUPPLIES. It threatens Jarly with dire consequences if he does not pay up in full.

Jarly takes a very large sheet of coarse grey paper of the sort used in primary schools and with a blunt blue crayon scrawls a reply in letters four inches high.

"Sorry not to reply sooner", he writes, "but they won't let me have anything sharp".

He never hears from them again.

Luna is sinking again. She is shapeshifting – nothing surprising in that – but the changes are beginning to happen too fast. Shapeshifts as we talk, Luna; morphs while I am looking at her: one moment sloe eyed and delicious in Balençiaga, the next one-eyed and crone. Long gone the imperious grand dame of the Narnian woods. Her guise-shifting has become erratic, matching the rollercoastering moods. Worst of all, she is no longer holding her characters. Blue-eyed Annie or dark-eyed Leah will stare at you through 'gashes of viridian' and she is using that word 'feral' too often. Me, I've tried everything to amuse, to cajole, to soothe away her turmoil. Lily spends hours every night with her. I've dragged out all my forms and shapes, run through my entire repertoire of characters – all the ones she likes – Begby, fool-moothed, troosers held up wi' string, pissin' in the aspifuckindistra, reekin' ay beer and spite. I conjured up Ophiolatreia, a fiend in cobra form, who wraps himself round your ankle and slides upward, soft poisons aflutter on the tips of his forked tongue. It's these dark characters that Luna likes, but even they don't make her smile. What is wrong? How can one know? Other than talking, there's no way to help but nowadays she refuses to talk about anything in the terrifying world outside the Vortex.

When Luna is depressed, she likes to sit by the bonfire in the fairground. She picks her way past the shooting galley and the dodgems, through the maze of stands and sideshows and goes to the fire that always burns in the private garden behind her caravan. This bonfire never goes out. Here we sit side by side on the log and she moodily tosses pine cones into the flames where they hiss damply, and occasionally sizzle, flare and spout sparks. You can follow the sparks as they fly up, hot pinpoints of flame against the deep blue of night. So beautifully constructed is the Vortex that the light of the fire obscures the night sky. But one step away in any direction the sky is dark and alive with stars.

She says, 'I was scared last night.'

Behind us the fairground's big ride catherine-wheels in the cybernight, lights blurred to circular streaks.

'What frightened you?'

She says, 'I . . . the human . . . was in bed. It couldn't sleep, but it must have been dreaming. In the dream I saw myself, lying in bed. But instead of my head, there was a mirror on the pillow with a reflection in it. As I looked at this, Bear, *I knew what it meant.'*

On the wheel the passengers begin to scream, their cries ringing out forever like the frozen songs of icicles. Unlike Luna and me they are locked into the game, hard-coded in, for them there's not even the possibility of escape.

'What did it mean? What did you see in the mirror?'

'Myself. I saw myself. But I didn't recognise any of myselves. Then it shattered. Pieces flew all over the room. One hundred times seven years bad luck all concentrated into one life. I got down on my hands and knees and started trying to pick up the pieces. It was hard. But I did it. And that was worse, because I was reflected in every piece, but in each one I was a different person.'

I can't think of a good thing to say.

'Maybe I'm going crazy,' says Luna. 'Good timing if so, because tomorrow I, or rather my human, is going to look at an exhibition of art by schizophrenics, at the Hayward.'

She looks at me. 'Why don't you come too? You keep saying you want to meet me. I'll be there at eleven.'

'How will I recognise you?'

Luna mischievously brings her face close to mine, so close that our foreheads are touching and I can feel her breath on my lips.

'Ah, Bear, old friend, that's up to you.'

'How will you recognise me?'

'Bring Eve too,' she says. 'I'll recognise her.'

>*park car*

You neatly park the car and step out.

>*time*

>You consult your watch, it reads 10.32 a.m.

>*e*

>Exiting the car-park you come to a flight of concrete steps. There is a malevolent atmosphere here, a reek of neglect, yet once the place must have been more pleasant, for posters advertising artistic and musical events are flyposted on the concrete walls.

>*u*

>Ascending the stairs, you come to a flat terrace. Immediately ahead of you is a statue of an African man with a half smile on his lips. There is a plaque below.

>*read plaque*

>The plaque reads 'Nelson Mandela'.

What a location. London's South Bank: built entirely in concrete, like the piss-stained tenement blocks that were its contemporaries. I had seen one of these blown up once, in Newcastle. Gentle puffs of smoke at the foot of the building. A few seconds later, the crack of small explosions and low grumblings. For a long time nothing seemed to happen and then, abruptly, the building sighed and sagged, as if resigned to its fate, and pancaked to the ground in a roiling storm of dust. The man next to me said, 'Die, wicked bitch.'

Eve and I enter the Hayward, looking for people who might be Luna. Downstairs there is a big exhibition of Howard Hodgkin paintings, bright jewels that overflow their boundaries. On a vast video screen is Hodgkin himself, complaining that his work is not taken seriously. 'The titles of my paintings are not arbitrary,' he is saying. 'They're carefully chosen.'

10.55 a.m. I am nervous as hell. We stand in front of a painting called *After Degas*. It's a brushsweep of tawny brown on a grass-green background, the frame over-painted in the same green.

'Can't see the Degas connection.'

'Degas used to paint figures sometimes with the limbs cut off,' says Eve. 'The colours are like Degas.'

We consult the catalogue, whose author quotes a critic as saying: *'It still mystifies me how such simple means can generate so much resonance, how an errant brushstroke hints at clouds, wind, a sweep of hair – or none of these things, in such a deeply satisfying way.' This seems quite conclusive to me.* (Wrote the cataloguer).

'Wanker.'

'Oh you mustn't say things like that,' my wife tells me, a trifle smugly, 'you must say "I don't understand it yet".'

At eleven we go up to the schizo exhibition. The programme informs us that many of the mental patients whose works we are about to see were killed by Nazis. Then the first paintings start screaming at us. What a difference between up here and down there. There a highly controlled artist bypasses convention so that we may directly receive the shock of his vision. He breaks rules (and frames) in the hope of pressing his soul to ours. Up here is no question of artifice, the artists are struggling to survive the demons wrestling for their souls. Their pain pours out like scorching acid and what they touch, burns. A woman has written to her husband, begging him to remove her from the asylum. Her letter is a model of concision, a page on which she has written, over and over again, more than a thousand times, the words *darling come darling come darling come darling come darling come* . . . Nothing could be clearer, or less likely to serve her purpose. The gallery is full of people. Which of them is Luna? Automatically I look for an old woman, but Luna might just as easily be the elderly man in the corner. Or the student in jeans who is busily copying a sketch of a witch riding on an upside-down umbrella. A middle-aged woman porks past with two attractive girls. They stop in front of the painting I was going to look at next. I hover, waiting for their interest to subside. She speaks a guttural kind of English, of course she must be Viennese.

Der Göttin SybillensGefilte, Roman der Burgverlliese. "The Goddess Sybilla's Domain: a novel of the castle dungeons." Pencil on paper. 'The publisher of this work invites his apponents (sic), if the reality of castles, ruins, groves, parks & palaces &, c, cannot be viewed, to call them up in the mind's eye, in order to partake fully of the symbol of the pleasures. Ah! what rustles in silken garments of the castles, from the strongholds' distant past, where jewellery's glittering elements, shine forth the noblest splendour of finery.' Franz Malter, a Catholic fisherman turned arsonist, who died in the Bayreuth asylum, in 1909.

This description of a cybergypsy hideaway is written in Gothic script below sigils that writhe and recurse like witch writing or the signatures of demons. Do these curves describe the wand-wavings of Luna during the rituals she claims to perform in her pentacle-inscribed kitchen by the cold square light of the moon? Withered, old, dry-dugged, could she be? – evoking who knows what horrors into beingness in her tired mind?

Eve and I are examining a drawing of birds. They are flying up in a cloud, in panic, wings fanning over the page, surrounded by handwriting that slopes everywhere, filling every interstice. The words are interesting. I pull out my notebook and make some notes, noting also the people near us, in case any might be Luna. Here is a young woman, pretty, cool, stylish in a camelhair coat, dark neat hair. Is she Luna? She is reading her programme notes and smiling. She takes out a pencil and begins to jot. Now, an unsmiling man of about fifty, hair swept back. Luna? He moves on and here are the fat woman and her two daughters again. Phases of Luna? *Die Herrlichkeiten das Schrot dem Jagdgewehr* done in pencil, pastel, body colour, pen on office paper by Johann Knopf. At lower right is a shotgun, a little cloud of lead shot expressing from its muzzle. Knopf was a locksmith, suffering from dementia praecox. In *Bitte No 2345 die geheimnisvolle Affären der Mordanschlägen,* pencil, pen on paper, he scribbled furiously between his birds about *'The mysterious affair of the murderous attacks'.*

The images and themes of cybergypsy sites, castles, ravens, demons, immortality, crop up time and time again. Now I know why Luna had to come here. Like her, I recognise through these paintings my intimate kinship with their authors. They too were cybergypsies, of an earlier and deadlier tradition than Coleridge and de Quincey, psychonauts who ventured into non-human realms without protective gear and had no way to escape from their terrifying reality. Looking into these pictures one can see what it would be like to live entirely in cyberspace, to have one's being entirely in the shifting relativities of the imagination. One can see what it must be like to be Luna.

'The marvels the lead-shot to the sporting gun,' wrote Knopf, '+ am now moved to write a picture of the Evil and good spirit + But I have yet to draw the devilish (?) pictures their evil figures of the evil spirits...'

The things they used to draw their devilish pictures. (Still no clue as to which of these people is Luna. Perhaps she is not here.) Contemporary artists can pickle sharks or chainsaw babies in half, the ICA can exhibit a wall of soiled nappies and call it art, but beside the efforts of these poor German madfolk, such art seems ploddingly contrived. In her desperation to make sense of anguish, a woman tore up scraps of paper to make giant patterns on the floor of her cell. She broke new ground without knowing it. Necessity mothered – certainly Luna is not here, none of the people we can see could possibly be her – their iconoclasms. Their drawings and paintings were poured out onto coarse asylum paper, packing and orange paper, newspapers, tissue, sugar-bag and toilet paper, margarine cartons, the margins of newspapers torn off and pasted together to make a page, envelopes, pages from books (cf Tom Phillips), brochures, school exercise books and scraps of cloth. 'Things were torn out, cut up, collaged, varnished; booklets, books, even giant folio volumes, were manufactured out of cardboard or newspaper; drawings were enriched by collages of fliers and art reproductions. The commonest drawing implement was the indelible pencil, as used by nurses and administrators, which writes in purple when wetted with spittle. Other media used in the collection included pastels, vegetable dyes, watercolour, india ink and oil; idiosyncratic varnishes, chalk washes or overpaintings modify or obscure the beholder's view. Photographs record designs for universal constructs, interior designs, body paintings, tattoos and a gigantic ragman. There was also a mass of written documentation: letters intercepted by the institutional authorities, petitions, texts, text and picture combinations and literary productions of all kinds, as well as musical notations, embroideries and woodcarvings.' Of course by now I am quoting the catalogue – there is something delicious about the texture of a list. But still no sign of Luna.

11.50 a.m. We are queuing to get a coffee in the cafe, when a woman's voice exclaims 'Eve! Bear!' The voice belongs to a friend from Sussex, Fanny, as surprised to see us as we her.

Two nights later, Luna makes a rare visit to *The Butterfly Effect.* 'Saw you at the Hayward on Thursday. It must have been you. I came and stood behind you. You didn't see me. You were looking at Knopf's birds, jotting something. Eve was beside you. I was near enough to touch her.'

Luna describes Eve's clothes in detail. Suddenly, surrounded by madness, I am afraid.

Q95 is dead

Eve turns on the radio.

Out of the ether a deep voice says, very clearly, 'Q95 is dead and buried.' Pause. Adds, 'But the grave is empty.'

A play? But no, the voice repeats.

'Q95 is dead and buried. But the grave is empty.'

And again. Again. Over and over.

'Q95 is dead and buried. But the grave is empty.'

'Q95 is dead and buried. But the grave is empty.'

'Q95 is dead and buried. But the grave is empty.'

'But the grave is empty.'

'Q95 is dead and buried. But the grave is empty.'

'Q95 is dead and buried. But the grave is empty.'

'Q95 is dead and buried. But the grave is empty.'

'Q95 is dead and buried. But the grave is empty.'

'Q95 is dead and buried. But the grave is empty.'

'But the grave is empty.'

'Q95 is dead and buried. But the grave is empty.'

Repeating endlessly, with that one slip-up regularly occurring to show that it is a looped recording. 99.4 FM. But who? Why? A test transmission? A coded message from a paramilitary gang, or one of the intelligence services? Like many other things that happened in Ireland, it had a mythological quality. The loopy logic of myth.

Hard Knot

On such a day on such a road Macbeth met his crones. So fair and foul a day. It hailed, sun snew and wind blew icy raspberries. A cold spring. Day and place made for meetings with witches, wizards and demons. Sere, blasted landscape. The Langdales still brown with last year's bracken, tarns a-glisten, slate and turquoise gems. Up the Wrynose, twisty road, narrowing in spasms where you can easily drop a wheel over the edge. On top, a brook babbles over stones past sheep in the meadows, we judder over cattle grids, then up a series of hairpins to the brink of the Hard Knot, the steepest unholiest descent in Britain. Visitors to this remote place – upon reaching the brink of the precipice you look up and, suspended impossibly high, catch the silver of the Irish Sea – seem nonplussed to see two men sitting on the rocks, one holding a twelve-foot long fax, which has unravelled and is writhing in the wind like a paper python; the other hunched over a laptop which, although the tourists in their cars cannot see this, is hooked to a mobile phone, receiving data from the internet.

Magnus and I have spent the morning watching the filming of the strange commercial I wrote for British Nuclear Fuels: a multi-jointed metal robotic arm clicking a finger cymbal, leads a circle of half-naked yogis in *hathayoga* exercises on a Cumbrian felltop. The agency thinks the film demonstrates scientific achievement, but to Magnus and me it's a cybergypsy paean to the weird realm that hides behind our eyelids. In truth, I am ruined for the nugacities and hebetudes of advertising. A decade of cybergypsying has cast me adrift in a world where things do not exist in their own right, where nothing exists except in relation to everything else.

'What else than a natural and mighty palimpsest is the human brain? Such a palimpsest is my brain; such a palimpsest, O reader! is yours. Everlasting layers of ideas, images, feelings, have fallen upon your brain softly as light . . .'

Strange to think that de Quincey and Coleridge lived here and knew these mountains. Opium-eating de Quincey had a vision of the architect Piranesi, the Scarpa of his day, climbing an eternal stair. Was that a de(e)scrying of the future, a metaphor for the finite recyclability of uranium? Or of the unending energy of sunshine? I think of Sipple – dreamer, ally, imagineer – who detested nuclear power. Ironically, a technology developed to enrich uranium has spawned a fridge-sized centrifuge that could make his solar dream come true . . . *"I know that God told you in a vision to leave Kuwait,"* his letter to Saddam had concluded. *"I have had similar experiences and know that they are meant to be acted on."*

Spirits from the deep mind used to irrupt in the most unwelcome fashion into de Quincey's everyday life. In *Confessions of an English Opium Eater*, he recorded that: 'One day a Malay knocked at my door. What business a Malay could have to transact amongst English mountains, I cannot conjecture: but possibly he was on his way to a sea-port about forty miles distant.'

Magnus has begun checking his mail. There's an email from the Detonator.

'The servant who opened the door,' writes de Quincey, 'was a young girl born and bred among the mountains, who had never seen an Asiatic dress of any sort: his turban, therefore, confounded her not a little: and, as it turned out, that his attainments in English were exactly of the same extent as hers in Malay, there seemed to be an impassable gulf fixed between all communication of ideas, if either party had happened to possess any. In this dilemma, the girl, recollecting the reputed learning of her master (and, doubtless, giving me credit for a knowledge of all the languages of the earth, besides, perhaps, a few of the lunar ones), came and gave me to understand that there was a sort of demon below, whom she clearly imagined that my art could exorcise from the house.'

'The Detonator wants to know if you've got hold of the Thorp operating system.'

'Tell him, yes. He can soon reduce this place to a smoking ruin.'

'Okay,' says Magnus, typing.

'I did not immediately go down,' (writes de Quincey) 'but, when I did, the group which presented itself, arranged as it was by accident, though not very elaborate, took hold of my fancy and my eye in a way that none of the statuesque attitudes exhibited in the ballets at the Opera House, though so ostentatiously complex, had ever done. In a cottage kitchen, but panelled on the wall with dark wood that from age and rubbing resembled oak, and looking more like a rustic hall of entrance than a kitchen, stood the Malay – his turban and looser trowsers of dingy white relieved upon the dark panelling: he had placed himself nearer to the girl than she seemed to relish; though her native spirit of mountain intrepidity contended with the feeling of simple awe which her countenance expressed as she gazed upon the tiger-cat before her. And a more striking picture there could not be imagined, than the beautiful English face of the girl, and its exquisite fairness, together with her erect and independent attitude, contrasted with the sallow and billious skin of the Malay, enamelled or veneered with mahogany, by marine air, his small, fierce, restless eyes, thin lips, slavish gestures and adorations . . . My knowledge of the Oriental tongues is not remarkably extensive, being indeed confined to two words – the Arabic for barley, and the Turkish for opium (*madjoon*), which I have learnt from Anastasius. And, as I had neither a Malay dictionary, nor even Adelung's *Mithridates*, which might have helped me to a few words, I addressed him in some lines from the Illiad.'

Ten minutes later, the Detonator has replied.

'He's keen,' says Magnus. 'Wants to go to work right away.'

'Good. Tell him not to worry about radioactivity circling the globe, children getting leukemia, contaminated grass, milk, farm animals . . . The thing is to get his point across good and hard.'

'Hang on, hang on,' says Magnus, taking this down.

The madness of de Quincey addressing to a Malay sailor in Homeric Greek such words of welcome as, say, Calypso spoke to Odysseus when he was washed up on her magic island, or Achilles to the luckless Hector; just such *coups de foudre*, such stunningly crass victories, are also ours. We are terrified that nuclear power may be unsafe, so fuck, let's prove we're right by trying to cause a major international incident.

Magnus and I sit side by side, arsed to granite, laughing like crazies. Around us, the mountain domes are wrinkled as the snouts of dinosaurs.

Geno has vanished. No sign of him for weeks. The bulletin board line appears to be down. The last time I talked to him, he told me that a lightning storm had taken out his hard drive. I wonder if someone, possibly Cleton, has wreaked cynical revenge by slipping him a trojan, one of those that instructs the victim's computer to perform the simple sequence

c:

format c: | y

which reformats, ie, wipes clean, your hard drive. I try for some days, but *The Oklahoma Institute of Virus Research* does not reply. One night, I get a recorded message which says, 'The number you have dialled has been disconnected.' I try Geno's voice line, but it's the same story. No trace on NuKENet, nor in several other obvious hacker haunts. No spoor on Cleton's reclaimed virus echo. Then one day I am on a board in Miami called *Brokedown Palace.* This is run by Newbomb Turk, NuKE sympathiser, friend of Geno's and ARiSToTLE's.

'Geno got his ass busted by the FBI,' Turk tells me. 'He's in jail.'

It appears that Geno had dialled up the FBI's National Crime Information Center computer and gingered it up with a virus. This seemed such a jolly idea that next day he decided to do it all over again. This time, words began appearing on his screen, an FBI system operator doing a sort of 'halt-who-goes-there?' routine. Geno immediately broke the connection and because he'd taken the usual hacker precaution of routing the call via two or three hard-to-trace nodes, breathed a sigh of relief. But a minute later his phone rang and a deep voice said with a chuckle, 'Gotcha!'

'Hit 'em with the Backtime virus,' says Turk gloomily. 'Yep, Geno's inside. Looks like he's gonna be away a loooong time.'

We've been in Ireland two weeks and Gliomach's clues are leading us nowhere. But in truth neither of us either minds or notices, because we are in a world of our own, neither of us quite certain what the future holds for us, or whether it will hold.

The storm catches us in MacGillicuddy's Reeks, huge, towering shoulders of moorland where golden eagles still fly. There is a crash of thunder overhead, a flash that turns the sky pond-green. It is summer, warm, the car is filled with green-yellow storm light. Fat drops of rain begin to fall, smearing the windscreen, making it hard to see. The road ahead is narrowing as we get higher, passing in and out of patches of cloud. Without warning a car as big as ours, in fact it's another Land Rover, comes at us round a corner. I stand on the brakes and somehow we fishtail past.

'That driver was Indian,' says Eve. 'How strange.'

The rain is rushing down outside. The surface of the road is a white haze of detonating water bombs.

'Even when the hurricane came, you played Shades,' says Eve.

All week, driving home from London there'd been lightning in the south; flickering, restless gusts. There were warnings that a big wind was on the way. Eve went to bed around eleven, as usual leaving me lost in the glow of the screen. There were lions in the wind. Line noise. Interference. We used to call it 'lions'. It looked something like . . . as if I were typing this sentence when wi{tho{{ut {{wa{{{rni{n{{g there{ {{w{ould {{{{begi{{{{n {{{{{{{{a{{{se{{{r{{{ies of in{{ter{{{{{{{{{u{{p{{{t {{io{{{{{n{s, {{{{{ {g{{ro{{{ wi{{{{{{ng worse. And the lions did roar, more and more loudly, and the brambles flung themselves at the windows as the wind picked up, wheewing, shrieking, whistling. A tall cypress bent forward, began rapping at the panes, which bulged inwards with each buffet of wind. When the 'lions' made play impossible, I went to bed.

Woke to a clear, bright sky. The bedroom seemed lighter. To the south, great gaps had opened up; we could see clear to the horizon, a field we had never seen before, a slope a mile or two away. Trees, big trees, were down, lying all around our boundary. I went out and stood in silent awe. No sound. No birds, what had become of them? Everywhere huge trees were down. Overhead electric wires writhed like a snake's honeymoon in our gateway. Grolius's apple trees were all gone, lying on their sides, roots in the air, oddly undignified, as though they had been pushed over by a child in a temper. Round the front of the house I found Eve standing silently, hugging her arms around herself, looking at her car. A tall pine had crashed down across it, bending it into a U, like a cartoon. She stood there very quietly. Then walked inside. She bore the blow like an animal, with trusting, helpless eyes.

'But I was wrong to trust you, wasn't I, Bear? I thought that if I stayed there for you, kept the house, brought up the children, that one day you would come back to me. But you never did. Nothing could stop you, could it? You nearly died of heart failure, but went straight back to Shades. Our rotten house was all we had in the world, but when the hurricane was trying to tear it apart, you went right on playing Shades.'

Actually I had stopped. I'd had to, the phone lines were dead and we had no electricity for weeks. It was a strange experience, driving back to Sussex from London those evenings after the storm. Central London was lit up, back to normal. On the outskirts, the damage was still there. In Kent, trees were lying by the roads, the lane where I'd rescued the two women was impassable, with big trunks lying across it. Even here there were still a few lights, but by the time you reached Sussex, the darkness was total. Here and there in the lanes, as in the days of the smugglers, were windows outlined in flickering candle-glow. The countryside had reverted to its past, but it was a joyful return. People were helping each other with axes and saws and pots of tea. The farmer from down the lane came with a tractor and lifted the tree off Eve's car. I bought a chain-saw and began logging our windfalls. We soon had a huge stack of firewood. Two of the pine trunks we dragged across the corner of a pond, to make a bridge. It was fun. With no electricity, people began to make their own music again. Guitars came out of attics; flutes and violins. From open windows came the tinkle of pianos. We got out the old wind-up gramophone and listened to Molly's collection of scratched 78s, records that in some cases had last been played in Ireland fifty years earlier. We cooked on wood and every meal tasted wonderful. Eve is right, I should have given up Shades and the modem at that point. Nothing I experienced in cyberspace ever came close to the beauty of those electricity-free weeks.

It is virtually impossible to drive. I cannot see the road even a few yards ahead. The mountain slopes around us are running with water. Brown torrents are careering off slopes which disappear almost vertically into the clouds. I stop the car.

'Eve, do you know when I realised what a bloody fool I've been? Not during our rows, but during one of our happiest times, when we'd been to the gallery where we were to meet Luna. Afterwards I felt sick with fear. I did not know who or what Luna was, yet I'd allowed it – she even called herself 'it' – to come within a yard of you. 'It' was standing right behind you. It could have reached out and touched you. My stupidity terrifies me. I can't believe what I did. Eve, bringing Luna so close to you was like evoking some unknown spirit to appearance. I had the strongest sense that she was jealous of you and now I understand why. I've been running that scene in my mind over and over, trying to see it through Luna's eyes. We are in the gallery looking at the picture of Knopf's birds. I am scribbling notes. What do I see when I look at you?'

'What?' Eve's face is wet, perhaps splashed by rain, although her window is closed.

'I see a flesh and blood woman. A woman you *can* reach out and touch. And that's what Luna's jealous of. She can only be who she wants to be in cyberspace, where she is a wraith, a voice, letters on a screen. You, Eve, are who you want to be, and you've got it all in real life. Imagine how galling for Luna. You have real hair to stroke, real lips to kiss. And then I had this utterly staggering thought. I thought, "Eve is warm. She breathes. She smiles and can talk to me. She is intelligent and amusing. We have done so many things together. We have shared so much. I held her hand when she gave birth to our children. Eve is far more wonderful, infinitely more compex and interesting than any character that has ever been or ever will be created in cyberspace."'

She is laughing and simultaneously half crying. 'You bloody fool, Bear, I suppose you think that's a compliment.'

'Eve, I have seen the fucking light. For years I have been living among shadows and reflections of reality. I've applauded people for making pathetic facsimiles of reality. I was amazed and thrilled by the woods in the Vortex. But now, Eve, I look at real woods, and I see that every single leaf is complex and mysterious. I came out while you were gardening the other day. I picked up the soil from the kitchen garden, it was rich, dark with compost. I thought, "Cyri the horse is marvellous, but this stuff is a miracle. It is full of living things too tiny to see. It's home to millions of nematodes, it has a smell, when rain falls it gives off a rich, deep aroma." I thought, "This is the world I want to live in. This lovely garden is infinitely more subtle, more enchanting, than anything we will ever see in cyberspace." Eve, I want to be with you in that garden.'

Eve has stopped crying. She says, 'Bear, you are ridiculous. You sound like an American.'

Then she takes a deep breath and says, 'I didn't want to tell you, I hoped I'd never have to hurt you. But I've fallen in love with someone else.'

Well, there's nothing left now but Gliomach. Irish roads are funny, they tell jokes. A stretch of loose chippings has three signs within a hundred yards of each other bidding us travel at, respectively, 20, 15, and 30 m.p.h. The verges are alive with scarlet crocosmia, purple loosestrife. A burst of cornflowers and scattered poppies brings us to Tralee.

We follow Gliomach's instructions to Harty's Bar, desperate for its facilities. On the door of the gents a notice proclaims *'Drop 2p in slot and slide knob'*. From inside comes the steady plop-plop-plop of a man at work. Eventually we reconvene at the bar.

'Will you be wanting cream at all in your coffee?' asks the barman. 'Tell you what, I'll give you a nice Irish coffee with cream, why don't I? That'll put you in the mood for celebration.'

On the walls are pictures of the barman with all sorts of people, local celebrities. People are constantly coming up and asking him questions. 'The Roses are coming tonight, aren't they Charlie?' 'There'll be fireworks, won't there Charlie?'

The atmosphere reminds me of Todd's barber of Fakenham.

Charlie the barman gives us a *Roses of Tralee* brochure and then, bizarrely, signs it himself.

We do not stay for the Roses festival, but carry on to Dingle where we find ourselves in a newsagent. Lounging in the doorway is a man who looks so much like Don McCullin that I want to go up and ask if he is related. Outside a fellow with matted hair is playing a didgeridoo, his small dog tied up nearby. A small girl tells her mother, 'Ah, I'm afraid some boys will come and kick it.'

'You mustn't always think the worst,' chides the mother.

There's a buzz in the supermarket, a tide of people drifting towards the door. Above the crowd of heads bob several large, floppy, beribboned hats. Beneath their wide, elegantly tilted brims are pretty young ladies. The Roses have followed us to Dingle. They sign autographs as a harassed-looking tour manager stands by the door consulting his watch.

'Block your ears during my <u>BAD</u> singing on the TV, Caroline, Perth'
'Eve, Greetings from Ulster Rose, Rosalie Howden'
'Eve, Greetings from South African Rose, Samantha Byre'

'I just don't know what came over me,' says Eve, holding out Charlie's makeshift autograph album.

When Eve says those words, we sit for a long time in silence. Silence, I say, but thought is locked in the brain by the deafening percussion of rain. It's an astonishing thing, the Coconet. It's at moments like that you really feel how complex and multi-layered are its processes. One part of my mind has gone blank, but at other levels, things are continuing as ever. Somewhere deep in my mind, sunlight is falling on a green trout stream, in another part a bus chugs up a hill, the raindrops are jumping off the bonnet of the car and a third part of my mind mimicks them, drumming imaginary fingers and saying 'pirrirrirrrimpirrirrimpirrimpirrrirrirrim'.

'How long?'
'About a year,' she says.
'Who?'
'You don't know him.'
'Ohmygod, ohmygod, what I am going to do?'
'You don't have to do anything.'
'Does anyone else know?'
'No, of course not.'

'You were always on the computer,' she says. 'I would walk the dogs. Take them for long walks. I met this man. He lived a couple of miles away. I used to stop and admire his garden. He grew lots of herbs. He was just very nice. Very kind, always smiling with something pleasant to say. I don't know, I didn't think you cared about me any more. I just suppose I melted. I began to think about what it would be like to be with him.'

'So what are your plans? You and him?'

For some reason this makes her laugh.

'Eve, when I was a boy, we lived in a place where there were mountains like these. Most of the year they were dry and brown. But then came the monsoon. Overnight the hills turned green. Puddles became trickles, then streams. At first the streams flowed brown and thick, like sweet tea, but after two weeks they'd be clear, full of weed, and crabs, and in the rice paddies there were small inexplicable fish among the stalks. My friend Dan and I, we would go fishing. We had bamboo rods with bits of peacock feather for floats. Sometimes we'd scoop out puddles with cloths, like village boys. We'd get covered in mud, caked with it. It'd get in our clothes and boots and between our fingers and ears and in our hair. Our mothers would get horribly angry. So we had a thing we used to do. We'd go to where the water was falling down the hillside and stand under a waterfall with all our clothes on. We would stand there until we were clean. And we'd feel very virtuous, as if it had washed off everything, mud, naughtiness, and guilt.'

Rain is beating a tattoo on the car, watery fingers drumming on the roof. I get out of the car and it shouts down on me. Nearby, water is pouring very loudly off the face of the mountain. A few steps to the right, these rocks, this ledge and then . . . A nudge, a shove. I open my eyes. Eve, hair glued to her face, clothes plastered to her body, is standing beside me.

The night before we are due to meet Gliomach (if we've read his clues aright) we stay at a little hotel near Dingle. At dinner someone begins singing in Gaelic. Others join in until the room is in full voice. At Dunquin, early in the morning, the appointed time, we walk down the steep zigzag of the harbour path to where black beetle curraghs wait. Piled in heaps are lobster pots, the old kind made of withies, bent by old men in peatsmoky rooms.

'*Gliomach* pots,' says Eve. 'This is the place.'

It must take skill to bring a boat in to Dunquin jetty. The waves come crashing in through rocks like teeth. The sea lifts the jetty's skirt of weed, probing with insolent fingers into its secret places. A little way off, at the foot of the cliff, stands a hut of whitewashed breezeblocks on which someone has lovingly painted a door, windows, and even curtains at the windows.

'Will you ever tell me about your plans?'

'Oh Bear, you are so ridiculous. There are no plans. How could there be plans?'

'How am I ridiculous? You say you are having an affair. Of course I want to know what your plans are.'

'I didn't say I was having an affair,' says Eve. 'I'm not having an affair. I said I had fallen in love.'

'But . . .'

'But nothing . . . The unfortunate man knows nothing about it. He thinks I'm just a woman with a couple of dogs who sometimes says "hello" over the garden gate.'

'You've never been inside the gate?'

'As a matter of fact, no. I often wished he'd ask me in, but for some reason he never did.'

'It's a strange thing,' says Eve, leaning on the sea wall and looking out towards islands lit by fine sunshine. 'But the other day, when I told you my secret, it was as though I'd pricked a bubble. It just vanished.'

'You mean you're no longer in love with this chap?'

I too lean on the sea wall, feigning nonchalance, watching the gulls dive and defecate.

'I don't know now that I ever was in love. And that makes me feel miserable. Because if even that was an illusion, a nothing, what have I got to show for all these years?'

'I'm glad if it was an illusion. I'm horribly jealous.'

'Good.' After a while, she says, 'I was just doing what you were doing. You went hiding in your imagination. So I hid in mine.'

A boat is combing towards us in heavy seas, foam churning at her bow. Minutes pass and she looks no nearer. It is a rock. Up there, on the island, we can see whitewashed houses. One of them, surely, is the café where we are due to meet Gliomach.

'Do you think he's there?'

'No,' says Eve, who has been reading about the Blaskets. 'Look, I'll give you a tour of the islands. That one there is Inishtooshkeart, and right out there is Inishvickallaun. Over there's the White Strand where Peig's daughter drowned and the little rabbit island, Beginnish, which they used to say was the gift of the tide.'

I'll play you jigs, and Maurice Kean,
Where nets are laid to dry,
I've silken strings would draw a dance
From girls are lame or shy;
Four strings I've brought from Spain and France
To make your long men skip and prance,
Till stars look out to see the dance
Where nets are laid to dry.

But where nets were laid to dry, we never did find Gliomach.

I'm at a book fair in Olympia, ploughing through lunchtime crowds when a man says, 'Bear?' Smiling, a pleasant open face. Wears a name tag that says 'Alain'.

'You don't remember me, do you? I was married to Clare, who used to play Shades. I met you a few times.'

'Calypso's husband?'

'Yes, that was it. Calypso.'

I cast my mind back to the high days of Shades, scan the snapshots of memory for a hundred faces seen at meets. Got it. Yes, I remember him now, how he leant on a pillar with a mug of beer in his hand, quietly watching his pretty wife at the centre of a group of excited young men. Now I know who he is.

'You say "was married". Aren't you still?'

'We had a parting of the ways,' he says, and quickly holds up a hand to forestall my condolences. 'It happens.'

Calypso's husband. Well, I am not surprised they've split up. Questions beg to be asked. How did it happen? How did you find out? Did you really never suspect, when she was so blatant? What about that holiday? I think these things and say none of them.

'You knew Clare pretty well, I think,' he says.

'No better than most,' I say, immediately pricked by the *double-entendre.* Does he know that I lay on his sofa while his wife paced up and down smoking and talking about her childhood wearing nothing but a tee-shirt?

'Do you fancy a drink?' he says, looking at his watch. 'I'm on the Litvinov stand over there and I've got a break coming up. Have you got time?'

Once again, even after all this time and at God knows what

distance, there's a big muffled drum beating, a disturbance of the breath, those wide green eyes, that shining fall of black spider silk.

'Before you ask,' he says when he has bought drinks and we are settled at a small table overlooking the throng, 'let me tell you what you are wondering. You are wondering if I know about you and my ex-wife. The answer is yes.'

He smiles and raises his glass.

In moments of extreme embarrassment I catch myself thinking 'how humiliating this is, it couldn't really be worse' before the awful realisation that the moment is still wide open all around me and my tongue is nailed to my palate. *vyãghrivasté jarã cayuryati bhinnãghatãmbuvata nighananti.* Old age leaps like a tiger . . . amazing how the mind drivels, I've said this before . . . in the swamps of the Sundarbans, woodcutters wear rubber masks painted with eyes, nose and mouth on the backs of their heads to put tigers off jumping them from behind. With a tiger on your back, you are pinned down, unable to move, unable to breathe.

'Sorry,' he says with a grin. 'Shouldn't have been so blunt.'

Composing myself, I raise my glass and say, 'If Calypso – I mean Clare – told you about the day we met, she must have also told you that nothing at all happened.'

'She told me exactly what happened,' he says. 'I was angry with her. I told her she should be more careful. It wasn't fair on you. You weren't like some who – well, I suppose we regarded as fair game.'

'*We?*'

'Clare was trouble,' he says, 'big trouble. She'd been out of order ever since she was a girl. All those stories about her childhood, well they're half true, partly true. I've met her father and stepmother. She didn't know. They refused to come to our wedding, so I rang up and arranged to meet them, get them to change their minds. But they wouldn't. They warned me against marrying her. They said, "She won't be faithful."

'I said, "I know that."

'"She has had dozens of men. She sleeps around."

'"I know that."

'They said, "Don't you mind?"

'I said, "Of course I mind, but I love her. And I love her exactly as she is, not as she isn't."

'I said, "I know everything about her. She's kept nothing back. She told me stuff that made us both weep. I'm going to marry her."

'They said, "you'll never change her."

'I said, "I don't want to."'

'You loved her for what she was?' I say incredulously. 'But what was she? Since we're being so frank, doesn't it strike you that she was a complete mess?'

'No,' he says. 'A mess is someone who doesn't know who they are. Clare knew exactly who she was. Most of the men she met tried to make her into something she wasn't. Take your friends. Chorley wanted to cuddle and protect her. To him, she was a bird with a broken wing. She wasn't at all. She was terrifyingly strong. For Steve, she was straight out of a top shelf magazine, the randy housewife looking for sex, an adolescent's dream, a conquest to flatter his ego till he grew out of needing her – she gave him his rites of passage you know – he was a virgin. We laughed about it.'

Again that inhuman "we".

'And Morgan?' I ask. 'And me?'

'Morgan? Morgan? Oh yeah, I remember. The big gloomy guy. Morgan couldn't believe she wasn't pure and immaculate. He tried to make her his goddess. He wanted her to let him worship her. Just as well he never got his wish, it would have destroyed him.'

'It nearly did anyway,' I say, remembering Morgan's credit card bills. 'But in the end it was someone else who destroyed him. And someone else whom she destroyed.'

I notice that he has not said a word about poor Droid.

'She nearly destroyed you,' says Alain. 'I've often thought about what happened to you. Like someone coming into contact with a very high energy source, a super high voltage. She was so good at hiding behind those incredible eyes. But whenshe dropped the disguise, you saw her as she really was and the experience nearly killed you.'

'That's a little fanciful,' I say, prepared to dislike him now. 'I had a serious heart problem. It chose that moment to announce itself.'

He says, 'There are no coincidences, Bear. Don't you know that?'

'What about you, Alain?' I say after several angels have flown past overhead. 'So you knew. Well we always thought you must. But I have to ask, because it became a legend on the net, how on earth could you go off on holiday with your wife and three blokes you knew she was sleeping with?'

He seems genuinely amused.

'What's so difficult? I've explained. I loved Clare for what she was, not something she wasn't. She never hid anything from me. She told me everything about herself. Absolutely everything. We met as students, at university. She had been leading a hellish life. She had done many many things she was ashamed of. I fell in love with her straight away. You understand. Those enormous eyes. Wide open and innocent. She had a talent, didn't she, for making every man she looked at feel that he and he alone was the centre of her universe. Of course, it wasn't very long before she slept with someone else. But when she told me, my response terrified her. I just smiled and said, okay, don't get hurt. I refused to be upset or angry or judgemental. She was amazed.

'She said she'd been slumming it in the gutter and I found her there and picked her up and brought her back from the brink. I told her that I loved her absolutely, which meant without conditions. I loved her just as she was. I said I wouldn't try to change her or force her to be anything she wasn't.

'She told me, "Men always seem to want sex and so I give it to them. But they never give me what I want, so I keep on looking."

'Sex wasn't a big deal to her. It was something she could take or leave. People who thought she was a tart never understood that. She was the very opposite. In her own way she was a complete innocent. And she was a romantic. She was waiting for someone.'

'She told me she was searching for a soulmate.'

For the first time he looks sad. 'Yes,' he says, 'and she told me that she was waiting, quote, for someone who could walk past her defences, find a way through the passages of her mind and the cave-cellars of her emotions until he came to the place where she lived, in darkness, all alone . . .'

'Was that you?'

He says, 'Unquote, I hoped so.'

'You helped her, didn't you? You actually helped her plan the gypsy caravan holiday.'

'Of course I did,' he says. 'But if you think it didn't hurt, knowing she was sleeping with other people, you must be crazy. It hurt like knives, hurt like death. But I never showed it, because if I had she'd have run a mile. She couldn't bear to hurt me. She loved me, in her way, as utterly as I loved her. That was my consolation. I gave her something she would never ever find again and she knew it. I was her rock, her anchor, her safe harbour. She could go out and have the adventure she craved because she knew I'd always be there to come back to, would always accept, always console.'

'So what happened? What the hell broke you up?'

He smiles. 'I met someone else,' he says.

The great room at the Grosvenor House Hotel, in London's Park Lane, is full of very young men in evening dress and young women wearing the very least that can be defined as evening dress. Waiters are circulating with trays of champagne. This is an advertising awards ceremony. It feels odd to be here, because I have quit my job and left the ad business. Even stranger is that beside me is Sathyu, clad in the garb of Bhopal's bazaars, wearing an embroidered skull cap and smoking a small Indian leaf-rolled cigarette called a *bidi*. We are accompanied by an elderly American in a crumpled suit, who never goes anywhere without dragging thirty kilos of books and papers behind him in a wheeled shopping bag (parked, for the occasion, under our table). This is Ward Morehouse, author and tireless campaigner for justice for Bhopal's gas victims. Each year Ward attends Union Carbide's annual stockholder meeting. Every year for more than a decade he has intervened to ask, 'When will this company honour its responsibility to the sick and injured of Bhopal?' Every year Ward is heckled and each year he goes back and asks his question again.

The appeal we have launched has raised enough money to open a free clinic in Bhopal. It has also won an advertising award. The latter news could be received with indifference (only the hardcore porn people feel the need to give themselves as many prizes as adfolk do), but I remember that last year, these awards had been televised. I called Sathyu and say, 'Come, if you can. When we go up to receive the prize, go to the microphone and make a short speech. This is strictly not done, but you don't know that and we'll get a free TV commercial.'

This, at any rate, is the plan, but as he begins to thread his way to the stage Sathyu whispers 'Bear, there is no mike!' The compère, Ned Sherrin, is using a lapel mike. The following exchange takes place, plainly audible to everyone in the room.

Sathyu: I want to say thank you on behalf of the people of Bhopal.

Sherrin: Okay, thanks, now you can sit down.

Sathyu: No, I must say thank you properly. I have come from Bhopal to do this.

Sherrin: You have received your award, now you must go back to your seat.

Sathyu: I cannot sit down until I have said thank you.

Sherrin (annoyed): In that case you'll have to speak here.

Ward and I, surrounded by incredulous admen, find ourselves cheering the curious sight of Sathyu leaning forward making his impassioned speech of thanks, announcing the opening of the free Sambhavna Clinic, into Ned Sherrin's bosom.

Later, when people are wandering around, a cigar-smoking creative director, one of the big names of the advertising business, on a legendary salary, comes up, ignores Sathyu and Ward, puts his arm round my shoulder, shakes his head and says, 'Bear, Bear . . . you just don't live in the real world . . .'

During my wanderings in worlds, real and unreal, I have often come into contact with currents of pure evil, but I have also known the touch of great goodness. I think of Morgan, unselfish to the point of self-destruction, searching for someone upon whom he could lavish his love. I remember Alastair McIntosh blowing his conch barefoot in the April slush, and how he once came home with me and narrated highland yarns to our saucer-eyed children, and played tunes on a penny whistle. But most of all I think of Sathyu, who lived in a slum, thanking the champagne drinkers at the Grosvenor House.

Acknowledgements

Grateful thanks to Peter Robinson at Curtis Brown, Martin Fletcher at Scribner and Wendy Wolf at Viking Penguin. To Urmilla Sinha, Claudia Gould, Sarah Palmer and Elizabeth Mortimer for reading early drafts and helpful suggestions.

To Roger Garfitt for allowing me to dislimb exquisite *Animula,* from his collection *West of Elm.* To Don McCullin for permission to quote from our conversations (good luck Don, with your new book *India*). To Rzgar Goran for *Cry* and Raf Atul Hussaini for *Leaves & Birds*. To the spirits of Thomas de Quincey, whose *Confessions of an English Opium Eater* inspired these confessions, of J.M. Synge, whose version of the Gaelic *Beg-Innish* is quoted by Eve on p.385, and of immortal Shailendra who wrote *Mera joota hai Japani.*

To Geno Paris, Stak Aivaliotis, Diane Allard, Karen Sherlock, James Adams, Neil Godfrey, Alastair McIntosh, Martyn Gregory, Edward Pilkington, John Salmon, Alexander Abian, Anita Roddick, Sarbast and Handren, John Hurt, Lord Jeffrey Archer, Nadhim, Brosk, Rzgar Goran, Zek and Misha Halu, Pustaq Keet, Ian Paisley Junior, Sadu Fisher, Aitan Arussi, Jim South, Madison, Palden Gyatso, Magnus Westerberg, Dan Phillips, Sathyu Sarangi, Ward Morehouse and Ned Sherrin for appearing as themselves. To Azad, Burhan and the boys in the KCC band, friends in Kurdistan and Bhopal. To Molly and Biffo (thanks to Biffo for translating *Der Magier als Kyberpunk* (a chaos-magic text from that notorious nest of hackers the Chaos Computer Club – cut from the book but on the website http://www.cybergypsies.com). To David Stoughton, Sander Kessels and Dirk van Dooren. To John and Penny Stuart and 'Gliomach'. To the folk in NuKE, Trident and Immortal Riot. To the sysops of Fidonet and the free internet. To all at the WELL, the Chaos Computer Club and Greennet.

To the cybergypsies, past and present, whom I've had the pleasure to know: Geno Paris, Savage Beast, Omega, Rock Steady, Michael Paris, The Wizard, ARiSToTLE, Ürnst Kouch aka Dr George Smith (author of the excellent *Virus Creation Labs*), Newbomb Turk, Sara Gordon. To the memory of TäLoN.

To Branwell, Hypatia, Merlin, Jarly, Arifax, Icecold, Gawain, Luna, Lilith, Morgan, Calypso, Chorley, Graeme, Chesh, Bouncy, Country Girl, Cthulhu, Pooh, Neuromancer, Shadow, Bond007, Hazeii, Peri, Chant, Ambushbug, Scarlet, Heloise, Lordant, Mak, Fluffs, Badriya, Phaid, Jik, Savannah, Zeon, Nongrata, Mouze, Catz, Dirk, Claudia, Jemima, Mina, Jaggery, Lady Janavan, Josie, Chipendale, Innocente, Zara, Oliphaunt, Malwen, Lizandith, Maryanne, Alcuin, Ninjette, Nymphette, Map, Pagan, Felicia, Delphi, Merilyn, Tammy, Dark, Pallium, Shaman, Euphoria, Jerri, Lor, Shoooty, Rheingold, Marina, Panacea, Zero, Fineas, Winseer, Slime, Rodney, Ender, Lender, Qadile, Panda, Ray, Seamoon, Vivian, Paladin, Galadriel, Lagolas, Precious, Assassin, Edelweiss, Zandramas, Boidae, Die, Diptheria, Ophelia, Ennui, Bulldog, Nathalie, Grittar, Electric, Ford, Hellborn, Mehitabel, Guiseppe, Damocles, Eyegor, Hemingway, Orddu, Saul, Minotaur, Pynkfloid, Gristle, Sparkhawk, Mrsa, Notrag, Lovabull, Centurion, Mnementh, Thesaurus, Riggins, Louise, Zarabeth, Seb, Ravena, Kali, Devil, Mindy, Pegasus, Linda, XXXX, Tenon, Hector, Polgara, Wizzo, Creature, Xena, Mylana, Zarquon, Gemini, Ahalya, Archaro, Azmodan and many others. A special message to Henry Cornelius Agrippa: the *Butterfly Effect* is still up on the old number. To those I do not, or dare not, name, you know who you are. This is your story as much as mine, a celebration of that peculiar world of ours which has all but vanished.

Finally, to Vickie, who has heard all these stories before, and whose strength brought us through.